Re-Imagining Class

Intersectional Perspectives on Class Identity and Precarity in Contemporary Culture

Re-Imagining Class

Intersectional Perspectives on Class Identity and Precarity in Contemporary Culture

Edited by
Michiel Rys & Liesbeth François

LEUVEN UNIVERSITY PRESS

Published with the support of the KU Leuven Fund for Fair Open Access, YouReCa (KU Leuven Young Researchers Career Centre), KU Leuven Research Unit Literary and Cultural Studies and FWO (Research Foundation - Flanders)

fwo

Published in 2024 by Leuven University Press / Presses Universitaires de Louvain / Universitaire Pers Leuven. Minderbroedersstraat 4, B-3000 Leuven (Belgium).

ISBN 978 94 6270 402 2 (Paperback)
ISBN 978 94 6166 569 0 (ePDF)
https://doi.org/10.11116/9789461665690
D/2024/1869/16
NUR: 610
Layout: Crius Group
Cover design: Annemie Mermans
Cover illustration: Michiel Rys, Untitled (2021).

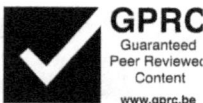

GPRC
Guaranteed
Peer Reviewed
Content
www.gprc.be

Contents

PART 3
NARRATING CLASS:
VOICE AND BELONGING

PART 4
PERFORMING CLASS:
MATERIALITY AND AFFECT

PART 5
CLASS BEYOND THE HUMAN:
WORK EXPERIENCES AND THE ANTHROPOCENE

Acknowledgments

This volume is the outcome of an interdisciplinary workshop on "Re-Imagining Class: Working-Class Identity and Intersectionality in Contemporary Culture" in Leuven in May 2022. We would like to thank all speakers and attendees for their participation and feedback on papers presented at this occasion. Furthermore, we want to express our deepest gratitude to Hannelore Roth and Stijn De Cauwer, who co-organised this event and without whose help this book would not have been possible. A special mention goes to Eva Gijsen, who assisted us in editing the manuscript. Finally, we want to thank YouReCa—the young researchers career centre at KU Leuven—, the Flemish Research Foundation (FWO), the KU Leuven Fund for Fair Open Access, and the Research Unit Literary and Cultural Studies for their financial support, which enabled us to publish this volume in the most democratic and accessible way possible.

Re-Imagining Class

Intersectional Perspectives on Class Identity and Precarity in Contemporary Culture

MICHIEL RYS AND LIESBETH FRANÇOIS

A lot has changed since the German sociologist Ulrich Beck declared class to be one of the 'zombie categories' in social theory, i.e. "living dead categories, which blind the social sciences to the rapidly changing realities" and which are in urgent need of critical revision (2002, 24). Writing from another context, the American feminist bell hooks famously noticed in 2000 that the topic of class was not as "cool" as other questions of identity, like gender, sexual orientation and race (2000, vii). She was just one of the many influential voices who strived to put class matters back on the agenda, and thereby made a convincing case for the need to address them through an intersectional perspective. Now, twenty years later, we cannot but confirm that matters have indeed changed drastically, and that class issues are sparking renewed interest from a wide range of artists and scholars, not in the least in the domain of humanities and social sciences. This situation responds to a social context which is characterised by the increasing hollowing-out of social protections that comes with the global rise of neoliberalism; as a consequence, 'class' re-emerged as a necessary category to make sense of social, economic and political changes more broadly. This volume is rooted in the observation that the idea of class haunts contemporary culture, which implicitly and explicitly evokes diverse concepts of the working class, but also problematises and appropriates them to fit a more contemporary perspective. Thus, recent engagements with class tend to draw on past traditions of working-class imaginaries but also introduce new concepts in the light of changing social realities and experiences, thereby acknowledging the need for an intersectional perspective. Through a wide range of examples from the Global North, this volume aims to study the ways in which artworks shed light on these ongoing processes of recuperation and re-imagination, and it does so from an interdisciplinary angle that brings advancements in sociology, critical theory, working-class studies, cultural studies and artistic research into a productive dialogue.

Class and the Expansion of Precarious Work

The insistence of class imaginaries in contemporary culture, and the concept of class in general, might at first seem a spectral remainder of an obsolete tradition of structuring social reality in antagonisms. Concepts of class have been adapted and transformed in the light of substantially different socio-economic contexts. The overt resurgence of class is first of all intrinsically related to the socio-economic developments initiated during the global turn to neoliberalism, understood here in the broadest sense as a set of beliefs based on the principle that the best way of improving human well-being lies in a society entirely organised according to free market principles (Harvey 2005, 2). This encompassing societal transformation, which started in the 1970s, has had a lasting impact on today's crisis-ridden societies, both in terms of labour relations and social experience. Even though the extent of these transformations may vary in different socio-economic contexts, there is a consensus that the labour market has changed significantly on a global level. This is the result of policy decisions in function of deregulation and flexibilisation, which have led to a general rise in insecurity among workers that cuts across sectors. In the Global North, this situation has led to the demise of the "social compromise of industrial capitalism" made in the aftermath of the Second World War and, subsequently, the "comeback" of the social question in Western economies (Castel 2009, 21). As a consequence of the debilitation of the post-war social pact, scholars have observed an evolution in recent years that gradually introduces these societies to the structural experience of precarity and insecurity that largely characterises employment in the Global South (Lazar 2017, 12). The latter can be partly explained by the widespread and historically engrained character of informal labour in this region: informal and informalised labour represent more than half of the total employment rate in the Global South (Hammer and Ness 2023, 4), while "85 percent of all new employment opportunities in the world today are in the informal economy" (Goldstein, quoted in Poblete 2021, 216). At the same time, it should be noted that Western societies still very much depend on a global division of labour that relies on the availability of a cheap, poorly protected and majorly unskilled workforce in regions that occupy secondary or directly peripheral positions with respect to the traditional centres of economic and political power (Suwandi, quoted in Hammer and Ness 2023, 6). Even if local conditions vary significantly both between and within these spheres, the dismantling of social protections garnered renewed attention in Western societies to the ravaging impact of uneven development and to the way in which capitalism fundamentally depends on geographical inequality (Soja 1989, 107–117).

Due to the dismantlement of collective social safety nets in the Global North, socio-economic risks are increasingly placed on individuals, who are deemed to be responsible for their success and happiness in what only on a surface level presents itself as a meritocratic, i.e. *classless* economy providing equal opportunities (Castel 2009, 23–27; see also Cruz 2021, 41). Taking the German context as an example, sociologists Nicole Mayer-Ahuja and Oliver Nachtwey (2021, 13–20) retraced how the focus on *individual* performance and productivity has fundamentally changed which types of work receive the most social recognition and are rewarded with the most secure and—in some cases—even generous working conditions. What is more, they reconstruct how a self-enforcing circle, in which deregulation and privatisation of labour result in a rise of precarious labour contracts, has incrementally become the norm for more groups of the workforce. They argue that these developments led to new social inequalities and put in place new class divisions, as the increase in wealth does not create better living conditions but causes a general trend of downward social mobility (cf. Nachtwey 2018). Furthermore, the waning of the traditional workers' unions— not only the traditional defenders of workers' class interests but also important pillars of workers' sociability and culture—alongside the disappearance of class concerns from the discourse of the left have led to more social isolation and the feeling of being left behind, as Didier Eribon's *Retour à Reims* (2008, also in Jean-Gabriel Périot's film adaptation of 2022) and Christian Baron's *Proleten. Pöbel. Parasiten* (2016) so meticulously document. The role of digital technology in this process cannot be underestimated, as James Bridle warns us, because the increasing tendency towards specialisation "concentrates power into the hands of an ever-smaller number of people who grasp and control these technologies" (Bridle 2018, 55). This deeply affects the lived realities and hence agency of workers, whose work gradually loses its visibility and is organised by algorithms that are becoming ever more opaque to them.

Another element that has impacted concepts of class involves the altered nature of work itself, with the main trends being the ongoing process of de-industrialisation and the rise of the service economy and of immaterial labour, defined by Antonio Negri and Michael Hardt as all forms of labour that create "immaterial products, such as knowledge, information, communication, a relationship, or an emotional response" (2004, 108). This has happened in parallel to the sharp rise in temporary contracts, seasonal labour, the platform economy, informal work and other schemes of atypical employment (see Christiaens 2023 for a detailed discussion of how a digitised platform economy enforces precarious labour conditions). Ulrich Beck already argued in *Risk Society* (first published in 1986) that class relations have receded, as "each person's biography is removed from given determinations and placed in his or her own hands" (1992, 135), while on a professional level, a "system of pluralized, flexible decentralized underemployment" has as a result that biographies have become more episodic

(Beck 1992, 149). On the one hand, flexibility does come with more freedom, which many perceive as a positive and which has even been deemed fundamental for workers belonging to the so-called "creative class" (Florida 2002). On the other hand, these workers often turn to entrepreneurial models in a context in which they are, again, insufficiently protected by state policies (e.g. García Canclini 2017) and, in this sense, become more vulnerable to market fluctuations. Flexibility thus also comes with new challenges and risks, which are often mitigated or maximised by variables like gender and ethnicity (see Pulignano et al. in this volume, who examine gender and race as crucial factors in the building of networks that determine project-driven careers in the creative industry). In consequence, work is much less a factor of social integration and financial stability than it used to be (cf. Nachtwey 2018). Such a diagnosis not only applies to the 'traditional' working class, but also to artistic, cognitive and highly educated employment, resulting in what Robert Castel has called "zones" of social in- and exclusion (cf. Dörre and Castel 2009, 15).

It is indeed important to stress the various degrees, stages and phases in these transversal processes of precarisation, because of which the working force has become more diverse and fragmented (Castel 2009, 29–30). As a result, some groups of workers gradually have lost their capacity to generate sufficient means to cover basic needs and services—hence the increase in people who are (mostly pejoratively) referred to as, for example, the 'working poor,' a new 'Unterschicht' or the 'deplorables.' In the UK, sociologists of the London School of Economics proposed a new "seven class model" based on "people's experiences, attitudes and lifestyles," in order to "recognise [...] both social polarisation in British society and class fragmentation in its middle layers" (quoted in Radice 2015, 270). Of course, work at the assembly line in the factory has not entirely disappeared and is still a major mode of employment globally, and many types of (seasonal) work in the food industry and in logistics—think of Amazon warehouses—can be regarded as forms of deskilled labour that continue to exist besides high-skilled precarious work (see Christiaens and De Cauwer 2020, 118–127). In contrast, Joshua Freeman observes a change in the prototypical figures of the working class, arguing that "sales clerks, hospital aides, and school teachers [have become] more representative of the working class than the steelworkers, coal miners, autoworkers, and railroad men who dominated images of twentieth-century labor" (quoted in Entin 2021, 34).

In this state of flux and diversification, class positions are more volatile: while a growing number of people face the risk of downward social mobility, climbing the social ladder has become more competitive, yet not impossible, as demonstrated by the narratives of social climbers discussed in this volume (see the contributions by Irene Husser and Katrin Becker). It is perhaps no coincidence that a prolific body of testimonial literature by academics grapples to find a language for experiences of upward social mobility, like Eribon's influential *Retour à Reims,* or Cynthia Cruz's *The Melancholia of Class* (2021), in which she notes that she "had no language or concepts with which to work through this experience" (12), because "the concept of social class and the working class have been removed from discourse" (80). The working class, however, has not: "Existing between worlds […], the working class haunts. Though (symbolically) dead, we cannot be put to rest because we are still alive" (ibid.). Cruz is one among many trying to give a voice—in this case taking recourse to the semantics of spectrality, and breaking up generic boundaries between personal testimony, critical theory and cultural analysis—to a new (and lived) class reality. Related to these discussions, the moral undertones of the topological metaphor of upward and downward mobility have urged scholars like Chantal Jaquet to develop a different, more neutral concept: the 'transclasse' (Jaquet 2018). While this is an important development, it would also be important to consider how 'transclasse' experiences are valued differently in various (national) contexts. The chapters collected in this volume achieve exactly this: they show how social mobility and the concepts used to capture it can have different cultural, symbolical and affective meanings—with the term of the 'social climber' having negative connotations in the United Kingdom, for instance.

Social Diversification and the Emergence of New Class Categories

While, on the one hand, broader socio-economic shifts conjured up spectres of class and rendered class boundaries blurry and less evident, on the other hand the diverse backgrounds of those in comparable precarious situations complicate class affinities and solidarity: it becomes harder to find commonalities between the interests of individual workers. However, traditional class theories, especially in a socialist and/or Marxist tradition, have defined classes as more or less stable and homogenous entities defined by objective political, economic and cultural relations. In this case, the working class, much like its antagonist, the bourgeoisie, is defined by a relation of production, its connection to capital, and its potential for resistance and revolution (with a classless society as final aim). As Magnus Nilsson reminds us in his contribution to this volume, Marx explains in *The Eighteenth Brumaire of Louis Bonaparte* (1852) that this power to resist depends on a passage from a 'class in itself' to a self-conscious 'class for itself,' capable of collective action. In a similar, classical Marxist vein, Lenin was profoundly suspicious of the assumption that the oppression of the working class would spontaneously lead to revolution, and he famously advocated the necessity to fashion a theoretically informed class consciousness that would go beyond concrete and immediate demands in *What is to Be Done?* ([1902] 1987).

While it may seem that it is due to contemporary evolutions that the image of a homogeneous working class becomes shattered, the latter has in fact always been a myth, concealing a myriad of concrete personal biographies and desires that do not necessarily overlap with socialist theorems. In particular, Jacques Rancière's work on the archive of nineteenth-century worker-poets in the *Proletarian Nights* has fundamentally altered the cliché view on workers' identity and their hopes and dreams for the future. As Donald Reid argues, Rancière's project has to be understood against the backdrop of overly reductionist theories of class held by Marxist scholars in the 1960s and 1970s (see introduction to Rancière 2012). Indeed, the reception of Marx often downplays the fact that, until the very end of his life, he acknowledged the heterogeneity of classes. As Joseph Entin recently reminded us, even in the last sections before the third volume of *Capital* abruptly breaks off, Marx distinguishes between "three major classes—laborers, capitalists and property owners—defined by each group's respective source of income: wages, profit or rent" (2021, 32). Marx, however, in the same breath also acknowledges that these classes can be endlessly divided further based on their diverging "Interessen und Stellungen" [interests and positions], resulting in "unendliche Zersplitterung" [endless fragmentation] (1983, 892–893). Descriptions like these anticipate the sensitivity to fragmentation and diversification in contemporary debates, in which the plurality of the working class, i.e. its "nonidentity" with its unitary 'ideal type,' is, as a sidenote, rediscovered in past phases in class history, too (see, among others, Eiden-Offe 2017, 23–27).

The more recent attempts to develop a language to come to terms with current complexities of class identity, too, evoke and break up traditional ways of imagining class. For example, Toni Negri and Michael Hardt have introduced the figure of the multitude, defined from the outset not only as global capitalism's other, but also in opposition to other collective subjects like the people, the masses and the working class. In contrast to these collectives characterised by a high degree of unity and homogeneity, the multitude "is composed of innumerable internal differences that can never be reduced to a unity or a single identity," as an open, inclusive and potentially "global class" that subsumes not only waged industrial workers, but also those tasked with "the production of communications, relationships, and forms of life" (2004, xiv–xv). Opening up to plurality, which implies drawing critical attention towards "race, ethnicity, geography, gender, sexuality, and other factors," multitude "is a class concept," as it exists only as "a collectivity" of singularities insofar they "struggle[] in common" (ibid., 104). In a similar vein, but relying on a more fleeting and flexible conception of subjectivation, Judith Butler has highlighted the performative potential of public assembly as it "embodies the insight that [precarization] is both shared and unjust and [...] enacts a provisional and plural form of coexistence that constitutes a distinct ethical and social alternative to 'responsabilization'" (2015, 14).

Furthermore, Guy Standing has introduced the precariat as a concept to denote a "fragmented global class structure," i.e. an emerging "dangerous class," marked by a shared sense of insecurity and a weak connection with capital or the state (2011, 13). He explicitly contrasts it with the working class, as the precariat "has none of the social contract relationships of the proletariat, whereby labour securities were provided in exchange for subordination and contingent loyalty" (ibid., 14). As a figure of the dispossessed and disenfranchised, the precariat lacks an occupational identity; its members are trapped "in career-less jobs, without traditions of social memory, a feeling they belong to an occupational community steeped in stable practices, codes of ethics and norms of behaviour, reciprocity and fraternity" (ibid., 20). These characterisations have urged critics like Bryan Palmer, writing from a traditionally socialist point of view, to reject Standing's precariat as a mere "ideology," which presumably neglects the fact that social vulnerability "has always been the fundamental feature of class formation rather than the material basis of a new, contemporary class" (2014, 44–45). Similar criticisms have emerged with respect to the geographical assumptions that underlie the notion of the precariat: while Standing suggests the global projection of the precariat, others have highlighted the risks of applying an overly homogenising approach to specific local conditions, which are often characterised by unequal power relations and different needs and forms of social struggle (Hammer and Ness 2023, 6). Aside from the links with actual protest movements like Euro-MayDay, Precarias a la deriva and Occupy—at times suggested by Negri, Hardt and Standing—this conceptual work has sparked a broader debate on the actuality and use of class categories, both as tools for sociological analysis and for protest, able to grasp, imagine or inspire actual outbursts of social protest of people with the most diverse backgrounds. These discussions have shifted attention to the singular, fragmented and intersectional dimensions of individual and social identities.

Intersectional Perspectives: Class vs. Identity?

In parallel to these political, socio-economic and cultural trends, in the mid-1990s the interdisciplinary field of working-class studies emerged, "out of a concern with those negatively impacted by these changes" (Fazio et al. 2021, 2) and with the central aim "to conceptualize the social differences, tensions, and

contradictions that have in fact always been constitutive of working-class collectivity" (Entin 2021, 32). Working-class studies put considerable emphasis on
plurality, relationality and change. In this context, a crucial question becomes
how class is inflected by race, ethnicity, nation, religion, gender and sexuality,
and approaches to class have been accordingly reformulated through the prism
of intersectionality. As a consequence, the focus has shifted away from class as
an objective relation to "class as an identity—shaped by economics and exploitation, to be sure, but most urgently stood as a form of belonging" (Entin 2021, 33).
In the words of Ben Clarke, "working-class studies is [...] necessarily a form of
'intersectional analysis,' its diversity founded, in the last instance, on that of the
working class itself" (2021, 363). As Patricia Hill Collins explains, intersectionality refers to a "constellation of ideas and practices that maintain that gender,
race, class, sexuality, age, ethnicity, ability, and similar phenomena constitute a
mutually constructing constellation of power relationships" (2020, 122). She also
emphasises that it refers to a knowledge project which implies both inquiry and
practice, and that the entrance of the term into academic discourse, most frequently attributed to Kimberlé Crenshaw (1991), was preceded by a long and
vibrant history of intersectional movements and practices, in which Black feminism in particular played a pivotal role. This prism, as she has argued elsewhere,
is fundamental in that it allows previously established knowledge to be interro-
gated, for instance with regard to the predominance of white, male experiences
in studies of work (Hill Collins 2019, 36).

Among the manifold approaches that have put intersectionality on the research agenda, even if they were not (explicitly) labelled as such at the time they
emerged, an important section of them have undertaken a considerable effort to
revise traditional Marxist categories. The project of rethinking Marxism from
the viewpoint of the intrinsic connectedness of class, gender and race relies on
a tradition of feminist—and particularly Black feminist—thought that spans the
whole twentieth century (see Lewis 2022, 93–186 for an overview). From the
perspective of gender, feminist scholars such as Silvia Federici and Angela Davis,
to name just two well-known examples, have pointed not only to the problem
of workplace discrimination and unequal remuneration, but also to the issue of
reproductive labour. Federici's criticism of Marx's work denounces the lack of
attention in his writings to the fundamental role of domestic work in the reproduction of the very conditions of possibility for capitalism. As one of the key pro-
ponents of the Wages for Housework movement, Federici ([1975] 2020, 40–44)
contended that women performing housework are in fact invisible—and hence,
unwaged—workers whose labour is being naturalised and obscured so as not
to reveal the essential part they play in the functioning of capitalist economies.
Correcting the idea that this situation affects all women equally, Davis pointed

out that Black women historically have had to endure the "double burden of wage labor and housework" ([1981] 1983, 192) because of slavery and its legacies—a burden shared by working-class white women, albeit not to the same extent, and in markedly different ways. She likewise problematised the assumption that capitalism was interested in maintaining the reproductive capacities of (all) women for the production of the labour force, pointing out how the reproductive rights of Black women have been consistently curtailed (cf. ibid., 178–185).

At the same time, the Eurocentric, Western and race-blind assumptions of Marxism became increasingly questioned by scholars working within in the Black Radical tradition (see Robinson [1983] 2000), while the intrinsic connection between capitalism and coloniality—as a constellation of "long-standing patterns of power that emerged as a result of colonialism, but that define culture, labor, intersubjective relations, and knowledge production well beyond the strict limits of colonial administrations" (Maldonado-Torres 2007, 243)—became a major preoccupation in post- and decolonial theory, accounting, for example, for the way in which colonial assumptions underpin the lack of valorisation—and hence, the unequal remuneration—of the indigenous and black workforce (Quijano [2000] 2020, 869). These inequalities are further exacerbated by migration, as migrants often face precarious and insecure conditions because of their incomplete access to full citizenship rights (see Ramírez et al. 2021). More recently, scholars such as Holly Lewis have worked to reconcile Marxist thought with the demands and struggles of queer people by problematising the heteronormativity that underlies capitalism's control of women's sexuality (2022, 183–186). Needless to say, these are only a few examples of the vast bibliography of critical thinking on which intersectionality relies, which should be complemented by approaches to other factors of discrimination such as ethnicity, ability and age, and should, ideally, be extended beyond the human as well, as the contributions to this volume by Tim Christiaens and by Joeri Verbesselt and Syaman Rapongan suggest.

A recurring topic in the bibliography on intersectional approaches to working-class studies is the encounter between identity politics and class-based demands and analyses. Especially in the US, approaches to class became entangled with questions of identity politics. These approaches have been criticised for conflating class as an objective social relation and as an individual way of life, i.e. an identity. In doing so, they are rooted in the broader post-structuralist suspicion against totalising narratives and essentialising categories. In opposition to these strands of research, critics like Tove Soiland (2012) have rejected the tendency to consider class as an identity category, refocusing its meaning to what it initially was: a heuristic tool to expose, analyse and problematise an objective, primarily economic relation that engenders mechanisms of hierarchisation and exploitation. Subsequently, she points out—correctly—that merely deconstructing a category like class will not alter the power structures it helps to conceive of. She pleads for reinstating the original meaning and purpose of class as a purely objective, materialist category.

Other scholars have warned against the neglect of class-based power inequities that can result from the predominant focus on (racial) identity politics (see Wilson [1987] 2012), as well as against the increasingly frequent cases in which movements of resistance based on identitarian demands have been hijacked by an economic and political elite (Táíwò 2022).[1] This uneasy combination of class and identity on a theoretical level also resonates strongly with the perception of their antagonism in the political sphere. Among other things, this phenomenon explains why voters in disadvantaged positions nevertheless endorse candidates and policies that are detrimental to their well-being as they perceive elitist political correctness and 'woke' movements as a more imminent threat—see the rise of populism in all Western societies (cf. Nachtwey 2018, 213–231 on the German situation), but especially the anger and hopelessness experienced by the precarised white working class in the US (Poblete 2021, 216–218).

This tension is the result of recent historical re-evaluations of identity concepts as such. For example, Marie Moran has shown that the emergence and salience of notions (and subsequent deconstructions) of both personal and social identity as a device of classification and of mobilisation is a fairly new phenomenon, "only emerg[ing] with the explosion of consumption in the late twentieth century" (2016, 4). A cultural materialist approach reveals that "what we now think of as different social and political 'identities' only came to be framed as such with the emergence of exclusive group-based politics, new social movements and 'multiculturalism' in the 1960s and 1970s" (ibid.). This is evident in an increasing occurrence of the term in political and cultural discourses, as well as a broadening range of its possible meanings. According to Moran, identity is a concept that "carries and encapsulates a new way of thinking about and engaging with a range of social, political and human concerns," which also includes activist struggles of/against collective identities (ibid., 26). By historicising the very idea of identity, it becomes possible to move beyond the aforementioned rift between a "social left" that maintains that "identity politics conceal the material bases of oppression and fracture any coherent, class-based movement" and a "cultural left" defending the use of identity categories and the attempts to mobilise along the (intertwined) axes of gender, sexuality, ethnicity or race (ibid., 7). The task, instead, is

> to examine how exactly this device [the concept of identity] has been operationalised, culturally, politically and commercially, in a capitalist context. Instead of asserting the priority of economic over cultural concerns, or of class over identity concerns, or vice versa, this approach allows us to explore and evaluate their

inter-relation—by examining how the idea of identity is used and acted upon to great political and commercial effect within capitalist societies, in ways which do not always or automatically reinforce a capitalist logic, but which may also challenge it. (ibid.)

This volume follows the thesis that personal and social identity concepts should not be neglected but rather studied in relation to the material and cultural contexts in which they are embedded. Objective economic relations are after all always experienced by individuals, and class is more than just a structural, economic category (Felski 2021, 98–99). In Pierre Bourdieu's influential theory of class (*La distinction*, 1979), this aspect already plays a fundamental role, insofar as it is intrinsic to his notions of social reproduction and habitus: he shows how a system of inequality, exploitation and class injury reproduces itself through everyday modes of being, i.e. engrained patterns of behaviour and thought. Social differences manifest themselves symbolically, as taste differences. Moreover, Bourdieu's concepts of class and habitus point to realms of social experience outside of the workplace, which sustain and enforce class differences, like the domestic sphere, school, the judiciary and penal system. These institutions of socialisation normalise power structures through habituation and discipline, keeping class subjects in place—an exertion of power Bourdieu also called "symbolic violence" (Bourdieu 1998).

Intersectional approaches to class and identity are also strongly dependent on the geopolitical factors that condition social relations. While class concepts that acknowledge the heterogenous and fragmentary nature of the working class, like the 'multitude' or 'precariat,' have an international—even aspirationally global—scope, contemporary class imaginations remind us of the many national, local and individual situations that affect these identities and are in their turn mediated and reconfigured through culture. As mentioned earlier, the neoliberal turn has taken on various guises in different locations, and so has its impact on work and class experiences. The contributions in this volume focus on societies that are commonly considered part of what has been called the "Global North." There is, however, a lot to learn from the so-called "Global South" when taking into account the evolution towards ever more precarious labour conditions in Western societies and from the aesthetic projects that address heavily entrenched forms of work-related vulnerability and precarity—for instance, Chilean author Diamela Eltit's recent novels on sex workers (*Fuerzas especiales*, 2013) and street vendors (*Sumar*, 2018), Mexican writer Vivian Abenshushan's experimental multimedia (*Permanente obra negra*, 2019) and essayistic work (*Escritos para desocupados*, 2013) on art as a form of precarious employment, or the immense literary production in Argentina that set out to diagnose the causes and consequences of the economic crisis and accompanying social upheaval of 2001. What is more, de-colonial scholars have identified the antagonism between class and identity poli-tics as a central feature of the Eurocentric perspective, and have highlighted the importance not only of deconstructing these assumptions, but also of taking so-called "epistemologies of the South" seriously (de Sousa Santos 2016). These offer different and potentially more productive models to approach these phenomena because, among other factors, of the way in which some of them are inherently non-binary (cf. Rivera Cusicanqui 2012). A proper engagement with such episte-mologies falls largely outside of the scope of this book (with the sole exception of Verbesselt and Rapongan's chapter, which adopts a perspective informed by Tao critical thought in Taiwan). However, we hope that the intersectional perspective on class that we adopt here can be a first step in addressing some of the concerns that have arisen regarding the exclusions generated by Western-based discourses of knowledge.

In the Global North as well, however, research that wants to do justice to the complexities of the local has to compare key examples taken from 'major' econo-mies (the US, UK, France, Germany) with class imaginaries that have not re-ceived much international attention by scholars (Sweden, Spain, Taiwan). This goal, pursued in this volume, can help us obtain a differentiated understanding of how complex class identities are articulated in contemporary culture. By read-ing contemporary class stories against the backdrop of class imaginaries and vo-cabularies from the past and the present, it is possible to shed more light on the different kinds of working-class culture that exist in different contexts and are reconfigured and actualised in concrete texts and images.

Class Imaginaries in Contemporary Culture

What the aforementioned debates show is that the questions of what constitutes a class and how the individual subject relates to class as an objective reality and subjective identity are constantly being renegotiated, under the pressure of shift-ing political, social, economic and cultural contexts. These reconceptualisations of class are presented with awareness of its inner tensions and differences, its dy-namics and historical variability, its intersections with other structures of power and exploitation—this in opposition to static, universal and essentialist defini-tions of the working class. Cultural representations of class *reflect and actively take part in* this myriad of positions, as becomes clear from the vast, rhizomati-cally expanding archive of narrative and visual stories dealing with the most het-erogenous intimate and social, personal and collective class experiences (even if they are not always explicitly framed in terms of class).

This volume wants to zoom in on specific aspects of this vast archive of stories, by looking at the strategies to negotiate and renegotiate, to mediate and remediate complex, intersectional identities in various narrative genres. Its premises are that this archive offers a highly diverse set of imaginaries and stories of class. Whereas there is a prolific body of scholarship dealing with working-class culture and representations of class, poverty and precarity (see, for example, Korte and Regard 2014, Böhm and Kovacshazy 2015, Lennon and Nilsson 2017–2020, Hogg and Simonsen 2021, Rys and Philipsen 2021, Fazio et al. 2021), contemporary cultural production urges us to revise some common premises and prejudices about class identities and imagine new ones (Fazio et al. 2021). The neoliberal condition, the new trajectories for up- and downward social mobility and the scattered nature of what could today be described as a working class—all recurrent themes in present-day culture—urge us to develop more differentiated analytic frames. Exactly because cultural narratives of and about class articulate this diversity, these have a crucial role to play in this process. The contributions to this volume show that the frames evoked by the diversifying and critical gestures of these stories complement and refine theoretical insights.

Furthermore, cultural representations of identity are related to the strife towards recognition of class experiences and injuries. It is no coincidence that both in sociology and in literary and visual text genres the role of *storytelling* occupies a central place, as narrative strategies are needed which construct and give access to class experiences. Informed by Axel Honneth's analysis of social struggles in terms of recognition, Rita Felski has argued that as soon as lived experiences of class are made accessible in the public realm, they acquire a different status, thereby shedding their anonymous and everyday character. As public goods and objects of representation, they are to various degrees legitimised as being "worthy of wider attention—as counting" (2021, 104). In contrast to sociological accounts of class and precarity, culture does more than registering that class exists, by showing "*how* it permeates one's being in the world, affects one's body, and enters into one's soul" (ibid., 103). In that respect, culture does "not simply portray struggles over recognition; they also *enact* them," as "a key *mechanism* of recognition" (ibid., 102). Culture thus influences the place and weight of layered class identities within the public debate.

These identities are also strongly dependent on the study of the narrative and visual techniques with which writers and artists construct and negotiate class experiences. As Jacques Rancière has it, aesthetic practices are fundamental for processes of subjectivation, by which traditional and common-sense identities are rearticulated, affirmed or called into question (1992, 58–64). It is this subjectivating power, indeed, that harbours a great deal of the performative potential of these stories for re-imagining class identity, for redistributing the sensible. It should be noted, as well, that these subjectivation processes can best be thought of as mobilised both by discourse and non-discursive regimes, in which affect plays a major role as a fundamentally transindividual force—see, for instance, Maurizio Lazzarato's (2014, 16) criticism of what he considers Rancière's excessive reliance on discursive practices. Already before Rancière, Raymond Williams argued that, because "no mode of production, and therefore no dominant society or order of society, and therefore no dominant culture, in reality exhausts the full range of human practice, human energy, human intention," culture always pushes the boundaries of what is perceived as normal further, teasing out "emergent," i.e. "alternative[,] perception[s] of others," "new meanings and values, new practices, new significances and experiences" (1980, 41–43).

Against this background, the study of artistic imaginaries of class helps to elucidate the importance of narrativity for sociological analyses more generally; it can also enrich existing models, by foregrounding the personal, plural and experiential. Class as subjective experience is, for example, prompted in projects that collect individual voices and personal stories of those in precarious positions, thereby not only foregrounding the diversity within the working force, but also emphasising that class is a lived experience. Acknowledging the voices *from the inside* is an important method of working-class studies, which contributes to a better understanding of "the tension between specificity and generalization" that underpins class theory. Stories help to "highlight gaps and oversimplifications" in our conceptualisations of class, and often this urges us to confront issues of social reproduction, or of class as experienced in its intersections with race, ethnicity, gender and sexuality (Linkon 2021, 23). Individual stories are Julia Friedrichs' (2021) and Nicole Mayer-Ahuja and Oliver Nachtwey's (2021) method to elucidate how insecurity disproportionately affects the non-white and non-male groups—a fact that had to a large extent remained invisible. Equally marginalised were the class experiences of social climbers, which statistical models neglect as mere anomalies. Chantal Jaquet (2018) shifted focus towards exactly these biographies as part of a project to revise Bourdieu's theory of social reproduction. Bourdieu leaves little room to acknowledge or explain what Jaquet labels "transclasse," even though these exceptional biographies can help to shed new light on class society: their existence itself reveals that class boundaries are still in place. Jaquet convincingly shows that, in particular, various strands of autobiographical narration, ranging from memoirs and testimonies to autofiction, have become a central medium to interlink self-exploration and broader sociological analysis, as it presents individual lives as embedded in class contexts. Autosociobiographical texts—texts that combine the narration of individual experiences with sociological analysis—like Annie Ernaux's *La Place* (1983) and *La Honte* (1987) or Eribon's *Retour à Reims* (2009) offer a theoretically informed analysis of a social reality exemplified in the narrating self's singular experience as a transclass, moving between classes, unable to fully break with their origin nor to integrate in the class of arrival.

The focus of these narratives lies on individual subjects growing up in a working-class environment from which they gradually become estranged; they also articulate complex identities, caught between classes and on the intersections with gender, sexuality and ethnicity. While Bourdieu urges us to confront how individuals are affected by their surroundings and social networks, more recent conceptualisations of class show that they are never fully determined by them. Accordingly, the focus on the individual exposes the role of affective relations that underpin the dynamic processes of class identification and de-identification, of social reproduction and non-reproduction. Teachers or family members who were able to cross class boundaries and with whom individuals have a positive relation can set an example and inspire them to make a jump themselves. Social non-reproduction is always a transindividual phenomenon, which can only be understood by taking into account a variety of changing social, economic and affective variants that inform singular biographies. In short, Jaquet offers a way out of the controversies as to whether the objective and collective *or* the subjective and personal should be foregrounded, and she shows that the complexity of class as relation and experience is paradigmatically grasped in concrete stories of factual or fictional selves, i.e. in cultural artefacts.

The cultural recognition of layered class identities in concrete stories and narratives has to be studied with attention to the variety in the corpus under consideration that manifests itself on multiple levels, culturally, historically and geographically. In order to do justice to this heterogeneity, we deliberately define working-class imaginaries in a broad sense, focusing not only on artefacts and voices by members of the working class themselves, but also by those depicting social realities and experiences they have not necessarily lived through themselves. This entails the risk Cynthia Cruz describes in *The Melancholia of Class*, where she signals that "there are very few contemporary poets or fiction writers from the American working class, and these few who are, tend either to incorporate culturally shared stereotypes and caricatures about the working class in their writing, or they abandon their working-class background entirely" (2021, 48). Cruz prompts us to reflect on the ethics of storytelling. This has to do not only with issues of representation and narratability, but also with the implicit power relations that necessarily define the position from which a writer or an artist speaks: who is in a legitimate position to speak about precarious workers from various backgrounds in the first place? Can someone who has not lived through the hardships of a life in precarity understand and talk about that? Cruz's position is clear: "Artists who attempt to depict the lives of the working class who are not from the working class must necessarily write from a detached point of view. As a result, such projects become anthropological: the writer and reader stand outside the experience being depicted, creating yet one more layer of marginalization" (ibid., 183). We believe, however, that excluding those 'external' class imaginaries would limit our capacity to reconstruct the myriad, hybrid and often fragmented cultural lives of class in contemporary culture—we would run the risk of reifying them and rendering them incommunicable to anyone who does not find herself in the exact same intersectional position in the field of power—as well as the parallel processes of recognition and misrecognition, of stereotyping and diversification.

Three fundamental questions follow from the call for an aesthetics of intersectional working-class identities. First, who or what is being recognised as being what? When do representations become stereotypical and/or voyeuristic, further enforcing cultural dynamics of othering? What realities and experiences are explicitly connected with concepts of class, or how do cultural artefacts indirectly conjure up imaginations of class? What ideological, political, activist meanings are projected onto figures of class? If the texts, images and filmic narratives from the archive of and about working-class culture articulate complex, intersectional identities, it should be analysed how these identities are constructed. In particular, the narrative works here studied explore new alliances and dividing lines both within the traditional working class and at its boundaries, which connect in different ways with questions of race, gender and sexual orientation. Second, through what genre- and medium-specific means is the process of recognising intersectional class identities realised? While present-day class imaginations respond to the neoliberal juncture in socio-economic history, it is also true that they often actualise existing narrative and visual strategies to narrate class identity and agency, like the *Bildungsroman* or certain types of social and critical realism. These lineages of writing and rewriting conceptual and aesthetic traditions from the past can best be reconstructed by moving back from specific cases to explore the dialogue with their antecedents. It is likewise important to note that many of the examples elude traditional genre categories and navigate on the scale of documentary and fictional narration. This hybridity is exemplified in the many examples of autobiographical and autofictional novels in which narrators seek a new voice to articulate their identities, like Didier Eribon, Édouard Louis and Deniz Ohde. Even though the textual, visual and performative narratives rely on different aesthetic strategies, it will be important to question how diverging stories of class resonate: what are the recurring patterns that become visible across the variety of individual experiences and artistic practices? Third, how do class texts and images position themselves socially, and what are the strategies by which they aim to affect readers, viewers and audiences? This points in the direction of a cultural reception that is itself affected by class boundaries, which impact the distribution and accessibility of texts and images. In their processes of affective world-making, textual and visual artefacts mobilise a wide range of structures of feeling which supersede the level of the individual mind and conscious interpretation (Breger 2020).[2] Several examples of contemporary literature related to the working class seek to involve their audience by interpellating them directly, or to make them participants of their performative gestures. Against this background, questions of aesthetics and ethics appear deeply entangled.

The Contents of this Book

This volume is the outcome of a symposium on *Re-Imagining Class*, which took place in May 2022 in Leuven and was organised by the IdeaLab *Figures and Narratives of Precarity* (a forum for ground-breaking and interdisciplinary research of early-career scholars, funded by KU Leuven, Belgium). The volume includes contributions by international researchers and widely recognised experts, active in a broad range of geographical and linguistic fields. The innovative aspect of this volume lies in its transnational, multimedial and interdisciplinary approach to examine the proliferating archive of class imaginaries. While most studies of working-class culture tend to zoom in on a national context, this volume's starting point is the diversification as well as the interaction and even transfer of texts and images within and across national boundaries or traditions of countries that are part of the Global North. One of its goals lies in its comparative approach, which traces how (rearticulations of) working-class identities are constructed across various media that have to be studied as complementary in order to get a fuller and more nuanced grasp of the diversity of the archive of working-class culture, its many manifestations and functions. Hence this volume does not claim exhaustivity, though it wants to offer models to analyse concrete artefacts. Lastly, the scope of the volume is interdisciplinary in order to map out the way in which art and storytelling can contribute to a better understanding of contemporary society. Together, the chapters elicit a dialogue between literary and cultural studies, artistic research, sociology and political theory, including perspectives on the function of testimonial narratives in qualitative sociological research.

The contributions are structured into five parts that set out possible trajectories through the maze of contemporary class imaginations. The first part, **"Rediscovering Class: Continuities and Ruptures,"** is comprised of two chapters that explore the way in which contemporary literature addresses the (recent) historical evolution of class imaginaries in different national contexts. They identify how these works engage with more traditional working-class figures, thereby examining both the factors of continuity and the breaking points which inform contemporary imaginings of class. Fundamental to these analyses are the questions as to which elements are selected from the traditional archive of working-class narratives, and which conditions govern the fluctuations in the visibility of class in a wider social and literary context. In both chapters, the question of precarity and the concept of the precariat play a fundamental role as heuristic devices to elucidate contemporary tendencies and to examine their (supposed) newness. What is more, both insist on the necessity of adequately accounting for geographical and historical specificity, as traditions and literary evolutions vary greatly between national contexts. This argument is made explicit by Magnus Nilsson's opening chapter "Writing (for) the Precariat: Mats Teglund's *Cykelbudet* (2021) and Pelle Sunvisson's *Svenska Palmen* (2021)" (1.1), which zooms in on the way in which contemporary Swedish novels engage with a local tradition of working-class literature which, in contrast to other national contexts, configures class as depending more on political and ideological parameters than on cultural factors. His readings of Pelle Sunvisson's *Svenska palmen* (2021) and Anders Teglund's *Cykelbudet* (2021) rely on Marx's distinction between an economically defined 'class in itself' and a 'class for itself' that implies a deeper level of class consciousness in order to address these works' similarities—and, to a lesser degree, their differences—with working-class novels published in the first half of the twentieth century.

In "Making Visible the Invisible: Spanish Post-Crisis Fiction" (1.2), Christian Claesson identifies post-dictatorial optimism after the return to democracy in Spain in the 1970s as an important factor in the obscuring of precarious experiences and of class-related concerns both in the public sphere and in literary discourse, and deems the particularly harsh way in which the financial crisis of 2008–2009 hit the Spanish economy at least partly responsible for their resurgence. He proposes the category of 'post-crisis literature' to amend the much-invoked label of the 'novela de la crisis' in a bid to signal how tendencies in literature evolve beyond the temporally limited framework imposed by the idea of 'crisis.' Drawing on the similarities and contrasts between Isaac Rosa's *La mano invisible* (2011) and Cristina Morales's *Lectura fácil* (2018), Claesson registers an increasing politicisation of post-crisis literature in the sense that it points to new possibilities for action on the basis of a recognition of (unequally) shared conditions of precarity.

The second part, **"Personalising Class: Individuals and Collectives,"** deals with the tensions between personal, at times also deeply intimate, experiences and the idea of shared socio-economic relations and interests that underpin collective class identities in the first place. As outlined above, class identities have become more fragmented because of socio-economic shifts and the growing awareness of their intersectional layering. This tension not only manifests itself in contemporary literature, but also plays a fundamental role in the narrative biographical interviews that form the basis of qualitative sociological research addressing the embedment of individuals in larger networks.

The chapters in this part zoom in on the tension between individual and class experience, and they explore how new forms of solidarity that are nonetheless respectful of individual differences can be imagined. In his contribution on "The Poetics of Personal Authenticity: Diversity, Intersectionality and the Working Class in Contemporary German Literature" (2.1), Christoph Schaub focuses on the new attention towards intersectional class identities in contemporary German literature, which finds its most poignant expression in genres of self-exploration, like autobiography and autofiction. Through the analysis of Deniz Ohde's autofictional novel *Streulicht* (2020) and the anthology of stories *Klasse und Kampf* (2021; ed. Maria Barankow and Christian Baron), Schaub shows how heterogeneity is vindicated by these authors through the narration of individual experiences, and how these are mobilised against homogenising views of the working class. In this context, ideas of personal authenticity appear key to understanding the diversifying strategies to which these authors turn in their works.

In his chapter "Narrating the Precariat: Social Wounds in Terézia Mora's and Wilhelm Genazino's Novels" (2.2), Olaf Berwald addresses how the narration of individual experiences and their confrontation with the perspective of external observers shed light on the consequences of intersectionally distributed precarity and their dehumanising dimension in the work of these two authors. He focuses on Mora's novel *Das Ungeheuer* (2013) and her notebooks published as *Fleckenverlauf* (2021), and on Genazino's novels *Die Kassiererinnen* (1998), *Außer uns spricht niemand über uns* (2016), and *Kein Geld, keine Uhr, keine Mütze* (2018), as well as his posthumously published lectures, *Die Angst vor der Penetranz des Wirklichen* (2020).

Crossing the disciplinary divide between literary studies and sociology, the chapter "'Know Where to Fish': Class and Gender Precarity and Project-based Networks in Creative and Cultural Industries" (2.3) underlines the importance of individual storytelling as a heuristic tool for the uncovering of broader tendencies in the rearticulation of class experiences in relation to race and gender. The authors of the chapter, Valeria Pulignano, Deborah Dean, Markieta Domecka and Lander Vermeerbergen, analyse the precarisation of work in the creative sector by mapping out the networks on which workers depend for project opportunities. Based on narrative biographical interviews with project workers, and semi-structured interviews with experts, in the film, TV and dance sectors across four European countries, their findings point to commodification in project work as one of the generative forces leading to precarious class-based outcomes, and identify the unequal positioning within and incomplete access to networks of sociability and recognition as detrimental to upward mobility.

In the third part, **"Narrating Class: Voice and Belonging,"** the contributors seek to flesh out the literary strategies with which writers construct a narrative voice able to adequately recognise layered class identities and affective structures of belonging. While the first chapter analyses the implications of the hybridity of the narratorial voice, the subsequent two chapters zoom in on the construction of the figure of the transclass in order to address the ambiguities that surround the characters' relationships to the differently positioned others that have influenced their professional trajectories. The trope of social advancement occurs in many contemporary novels that deal with experiences and injuries of class, not in the least in a societal context that often still allegedly adheres to the idea of meritocracy. All these chapters explore the way in which characters' voices reflect the hesitations, insecurities and traumatic experiences related to their (shifting) belonging to the working class. "Double(ing) Voices: Narrating Precarious Class Status and Class Identities" (3.1) by Sula Textor explores the hybridity of the narrative voice as a complement to—and, to an extent, a problematisation of— the increasing prominence of autosociobiographical narratives. In her analysis of Canadian author Megan Gail Coles' novel *Small Game Hunting at the Local Coward Gun Club* (2019), Textor shows how precarious class consciousness does not emerge in this text as an individual experience presented through the perspective of a classical homodiegetic or omniscient narrator. Rather, the multiperspectivism of the narrative voice emphasises its transindividual dimension as the chapter explores the way in which voices and discourses become blurred to the point that it becomes difficult to attribute them to singular characters. Thereby it points to the fundamental tension between lines of division and the very fluidity of identity concepts.

In "Obstacles to Leaving, Problems of Arriving: Gender and Genealogy in Contemporary German Narratives of the Social Climber (Christian Baron, Bov Bjerg, Deniz Ohde, Anke Stelling)" (3.2), Irene Husser advocates for a sustained engagement with narrative techniques and genres in order to avoid reducing literary analysis to the identification of sociological categories within texts dealing with precarious class experiences. Tracing narratives of the social climber back to the genre of the *Bildungsroman*, Husser unpacks the gender norms that interact with ideas of meritocracy in a comparative analysis of four contemporary novels by German authors: Christian Baron's *Ein Mann seiner Klasse* (2020), Bov Bjerg's *Serpentinen* (2020), Deniz Ohde's *Streulicht* (2020) and Anke Stelling's *Schäfchen im Trockenen* (2018). By comparing the ways in which these texts construct discursive and affective genealogies with father and mother figures in the context of upward social mobility, the chapter unveils how they punctuate overly optimistic accounts of individualised agency and explore the gendered construction of class-based models and anti-models of aspiration.

The last chapter of this part, Katrin Becker's "Narrating Class and Classlessness in Contemporary British Novels of Black Women's Social Climbing" (3.3), similarly explores the ambiguities that surround the figure of social ascent by focusing on narrative techniques and by situating them against the reappraisal of class in British sociology after its demise in the political repertoire in neoliberal Britain. She analyses how Natasha Brown's *Assembly* (2021), Zadie Smith's *NW* (2012), Bernadine Evaristo's *Girl, Woman, Other* (2019) and Nicola William's *Without Prejudice* (1997) rely on strategies such as the narrative distribution of information to deconstruct the individualist myths of meritocratic class imaginaries. In these texts, the tension between visibility and invisibility surrounding helper figures and the asphyxiating consequences of the imperative of individual advancement are mobilised to renegotiate the pitfalls of upward mobility from an intersectional and transindividual vantage point. In so doing, Becker argues, some of them also point to the desire to re-explore the modes of collective agency still sidelined in current political debates.

The fourth part, **"Performing Class: Materiality and Affect,"** deals with stagings of class in contemporary theatre, performance art and cinema. The contributions are especially interested in the way in which these works invite affective responses from their audiences. First of all, the contributions in this part analyse the techniques that are intended to create a shared space of feeling and, ideally, to mobilise their spectators. Here, gestures that are aimed at producing and directing affect come to the fore as recurrent tactics to foster audiences' critical reflection about their involvement in class structures and identities. In parallel, all the contributions foreground issues of materiality, both with regard to the circumstances in which artists and playwrights have to work, and as a formal strategy, particularly in relation to the material living and working conditions that are thematised on the level of plot and content. Furthermore, it becomes apparent that contemporary playwrights and film makers develop techniques that often involve reconfiguring past traditions in order to adequately address the structures of feeling that arise in the evolution towards today's heterogenous precarious classes.

The first chapter in this part, Marissia Fragkou's "Affected by Discomfort: Class and Precarity in Twenty-First-Century Theatre" (4.1), analyses performances that aim to submerge their audiences in the experience of precariousness tied to being an artist with a working-class and otherwise intersectionally disadvantaged background. Based on three examples of autobiographical work by UK-based performance makers Scottee (*Bravado*, 2017, and *Class*, 2019) and Travis Alabanza (*Burgerz*, 2018), the chapter explores the use of discomfort as an affective strategy to induce ethically informed spectatorial engagement. Situating the performances in the context of initiatives that aim to promote diversity in the artistic sector and problematising the gap between some of the latter's intentions and outcomes, Fragkou scrutinises how the active participation of members of the audience becomes the ground for the construction of an ethics of care that would transcend the boundaries instated by class, race, gender, sexuality and ability.

While Fragkou demonstrates how theatre makers experiment with new modalities of performing class, Sarah Pogoda's contribution "The Redundancy: Playing Production in Academic Capitalism" (4.2) shows how existing theatre plays from the past acquire new uses and meanings in contemporary contexts. Here, Pogoda presents her artistic research project "The Redundancy,"[3] staged in June 2019, which confronted working conditions at UK universities with German author Heiner Müller's socialist production play *Der Lohndrücker* (*The Scab*, 1957). The multi-medial, site-specific performance addressed the dangers of self-exploitation academics face when confronted with the increase in competitivity, consumer-oriented policy changes and top-down managerial practices in higher education. By recontextualising quotes from Müller's play and drawing on its underlying criticisms of an excessive emphasis on productivity, "The Redundancy" staged spaces in which visitors could interactively engage with reflections on the precarisation and commodification of academic labour. Equally central to Pogoda's performance is the self-reflexive attention towards its conditions of realisation and reception as its evolution was impacted by the limited availability of overworked academic participants and gave way to, in the very writing of her chapter, its own recuperation as academic labour.

The afterlife of material detail in visual culture is highlighted in Daniel Brookes' contribution "'The View Is Nice, but You Can't Eat It': A Poetics of Precarity in *Bait* (2019)" (4.3) about the aesthetics of the highly diverse precariat in Mark Jenkin's *Bait*. The experimental and fragmentary film zooms in on a Cornish fishing town in which social life has been gravely affected by the expansion of tourism and rentier capitalism. Brookes shows how the film's proximity to the genre of the pastoral and its visual counterposition of scenes starring villagers and visitors sheds light on the increasing difficulty of mobilising structures of feeling for the development of class consciousness, as these depend on the existence of a community that has now been torn apart. In its exploration of the obstacles to intra- and inter-class solidarity, the film centrally relies on tactility both as an invitation to consider the material conditions of physical labour and as a strategy of defamiliarisation.

The final part of this volume, **"Class beyond the Human: Work Experiences and the Anthropocene,"** further extends the intersectional perspective adopted in the preceding contributions to the domain of the non-human and more-than-human. It emphasises the fact that the worldwide intensification of precarity cannot be disentangled from the ecological damage to the planet brought about by human beings—as the term 'Anthropocene' is intended to convey—and specifically by the rise, consolidation and subsequent neoliberalisation of capitalism—captured by the concept of the 'Capitalocene,' which emerged as a correction to the assumption that human beings share responsibility over climate change equally (Moore 2016; Haraway 2016, 263). Re-imagining class in ecological terms implies, in the two contributions that make up this part, an effort to conceive of the ways in which certain sectors of the both human and non-human populations of the planet are disproportionately affected by anthropogenic natural disasters and processes of ruination; it also entails thinking beyond anthropocentric perspectives and, in a sense, learning from the earth itself.

Tim Christiaens's "Bare Land: Alienation as Deracination in Anna Tsing and John Steinbeck" (5.1) confronts Tsing's contention that capitalism alienates living beings from their capacity to form sustainable alliances across species and environments with a rereading of John Steinbeck's *The Grapes of Wrath* (1939) in an effort to show how literature can work to imagine a new ecological class politics. As Christiaens suggests, even if it is impossible to consider Steinbeck as a posthumanist writer *avant-la-lettre*, his novel nonetheless provides insights into how capitalism simultaneously disturbs human and non-human realities by exhausting agricultural grounds, which, in turn, leads to the uprooting of rural workers. The book thereby relies on what could be called a 'strategic anthropocentrism' in a bid to affectively engage its human readers. Christiaens proposes the category of 'bare land,' by analogy with Agamben's 'bare life,' to make sense of how, in the age of intensified planetary destruction, the conditions of reproduction rather than of production become essential to understand class struggle in an ecological sense.

The preoccupation with sustainable modes of living together is shared by Joeri Verbesselt and Syaman Rapongan's chapter, "Interspecies Storytelling for Prudent Predation" (5.2), which proposes a close reading of the latter's story 'The Eyes of the Sky' (2012). In this story, Rapongan, a Taiwan-based Tao writer draws on Tao mythology as a way of urging humans to consider and learn from animal populations—in this case, the fish living in the ecosystem surrounding the island of Pongso no Tao. Situating their contribution within contemporary Western academic debates on the Anthropocene and ecological precarity but decidedly prioritising the Tao perspectives and traditions that have advanced these insights independently from —and often considerably before—the latter for their analysis, the authors point out how interspecies storytelling can help envisaging modes of 'prudent predation' as opposed to the unsustainable fishing practices that respond to the needs of international markets. Thus, within the contours of literary and critical practice, the possibility emerges to imagine an international interspecies alliance that would reframe and correct the notion of class in the context of the Anthropocene.

In short, the chapters in this volume explore multiple ways in which contemporary culture engages with, diversifies and in some cases radically transforms existing imaginaries of class in a deeply intersectional way. The contributors explore how class intersects with race, ethnicity, sexuality, gender and ability, and also how different spatio-temporally anchored concepts of class co-exist. What is more, they show how representations of class have adapted to rapidly changing socio-economic realities that, indeed, force us to constantly re-imagine class in terms of precarity, social mobility and social fragmentation, to name just a few factors. We believe that it is precisely this diversity that requires us to engage in an interdisciplinary dialogue that involves, among others, artists and writers, literary scholars and cultural critics, sociologists and political theorists. The conversation started in this book, however, is limited to the region and time in which its objects of study are situated. Most of the contributions deal with cultural concepts that originated in societies shaped by post-industrialisation and waning social security schemes. Nevertheless, we hope that the last part of this volume anticipates a wider discussion of new perspectives on class imaginaries on a planetary scale, which would include the Global South and would require, among other things, a deeper engagement with decolonial and post-humanist approaches. This can pave the way for further research on the conditions under which contemporary culture imagines class in a more global sense.

Notes

1. Táíwò also reminds us that early advocacy groups such as the Combahee River Collective practised identity politics as a way to engage in politics more generally, in stark contrast with some movements' present tendency to "close ranks—especially on social media—around ever-narrower conceptions of group interests" (2022, 18).

2. In her analysis of Didier Eribon's *Retour à Reims*, Felski warns of the risk of misrecognition, by artists (writers, filmmakers, etc.) and audiences (readers, spectators, etc.) alike, pointing to the work of (self-)interpretation: "while others may not recognize us as we recognize ourselves, our own sense of self also fluctuates over time and is, of course, far from fallible. [...] People disagree about the extent to which they want to be acknowledged by others [...] and what forms such acknowledgement should take. [...] An attempt at acknowledgement—even if undertaken with good intent—may be perceived as graceless or condescending. And if a person chooses to disidentify with social categories they're associated with—around gender, sexuality, race, or class—an acknowledgement of such categories by others may feel like an affront rather than an affirmation" (2021, 101–102).

3. The project can be found on Vimeo via https://vimeo.com/336614669; there is a password to watch the trailer, "HeinerMüller".

References

Baron, Christian. 2016. *Proleten. Pöbel. Parasiten: Warum die Linken die Arbeiter ver-achten*. Berlin: Das Neue Berlin.

Beck, Ulrich. 1992. *Risk Society. Towards a New Modernity*. London, Newbury Park, New Delhi: SAGE.

Beck, Ulrich. 2002. "The Cosmopolitan Society and its Enemies." *Theory, Culture & Society* 19, no. 1–2: 17–44.

Böhm, Roswitha, and Cécile Kovacshazy, eds. 2015. *Précarité. Littérature et cinéma de la crise au XXIe siècle*. Tübingen: Narr Francke Attempto.

Bourdieu, Pierre. 1998. *La domination masculine*. Paris: Seuil.

Breger, Claudia. 2020. *Making Worlds: Affect and Collectivity in Contemporary European Cinema*. New York: Columbia University Press.

Bridle, James. 2019. *New Dark Age: Technology and the End of the Future*. Old Saybrook CT: Tantor Media.

Butler, Judith. 2015. *Notes Toward a Performative Theory of Assembly*. Cambridge MA, London: Harvard University Press.

Castel, Robert. 2009. "Die Wiederkehr der sozialen Unsicherheit." In *Prekarität, Abstieg, Ausgrenzung. Die soziale Frage am Beginn des 21. Jahrhunderts*, edited by Robert Castel and Klaus Dörre, 21–34. Frankfurt, New York: Campus.

Christiaens, Tim. 2023. *De kluseconomie. Voor uitbuiting: klik 'aanvaard'*. Berchem: EPO.

Christiaens, Tim, and Stijn De Cauwer. 2020. "The Multitude Divided: Biopolitical Production During the Coronavirus Pandemic." In *Pandemic and the Crisis of Capitalism*, edited by Vincent Lyon-Callo et al., 118–127. Brighton: ReMarx.

Crenshaw, Kimberlé. 1991. "Mapping the Margins: Intersectionality, Identity Politics, and Violence against Women of Color." *Stanford Law Review* 43, no. 6: 1241–1300.

Cruz, Cynthia. 2021. *The Melancholia of Class: A Manifesto for the Working Class*. London: Repeater.

Davis, Angela Y. 1983. *Women, Race, & Class*. New York: Random House.

Eiden-Offe, Patrick. 2017. *Die Poesie der Klasse: Romantischer Kapitalismus und die Er-findung des Proletariats*. Berlin: Matthes & Seitz.

Entin, Joseph. 2021. "Reconceiving Class in Contemporary Working-Class Studies." In *Routledge International Handbook of Working-Class Studies*, edited by Michele Fazio, Christie Launius, and Tim Strangleman, 32–44. Abingdon, New York: Routledge.

Eribon, Didier. 2009. *Retour à Reims*. Paris: Fayard.

Fazio, Michele, Christie Launius, and Tim Strangleman, eds. 2021. *Routledge International Handbook of Working-Class Studies*. Abingdon, New York: Routledge.

Federici, Silvia. 2020. *Revolution at Point Zero: Housework, Reproduction, and Feminist Struggle*. PM Press. E-book.

Felski, Rita. 2021. "'Recognizing Class.'" *New Literary History* 52, no. 1: 95–117.

Florida, Richard L. 2002. *The Rise of the Creative Class: And How It's Transforming Work, Leisure, Community and Everyday Life*. New York: Basic Books.

Friedrichs, Julia. 2021. *Working Class: Warum wir Arbeit brauchen, von der wir leben können*. Berlin: Berlin Verlag.

Garcia Canclini, Néstor García. 2017. "Urban Spaces and Networks: Young People's Creativity." *International Journal of Cultural Studies* 20, no. 3: 241–252.

Hammer, Anita, and Immanuel Ness, eds. 2023. *Global Rupture: Neoliberal Capitalism and the Rise of Informal Labour in the Global South*. Leiden: Brill.

Haraway, Donna. 2016. *Staying with the Trouble: Making Kin in the Chthulucene*. Durham: Duke University Press.

Harvey, David. 2005. *A Brief History of Neoliberalism*. Oxford: Oxford University Press.

Hill Collins, Patricia. 2019. *Intersectionality as Critical Social Theory*. Durham: Duke University Press.

Hill Collins, Patricia. 2020. "Intersectionality as Critical Social Theory." In *The Cambridge Handbook of Social Theory: Volume 2: Contemporary Theories and Issues*, edited by Peter Kivisto, 120–142. Cambridge: Cambridge University Press.

Hogg, Emily, and Peter Simonsen, eds. 2021. *Precarity in Contemporary Literature and Culture*. London: Bloomsbury Academic.

hooks, bell. 2000. *Where We Stand: Class Matters*. New York: Routledge.

Jaquet, Chantal. 2018. *Zwischen den Klassen: Über die Nicht-Reproduktion sozialer Macht. Mit einem Nachwort von Carlos Spoerhase*. Translated by Horst Brühmann. Göttingen: Konstanz University Press.

Korte, Barbara, and Frédéric Regard, eds. 2014. *Narrating Poverty and Precarity in Britain*. Berlin: De Gruyter.

Lazar, Sian. 2017. *Where Are the Unions?: Workers and Social Movements in Latin America, the Middle East and Europe*. London: Zed Books.

Lazzarato, M. 2014. *Signs and Machines: Capitalism and the Production of Subjectivity*. Translated by Joshua David Jordan. Los Angeles: Semiotext(e).

Lenin, Vladimir Il'ich. 1987. *Essential Works of Lenin: 'What Is to Be Done?' And Other Writings*. Edited by Henry M. Christman. New York: Dover Publications.

Lennon, John, and Magnus Nilsson. 2017–2020. *Working-Class Literature(s). Historical and International Perspectives*. 2 vols. Stockholm: Stockholm University Press.

Lewis, Holly. 2022. *The Politics of Everybody: Feminism, Queer Theory, and Marxism at the Intersection: A Revised Edition*. London: Bloomsbury Academic.

Linkon, Sherry Lee. 2021. "Class Analysis from the Inside: Scholarly Personal Narrative as a Signature Genre of Working-Class Studies." In *Routledge International Handbook of Working-Class Studies*, edited by Michele Fazio, Christie Launius, and Tim Strangleman, 20–31. Abingdon, New York: Routledge.

Maldonado-Torres, Nelson. 2007. "On the Coloniality of Being." *Cultural Studies* 21, no. 2–3: 240–270.

Marx, Karl. 1979. "The Eighteenth Brumaire of Louis Bonaparte." In *Collected Works*, by Friedrich Engels and Karl Marx, 11:99–197. London, New York, Moscow: Lawrence & Wishart, International, Progress.

Marx, Karl. 1983. *Das Kapital III: Der Gesamtprozeß der kapitalistischen Produktion*. Berlin: Dietz.

Mayer-Ahuja, Nicole, and Oliver Nachtwey, eds. 2021. *Verkannte Leistungsträger:innen. Berichte aus der Klassengesellschaft*. Frankfurt am Main: Suhrkamp.

Moore, Jason, ed. 2016. *Anthropocene or Capitalocene? Nature, History, and the Crisis of Capitalism*. Oakland: PM Press.

Moran, Marie. 2016. *Identity and Capitalism*. London: SAGE Publications.

Nachtwey, Oliver. 2018. *Germany's Hidden Crisis. Social Decline in the Heart of Europe*. London, New York: Verso.

Negri, Toni, and Michael Hardt. 2004. *Multitude. War and Democracy in the Age of Empire*. London: Penguin.

Palmer, Bryan. 2013. "Precariousness as Proletarianization." *Socialist Register* 50: 40–62.

Poblete, Juan. 2021. "Formal and Informal Citizenships: The Spectrum of Practices and Statuses in Latin America and the United States." In *Precarity and Belonging: Labor, Migration, and Noncitizenship*, edited by Catherine S. Ramírez et al., 209–226. Camden NB, Newark NJ, London: Rutgers University Press.

Quijano, Aníbal. 2020. "Colonialidad del poder, eurocentrismo y América Latina." In *Cuestiones y horizontes: de la dependencia histórico-estructural a la colonialidad/descolonialidad del poder*, 861–919. Buenos Aires: CLACSO.

Radice, Hugo. 2014. "Class Theory and Class Politics Today." *Socialist Register* 51: 270–292.

Ramírez, Catherine S. et al., eds. 2021. *Precarity and Belonging: Labor, Migration, and Noncitizenship. Precarity and Belonging*. Camden NB, Newark NJ, London: Rutgers University Press.

Rancière, Jacques. 1992. "Politics, Identification, Subjectivization," *October* 61: 58–64.

Rancière, Jacques. 2012. *Proletarian Nights. The Workers' Dream in Nineteenth-Century France*. London, New York: Verso.

Rivera Cusicanqui, Silvia. 2012. "Ch'ixinakax Utxiwa: A Reflection on the Practices and Discourses of Decolonization." *South Atlantic Quarterly* 111, no. 1: 95–109.

Robinson, Cedric J. 2000. *Black Marxism: The Making of the Black Radical Tradition*. Chapel Hill NC: University of North Carolina Press.

Rys, Michiel, and Bart Philipsen, eds. 2021. *Literary Representations of Precarious Work, 1840 to the Present*. Cham: Palgrave Macmillan.

Soiland, Tove. 2012. "Die Verhältnisse gingen und die Kategorien kamen: *Intersectionality* oder Vom Unbehagen an der amerikanischen Theorie." Portal Intersektionalität. Accessed 7 April 2023. http://portal-intersektionalitaet.de/theoriebildung/ueberblick-stexte/soiland/.

Soja, Edward W. 1989. *Postmodern Geographies: The Reassertion of Space in Critical Social Theory*. London, New York: Verso.

Sousa Santos, Boaventura de. 2016. *Epistemologies of the South: Justice against Epistemicide*. London: Routledge.

Standing, Guy. 2011. *The Precariat: The New Dangerous Class*. London: Bloomsbury Academic.

Táíwò, Olúfẹmi O. 2022. *Elite Capture: How the Powerful Took over Identity Politics (and Everything Else)*. Chicago: Haymarket Books.

Williams, Raymond. 1980. *Problems in Materialism and Culture*. London: Verso.

Wilson, William J. 2012. *The Truly Disadvantaged: The Inner City, the Underclass, and Public Policy*. Chicago: University of Chicago Press.

PART 1

REDISCOVERING CLASS: CONTINUITIES AND RUPTURES

1.1
Writing (for) the Precariat

Mats Teglund's *Cykelbudet* (2021) and Pelle Sunvisson's
Svenska palmen (2021)

MAGNUS NILSSON

In recent years, scholarly interest in the relationship between literature on the one hand, and precarity, precariousness and the precariat on the other has increased, and a rather substantial research literature on the topic has emerged (see e.g. Connell 2017; Rys and Philipsen 2021b; Hogg and Simonsen 2021).[1] I find two features of this literature especially interesting. The first is the insistence that the relationship between literature and precarity is dialectical. Emily Hogg, for example, argues that "culture and the precarity concept can elucidate each other" and that "reading notions of precarity through and with contemporary cultural forms can generate new insights into both" (Hogg 2021, 2). The second interesting feature is an emphasis on literature's potential to contribute to struggles against the injustices suffered by the precariat. A good example of this can be found in Michiel Rys and Bart Philipsen's introduction to their edited collection about literary representations of precarious work, where they argue that literature is "co-constitutive of a shared socioeconomic imaginary, which allows one not merely to speak about precarity," but also to *act against it* (Rys and Philipsen 2021a, 3).

However, even if I very much sympathise with these research approaches and see great potential in them, I also think that they need to be refined. Above all, it is necessary to insist much more than most scholars have hitherto done on the historical and geographical specificity on both sides of the equation, of both literature and precarity, that is. This is important not least when discussing questions about the *politics* of precarity and literature.[2]

I subscribe to Marx's view—expressed throughout his writing from the so-called Paris manuscripts and onwards, and analysed by S. S. Prawer in his remarkable book *Karl Marx and World Literature*—that literature, among many other things, is something we use to *transform* and *create* both the world and ourselves (2011, 144). This includes making sense of the societies we live in and our places in them. For example, literary works about precarious work might contribute to our understanding of capitalism and to the imaginaries on the basis of which we construct class identities (see Thompson 1977; Eiden-Offe 2017, 15). However, such literary meaning-making always takes place in concrete historical situations that change over time and vary between different places; precarious working conditions are not the same everywhere, since, for example, legislation varies from country to country, as does the strength of unions; literary representations of precarious work enter into dialogue with literary, political, etc. discourses that also vary over time and between contexts; furthermore, literary meaning-making is conditioned by the specific economic, ideological, etc. conditions in the sites of literature where it emerges. To put it as simply as possible, authors who write about precarity, precariousness and the precariat in different places and at different times do not necessarily write about the exact same things. Furthermore, they write under different economic, political, literary, etc. conditions. Thus, questions about the relationship between literature on the one hand, and precarity, precariousness and the precariat on the other can never be answered generally, only specifically.

In this chapter, I will try to illustrate these claims, with the point of departure in an analysis of two contemporary Swedish works of literature, both published in 2021, that describe and criticise precarious employment: Anders Teglund's (b. 1983) *Cykelbudet* (*The Bicycle Courier*) and Pelle Sunvisson's (b. 1980) *Svenska palmen* (*The Swedish Palm Tree*).

Tourists in the Precariat?

Both *Cykelbudet* and *Svenska palmen* are based on the authors' first-hand experiences of precarious work. *Cykelbudet* is an autobiographical diary-novel about working as a bicycle courier for the platform company Foodora, delivering restaurant food in Gothenburg during the COVID-19 pandemic, and *Svenska palmen* draws on Sunvisson's experiences of working under a false identity as an Eastern European migrant worker in Stockholm, mainly doing construction work. Sunvisson is a writer, but also works as a negotiator and a translator for a trade union. His stint in the precariat—which also included work as a berry-picker—was short and voluntary; he did not do precarious work because he needed to, but because he wanted to do research for his writing, and, perhaps, for his union work. For Teglund, the situation is somewhat different: he is a concert pianist who also does freelance work in the cultural sector and runs a small publishing house. He began working as a bicycle courier because the pandemic destroyed most of his work opportunities as a cultural worker. However, he soon came up with the idea of writing about his experiences, and thus his work can also, at least in part, be characterised as research for writing. Teglund worked as a bicycle courier for eighteen months before he was sacked, probably because he had become a union organiser (see Teglund 2021b, 15).

When *Cykelbudet* was published, several critics pointed out that its author only had short-term experience of precarious work. One of them, Lars Henriksson (2021b, 40), even launched an attack on Teglund, arguing that he belonged to a tradition of writers who "descend in class society to write for other members of the educated middle class." As well as George Orwell, he mentions Ester Blenda Nordström (1891–1948), a Swedish reporter famous for her reportages, for example about working as a maid on a farm under a false identity (he scathingly also compares Teglund to Günter Wallraff). In a Swedish context, the tradition described by Henriksson constitutes the antithesis to that of working-class literature. According to Lars Furuland—who is the founding father of the academic study of this literature in Sweden—it is constituted by its "ideological anchorage" in the working class and the labour movement (Furuland and Svedjedal 2006, 24), and, according to most critics and commentators, what guarantees this anchorage is the working-class writer's proletarian biography. A paradigmatic example of this can be found in an article from 1903 about the working-class poet K. J. Gabrielsson (1861–1901), written by the leader of the Social-Democratic Party, Hjalmar Branting. He stresses the importance of Gabrielsson's proletarian background and celebrates him as "the first worker in our country who, without leaving his class [...] reached a mastery of form and a scope in his production that grants him a place in the literature of our age" (Branting 1930, 174). Because of this, Branting argues, Gabrielsson could understand the workers in a way that was impossible for bourgeois writers, no matter how politically progressive they were. Branting also claims that this is of fundamental political importance, stating that the Marxist slogan that the emancipation of the working classes must be conquered by themselves is also valid in literature. The idea that the political function of working-class literature is dependent on the writer's working-class background is at the heart of Henriksson's criticism of Teglund. Just like Branting, he stresses the importance of authors having substantial first-hand knowledge of the social conditions in the classes they write about. For example, he claims that "the special community that can emerge from shared experiences takes time to materialize and doesn't include tourists" (Henriksson 2021b, 40). Just like Branting, he also mobilises a Marxist understanding of literary class politics, by arguing that the emancipation of gig workers must be achieved by themselves. "Even if the need for solidarity is stronger the more insecure our jobs are," Henriksson (2021a) writes, "emancipation can only be conquered by us ourselves."

Teglund expresses an ambivalent attitude to this criticism. On the one hand, he stresses that he actually does have long-time experiences of precarious work, since, as a cultural worker, he is no stranger to freelance and gig work. On the other hand, he also acknowledges that, in some respects, he is an outsider, for example since most of the other couriers have a different skin colour and that, unlike him, they have no voice in the public sphere (Teglund 2021c). And, when the protagonist in *Cykelbudet* sums up his predicament—being a cultural worker who has to become a bicycle courier—he describes it as "falla djupare ner i prekariatet"[3] (Teglund 2021a, 46). Thus, Teglund claims membership in the precariat, while also acknowledging its heterogeneity.

That Teglund feels the need to emphasise his experiences of precarious work could be read as an indication that in Sweden the political importance of class authenticity, of writers belonging to the collectives that they write about, is still strong. Coming across as a tourist writing about the work of others is not desirable. But Teglund is also critical of the idea that outsiders should not write about precarious work. He insists that it is very difficult for many within the precariat to make their voices heard in the public sphere, implicitly pointing to the *need* for assistance from outside, thereby indicating that he does not fully embrace the literary politics traditionally associated with working-class literature in Sweden.

This, I believe, should be connected to the fact that the precariat—as Guy Standing (2011) emphasises—is not a class *for* itself. One of the most important sources for the distinction between a class in itself and a class for itself is the famous passage in Marx's *The Eighteenth Brumaire of Louis Bonaparte* about peasant smallholders in nineteenth-century France. What makes them a class in itself, Marx argues (without actually using that concept), is that they share certain "economic conditions" that give rise to specific "interests" that are in conflict with those of other classes. At the same time, however, they do not constitute a class for itself—i.e. a self-conscious collective that acts politically in its own interest (2002, 100–101).

Marx's description of smallholders in mid-nineteenth-century France fits the contemporary precariat rather well. While sharing some conditions and interests—for example the lack of different kinds of "labour-related security" that is at the heart of Standing's (2011, 10–11) definition—the precariat is also characterised by a high degree of heterogeneity in terms of education, ethnic background, legal status, income, kind of work, etc. Furthermore, like the smallholding peasants, the precariat is often characterised by a "mode of production" that "isolates" its members "instead of bringing them into mutual intercourse," as Marx (2002, 100) puts it. For example, short-time and temporary employments, as well as the fact that the actual work is seldom performed collectively, prevent the formation of worker collectives.

Thus, criticising those who write about the precariat for not being as well integrated into the class they depict as older working-class writers were is not very meaningful. Since the precariat is not a class for itself, there is—quite simply—not much for the writers to be integrated *in*: no identity, no community, no culture, no political organisation.

Writing Class

Since the precariat does not display the kind of class consciousness often associated with the traditional working class, those writing about it must adopt another role than that of representing an already existing class (for itself). In the case of Teglund and Sunvisson, this role seems to be modelled on the one assigned by Standing (2014, 30) to artists experiencing precarious conditions, namely inducing others "to share a common vision." Or, to put it in Marxist terms, to contribute to the precariat's fulfilment of the potential that Standing attributes to it—its transformation into a class for itself—through the promotion of class consciousness.[4] Teglund and Sunvisson do this by highlighting the economic conditions and political interests shared by those who work under precarious conditions, whilst at the same time acknowledging that as a group they are heterogenous. They also discuss the relationship between the precariat and the working class.

In *Svenska palmen*, Sunvisson tells the story of Ukrainian migrant worker Ruslan. On the surface, it seems to have great similarities with a classic Swedish working-class novel: Ivar Lo-Johansson's (1901–1990) *Kungsgatan* (1935, literally: King Street; published in German as *Kungsgatan: Roman einer Strasse* in 1949). The protagonist in that novel, Adrian, is a young man who moves to Stockholm from the countryside with the goal of shedding his identity as the son of a farmer and instead becoming a worker, and thus placing himself at the centre of Sweden's transformation from an agrarian class society to a modern social-democratic welfare state (see Nilsson 2019). Ruslan's background is similar to Adrian's, as he too migrates from the periphery to the metropolis. But his goal is simpler than Adrian's: he just wants to make money. However, when working as a paperless migrant, he begins learning what it is to be a worker: it is someone who, together with others, performs labour that is so important that employers cannot ignore their demands. Ruslan begins dreaming of becoming one, but—unlike Adrian's in *Kungsgatan*—his individual development does not take place against any backdrop of collective progress for workers, but in a cold capitalist world characterised by precarity. For example, his status as a paperless migrant worker means that he is excluded both from the welfare granted to Swedish workers by the state and from the labour movement. And unlike Adrian he never becomes class-conscious. Instead, the novel ends with him facing deportation, and with his identity as a worker falling apart:

> Han hade trott sig tillhöra staden, liksom han trott sig tillhöra de arbetare som kunde ställa krav […]. Han hade trott, men trodde inte längre.[5] (Sunvisson 2021, 252)

Sunvisson not only emphasises the differences between the contemporary precariat and the traditional working class, but also points out similarities. When

Ruslan and a couple of other migrant workers renovate an apartment, they begin to realise that their labour makes their employers rich:

> – [...] Vi gör en renovering och priset går upp med en miljon. Materialet kostar kanske tvåhundrafemtio tusen, vi får femtio var och chefen får kanske hundra. Sammanlagt är det en halv miljon. Varifrån kommer resten? Priset har ju gått upp med en halv miljon till.
> [...] [D]en där halvmiljonen extra är det riktiga priset på vårt arbete.[6] (ibid., 191)

This is a condensed version of Marx's theory of exploitation. Thus, even if Sunvisson points to the differences between the contemporary precariat and the traditional working class, he also highlights the fact that their fundamental relationship to capital is the same. In addition, he tries to conjure forth a possible class identity based on these shared economic interests. The primary example of this is the ending of the novel, where he describes a future transformation of Ruslan and other migrant workers into a politically powerful collective: "I det försvinnande ögonblicket av klarsynthet såg han den rätta tiden komma [...], såg han deras samlade växtkraft spränga stadens väggar inifrån"[7] (ibid., 252).

Working-Class Literature Revisited

So far, when comparing contemporary Swedish literature about precarious work with older working-class literature, I have mainly emphasised the *differences* between them. I have also argued that they are conditioned by differences between the traditional working class and the precariat, the most important of which being that the latter is not a class for itself. But I have also shown that Sunvisson points to similarities between the precariat and the working class. In the following, I will try to demonstrate that the differences between his and Teglund's works about the precariat and older working-class literature are perhaps not as great as is generally assumed.

First, contributing to the promotion of *class consciousness*—as Teglund and Sunvisson do—has always been an important function of working-class literature in Sweden. Gabrielsson and other working-class poets tried to win workers for the socialist labour movement by making them share its political ideals and adopt a proletarian identity (see e.g. Mral 1985). The same is also true for many later working-class writers, even if their works have usually been less explicitly political. For example, as I have shown elsewhere, during the decades following the Second World War, when many within the labour movement argued that the welfare state had put an end to class antagonism, the working-class poet Stig Sjödin (1917–1993)—who is often viewed as the poet laurate of Swedish social de-mocracy—promoted a working-class consciousness that was founded in a Marx-ist understanding of the antagonistic relationship between capital and labour (Nilsson 2021). Thus, even if the working class at this time was indeed a class for itself, Sjödin—as well as other working-class writers (see Nilsson 2014)—con-tributed both to its *expansion* (by trying to make *more* workers class-conscious) and to its *development* (by promoting a *specific* kind of class consciousness).

Secondly, even if traditional working-class writers promoted class con-sciousness from the inside of an already existing class, their anchorage in this class was seldom as strong as is usually assumed. This is true even for Lo-Jo-hansson, generally considered to be the archetypical Swedish working-class writer. He made his breakthrough in the 1930s with a series of novels and col-lections of short stories about the so-called *statare*: agricultural workers who were paid in kind and constituted the lowest stratum of the Swedish working class. The best known of these is the novel *Godnatt, jord* (1933, published in English as *Breaking Free* in 1991). However, Lo-Johansson himself was never a *statare*. His parents had been, but they managed to become tenant farm-ers—which represented an important step on the social and economic ladder at the time—when he was still a small child. After leaving home at a young age, Lo-Johansson briefly tried his luck as, among other things, a peddler, a stone mason and a postman, but soon started working as a journalist, and eventu-ally literary writing became his main occupation. One consequence of this was that when writing a novel about contemporary agricultural labour in the early 1940s, Lo-Johansson had to do extensive research. However, unlike Sunvisson and Teglund, he limited himself to theoretical research, rather than returning to the countryside to work.

This means that Teglund and Sunvisson are actually as well anchored in the precariat as working-class writers like Lo-Johansson were in the working class. At least they have as much personal experience of the *work* done in this class. One could also argue that some of the writers writing about the precariat share the economic and social situation of this group to a greater degree than older working-class writers shared those of the working class. That Lo-Johansson be-came an author did indeed mean that he distanced himself radically from the proletarian world in which he grew up. For Teglund, on the other hand, being an entrepreneur in the cultural sector does not necessarily mean that he enjoys much better economic conditions than bicycle couriers or other gig workers. During a pandemic, when the cultural world grids to a halt, he might even be worse off. Thus, if one subscribes to the idea that being anchored in a class is important for those who want to represent it in literature, and if one argues that contributing to the formation of this class as a class for itself is an important fea-

ture of literary class politics, then Teglund and Sunvisson might appear to be in
no worse a position than were many older working-class writers.

Furthermore, it is not at all obvious that it is sharing a life world or experiences of work that constitutes the best foundation for literary class politics. In
Marx's analysis, the distinction between a class in itself and a class for itself is
often somewhat blurred. As an ideal type, a class in itself could be viewed as an
entity united solely by shared economic interests, without any social, cultural
or ideological bonds necessarily existing between its members. For example, in
Capital Marx (2000, 730) points out that a schoolmaster in a private school and
a worker in a sausage factory both produce surplus value for capitalists. Thus,
economically, they stand in the same relationship to capital, and could therefore
be said to belong to the same class (in itself), even if they might have nothing in
common culturally and socially. A class for itself, in contrast, is characterised,
as an ideal type, not only by a consciousness about common interests, but also
by political organisation and action. It is this that the small-holding peasants
in France lacked, but that workers in the labour movement had. Between these
ideal types, Marx seems to place various intermediate stages. The smallholding
peasants described in *Brumaire*, for example, are said to share a "culture," but still
do not yet constitute a class for itself. Earlier in the work, Marx also writes about
how on "the social conditions of existence" of a class "*arises* an entire superstructure of different and peculiarly formed sentiments, delusions, modes of thought
and outlooks on life" (2002, 43, emphasis added). Thus, according to Marx, a
class in itself will eventually evolve into a class for itself characterised by cultural
and ideological homogeneity.

I think that it is worth challenging this idea about class consciousness being
a product of a shared culture that, in turn, is a superstructural reflection of economic interests (see e.g. Eiden-Offe 2017, 16). For example, the working classes
in different countries have displayed differences that cannot be reduced to differences regarding their economic interests. They have also changed over time—in
terms, for example, of political orientation—in ways that cannot be explained
only by reference to changes in the economic infrastructure. Furthermore, every
real labour movement—which can be seen as the political manifestation of a
class-conscious working class, or as *the working class for itself*—has encompassed
workers from different industries and regions, of different genders and religions,
etc. Thus, neither their economic "base" nor their cultural "superstructure" have
been homogenous. In Sweden, the working class has been particularly heterogenous when it comes to social and cultural characteristics. Because of the country's
late industrialisation, historian Henrik Berggren argues, Sweden's working class
never developed the "tight socio-cultural community" that characterised it in
places like England, Belgium or northern Germany (2010, 415). Instead, its "class

solidarity" was "born together with the organized labour movement" and thus became *political* rather than *cultural*. "The labour-movement municipal building and the trade union became the natural gathering point, rather than the pub and the neighbourhood," Berggren writes (ibid.). If this is true, then a writer's anchorage in the life world of a class might be less important than his or her engagement in the organisations trying to mobilise it politically. And so the differences between contemporary writers writing for the precariat and traditional working-class writers are perhaps not so big after all, at least not in a Swedish context.

I have already mentioned that Sunvisson works for a union, and that Teglund became a union organiser of gig workers when he worked as a bicycle courier. Older working-class authors also often had strong ties to the labour movement. In Furuland's words, Swedish working-class literature has had an "ideological anchorage" in the labour movement. Often, working-class writers have also taken active part in labour-movement organisations. Lo-Johansson and Sjödin, mentioned above, are good examples. The former worked in close collaboration with the agricultural workers' union, and the latter frequently published poems and short stories in the trade union press, where he was also employed as a journalist. Both contemporary Swedish literature about precarious work and older Swedish working-class literature can, in other words, be conceptualised as *ideologically* and *politically*, rather than *socially*, defined kinds of literature.

My argument that there are similarities between traditional working-class writers and contemporary authors writing about the precariat does not mean that I think that the differences between them should be ignored. However, I do want to stress that they should not be taken for granted, or be exaggerated, and that it could be a good idea to look for similarities as well. For example, while there are major differences between *Svenska palmen* and a classic working-class novel like Lo-Johansson's *Kungsgatan*, the former also displays thematic links to other examples of working-class or proletarian literature. Its descriptions of the exploitation of migrant workers, for example, sometimes resemble those in Upton Sinclair's *The Jungle* from 1906, and one critic has pointed out similarities with John Steinbeck's *The Grapes of Wrath* (de Veen 2021). And there are even stronger resemblances with another working-class literature classic, namely Robert Tressell's *The Ragged-Trousered Philantropists* from 1914. The philanthropists of the title are construction workers who, while renovating a villa, develop a labour theory of value and come to the conclusion that their work can be considered charity, since it makes their employers rich. As I have already mentioned, the workers in *Svenska palmen* come to a very similar conclusion when, more than a century later, they work under conditions that differ very little from those described by Tressell.

Teglund too makes comparisons between contemporary precarious work and the working conditions suffered by workers a hundred years ago. When the protagonist in *Cykelbudet* discusses his work as courier with his father, they make comparisons with older relatives, especially with the protagonist's great-grand-father Jonas, who worked in a paper mill at the turn of the twentieth century, and his son, the protagonist's grandfather. The protagonist puts special emphasis on how the welfare state represented a radical change for workers, and how his grandparents—Ernfrid and Siri—could lead much better lives than their parents:

> Ernfrid och Siri får ta del av många sociala framsteg. Fem år efter Jonas död, 1938, kommer den första lagstadgade semestern. Tolv dagars betald ledighet per år. Det ska komma att bli bättre succesivt. Fyra decennier senare, mot slutet av Ernfrids arbetsliv, är industrisemestern uppe i fem veckor. Han blir kvar på fabriken hela livet och lever pensionärsliv under åttiotalet innan han dör 1990 efter en kort tids sjukdom. En politisk retoriker skulle kunna hävda at than levde och dog parallellt med den traditionella socialdemokratins gyllene era.[8] (Teglund 2021a, 111)

The protagonist then goes on to reflect upon the emergence of the labour move-ment in Sweden, and what today's precariat can learn from it. He grounds this in a discussion of Per Olov Enquist's (1934–2020) novel *Musikanternas uttåg* (1978, published in English as *The March of the Musicians* in 1985):

> *Musikanternas uttåg* skildrar en brytpunkt där något började röra på sig. Men det var inget som kom från ovan. Det var enskilda personer som tog strid i det lilla: i familjen, på arbetsplatser och i samhället. Dessa människor riskerade stora saker för små framsteg, de gjorde det för sin överlevnads skull och misslyckades ideligen. Med tiden fick de dock fler att ansluta sig, och stegvis skapades en förän-dring. Det kom inte gratis. I boken upprepas ett mantra som fångar denna prem-iss: *Det gives alltid något bättre än döden.*
>
> [...] Även om de fackliga framstegen gjordes i en annan tid, under en indus-triell blomstringsperiod och i ett annat politiskt klimat, så har det likafullt gjorts en gång i vårt land av människor som aldrig hade gjort det förut.[9] (Teglund 2021a, 112–113)

Thus, Teglund emphasises the differences between the precariat and the working class of the welfare state, while at the same time identifying similarities between today's precariat and the working class during the period before the welfare state. That he anchors this comparison in a discussion of a novel is interesting, since it points to the possibility of using literature to understand and criticise class society, and even to inspire struggles against class injustices. It is also interesting that the discussion is anchored in this particular novel. *Musikanternas uttåg* be-gins with a scene describing how an agitator who has come to organise workers in northern Sweden is lynched by the very same workers. In *Cykelbudet* this is interpreted as a consequence of the agitator being an outsider. "Det går aldrig att bara komma utifrån och tro att man ska få med sig vem som helst,"[10] the protagonist's father concludes (Teglund 2021a, 112). Thus, *Cykelbudet* thematises in advance the critique that would be directed at its author upon its publication by some critics. But it also shows that there has always been a distance between workers (who have not yet become a class for itself) and organisers. And the story about the lynched agitator is actually presented as a story about the beginning of the rise of the Swedish labour movement, which would soon become one of the most powerful such movements in the world.

Of course, narratives about the precariat that stress its resemblance to the working class and argue that the solution to the injustices it suffers is traditional labour-movement politics could be read as examples of the kind of anachronism that Marx ridicules in *Brumaire*, where he discusses how during revolutionary processes people often "summon up the spirits of the past." This is something that Marx warns socialists about. "The social revolution," he writes, "cannot create its poetry from the past but only from the future" (2002, 22). It might be that in Sweden, where the labour movement was the dominant political power throughout most of the twentieth century, those who oppose the exploitation suffered by the precariat are stuck in older kinds of political thinking, and that the works of Teglund and Sunvisson should thus be viewed as "poetry from the past."

However, in Sweden it has been the labour movement, and especially the unions, that have historically secured for workers the labour-market security, the absence of which constitutes the precariat. And even if Swedish unions are not quite as powerful today as they once were—after all, if they had been, there would exist no precariat—they are still more potent than in most other countries. For example, as Teglund details in *Cykelbudet*, the bicycle couriers working for Foodora in Sweden did eventually manage to get a collective agreement between their employer and the transport workers' union. The union for which Sunvisson works has also been quite successful in their efforts to help paperless migrant workers. For example, in many cases they have managed to help workers secure wage settlements from employers that have tried to cheat them. Thus, it is hard to see why unionising should be a bad strategy for fighting precarious working conditions.

Furthermore, Marx's ridiculing of bourgeois revolutionaries dressed up in Roman costumes does not mean that he dismisses history as a political resource. For example, he stresses that in its Roman costumes, the bourgeoisie developed an unexpected but much needed heroism.[11] When contemporary writers conjure up images of older class struggles and narratives about how in the past workers have managed to overcome problems similar to those faced by the precariat today, this might very well be an important source of inspiration for contemporary struggles. In fact, this is no new literary-political strategy. At least since the 1940s, many Swedish working-class writers—the earlier-mentioned poet Sjödin (Nilsson 2021) for one, but also the prominent working-class novelist Folke Fridell (1904–1985) (Nilsson 2014)—have promoted a revival of the ethics and politics of the early socialist labour movement.

Trying to create class consciousness beyond differences and divisions is also nothing new. The formation of the Swedish working class as a class for itself through the labour movement did include the creation of alliances between different groups, such as agricultural and industrial workers or workers in the public and private sectors. In addition to this, the social-democratic labour movement also forged an alliance between blue-collar and white-collar workers under the umbrella term of "wage earners." Working-class literature contributed to this process. Lo-Johansson's works about *statare* not only made it possible for *that* collective to develop a shared consciousness, but also contributed to the creation of solidarity and political alliances *between* the *statare* and other groups of workers within the labour movement, and thus to their *joint* formation as a class for itself, despite the many differences between them. This is a good reminder that the formation of a class for itself is a creative process that always involves a constant *making*—or re-making—of a common identity (Eiden-Offe 2017; Thompson 1977) beyond differences and divisions.

Concluding Remarks

In their works, Teglund and Sunvisson contribute to the creation of what Philipsen and Rys call "a shared socioeconomic imaginary, which allows one not merely to speak about precarity," but also to *act against it*, or, to put it in Marxist terms, a class consciousness that could transform the precariat into a class for itself. A key feature of this imaginary is the portrayal of the precariat as a *heterogenous* collective with blurred borders, made up of people who nevertheless, despite their differences, share certain economic conditions and political interests, not only with each other, but also with other workers. Another important feature is the insistence that it is through more or less traditional labour-movement politics—and, in particular, through unions—that the injustices suffered by the precariat can be overcome. This means that the foundation for the precariat's formation as a class for itself suggested by Teglund and Sunvisson is perhaps not best described as a "socioeconomic" but as an *economic and political* imaginary.

At first glance, this seems to indicate that contemporary Swedish literature about the precariat is rather different from traditional working-class literature, which is generally described as the literary expression of a social class sharing not only economic and political interest but also—or even primarily—a life world, a culture and an identity. But even if there are differences, they should not be exaggerated. As I hope that I have managed to demonstrate above, Sunvisson and Teglund's relationship to the precariat is actually much like that between older working-class writers and the working class, and their aesthetical-political strategies to a large degree resemble those found in traditional working-class literature.

As I pointed out in the beginning of this chapter, many scholars argue that "culture and the precarity concept can elucidate each other," as Hogg puts it. My analyses seem to confirm this. First of all, I hope that I have been able to show that literary responses to precarious employment bring to the fore questions about literature and its relationship to class that might function as catalysts for revising some received ideas, not least about the tradition of working-class literature and its politics. I also think that my analysis of Swedish novels about precarious work can challenge an often-repeated argument in contemporary research, namely that, in general, literary representations of the precariat are pessimistic. For example, Liam Connell has claimed that novels about the precariat are mostly characterised by political hopelessness, and Mads Simonsen has argued that "in the art and literature that engages with the precariat" it is hard to find much validation of Standing's optimism regarding the possibilities for authors to create community and solidarity (Simonsen 2021, 59; Connell 2021, 35). In contemporary Swedish literature, things look somewhat different. While recognising that the precariat is politically weak, authors such as Teglund and Sunvisson nevertheless insist that it is meaningful to fight for its rights. This, I hope, can serve as a good illustration of the need not to generalise about the relationship between literature and the precariat, but always to analyse it in its specific contexts.

I also think that my analysis can say something about the precariat. If nothing else, it can provide input to discussions about how to understand its possible transformation into a class for itself. According to Standing (2011, 155), "twentieth-century labourism" is "unattractive" to the precariat. Teglund's and Sunvisson's novels contradict this claim, showing that—in a Swedish context!—traditional working-class politics seems to be a quite attractive, but not unproblematic, option in the struggle against precarious working conditions. Perhaps my analysis can also contribute to the discussion of the much-debated question about the precariat's relationship to the working class. Standing's conceptualisation of the precariat is based on it being different from the traditional working class, especially that of the welfare-state era. Others, however, have argued that it should rather be viewed as a part of the working class and have emphasised its similarities to the proletariat during the period before the emergence of welfare states (Breman 2013; see e.g. Bieler 2013). The facts that Sunvisson's *Svenska palmen* has similarities with older working-class literature, that Teglund in *Cykelbudet* proposes unionising as the way forward in the struggle against precarious work, and that both authors highlight similarities between the contemporary precariat and the working class before the emergence of welfare states all seem to support the latter idea. Thus, these works could be read as a warning against creating (and generalising) a radical opposition between the precariat and the working class.

Teglund's and Sunvisson's literary representations of the precariat are, to some extent, different from those found in literature from other countries, being (relatively) optimistic about the possibility of fighting precarious working conditions, and promoting (relatively) traditional working-class politics. This is a result of differences pertaining to both the literary and political situation, which need to be analysed further. Hopefully, such analyses could function as catalysts for a better understanding of the precariat, the literature about it and the relationship between them. And that could make it possible not only to talk about precarious work with more precision, but also to act against it with greater force.

Notes

1. The research presented in this text has been conducted within the research environ-ment *Precariat, Precarity and Precariousness in (Post) Welfare-State Scandinavian Lit-eratures*, which is funded by the Swedish Research Council (Project ID: 2022–01839).
2. In the study of working-class literature, there has been a turn in recent years to an increased focus on the specificity of working-class literatures from different times and places, and to an increased interest in comparisons between them, which constitutes an important source of inspiration for this chapter (see e.g. Lennon and Nilsson 2017, 2020).
3. "[F]alling deeper into the precariat."
4. The political functions of literature are not always results of the authors' intentions. In general, it is the uses of literature by its readers that generate political effects. In this chapter, I analyse how Teglund's and Sunvisson's representations of precarious work *could* be used as platforms for the construction of class consciousness. However, both writers have expressed political intentions that point in this direction. At the literary festival Littfest in Umeå 2022, Teglund was asked how literature (including *Cykelbu-det*) can contribute to better conditions on the labour market. In his answer, he empha-sised the importance of making those working under precarious conditions visible, and aware of their visibility. That could certainly be read as an ambition to make them class-conscious. And the same can be said of Sunvisson's (2021, 6) statement, in his foreword to *Svenska palmen*, that he wants to use literature to turn the migrant work-ers he describes into "subjects."

5. "He had thought that he belonged to the city, just like he had thought that he belonged to the workers who could make demands [...]. He had thought so, but didn't think so anymore."

6. "We renovate, and the price goes up one million. The material costs two hundred and fifty thousand, we get fifty each and the boss maybe gets a hundred. Where does the rest come from? After all, the price has gone up another half a million. The extra half-million is the real price of our labour."

7. "In the passing moment of clarity, he saw the right time coming, he saw their combined power tearing down the city walls from within." It is worth noting the similarities between this ending and that of Sinclair's *The Jungle* (2006). There too, the ending is utopian, and the coming triumph is described as a conquering of the city: "*Chicago will be ours!* Chicago will be ours! CHICAGO WILL BE OURS!". In both cases, the triumph of working-class politics is expressed in terms of a conquering of the city.

8. "Ernfrid and Siri benefit from numerous social improvements. Five years after Jonas' death, in 1938, comes the first-ever legislation about paid vacation. Twelve days of paid leisure every year. It will get even better gradually. Four decades later, toward the end of Ernfrid's working life, paid vacation for industrial workers has been extended to five weeks. He works in the factory his whole life and is a pensioner in the eighties, before dying in 1990 after a short period of illness. A political historian could argue that he lived and died in parallel with the golden era of traditional social democracy."

9. "The *March of the Musicians* describes a turning-point when something began to move. But it wasn't something that came from above. It was individuals who fought where they were: in their families, in their workplaces and in society. These people took big risks for little progress, they did it for their survival and they often failed. In time, however, they convinced more and more people to join them and gradually they created change. It wasn't for free. In the book a mantra that captures this premise is repeated: *There is always something better than death*. [...] Even if the rise of the unions happened in another time, in a period of industrial flourishing and in a different political climate, it is a fact that it has been done once before in our country, and that it was done by people who had never done it before."

10. "It never works to come from the outside and believe that everyone will join you."

11. See also Eiden-Offe's analysis of so-called romantic critique of capitalism (i.e. critique founded in values from the past). Against its condemnation by, among others, Georg Lukács for being backward-looking, Eiden-Offe (2017, 18) stresses that it expresses a critique of contemporary conditions and thus can have real political effects here and now.

References

Berggren, Henrik. 2010. *Underbara dagar framför oss: En biografi över Olof Palme*. Stockholm: Norstedts.

Bieler, Andreas. 2013. "Guy Standing *The Precariat*." *Capital & Class* 37, no. 2: 322–325.

Branting, Hjalmar. 1930. *Litteraturkritik och varia. Vol. XI: Tal och skrifter*. Stockholm: Tidens förlag.

Breman, Jan. 2013. "A bogus concept?" *New Left Review* 84 (November/December): 130–138.

Connell, Liam. 2017. *Precarious Labour and the Contemporary Novel*. New York: Palgrave Macmillan.

Connell, Liam. 2021. "Anxious Reading: The Precarity Novel and the Affective Class." In *Precarity in Contemporary Literature and Culture*, edited by Emily J. Hogg and Peter Simonsen, 27–41. London: Bloomsbury Academic.

de Veen, Lucas. 2021. "Utländsk arbetskraft sliter för våra blåbär." *Dala-Demokraten*, 15 July 2021, 14.

Eiden-Offe, Patrick. 2017. *Die Poesie der Klasse: Romantischer Antikapitalismus und die Erfindung des Proletariats*. Berlin: Matthes & Seitz.

Furuland, Lars, and Johan Svedjedal. 2006. *Svensk arbetarlitteratur*. Stockholm: Atlas.

Henriksson, Lars. 2021a. "Gigarbetaren måste föra sin egen talan." *Göteborgs-Posten*, 4 October 2021, 29.

Henriksson, Lars. 2021b. "Varför infiltrerar journalisterna bara arbetarklassen?" *Göteborgs-Posten*, 23 September 2021, 40–41.

Hogg, Emily J. 2021. "Introduction." In *Precarity in Contemporary Literature and Culture*, edited by Emily J. Hogg and Peter Simonsen, 1–24. London: Bloomsbury Academic.

Hogg, Emily J., and Peter Simonsen, eds. 2021. *Precarity in Contemporary Literature and Culture*. London: Bloomsbury Academic.

Lennon, John, and Magnus Nilsson, eds. 2017. *Working-Class Literature(s): Historical and International Perspectives*. Vol. 1, Stockholm Studies in Culture and Aesthetics. Stockholm: Stockholm University Press.

Lennon, John, and Magnus Nilsson, eds. 2020. *Working-Class Literature(s): Historical and International Perspectives*. Vol. 2, Stockholm Studies in Culture and Aesthetics. Stockholm: Stockholm University Press.

Marx, Karl. 2000. *Capital, Volume I*. London: Electric Book Company.

Marx, Karl. 2002. "The Eighteenth Brumaire of Louis Bonaparte." In *Marx's 'Eighteenth Brumaire': (post)modern interpretations*, edited by Mark Cowling and James Martin, 19–109. London: Pluto Press.

Mral, Brigitte. 1985. *Frühe schwedische Arbeiterdichtung: Poetische Beiträge in sozialdemokratischen Zeitungen 1882–1900*. Uppsala: Avd. för litteratursociologi, Litteraturvetenskapliga inst., Uppsala universitet.

Nilsson, Magnus. 2014. *Literature and Class: Aesthetical-Political Strategies in Modern Swedish Working-Class Literature*. Berlin: Humboldt-Universität.

Nilsson, Magnus. 2019. "Class, Taste, and Literature: The Case of Ivar Lo-Johansson and Swedish Working-Class Literature." *Journal of Working-Class Studies* 4, no. 1: 24–36.

Nilsson, Magnus. 2021. *Kampdiktare i folkhemmet: Arbetarpoeten Stig Sjödin*. Stockholm: Verbal.

Prawer, Salomon Siegbert. 2011. *Karl Marx and World Literature*. London: Verso.

Rys, Michiel, and Bart Philipsen. 2021a. "Introduction: Poetics and Precarity—Literary Representations of Precarious Work, Past and Present." In *Literary Representations of Precarious Work, 1840 to the Present*, edited by Michiel Rys and Bart Philipsen, 1–19. Cham: Palgrave Macmillan.

Rys, Michiel, and Bart Philipsen, eds. 2021b. *Literary Representations of Precarious Work, 1840 to the Present*. Cham: Palgrave Macmillan.

Simonsen, Peter. 2021. "Performing Precarity: Threatening the Audience in Gary Owen's *Iphigenia in Splott*." In *Precarity in Contemporary Literature and Culture*, edited by Emily J. Hogg and Peter Simonsen, 56–71. London: Bloomsbury Academic.

Sinclair, Upton. 2006. *The Jungle*. Project Gutenberg. Accessed 14 April, 2023. https://www.gutenberg.org/cache/epub/140/pg140-images.html.

Standing, Guy. 2011. *The Precariat: The New Dangerous Class*. London: Bloomsbury Academic.

Standing, Guy. 2014. *A Precariat Charter*. London: Bloomsbury Publishing.

Sunvisson, Pelle. 2021. *Svenska palmen*. Stockholm: Verbal.

Teglund, Anders. 2021a. *Cykelbudet*. Luleå: Teg Publishing.

Teglund, Anders. 2021b. "Foodoras last." *Ord & Bild* 124, no. 5: 14–29.

Teglund, Anders. 2021c. "Vem ska tala för den mest utsatte gigarbetaren?" *Göteborgs-Posten*, 1 October 2021, 37.

Thompson, E. P. 1977. *The making of the English working class*. Harmondsworth: Penguin Books.

1.2

Making Visible the Invisible

Spanish Post-Crisis Fiction

CHRISTIAN CLAESSON

Introduction

The year 2008 was a watershed moment in Spanish post-dictatorship politics and culture. Before that, the national narrative declared that Spain was a prime example of political, economic and cultural progress, from the peaceful transition to democracy in the 1970s to the politically stable and economically successful country of the 2000s (see for example Muñoz Molina 2013). Spain had surely had its problems—widespread and engrained corruption, ETA's political violence, growing unemployment and inequalities—but, on the whole, both from within and without, the country was seen as a solid western European democracy. The far-reaching economic, political, cultural and social consequences of the financial crisis of 2008, ignited by the fall of Lehman Brothers, shook Spanish society to the core: the housing bubble exploded, unemployment rose to 27% (57% among adults under 25), the general labour market was increasingly precarised, over 1.7 million people were evicted from their homes between 2008 and 2019, newly built twenty-story buildings and airports were finished but never used, emigration outstripped immigration, and prostitution, trafficking and drug abuse increased significantly (Naredo 2010; El País 2011; Universidad de Barcelona n.d.; Cúneo 2020). The crisis also sparked a wide array of grassroots mobilisation, political changes, intellectual debate and cultural activity. The massive demonstration and occupation of Madrid's central square on 15 May 2011, led to the 15M, a multifarious movement that rejected party politics and organised in popular assemblies, intent on targeting what was perceived as a political class out of touch with society and on fostering consciousness-raising campaigns. New parties were founded: the left-wing Podemos sprung out of the political energy of the 15M (and, in some way, also neutralised it), and the extreme right party Vox rose to be the country's third political power, partly as a reaction to the Catalan independence movement. In the wake of these events, writers, artists and intellectuals studied and represented the effects of the crisis, fostering a general repoliticisation of Spanish culture (Claesson 2018b). In this chapter, I will explore how the crisis has made visible what used to be out of sight, veiled, repressed and unconscious, and how it is represented in what might be termed 'post-crisis fiction'. I will focus on the development of the concept of precarity in the Spanish context, which largely has replaced the notion of class, and how work, gender and subjectivity are represented in Isaac Rosa's *La mano invisible* (2011) and Cristina Morales's *Lectura fácil* (2018).

Spanish Precarity in the 2000s

During the 2000s, the concept of precarity was beginning to enter the critical vocabulary as a way of referring to working conditions under neoliberalism. It is described by Maribel Casas-Cortés as a "toolbox concept" (2014, 221), whose validity and use depend on time, place and from what perspective and for what purposes it is discussed and used. As Emily Hogg says, "the term's descriptive precision—the extent to which it explains actually existing social reality—is less important than the way it is put to work by individuals and groups in order to contribute to the reshaping of those social realities" (2021, 1). The term comes from the Latin *precārius*, meaning "supplicant" or "dependent on the favor of another"; a precarious person is, therefore, one who, instead of having rights and legal protection, is at the mercy of the favours of others. Precarity itself is neither Western nor contemporary—in many parts of the world it is more the norm than the exception, which has also been the case for most of the history of Western capitalism—but it is in Europe that it enters the critical and theoretical dictionary. When it is formulated as a concept, it is precisely because it comes to define the change in the labour market after the first neoliberal reforms in the 1980s. In the 1990s, Pierre Bourdieu theorises the notion and underlines the effect that job insecurity has on individual subjectivity and the possibility of collective action; the problem is not only the lack of regularity and permanence in the labour market, but also the uncertainty, disorientation and loss of meaning that this lack causes (1998, 82). The inability to anticipate the future makes existence more uncertain and leads to the deterioration of the entire relationship with the world, time and space, permeating both the conscious and the unconscious (ibid., 3). The effects of precarity, therefore, go far beyond mere working conditions, affecting the existential dimension of life.

Judith Butler's post-9/11 work is foundational in scholarship on precarity, and distinguishes between this term and 'precariousness'. Precariousness is the inevitable vulnerability of social existence, the fact that our lives are, in a sense, always dependent on others. This meaning is established in opposition to the definition of the masculine, autonomous and free subject; this view is a fantasy, since what constitutes a body to a certain extent is its dependence on other bodies (Hogg 2021, 6). Precarity, on the other hand, is the way in which vulnerability is organised in social situations, intensified for some subjects and minimised for others, according to the corresponding political structures. Hence the value and complexity of understanding these two sides of the concept in conjunction: "it encompasses the risk, insecurity and instability that are intrinsic to sociality, but draws attention to the mutable and historically variable practices that intensify the experience of vulnerability in particular times and places and allow certain individuals and groups to evade reckoning with their dependence on others" (ibid., 8). Something similar occurs with the concept of subject, whose double condition Butler summarises in the following question: "How can it be, that the subject taken to be the condition for and instrument of agency, is at the same time the effect of subordination, understood as the deprivation of agency?" (1997, 10) These thoughts are developed by Isabell Lorey, in her important *State of Insecurity: Government of the Precarious* (2015). Lorey's book focuses on the Foucauldian idea of governmentality, which denotes the overlap of individual self-rule and the political rule of the nation-state, and she studies precariousness as a technique of the neoliberal era, ruling through insecurity. In this regime, the double nature of the subject is exploited: the modern individual is both active and passive, both free and subjugated, to the point where it is impossible to separate one from the other. Exposure to uncertainty and danger is not only restricted to working life, but to existence—the body and subjectivation—in general. It can open up new potential for life and work at the same time that it is a threat; it is important to remember that neoliberalism takes advantage of the countercultural rejection of Fordist labour monotony, and offers a more flexible, cultural, cooperative and communicative alternative, often centred on immaterial labour. However, it is not necessarily an emancipatory change, but rather something that is decidedly ambivalent, "modes of self-government that represent a conformist self-development, a conformist self-determination enabling extraordinary governability" (Lorey 2015, 14). As Jornet Somoza points out, the disciplinary mechanisms imposed by the neoliberal order are various: "individualismo institucionalizado, régimen de competitividad como principio básico de todas las relaciones socio-productivas, gestión del yo convertido en emprendedor-de-sí, financiarización de la propia vida, imposición de un estado securitario que decide qué vidas son vivibles"[1] (2017, 158).

The first time these thoughts had a concrete political mobilisation on an international scale was through EuroMayDay in 2001, with demonstrations that began in Italy and quickly spread to Spain and other countries. For the precarious

Posters for EuroMayDay demonstrations in Madrid, Milan and Barcelona.

at the beginning of the twenty-first century, traditional 1 May demonstrations stood for the nostalgia of a unionist past that had little to do with the present and that did not represent the situation of young people who had just entered the labour market. To some extent, the historically strong Spanish unions had lost legitimacy and support during the 1990s (partly because they were perceived as having allowed unemployment benefits cuts and the legalisation of temporary work agencies) and younger people, also wary of the unions' ties to political power, tended not to unionise (Casas-Cortés 2014, 207–209). According to Casas-Cortés, the EuroMayDay phenomenon introduced an element of ambiguity to the discourse on precariousness, criticising its negative consequences, but also showing some of its potential: "A series of emerging actors, texts, and interventions linked to EuroMayDay networks continued a resignification of precarity based on the logic of *and, and, and* ... (in the sense of Deleuze's call for complex multiplicity rather than reductionist exclusion), clustering multiple and at times contradictory meanings" (2014, 210; emphasis in original). Indeed, until the last demonstration in 2011, EuroMayDay increased its ambitions: the poster for the demonstration in Madrid in 2008 mentions basic income, papers for everyone, decent housing, social rights, free culture, redistribution of work and wealth, public services and sexual freedoms as its demands.

In 2004, before the publication of the texts that are considered foundational in the study of precariousness (the works of Butler and Lorey, as well as Guy Standing's *The Precariat*), the Spanish collective Precarias a la deriva published *A la deriva por los circuitos de la precariedad femenina* (*Drifting through the circuits of female precariousness*), a truly pioneering book in its situated research of precarity. For the Precarias, precarity is the "conjunto de condiciones, materiales y simbólicas, que determinan una incertidumbre acerca del acceso sostenido a los

Cartoon by Martin Ferran depicting the mileurista.
Reproduced with permission © Martin Ferran

recursos esenciales para el pleno desarrollo de la vida de un sujeto"[2] (2004, 28). The inspiration comes from the French situationists, but here the project is given a clearly feminist cue: it is no longer about the fluid itinerary of the autonomous and free man, but about walking interviews with a series of diverse precarious women to some very specific places in a city that limit and condition experience and possibilities, and often blur the boundaries between work and life. The project's ambition was to constitute a situated and heterogeneous knowledge: "partir de sí, para no quedarse en sí (como querría el capital y el patriarcado); desobedecer las segmentaciones y fronteras del capitalismo global integrado para estar juntas y revueltas; aferrar la ciudad-empresa como terreno común y de conflicto: situarse dentro y contra (la precarización, la movilidad forzada, el acceso desigual a los recursos, la explotación, el miedo, la soledad…)"[3] (ibid., 11). More specifically, the idea of the "drifts" is to locate and map the ways of living, thinking and feeling time, space, income, communication, relational and care networks, conflict, hierarchy, risk and the body (ibid., 18). Although neo-Marxism had already pointed out the importance of immaterial work (affective, communicative, creative), especially through the work of Silvia Federici, the Precarias wanted to maintain their singularity so as not to reproduce "false homogeneities"; the conditions that determine a precarious experience vary greatly and combating them requires specific strategies. Likewise, *A la deriva* emphasises that the critique of affective and immaterial work tends to forget the feminist aspect according to which reproductive work is unpaid, but at the same time essential for the functioning of the capitalist economy. The result of the ambitious investigation of the Precarias is a very varied series of testimonies of urban life in the neoliberal economy, with immediate strength and concreteness, which defines and studies the female experience of precarity. In this period, the term *mileurista*, popularised by Espido Freire in two books—*Mileuristas: Retrato de la generación de los mil euros* (2006) and *La generación de las mil emociones: Mileuristas II* (2008)—came to denote the young educated professional who earned only a thousand euros per month, despite having a full-time job. Only a few years later, the *mileurismo* would not be seen with pity, but with envy.

Spanish fiction was largely oblivious to the underlying conflicts of Spanish society: on the one hand, the consequences of neoliberal capitalism and any sort of class antagonism; on the other, the narrative of Spain's peaceful and unproblematic transition from an almost forty-year-long Fascist dictatorship to a capitalist, liberal democracy (for a study on the presence of Francoism in Spanish society today, see Faber 2021). Referring to pre-crisis fiction, David Becerra Mayor talks about "la novela de la no-ideología," novels that displace any kind of class conflict in favour of individual and subjective accounts:

> La novela española actual reproduce, inconscientemente (y acaso muy conscientemente, cuando la *carrera literaria*, las ventas, la fama, el reconocimiento público, etc., predominan sobre la escritura), la ideología del capitalismo avanzado al desplazar las contradicciones radicales del sistema por otras asumibles por su ideología. La novela de la no-ideología borra las huellas de lo político y lo social para ofrecer una interpretación de la realidad en que todo conflicto se localiza en el interior del sujeto. Este desplazamiento de las tensiones sociales hacia las pulsiones subjetivas contribuye, por defecto, a la construcción imaginaria de un mundo perfecto y cerrado, aconflictivo. Esto es, el "Fin de la Historia."[4] (2013, 65)

Becerra points out that this not only applies to novels set in the present, but also in the past: for example, the popular Civil War novel rarely focuses on ideological conflict, but rather uses the War as a setting for individual dilemmas, or even as a dramatic backdrop for thriller or romantic stories (Becerra Mayor 2015). However, there were exceptions. Belén Gopegui thoroughly investigates the ideological bearings of Spanish society in fictional form in *Lo real* (2001), as well as the possibilities of real class struggle in *El padre de Blancanieves* (2007). Marta Sanz places her fiction on the intersections between class, gender and subjectivity in *Susana y los viejos* (2006), and from a more bodily-situated perspective in *La lección de anatomía* (2008). Isaac Rosa studies the ideological cover-ups related to the transition to democracy (in Spanish, significantly, capitalised as *la Transición*) in *El vano ayer* (2004) and to the Spanish Civil War in *¡Otra maldita novela sobre la guerra civil!* (2007). Rafael Chirbes, the most meticulously realist of these four writers, relates the political tensions by the time of Franco's death in

La caída de Madrid (2000), the dreams of revolution in *Los viejos amigos* (2003) and the construction bubble in *Crematorio* (2007); his 2013 novel on the corruption in Spain, *En la orilla*, was awarded the prestigious Premio Nacional de Literatura and hailed as the great novel of the crisis (Rodríguez Marcos 2013). Particularly interesting are two books published under a pseudonym: *El año que tampoco hicimos la revolución* (*The Year We Didn't Make the Revolution Either*, 2005), published by the collective Todoazén (two writers and one economist, all anonymous), and Fernando Díaz's *Panfleto para seguir viviendo* (*Pamphlet to Keep on Living*, 2007). Todoazén's book is a chronological collection of hundreds of authentic newspapers clippings from 2003 that, read together as a continuous narrative, display a country sleepwalking toward economic and social catastrophe, making clear that anyone who was surprised by the 2008 crisis had not read the papers carefully. The *Panfleto*, on the other hand, is a hard-hitting story of a youngster who, out of lived experience and autodidact ideological schooling, realises that aggressive political militancy, or even taking up arms, is the only way to break the current neoliberal chokehold. The fact that both books are published anonymously points to the reluctance of Spanish society to face the growing tensions in the country (Bértolo 2015). Despite the generally apolitical tendencies of Spanish literature, then, these novels are testimonies to the fact that there was a staunchly political pre-crisis literature, a literature that laid bare the ideological underpinnings, social inequalities and class frictions of contemporary Spanish society.

The 2008 Crisis

If the 2000s were the decade in which precarity became part of the working conditions under the neoliberal regime in the Western world, in the 2010s, it has spread throughout society on a much greater scale. The situation has deteriorated for the already vulnerable and has fully reached a middle class that believed itself to be protected; the gig economy has turned many workers into day labourers, without stability, security or access to the welfare system; and migration flows have provided an army of the needy as cheap labour. Some critics deny the existence of a new precarity, arguing that precarity has always been and always will be, plain and simple, the condition of the working class under capitalism (Di Bernardo 2016), but it seems certain that the situation has changed for the worse for large part of the population in the last decade. If anything, the concept of precarity has spread far beyond the labour sphere, being "una condición social y geográficamente determinada que se plasma, de manera visible (a veces obscenamente), en una multitud de coyunturas laborales, educativas, sanitarias, migratorias, habitacionales y salariales, pero también psicológicas, afectivas y simbólicas"[5] (Álvarez Blanco and Gómez L. Quiñones 2016, 12). Among these precarities, "también hay que tener muy presente la precariedad para imaginar, pensar y actuar coherentemente contra la precariedad"[6] (ibid., 14).

The 2010s began with the economic recession as a result of the bankruptcy of Lehman Brothers and ended with the COVID-19 pandemic, that is, beginning with one crisis and ending with another. The crisis of 2008 has not led to an economic and social recovery, a return to the "normality" of before or, much less, the advent of a "more humane capitalism." If the events of recent years have revealed anything, it is that "normality" will never return. Moreover, it is even necessary to ask whether that era—a relatively stable Fordism managed by a welfare state that offered security in exchange for labour in the post-war era—was so normal or if it was, instead, a historical anomaly that in Spain lasted about thirty years and in a handful of Western countries a little longer. Luisa Elena Delgado uses the concept of psychoanalytic fantasy, the one that "hace posible e imposible a la vez la identificación colectiva"[7] and that "no es la antagonista de la realidad social, sino, por el contrario, su condición preexistente, su pegamento psíquico"[8] (2014, 68) to characterise that supposed Spanish normality from which the conflicts of national identity and the Franco dictatorship have been suppressed. The same could be said of "normality" before the 2008 crisis: what are now longed for as times of abundance and stability were actually inflated by loans and disguised by a "left" that had long since ceased to have the interests of the people as their greatest concern, with clearly appreciable cracks. As Palmar Álvarez Blanco and Antonio Gómez Quiñones state, "sin el teatro alucinado de auto-representaciones y auto-celebraciones, sin ese retablo de las maravillas del progreso en la (post)modernidad ibérica, no se entiende la *belle époque* de la nueva España democrática y de su experiencia cotidiana"[9] (2016, 14).

In what follows, I will define what could be called Spanish 'post-crisis fiction', rather than the occasionally used crisis fiction (or *novela de la crisis*). As I discuss elsewhere (Claesson 2015), the latter label is perhaps too restrictive, since it seems to refer (as in Rodríguez Marcos 2014) to a relatively uniform subgenre of novels that include the crisis and its consequences as their main topic. Some commentators question whether the Spanish crisis has actually ended, since the social and economic situation of the country is still considerably worse than before 2008. Nevertheless, a crisis is, by definition, something sudden and decisive—a turning point—so, in that sense, it is more accurate to say that Spaniards are living the consequences of the crisis rather than the crisis itself. Likewise, the 'post' prefix does not entail an overcoming of the effects of the crisis, but rather the questioning or reconfiguration of these effects, as a way of understanding the changing social, cultural and political landscape. The post-crisis novel, then, would be a novel that attempts to understand the social, cultural and political changes by questioning the effects of the crisis, and not merely fiction that registers the consequences without further consideration.

La mano invisible: the Narrativity of Work

One of the most thorough, researched, overwhelming and insightful novels ever written on the phenomenon of work in Spain, Isaac Rosa's *La mano invisible* (*The Invisible Hand*, 2011), also stands as a bridge head between the before and after the crisis: it describes the labour situation of the 2000s, with mostly traditional jobs and a subjectivity formed during the years of a relatively functional welfare state, but points toward a more precarious future—and toward fiction's heightened interest in work and class issues. In this novel, we follow twelve unnamed workers—a bricklayer, a butcher, a car mechanic, a cleaner, a secretary, a programmer, a bartender, a security guard, a jack-of-all-trades, a telemarketer, an assembly line worker and a seamstress—while they are really at work, through all their movements, pain, monotony, stress, tiredness, pride and rivalry, but also their own reflections on the work they are performing as well as on the meaning, place and function of work itself. The particular circumstance of these (manual) workers is that they are not doing at all typical work in a typical workplace; they perform the same tasks over and over again—the bricklayer builds a wall only to tear it down, the butcher slaughters only sick animals that are thrown away, the car mechanic takes a car apart only to put it together again—in an enormous warehouse, lit up by spotlights and in front of an audience. Nobody knows neither the organisation nor the rationale behind the setup, but it becomes a major event over several months, with large audiences and discussions among intellectuals, academics, trade unionists and the general public in newspapers and on television. Is it a performance, a piece of theatre, a circus, a protest or perhaps a publicity campaign? Can the workers actually be said to be working when their labour does not lead anywhere, even though they are paid and their bodies hurt at the end of an eight-hour workday? After a first few weeks of stable work, the invisible employer raises demands that causes frictions and conflicts in the group, both in front of the audience (who love the sight of conflict) and during the after-work drinks. At the end, the rising tempo, the sense that the workers are taken advantage of and the diminishing audience leads to resignations and finally to a complete shutdown, and neither the characters nor the readers ever learn who was behind the whole thing.

Among other things, the novel is an exploration of the dynamics of visibility and invisibility of the modern labour market. The title is of course a nod to Adam Smith's market metaphor (never more than a utopian liberal idea), but more spe-

cifically to the opaque labour relations under neoliberal capitalism. The workers
are hired by a temporary work agency and never meet any managers—they do
not know who the employer is, nor, indeed, what kind of employer it is. Each
time they drag their feet or silently protest against an already utterly meaningless task (typing fewer pages or building fewer walls than expected) they are
penalised through a salary reduction. It is not until several months later that they
discover the supervisor has been right among them: the programmer is surveilling his co-workers' every step, in order to develop a computer programme to
improve labour efficiency. The programme is aptly called Panoptic, as a reference to Bentham's panopticon, and particularly to its application to modern-
day working life, as predicted in Shoshana Zuboff's now classic *In the Age of the
Smart Machine: The Future of Work and Power* (1988). Surveillance is moreover
exercised by the audience of the spectacle: invisible behind the powerful spotlights, they laugh, boo and urge the workers to talk less and work more.

The invisibility also applies to work and workers themselves—the hand that
cleans the toilet, slaughters the animal, sews the shirt—in modern society. To the
middle class, mainly working in the service sector, it may seem as if things grow by
themselves. Thinking about the audience, whom he labels 'work tourists', the bricklayer wonders whether they ever reflected upon who actually built their buildings:

> si alguna vez al llegar desde la calle levantarán la vista y al ver el edificio se pre-
> guntarán cómo fue su construcción, cómo aguantaron el frío y la lluvia hombres
> subidos a un andamio para enfoscar la fachada; si alguna vez han dedicado un
> solo pensamiento por pequeño que sea a quienes se esforzaron, se fatigaron, su-
> daron, se dolieron y desgastaron sus cuerpos para hacer posibles esas paredes, ese
> techo, esa escalera, ese hueco del ascensor por el que alguna vez cae un albañil que
> nunca será recordado con una placa de agradecimiento en la entrada a la casa;
> incluso si se les ha ocurrido pensar que ese edificio lo hicieron hombres, no se
> hizo solo, no fueron las máquinas ni trajeron módulos prefabricados, como esas
> parejas que se compran un piso y cada domingo van a ver cómo avanza la obra, y
> al no ser día de trabajo ven de una semana a otra que la casa va creciendo como si
> lo hiciera sola[10] (Rosa 2011, 31–32)

On another level, the novel is an attempt to fill the perceived void of actual working fictions in literature, the presumed *inenarrable* or even inhumane quality of
work, epitomised by a quote by José Luis Pardo included as a postscript to the text:

> Ciertamente, hay muchas narraciones que transcurren total o parcialmente en
> lugares de trabajo, pero lo que estas narraciones relatan es algo que ocurre en-
> tre los personajes *al margen de su mera actividad laboral*, y no esa actividad en

cuanto tal, porque su brutalidad o su monotonía parecen señalar un límite a la narratividad (¿cómo contar algo allí donde no hay nadie, donde cada uno deja de ser alguien?).[11] (379)

In *La mano invisible*, working workers occupy centre stage in a double sense, both literally on the warehouse stage in front of the audience, and as the main characters of the novel we are reading. Fiction fertilises and multiplies the meaning of the work at the centre of the novel. On the one hand, the fictional setup of the labour produced (or reproduced) in the warehouse makes us reflect on what work is and whether it still counts as work when done in an unproductive setting, which, in turn, leads to a whole array of questions as to what actually constitutes a productive and meaningful job, and whether there is any real difference between this staged work and David Graeber's 'bullshit jobs' (2018). On the other hand, the fiction of the thoroughly researched representations of work that make up the novel denotes a real break in the hegemony of mainstream fiction. Carmina Gustrán Loscos relates this to Jacques Rancière's idea of the distribution of the sensible—"the system of self-evident facts of sense perception that simultaneously discloses the existence of something in common and the delimitations that define the respective parts and positions within it," that is, "the delimitation of spaces and times, of the visible and the invisible, of speech and noise, that simultaneously determines the place and the stakes of politics as a form of experience" (2004, 7–8). "Placing precarious workers on a stage," argues Gustrán Loscos, "disrupts the distribution of the sensible" (2020, 44), and gives these otherwise unheard workers a voice with which to stick out from that which is normally only perceived as noise. Moreover, she also talks about work as a fiction in itself—a story that is told to us about power relations that are constructed and therefore might be upset and changed (ibid., 47). In some sense, what is questioned is work itself, although this idea is never fully articulated.

However, even more central than workers is work itself. Intermixed with the reflections on the work situation, daydreaming, associations and memories are descriptions of the labour performed, often mimicking the monotony of the working situation: "Redonda, cuadrada, redonda, cuadrada, triangular, rectangular, triangular, rectangular, mira el reloj para ver cuántos segundos tarda en tomar una caja, llenarla y ponerla en su sitio, redonda, cuadrada, redonda, cuadrada, triangular, rectangular, triangular, rectangular"[12] (ibid., 64). The novel gives voice to twelve workers in twelve chapters—the thirteenth worker represented, the prostitute, is significantly *not* given a voice and is not a part of the performative setup—and each chapter is narrated almost in one breath, without dialogue quotation marks or question marks, although dialogue and questions abound (see the bricklayer quote above as an example). The free indirect speech throughout the text makes for a realistic testimony ordered by the discipline and irony of the narrator, a sort of stream of consciousness, with page-long sentences and few paragraph divisions, that overwhelms the reader and puts her in the situation of the worker. Sometimes, as in the case of the telemarketer, the monotony of work is the monotony of language itself:

> Buenas tardes, podría hablar con el señor Herrera Abad, por favor. Encantada de saludarle, señor Herrera. Le llamo para. No, no es una venta telefónica. No, no voy a ofrecerle ningún. Disculpe, buenas tardes.
>
> Buenas tardes, podría hablar con el señor Herrera Acosta, por favor. Encantada de saludarle, señor Herrera. Le llamo para pedirle su. Sólo serán cuatro minutos, señor Herrera. No tiene que. Disculpe, buenas tardes.
>
> Buenas tardes, podría hablar con el señor Herrera Agudo, por favor.[13] (ibid., 117)

The representation of work at a concretely textual level is, ultimately, what makes an identification with these unnamed workers in their daily routine possible. Work may be missing even in working-class fiction, like that invisible hand that moves the story, as Pardo suggests, but here it is the core of the novel.

Published in 2011, Isaac Rosa's ground-breaking novel has come to be read as post-crisis fiction, standing at the beginning of the stream of novels that in some way deal with conditions and consequences of the crisis, but it refers to a labour situation in place well before the crisis. La mano invisible certainly depicts precarity, uncertainty and ever-increasing productivity demands, but also more general, work-related issues such as monotony, boredom, class, community, unionisation and exploitation. It thus straddles the Spanish crisis: it narrates a general working situation, especially poignant in the 2000s, but also opens up for the novelistic production of the 2010s. For all its irregularities, such as the performative setup, it relates a fairly regulated work situation. The novels published in the 2010s focus more on the lack of work, refusal to work and irregular work, as well as the general social consequences of the crisis.

Post-Crisis Fiction

In the last part of this chapter, I will briefly review how Spanish fiction[14] has responded to the precarity that has permeated society over the last ten years. Both Isabell Lorey (2015) and Precarias a la deriva, among others, underline the double face of precarity: it is associated with fear and profound uncertainty, but there is also a potential for making structural changes that may lead to a more just society. The same applies to literature on precarity, which both represents and challenges contemporary insecurity. On the one hand, there is a testimonial trend of narratives, generally realistic, that integrate precarity at the level of content and make visible the life circumstances of the precariat, recounting the multitude of consequences that the 2008 crisis has had from a human and situated perspective. In these cases, the capacity of the novel as a genre is used to put the reader in the place of the ordinary person, to humanise a crisis that tends to be abstract, to animate the testimony with the tools of fiction, and to be a counterpart of the many essays of all kinds that analyse the crisis from a general perspective and from above. In this sense, "la precariedad, novelada siempre desde un multiperspectivismo interseccional y multiescalar, se transforma en un *locus* de enunciación privilegiado desde el cual es posible *replicar* a la *hibris* del gran metarrelato supuestamente anónimo de la crisis, definiendo la movilización como procedente de una territorialidad en forma de 'planetaridad situada'"[15] (Bonvalot 2019, 201). On the other hand, although these aspects are clearly intertwined, there are texts that integrate precarity at the level of form, experimenting with the techniques and strategies they employ. This type of text is "un conjunto que se inclina cada vez más hacia el mestizaje de los géneros, de los lenguajes y de los planos comunicativos, y que convierte la reflexión metaliteraria en un espacio propositivo y propulsivo"[16] (Rossi 2021, ii). These texts reflect the disorientation, uncertainty and ambiguous and complex functioning of ideology also at the textual level, what I elsewhere have called "precarious narratives" (Claesson 2016; Claesson 2018b). Sometimes these novels create a "sense of equivalence": "The affect of crisis moves out from the narrative and is felt as a kind of reading experience. In this way the reader is able to image lines of affinity that are capable of extending the connection between the reader and the character to precarious subjects beyond the textual encounter" (Connell 2021, 29). Consequently, the text can create a subjective awareness of the situation that, based on the concept of precariousness as an operative notion, has the possibility of functioning as a place of political action (ibid., 30). In this sense, as Hogg asserts, what matters about artistic texts is not primarily what they say about precarity, but the way in which they forge new ways of seeing and describing, new possibilities of perception and new forms of representation, to break down some of the stagnant political structures and hegemonic narratives of the contemporary moment (Hogg 2021, 13).

The Spanish post-crisis has undoubtedly grown into a literary subgenre and a research field of its own. Nere Basabe (2018, 24–27) identifies six mayor literary categories: (1) novels on labour and existential precarity, often in a testimonial register, as in Javier López Menacho's *Yo, precario* (2013) or Elvira Navarro's oft-quoted *La trabajadora* (2014); (2) critiques of consumer society and explorations of modern subjectivity, as in the fiction of Sara Mesa and Javier Moreno; (3) fictions on the migratory experience, as in Miguel Ángel Hernández's *Intento de escapada* (2013); (4) political activism, as a testimony to the wide array of grass-roots movements that spread throughout Spain in the aftermath of the 15 May demonstration in 2011, as in Pablo Gutiérrez's *Democracia* (2012)—a key reference in Spanish post-crisis fiction—or Alberto Olmos's *Ejército enemigo* (2011); (5) rural exile stories, even called "the new rural novel," of urbanites who flee the city and all its ills to relocate (with a Wi-Fi connection) to the countryside; and (6) re-interpretations of the past—to the *movida* years of the 1980s, the Transition, the Franco dictatorship, the Civil War—in the wake of a crisis that shook the foundations of both Spanish society and historiography. To these categories, we might add novels on reproductive work, gender and class, like Elena Medel's *Las maravillas* (2020), or fiction that questions or openly shuns work, as in Santiago Lorenzo's best-selling *Los asquerosos* (2018), work tourism, as Munir Hachemi's *Cosas vivas* (2018), or novels of revolutionary violence, as in Bruno Galindo's *El público* (2012) or one of the greatest achievements of the post-crisis fiction era, Diego Sánchez Aguilar's *Factbook: El libro de los hechos* (2018). Federico López-Terra adds that, in addition to the crisis *in* the story, we also have the crisis *of* the story, signalling a halt in the production of meaning, where "la crisis como interrupción tanto de narrativas personales como colectivas derivó en la incapacidad de los sujetos de dotar de continuidad narrativa su propia historia, de hacerse con el relato"[17] (2018, 123).

A landmark event in the evolution of the genre was the surprising choice to grant the Premio Nacional de Literatura to Cristina Morales's *Lectura fácil* in 2018—born in 1985, she is the youngest woman writer to receive the prize. The prize is state-sponsored, bestowed by the Ministry for Culture and Sports, which "promotes a specific type of individualism that allows the state the annual opportunity to publicly appropriate the writer/citizen's labour for its own purposes, which are, of course, 'nationalistic' in the sense that the prize serves to promote literary value that is presented as representing the nation" (Perret 2015, 78). What the novels that have won this award have in common is that they are not "too militantly 'Other' from the state's perspective" (ibid., 83), but rather subscribe to the idea of a Spain that aligns with the political consensus formed by the transition to democracy and the Constitution of 1978. Strikingly, *Lectura fácil* is the complete opposite of the novels that normally receive this award. The novel tells the story of four intellectually impaired women living in a group home in Barcelona, in which different voices and genres coalesce and mirror each other—first-person narratives, court hearings, minutes from anarchist collectives in which the characters are involved, libertarian fanzines and the texts written in the mode of "easy reading" designed for people with reading or other intellectual impairments. On one level, it criticises a regime of Foucauldian biopolitics, in the way it deconstructs "el modo en que los dispositivos del Estado operan en la institucionalización de los cuerpos de quienes no encajan en la normalidad y la heteronormatividad construida"[18] (Becerra Mayor 2021, 145). Here, another kind of Panopticon is installed, in which bodies and behaviours deemed deviant are controlled by the State through sterilisation and medication as well as apparently well-meaning measures such as welfare checks (with a set of demands), reading groups (where reading and writing is controlled) or integral dance, which is inclusive of individuals with and without disabilities (but where difference is, paradoxically, homogenised). On another level, it is a furious attack on post-crisis Spain—or even Spain as state formation—in which almost nobody is spared. The political critique is expressed especially by Nati, who was about to complete her PhD in sociology when she suffered a nervous breakdown triggered by her pathological inability to tolerate class differences, capitalism "non plus ultra" (ibid., 139) or especially the racist "facho-machos" (fascist-machos) that dominate Spanish society, and through the discussions in the anarchist collective that are given ample space in this long novel.

Lectura fácil may be considered the most thorough anarchist critique of Spanish post-crisis society to date, although it looks slightly different from more conventional (if that is the right word here) anarchist writings. As such, it channels the most radical political energy of the 15M, the massive, horizontal and loosely bound movement that started with the occupation of the Puerta del Sol in Madrid on 15 May 2011. The fact that the novel was awarded the Premio Nacional, in spite of the character and history of the prize, seems to be an acknowledgment both of the force of the post-crisis novel in general and of the sprawling and radical legacy of the 15M movement. David Becerra calls the novel an example of *intransitive literature*: a literature that does not commit to a previously defined goal, that does not aim to overtake power (as would be the case of transitive literature), but rather to de-activate power from the margins, freeing itself from the mechanisms that discipline bodies and subjectivities, leaving room for anyone to discover the possibilities by exploring previously unknown territories (2021, 142). Likewise, when analysing the 15M, Amador Fernández-Savater underlines what he calls "la fuerza de los débiles, cuyos ingredientes son la activación de los afectos y los vínculos, la elección autónoma de los tiempos y los espacios, el valor de la igualdad y la pluralidad"[19] (2021, 66). The strength of the weak, therefore, is "una guerrilla-movimiento: un ecosistema, una red autoorganizada, un *mundo en marcha*"[20] (ibid., 76). This is what Standing (2011, 2021) is aiming at when he talks about the precariat as a class-in-the-making: it will never be like the working class, with its physical meeting places, unions, faith in progress, pride and revolutionary potential, but it can indeed constitute a common sensibility, a destituent force, a rhizomatic network, a shared condition. Morales's *Lectura fácil* goes beyond the focus on precarity so common in Spanish post-crisis fiction and hones in on precariousness and governmentality: by portraying a group of women who struggle against (or just are outside) institutionalised individualism, competitiveness as a core principle of society, self-entrepreneurialism, financialisation and the imposition of the security state, she questions the disciplinary mechanisms that are both a condition and a result of neoliberal society. Instead, the novel argues (if it argues for anything) for the acknowledgment of our mutual precariousness, for the strength of the weak, for resistance in multiplicity, for democratic horizontality and for a refusal of work and productivity. As such, Morales's novel becomes the most radical expression of thinking and fiction in the post-crisis, post-15M era.

As we have seen, there was certainly political fiction and thinking before the crisis, but it was scarce and tended to be buried under the narrative of an economically prosperous, democratically normalised and culturally homogeneous Spain. The crisis and the massive politicisation that followed—mainly through the 15M—made it much more difficult for writers, critics and scholars, as well as for society as a whole, to look the other way. It also became relevant to pinpoint the political potential of post-crisis fiction. Maria Ayete Gil defines the political novel as one that, with all the aesthetic resources of fiction, intends to intervene in the consensus view of reality, breaking the division of the common with the aim of revealing the possibility of a different, more just world (2021, 161). The political post-crisis fiction, in contrast to a fiction that merely registers the effects of the crisis, would thus be novels "que traten de visibilizar cuestiones derivadas de la ruina económica, moral, social y política invisibilizadas por el discurso oficial; que traten de señalar causas, culpables y contradicciones, o de imaginar, bien salidas, bien mundos alternativos"[21] (ibid., 202–203). The post-crisis novels that are truly political, then, are those that highlight the cracks in the hegemonic ideology, point to the possibility of other worlds and other subjectivities, and make visible the invisible. Spanish post-crisis fiction both depicts a political awakening in society and imagines a way forward.

Notes

1. "[I]nstitutionalised individualism, a regime of competitiveness as a basic principle of all socio-productive relationships, management of the self as self-entrepreneur, financialization of one's own life, imposition of a security state that decides which lives are liveable."

2. "[S]et of conditions, material and symbolic, that determine an uncertainty about sustained access to essential resources for the full development of a subject's life."

3. "[S]tart from oneself, so as not to remain in oneself (as capital and patriarchy would like); disobey the segmentations and borders of integrated global capitalism to be together and revolt; grasping the city-company as common and conflict terrain: situating oneself within and against (precariousness, forced mobility, unequal access to resources, exploitation, fear, loneliness…)."

4. "The current Spanish novel reproduces, unconsciously (and perhaps very consciously, when literary career, sales, fame, public recognition, etc., prevail over writing), the ideology of advanced capitalism by displacing the radical contradictions of the system by others that could be assumed by that ideology. The novel of non-ideology erases the traces of the political and the social to offer an interpretation of reality in which all conflict is located within the subject. This displacement of social tensions towards subjective impulses contributes, by default, to the imaginary construction of a perfect and closed, unconflicted world. That is, the 'End of History.'"

5. "[A] social and geographically determined condition that is reflected, in a visible way (sometimes obscenely), in a multitude of work, educational, health, migratory, housing and salary situations, but also on a psychological, affective and symbolic level."

6. "[W]e must also keep very much in mind the precarity that makes it difficult to imagine, think and act coherently against precarity."

7. "[I]t makes collective identification possible and impossible at the same time."

8. "[I]t is not the antagonist of social reality, but, on the contrary, its pre-existing condition, its psychic glue."

9. "[W]ithout the hallucinatory theatre of self-representations and self-celebrations, without that 'marvellous puppet show' of progress in Iberian (post)modernity, the belle époque of the new democratic Spain and its daily experience cannot be understood."

10. "[I]f ever, upon arriving from the street, they look up and, when seeing the building, wonder how it was built, how men on scaffolding to plaster the façade endured the cold and rain; if they have ever given a single thought, no matter how small, to those who toiled, tired, sweated, ached, and wore out their bodies to make possible those walls, that ceiling, that stairway, that elevator shaft where a bricklayer sometimes falls down who will never be remembered with a plaque of gratitude at the entrance to the house; if it has even occurred to them to think that this building was made by men, it wasn't built by itself, it wasn't machines or prefabricated modules, like those couples who buy a flat and go every Sunday to see how the work progresses, and, since it is not a work day, from one week to the next they see the house growing as if by itself."

11. "Certainly, there are many narratives that take place totally or partially in workplaces, but what these narratives relate is something that happens between the characters outside of their mere work activity, and not that activity as such, because its brutality or

monotony seem point out a limit to narrativity (how to tell something where there is no one, where everyone ceases to be someone?)."

12. "Round, square, round, square, triangular, rectangular, triangular, rectangular, she looks at the clock to see how many seconds it takes to take a box, fill it and put it in its place, round, square, round, square, triangular, rectangular, triangular, rectangular."

13. "Good afternoon, could I speak to Mr. Herrera Abad, please. Pleased to greet you, Mr. Herrera. I call you to. No, it is not a telephone sale. No, I will not offer you any. Excuse me, good afternoon.
Good afternoon, could I speak to Mr. Herrera Acosta, please. Pleased to greet you, Mr. Herrera. I'm calling to ask for your. It will only be four minutes, Mr. Herrera. You don't have to. Excuse me, good afternoon.
Good afternoon, could I speak to Mr. Herrera Agudo, please."

14. The term 'Spanish' refers to the language rather than to the country as a whole, since there are a large number of novels published in Spain written in Catalan, Basque and Galician. A more accurate denomination would thus be "Spanish Post-Crisis Fiction in Spanish" but, for the sake of stylistic elegance, I use the conventional term. See my article "One Country, Several Literatures: Towards a Comparative Understanding of Contemporary Literature in Spain" (Claesson 2018a) and *Novela política en la España plurilingüe*, a collection of edited essays that study post-crisis political fiction published in all the official languages of Spain (forthcoming in 2024).

15. "[P]recarity, always fictionalised from an intersectional and multi-scalar multi-perspectivism, becomes a privileged locus of enunciation from which it is possible to reply to the hubris of the great supposedly anonymous meta-narrative of the crisis, defining the mobilisation as proceeding from a territoriality in the form of 'situated planetarity.'"

16. "[A] set that leans more and more towards the miscegenation of genres, languages and communicative planes, and that turns metaliterary reflection into a propositional and propulsive space."

17. "[T]he crisis, as a disruption of both personal and collective narratives, resulted in the subjects' inability to provide narrative continuity to their own story, to take hold of the narrative."

18. "[T]he way in which the devices of the State operate in the institutionalisation of the bodies of those who do not fit into normality and constructed heteronormativity."

19. "[T]he strength of the weak, whose ingredients are the activation of affections and ties, the autonomous choice of times and spaces, the value of equality and plurality."

20. "[A]a guerrilla-movement: an ecosystem, a self-organised network, a world on the move."

21. "[T]hat try to make visible issues derived from the economic, moral, social and political ruin that had been obscured by official discourse; that try to point out causes, culprits and contradictions, or to imagine either solutions or alternative worlds."

References

Álvarez Blanco, Palmar, and Antonio Gómez L. Quiñones. 2016. "Introducción." In *La imaginación hipotecada: Aportaciones al debate sobre la precariedad del presente*, edited by Palmar Álvarez Blanco and Antonio Gómez L. Quiñones, 9–16. Madrid: Libros en acción.

Ayete Gil, Maria. 2021. "Ideología, poder y cuerpo: la repolitización de la narrativa española en castellano (2011–2020)." PhD diss., Universidad de Salamanca.

Basabe, Nere. 2018. "Memoria histórica, violencia política y crisis de identidades en la nueva narrativa española." In *Narrativas precarias: Crisis y subjetividad en la cultura española actual*, edited by Christian Claesson, 21–57. Gijón: Hoja de lata.

Becerra Mayor, David. 2013. *La novela de la no-ideología: Introducción a la producción literaria del capitalismo avanzado en España*. Madrid: Tierra de nadie.

Becerra Mayor, David. 2015. *La guerra civil como moda literaria*. Madrid: Clave intelectual.

Becerra Mayor, David. 2021. *Después del acontecimiento*. Barcelona: Bellaterra Edicions.

Bértolo, Constantino. 2015. "*Panfleto para seguir viviendo* de Fernando Díaz: El extraño caso del panfleto que no quería ser literatura." In *Convocando al fantasma: Novela crítica en la España actual*, edited by David Becerra Mayor, 283–298. Madrid: Tierra de nadie.

Bonvalot, Anne-Laure. 2019. "Nuevas territorialidades y ontologías políticas en la ficción española post 15M: horizontes estéticos y antropológicos de la 'literatura indignada'." In *España después del 15M*, edited by Jorge Cagiao y Conde and Isabelle Touton, 193–201. Madrid: Catarata.

Bourdieu, Pierre. 1998. *Acts of Resistance: Against the New Myths of Our Time*. Translated by Richard Nice. Cambridge: Polity Press.

Butler, Judith. 1997. *The Psychic Life of Power: Theories in Subjection*. Stanford: Stanford University Press.

Casas-Cortés, Maribel. 2014. "A Genealogy of Precarity: A Toolbox for Rearticulating Fragmented Social Realities in and out of the Workplace." *Rethinking Marxism* 26, no. 2: 206–226.

Claesson, Christian. 2015. "En busca del sentido: Exceso y crítica social en *Karnaval* de Juan Francisco Ferré." In *Convocando al fantasma: Novela crítica en la España actual*, edited by David Becerra Mayor, 395–420. Madrid: Tierra de nadie.

Claesson, Christian. 2016. "Precarious Narratives: Subjectivity in Rosarios Izquierdo's *Diario de campo* and Elvira Navarro's *La trabajadora*." In *Identities and Intersections in 21st-century Peninsular Fiction and Film*, edited by Jennifer Brady and Meredith L. Jeffers, 10–36. Cambridge: Cambridge Scholars Publishing.

Claesson, Christian. 2018a. "One Country, Several Literatures: Towards a Comparative Understanding of Contemporary Literature in Spain." In *World Literatures: Exploring the Cosmopolitan-Vernacular Exchange*, edited by Stefan Helgesson et al., 31–41. Stockholm: Stockholm University Press.

Claesson, Christian (coord.). 2018b. *Narrativas precarias: Crisis y subjetividad en la cultu-ra española actual*. Gijón: Hoja de lata.

Connell, Liam. 2021. "Anxious Reading: The Precarity Novel and the Affective Class." In *Precarity in Contemporary Literature and Culture*, edited by Emily J. Hogg and Peter Simonsen, 27–41. London: Bloomsbury Academic.

Cúneo, Martín. 2020. "Un estudio cifra en 684.385 los desahucios desde 2008 y concluye que la crisis se ha hecho crónica." *El Salto*, 14 June 2020. Accessed 14 April 2023. https://www.elsaltodiario.com/vivienda/analisis-684385-desahucios-2008-hipoteca-alquiler-pah-observatori-desc-concluye-crisis-permanente-cronica.

Delgado, Luisa Elena. 2014. *La nación singular: Fantasías de la normalidad democrática española (1996–2011)*. Madrid: Siglo XX.

Di Bernardo, Francesco. 2016. "The Impossibility of Precarity." *Radical Philosophy* 198 (July/August): 7–14.

Díaz, Fernando. 2007. *Panfleto para seguir viviendo*. Barcelona: Bruguera/Ediciones B.

El País. 2011. "España perderá medio millón de habitantes en la próxima década si se mantiene la tendencia demográfica." *El País*, 7 October 2011. Accessed 14 April 2023. https://elpais.com/sociedad/2011/10/07/actualidad/1317938404_850215.html.

Faber, Sebastian. 2021. *Exhuming Franco: Spain's Second Transition*. Nashville: Vanderbilt University Press.

Fernández-Savater, Amador. 2021. *La fuerza de los débiles: El 15M en el laberinto español. Un ensayo sobre la eficacia política, Pensamiento crítico*. Madrid: Akal.

Freire, Espido. 2006. *Mileuristas: Retrato de la generación de los mil euros*. Barcelona: Ariel.

Freire, Espido. 2008. *La generación de las mil emociones: Mileuristas II*. Barcelona: Ariel.

Graeber, David. 2018. *Bullshit Jobs: A Theory*. New York: Simon & Schuster.

Gustrán Loscos, Carmina. 2020. "An estranged gaze at the world of work: *La mano invis-ible* (Isaac Rosa 2011; David Macián 2016)." *International Journal of Iberian Studies* 33, no. 1: 41–59.

Hogg, Emily J. 2021. "Introduction." In *Precarity in Contemporary Literature and Culture*, edited by Emily J. Hogg and Peter Simonsen, 1–26. London: Bloomsbury Academic.

Jornet Somoza, Albert. 2017. "Nuestro cuerpo también: pensar en precario en la España de la crisis." *Artes del ensayo* 1: 153–182.

López-Terra, Federico. 2018. "Narrar la crisis: Representación y agencia en la España poscrisis." In *Narrativas precarias: Crisis y subjetividad en la cultura española actual*, edited by Christian Claesson, 121–153. Gijón: Hoja de lata.

Lorey, Isabell. 2015. *State of Insecurity: Government of the Precarious*. Translated by Aileen Derieg. New York: Verso.

Muñoz Molina, Antonio. 2013. *Todo lo que era sólido*. Barcelona: Seix Barral.

Naredo, José Manuel. 2010. "El modelo inmobiliario español y sus consecuencias." *Boletín CF+S* 44: 13–27.

Perret, Sally. 2015. "In the Name of the Nation? The National Award in Narrative Literature, and the Democratization of Art in Spain (1977–2013)." *Journal of Spanish Cultural Studies* 16, no. 1: 77–93.

Precarias a la deriva. 2004. *A la deriva por los circuitos de la precariedad femenina*. Madrid: Traficantes de sueños.

Rancière, Jacques. 2004. *The Politics of Aesthetics*. Translated by Gabriel Rockhill. London: Bloomsbury.

Rodríguez Marcos, Javier. 2013. "La gran novela de la crisis en España." *El País*, 2 March 2013. Accessed 14 April 2023. https://elpais.com/cultura/2013/02/28/actualidad/1362067884_779080.html.

Rodríguez Marcos, Javier. 2014. "Una crisis de novela." *El País*, 16 March 2013. Accessed 14 April 2023. https://elpais.com/sociedad/2013/03/16/actualidad/1363470608_130051.html.

Rosa, Isaac. 2011. *La mano invisible*. Barcelona: Seix Barral.

Rossi, Maura. 2021. "Literaturas de la crisis: precariedad y narración en el ámbito peninsular del siglo XXI. Introducción." *Orillas: Rivista d'ispanistica* 10: i–iii.

Standing, Guy. 2011. *The Precariat: The New Dangerous Class*. London: Bloomsbury Academic, 2011.

Standing, Guy. 2021. *The Precariat: The New Dangerous Class. Covid-19 Edition*. London: I. B. Tauris.

Todoazén, Colectivo. 2005. *El año que tampoco hicimos la revolución*. Barcelona: Caballo de Troya.

Universidad de Barcelona. n.d. "Proyecto crisis económica y confianza." http://www.ub.edu/crisis-desigualdad-confianza/factores-de-confianza.html.

Zuboff, Shoshana. 1988. *In the Age of the Smart Machine: The Future of Work and Power*. Oxford: Heinemann Professional.

PART 2

PERSONALISING CLASS: INDIVIDUALS AND COLLECTIVES

2.1

The Poetics of Personal Authenticity

Diversity, Intersectionality and the Working Class in Contemporary German Literature

CHRISTOPH SCHAUB

Diversity, Invisibility, Intersectionality

Over the last decade, literary, journalistic and sociological writing about class society and the working class has increased in Germany and gained broader public visibility. Such writing has been triggered by, and given shape to, discussions about the precariat (Standing 2021) and the society of downward mobility (Nachtwey 2018). At the same time, it was influenced by Didier Eribon's *Retour à Reims* (*Returning to Reims,* 2009), translated into German in 2016 with a field-forming impact. The rise of this writing appears to be as much a symptom of neoliberalism's "restoration of class power" through "accumulation by dispossession" (Harvey 2007, 31; 159) as it is an intellectual, artistic and political response to it. As I argue, the entanglement of the representation of the working class as a diverse group with a poetics of personal authenticity predominates in this strand of contemporary literature.

In recent publications, sociological and journalistic authors often highlight two characteristics of the working class, understanding it as the majority of the population who do not possess capital and have to sell their labour power, yet are increasingly unable to live off what they make. Authors emphasise the working class's diversity. The sociologists Nicole Mayer-Ahuja and Oliver Nachtwey (2021), for example, argue that "the labouring class [...] is everything but homogenous"; they contend that it has encompassed "very different persons since the beginning of capitalism" and has done so "despite its romantic reduction [*Engführung*] to the industrial proletariat" (30–31).[1] These new conceptions foreground a working class not limited to, nor even centred on, the white male worker in the factory, in mining or construction; instead it encompasses, to name only a few examples, care workers of all kinds, delivery and service personnel, and workers in the gig economy. The diversity of the working class stems both from the multiplicity of professional occupations (and their various legal frameworks and educational backgrounds) and from the heterogeneity of working-class social positions and identities, which are best understood through an intersectional lens that demonstrates how class is connected to, for example, gender, ethnicity and citizenship.

If authors stress diversity, they also emphasise the absence of self-representations by working-class subjects in the public sphere. Writing of the "unheard half," journalist Julia Friedrichs (2021) contends, in her book-length reportage *Working Class*, that the "voices" of the working class "are much too rarely heard" (17). Similar to Friedrich, Mayer-Ahuja and Nachtwey (2021) see the interview-based reportages they collect in their edited volume as a way to make working-class people "visible" and enable them to "report with their own voices about their work and their lives" (14). These books tend to arrange working-class first-person utterances within the authors' larger interpretative narratives. In contrast, Frédéric Valin, an author and care worker, does without such a framework to foreground the voices of the care workers he interviews in his *Pflegeprotokolle* (*Care Protocols*, 2021), a title that evokes Erika Runge's famous *Bottroper Protokolle* (1968) and points back to earlier writing about class society. All these publications register the need for different kinds of representations of workers, both in terms of *how* they are represented and *who* represents them.

Against the background of the long history of imaginaries of the working class, diverse self-representations of different working-class subjects seem to be relevant for at least two reasons (see also Nilsson in this volume). First, they complicate the homogenisation of the working class in parts of the labour movement: an operation that constructed a homogenous class position as the basis for a revolutionary subject to emerge and that was driven by "the *telos* of a unified working class" (Jay 2013, 390). Second, and more relevant today, self-representations of different working-class subjects counter classism—that is, the homogenising, othering and pejorative depiction of the working class that is entangled with the political, economic, cultural and social discrimination and subjugation of working-class subjects (Kemper and Weinbach 2020, 13–25). The new writing about the working class in Germany thus resonates with important concerns of certain strands within intersectional studies and politics: that is, the attempt to make visible groups and individuals not intelligible in the public sphere *and* to deconstruct generalising and othering representations of marginalised groups and individuals (Meyer 2017, 72–78), the latter point being a major concern of anti-categorical approaches in particular. However, this writing also addresses a relative blind spot in intersectionality studies itself, as such scholarship and politics have generally paid little attention to class by comparison with gender or race (hooks 2000). In contrast to earlier phases of politicised writing about the working class in (West) German literary history—such as the 1920/30s and 1960/70s—contemporary German literature proceeds in an emphatically inter-sectional way in order to represent the working class as a diverse group. In this regard, the new literature about class society is the result not only of discussions about socio-economic precarity, but also of the heightened visibility of Germany's post-migrant condition, and of debates about cultural diversity.

Didier Eribon and Personal Authenticity

For my argument, one more layer needs to be added. It relates more directly to the literary field. In contemporary German literature, texts about class that em-ploy modes of autosociobiographical, autobiographical and autofictional writing predominate. In a retrospective manner, they often tell the upward mobility of a protagonist of working-class origin who is also the autodiegetic narrator. They include Daniela Dröscher's autosociobiography *Zeige deine Klasse* (*Show your Class*, 2018), autobiographical testimonies like Christian Baron's *Ein Mann sein-er Klasse* (*A Man of his Class*, 2020) and Olivier David's *Keine Aufstiegsgeschichte* (*Not a Story of Upward Mobility*, 2022), and autofictional, or autobiographically influenced, novels such as Deniz Ohde's *Streulicht* (*Scattered Light*, 2020). That these particular modes of writing are so prevalent can be traced back, at least to some extent, to the success of the German publication of Eribon's *Retour à Reims* in 2016, in which the French sociologist returned home to explore his social origins in the working class by mixing sociological and autobiographical meth-ods and forms of representation.[2] That *Retour à Reims* was able to have such a field-forming influence must also be seen in terms of an absence: older German-language texts written in the autofictional mode about class and upward mobil-ity—such as Gerhard Zwerenz's *Kopf und Bauch. Die Geschichte eines Arbeiters, der unter die Intellektuellen fiel* (*Head and Stomach. The Story of a Worker who ended up among the Intellectuals*, 1971) and Karin Struck's *Klassenliebe* (*Class Love*, 1973)—did not have an influence on contemporary writing, something that seems to reflect a break in the (literary) discourse about class between the 1970s and now (Schaub 2020).

Various writers and critics, including Christian Baron (Schuhen 2020, 59), Daniela Dröscher (2020, 20–21), Anna Mayr (2020, 21–24) and Leander Scholz (2019, 127–129), have attested that Eribon's text triggered a broader discourse about class society, helped to position class topics in the literary field, and also heightened their own attention to issues of class and social origin; Eribon's autosociobiography is even briefly discussed in Bov Bjerg's novel *Serpentinen*

(2020, 100–111; *Winding Road*). Assessments of Eribon differ, however. While Dröscher (2018), who grew up in the middle class, celebrates Eribon as someone who "has opened a door" and made it possible to "talk again about social distinctions" (21), Mayr (2020), the daughter of unemployed parents, sees his influence more ambivalently, considering some of the publications that have followed in his vein as "bordering on social pornography" (24), which likely reflects a distancing between authors and the milieu of their social origin as well as possibly classist expectations in the targeted non-proletarian readership. Still, with respect to the German literary field, there can be little doubt about Eribon's field-forming impact (Schuhen 2020). His book had a "genre-forming function" since it paved the way for texts that "negotiate working-class origins in the form of an autobiographical narration and with attention to social conditions, and that approach these origins by way of a retrospective return and through the act of writing" (Ernst 2020, 79).

Retour à Reims would appear to provide an attractive model for representing a diverse working class for two reasons. First, although he does not use this term, Eribon looks at his social origins through a kind of intersectional lens, tracing the entanglement of class, gender and sexuality. His negotiation of class thus connects easily to public debates about social justice that have been increasingly dominated by questions of recognition, identity and diversity (Fraser 2003, 16). At the same time, his book resonates with burgeoning discussions about socio-economic inequality and redistribution.

Second, while Eribon's text makes use of sociological analysis, it also relies on an autobiographical narrative that contributes to the creation of knowledge about the working class. In this mode of writing that revolves around an individual, the analysis of society and the analysis of the self proceed simultaneously. The knowledge that it produces is not only legitimated—i.e. understood by the reading public as true and accurate—due to the use of sociological methods, but also because of the author's personal authenticity. I follow the philosopher Sybille Krämer (2012) in distinguishing 'material authenticity' from 'personal authenticity' as two ways through which authenticity is culturally constructed, or staged. While the former refers to the "property of a product whose creator cannot be identified" and is in the first place a descriptive term, the latter, a normative term, designates "the 'realness' [*Echtheit*] and credibility of a person. This kind of authenticity refers to the capacity for human beings to be genuine and truthful" (16). In other words, in the field of literature, both the personality and the social identity of an author, as entangled with each other, can be strategically employed to construct 'the truth' of what this author articulates about society and politics. Obviously, this is a connection between an artwork and authenticity that needs to be distinguished, for example, from the rather material authenticity of the work of art in Theodor W. Adorno's sense (Butler 2019, 270–271). Personal authenticity is a particularly useful concept with respect to the German literary field, where a specific discourse about autofiction now predominates. According to this discourse, "the subject of the autofiction intersects with the author and is thus grounded in the author's social position whereby the credibility of what is written is guaranteed without having to rely on facticity" (Ernst 2020, 78). To put it somewhat differently: a widespread expectation of the literary public is that the identity of the author authenticates what is related in the text, and this extends even beyond works of autofiction (Baßler 2022, 182–197). In recent German-language literary history, this is however only one available way of dealing with the intersection of autofiction and authenticity. In contrast, in the so-called pop-literature of the 1990s, autofictional modes of writing and the authors' related self-fashioning beyond their texts were emphatically used to deconstruct notions of authenticity (Butler 2019; Kreknin 2019), something influenced by post-structuralist thought and more recently again exemplified in Christian Kracht's *Eurotrash* (2021). With respect to my corpus of texts, the notion of personal authenticity is significant because contemporary writing about class often strategically employs personal authenticity, but rarely, I would contend, meta-poetically reflects or problematises it. The personal is then itself a category that has been mobilised in recent literature and its discourse about the working class, and particularly so since the personal, in the vein of Eribon, is understood and represented as socially co-formed. Moreover, the concept is important to the understanding of German writing after Eribon as this literature largely dispenses with a more formally sociological dimension and foregrounds individual and autobiographical narratives even more. It is necessary to engage the category of the personal and the poetical and political strategies of personal authenticity because they are characteristic of the ways many authors write about class today.

In literary representations of the working class as a diverse group, I argue, the poetics of personal authenticity, which to varying extents undergirds modes of autofictional, autobiographical and autosociobiographical writing, is particularly powerful because it serves a dual function: by its force, these texts represent the diversity of the working class as one of heterogeneous, interrelated socio-cultural groups—one (or more) of which the socially formed autodiegetic narrator/author stands in for. At the same time, it allows these texts to represent working-class diversity as a plethora of different, singular individuals. Because of this dual function, the poetics of authenticity can tie in with different strands in the discourse about diversity as authors use it to re-imagine the working class. In the following two sections, I discuss my arguments first with regard to an anthology of short autobiographical texts and then an autofictional novel, before closing with a critique of this trend in contemporary German literature.

Assembling a Plurality of Voices: The Medium of the Anthology

Published in 2021, the anthology *Klasse und Kampf* (*Class and Struggle*) gathers texts by contemporary authors about class society and the working class. The editors, Maria Barankow and Christian Baron, who has a working-class background, are well positioned to influence the literary and political debate: Barankow is an editorial director at the Ullstein publishing house and Baron, the author of the testimonial mentioned above, is a prominent journalist writing frequently about social inequality in leftist and left-liberal media such as the daily *Neues Deutschland* and the weekly *Der Freitag*. Separating the much more common compound noun *Klassenkampf* (class struggle), the anthology's title evokes labour movement politics and at the same time signals a distancing from it. Realistically, the editors contend that "the revolution is not imminent" and advocate for a social transformation "by little steps," which they consider to be most likely to lead to "a better world" (Barankow and Baron 2021, 11–12).

Barankow and Baron draw on feminist critic bell hooks and feminist-Marxist philosopher Frigga Haug, as well as sociologists Nachtwey and Andreas Reckwitz, to position their book as a collection of texts that explores "the contradiction between capital and labor" (ibid., 8) under the conditions of social and cultural pluralisation and through an intersectional perspective. Taking the plurality of German society into account, their book is meant to give voice to fourteen "different perspectives, backgrounds, and ways of storytelling" (ibid., 10). They write: "Die hier versammelten Stimmen sind so vielfältig wie unsere Gesellschaft"[3] (ibid.). Consequently, the anthology features texts by Afro-German, Black British and Turkish-German authors alongside those by white contributors, and it includes writers from the East and the West of the country: Bov Bjerg, Kübra Gümüşay, Clemens Meyer, Katja Oskamp, Sharon Dodua Otoo, Anke Stelling and Olivia Wenzel are among the contributors. Barankow and Baron's anthology testifies to a new literary discourse about class that is fundamentally marked by debates about cultural diversity.

More than simply surveying this corpus of literature, however, *Klasse und Kampf* contributes performatively to the formation of a new writing about class that revolves in multi-dimensional ways around the question of class inequality. The anthology explores class inequality's entanglement with social and cultural pluralisation in post-migrant Germany and promotes literature that contributes to this project. Since the anthology moreover functions as a genre that collects and combines diverse texts and authorial voices into a single publication to construct a polyphonic expression decentred from any individual authorship, the anthology accomplishes something that mostly escapes texts employing autofictional, autobiographical and autosociographical modes in isolation. *Klasse und Kampf* provides one possible formal answer to the question of how first-person narratives revolving around the biography of an individual can be used to enact a collective engagement with class society (Spoerhase 2017, 37) and how they may represent a diverse and polyphonic collective: such narratives can be assembled into a juxtaposition of voices that resonate with each other without becoming a single, uniform utterance.

Yet the editors express an uneasy relation to their anthology's potential role in the formation of a literary and political movement. They write: "Der von uns gewählte Titel *Klasse und Kampf* verspricht auf den ersten Blick eine Programmschrift, ein Manifest, eine Anklage. All das ist diese Anthologie nicht, und das ist sie irgendwie doch"[4] (Barankow and Baron 2021, 10). They moreover explain that neither the anthology nor any of its authors employ a logic of political or socio-cultural representation: "sie machen sich nicht zum Sprachrohr einer Gruppe, einer politischen Partei oder Strömung"[5] (ibid.; see also Frank 2021, 29). While the question of how any kind of organised political agency may result from this project remains unaddressed, it is at this point in the anthology's foreword that the poetics of personal authenticity finds an explicit, almost programmatic expression: "Wir wollen durch persönliche Perspektiven die Misstände greifbar machen und damit eine Einladung zur Empathie aussprechen"[6] (ibid.). The poetics of personal authenticity is supposed to help transform the experiential and affective foundation from which political acts may subsequently emerge. The force of personal authenticity, as a poetics that grounds stories about social origins in the working class, lies in the way that it makes social conditions more relatable to the reader because they are spoken about in personal and concrete terms by the person who has experienced them, rather than relying on a form of narration that abstracts from personal experience, a point that Otoo (2021) makes: "Bei [...] strukturellen Diskriminierungen ist es [...] so, dass Menschen viel besser in der Lage sind, einen Sachverhalt kognitiv zu erfassen, wenn er über eine persönliche Erzählung erklärt wird"[7] (123). Yet the prevalence of this poetics may simultaneously be read as the symptom of a lack of collective (literary) politics in the present.

In the anthology, authors mobilise personal authenticity and their individual life stories to counter stereotypical and generalising understandings of the working class and to produce non-hegemonic knowledge about it. Several authors position the stories of their social origin to complicate generalising terms such as 'the worker,' which do not capture their precarious and specific socio-economic and cultural experiences. For example, Francis Seeck (2021), an anti-discrimination activist, author and academic, who was the child of educated, and politically committed but poor parents, writes:

Ich bezeichne meinen Klassenhintergrund als Armutsklasse. Wir waren reich an Bildung und arm an Einkommen und gesellschaftlicher Anerkennung. Die

Gruppe der Menschen, die in materieller Armut leben, ist divers [...] Die Re-
alitäten meiner Herkunftsklasse lassen sämtliche Klischees über "die Hartz-IV-
Bezieher"[8] oder die "die Arbeiter" scheitern.[9] (68)

Contributors position themselves against those who "romanticise" the "so-called
working class" (Becker 2021, 151): "Was sollen wir romantisieren? In unserem
Viertel kursierte auch das Elend. Vor der Wende, nach der Wende. Trinker,
Kranke, Verwahrloste, Schrottsammler [...]" (Meyer 2021, 177).[10] Consequently, authors emphasise individual life stories and experiences that do not fit neatly
into prevalent stereotypes. Many contributors also describe their precarious occupations as writers and workers in the cultural field in terms of class. Their
"personal experiences" provide, as Otoo (2021) argues, a knowledge that is not
captured in statistics and does not "fit into [existing] theories" (123; 113). In
Klasse und Kampf, the poetics of personal authenticity works toward the creation
of anti-hegemonic knowledge about a diverse working class, even to the extent
that the usefulness of the term itself is put into question.

"Augenhöhe" ("Eye to Eye"), the contribution by Pinar Karabulut, exemplifies how personal authenticity functions in the anthology to represent diversity
both in terms of socio-cultural groups and individuals. Karabulut grew up as the
daughter of a Turkish immigrant, a so-called guest-worker (*Gastarbeiter*). Now
a member of the artistic direction of the theatre Münchner Kammerspiele, she
belongs, in her own words, to "the classical middle class of Germany" (Karabulut 2021, 83). On her text's fourteen pages, she relates her parents' life story—
specifically her father's—and her own as a shared, but different, story. It is the
story of two different kinds of upward mobility through labour and education,
respectively, and it is the story of an intergenerationally shared "invisibility in
the German mainstream society [*Mehrheitsgesellschaft*]" (ibid., 90). In her text,
which combines essayistic passages, autobiographical episodes and her parents'
memories, the poetics of personal authenticity and the mode of autobiographical
writing have a self-reflexively counter-hegemonic impetus: "Während es Menschen der Mehrheitsgesellschaft erlaubt ist, individuelle Biografien zu besitzen,
bleibt dies Menschen mit sogenanntem Migrationshintergrund verwehrt. Unsere Funktion scheint als Pars pro Toto für eine Gruppe zu dienen"[11] (ibid., 83).
By employing an autobiographical narrative and thereby stressing individuality,
the text's form itself challenges the boundaries of who is allowed to have a publicly visible individual story.

By complicating a mere politics of representation, as well as the idea of socio-
cultural embodiment alluded to in the phrasing *pars pro toto*, Karabulut understands and tells her father's life story in a twofold sense. Her father's life both
exemplifies what is typical for someone from his socio-cultural background and

exhibits something so particular and extraordinary that it can only be captured by comparing it to cinema: "Auf der einen Seite ist die Biografie meines Vaters eine sehr klassische und gewöhnliche Gastarbeiter-Biografie. Auf der anderen Seite muss ich oft an *Catch Me If You Can* denken—leider ohne Leonardo Di-Caprio und ohne Flugzeuge"[12] (ibid., 84). Karabulut describes the dehumanising practices Turkish guest-workers were subjected to and that culminated, during the recruitment process, in the de-individualising temporary assignation of a number for a name (ibid., 86). But she also highlights the inventiveness of her father and his various tricks to get jobs and advance, working in a bank for twenty-four years and eventually achieving an elevated standing in the local Turkish-German community. Narrating her father's story, Karabulut emphasises both what she considers typical for his migrant worker story and aspects where his individual character stands out. But Karabulut's intervention stresses individuality most, as she considers it the dimension largely neglected in many hegemonic representations of (working-class) migration and post-migrant society: "Wie soll ein einzelner Mensch [...] die komplette Migrationsgeschichte Deutschlands verkörpern können?! Die Schönheit jedes Menschen liegt in ihrer oder seiner Individualität—und somit auch in diesen individuellen Geschichten"[13] (ibid., 83–84). In "Augenhöhe," as elsewhere in *Klasse und Kampf*, the narrative and conceptual foregrounding of the individual works to further pluralise the representation of a working class seen through an intersectional lens.

Intersectional Invisibility, the Working Class and the Autofictional Novel

In her debut novel *Streulicht* (*Scattered Light*), published and shortlisted for the prestigious Deutscher Buchpreis in 2020, Deniz Ohde relies much less on the poetics of personal authenticity than the contributors of *Klasse und Kampf* or the authors of aforementioned books such as *Zeige deine Klasse* and *Ein Mann seiner Klasse*. On the one hand, this is an effect of genre as the text is peritextually designated a novel and framed as a work of fiction. On the other hand, it relates to the novel's epitexts. In interviews, Ohde has emphasised repeatedly that she does not understand her novel as autobiographical, pointing out differences between herself and the narrator (Walter 2021). Yet she also acknowledges similarities between the narrator's and her own socio-cultural and family backgrounds and their different, but resonant stories of upward mobility (Gerk 2020). The novel moreover includes signals of an autofictional dimension. The age of the author and narrator are close enough, as is their mixed-ethnic/national parental lineage (author: Turkish father, German mother; narrator: German father, Turkish mother); and while the town in the novel remains unnamed, it can be easily reconstructed as Frankfurt-Sindlingen, where Ohde grew up.

For these reasons, *Streulicht* can be understood as autofictional in the expanded sense explained above, even if there is no nominal identification of author and narrator. The author's socio-cultural position, social origin and biographical experience inform the extent to which the knowledge about class society that her novel produces is perceived as plausible by reading audiences that situate the novel within the dominant current of contemporary autofictional writing. While the novel invites such a reception, it simultaneously presents itself as a fictional work not to be easily identified with its author's biography. It is this tension that distinguishes Ohde's novel from texts by Baron or Dröscher. Yet *Retour à Reims* and *Streulicht* also share a structural similarity: an autodiegetic narrator explores her social origins through the chronotope of a return home. *Streulicht* then exists in the literary forcefield of a poetics of personal authenticity that is intertwined with the representation of a diverse working class and that makes it possible for an autofictional, or at least autobiographically influenced, novel to be understood as providing knowledge about contemporary class society that is grounded in, and authenticated through, the personal experience of the author.

Born in the late 1980s, the nameless first-person narrator grows up in a place dominated by an industrial park. In one of its factories, her German father "dipped aluminum sheets into lye [*Laugen*] for forty years, for forty hours a week" (Ohde 2020, 11). In her eyes, he has a "working-class pride" and shows "helplessness with regard to everything that goes beyond his immediate environment" (ibid.). For him, higher education is coded as foreign, something the narrator internalises (ibid., 84; 155). Driven by longing, her mother left Turkey to join her sister in Frankfurt and there started to work as a cleaner (ibid., 107–112). For the narrator, her mother, who temporarily leaves her husband without taking her daughter, remains as problematic as her father: "Nie war es ihr darum gegangen, mich zu beschützen. Nie war es ihr darum gegangen, mir diese Unabhängigkeit vorzuleben, die sie erfasst hatte, als sie mit zehn oder elf Jahren heimlich Schweinefleisch aß"[14] (ibid., 229) The parents are of little help to their daughter in understanding their family history as they rarely share their memories (ibid., 90; 109). The narrator thematises an unwillingness, or inability, of her working-class family members to tell their own history, or at least share it with their daughter, something the narrator overcomes by finding her own voice through narrating her life story (ibid., 165; 251–254). Both the retrospective form of narration and the changing position of the narrator between the classes leads to a multiplicity of perspectives in the novel. Kyung-Ho Cha (2023) has convincingly distinguished three points of view: "first, there is the perspective of the protagonist as a child and teenager who experiences social and racial discrimination, the nature of which she does not understand. Second, there is the perspective of the protagonist as narrator, who remembers and analyses her younger self" (142) and who looks at her parents like an "ethnographer" (ibid., 139). Finally, there is a third perspective that "is implied in the text and belongs to the reader" (ibid., 142). It shows the father as an "active and caring person," something that the narrator cannot recognise (ibid., 142). If only marginally, the novel thus implies a critique of the narrator's in some regards limited perspective on her working-class origins.

Overall, the novel depicts contours of a working class in Germany that is characterised by transnational connections and includes workers in standard employment and in more precarious jobs. *Streulicht* does so without romanticising this class as it tells a family history marked by unresolved trauma, intra-familial violence and an anxiety to go beyond what one is used to. The same de-romanticising impulse goes for the novel's story of upward mobility as well. Although the narrator manages to move beyond the educational background of her working-class parents and graduates from university, her financial and professional situation remains precarious throughout (Ohde 2020, 267–272; 284). She also continuously experiences shame and feelings of in-betweenness, both of which Chantal Jaquet (2018) has identified as characteristic of the figure of the transclass. Ohde's nameless narrator is one of many examples of this figure in contemporary German literature.

With respect to a social position that is constituted by the intersection of class, gender and ethnicity, *Streulicht* explores what theorists such as Kimberlé Crenshaw and Gudrun Axeli-Knapp term 'intersectional invisibility' (Axeli-Knapp 2013). On one level, the term intersectional invisibility criticises the lack of a language or communal space for addressing the various elements of the narrator's marginalised experience. Worried about German racism, her mother, for example, tells her that she is a "German" (Ohde 2020, 49) and could not be the target of racist language after the narrator was confronted with racist (and classist) slurs in school (ibid., 48). At the same time, intersectional invisibility refers to how the norms that make possible such othering remain invisible. The narrator's best friends in childhood and youth, Sophia and Pikka, embody the white middle-class norm so self-evident and naturalised that it determines any interactions, choices and feelings, constituting "an invisible wall" (ibid., 22) that separates the narrator from the mainstream society of her town (ibid., 38–42). By retrospectively telling her story, the narrator lays bare this norm, makes legible intersectional invisibility, and shows how it leads to feelings of shame.

If the novel explores the invisibility of intersectional working-class positions, it also stages itself as a counter-representation. This aspect is foregrounded, on a more individual level, when, in one episode, the narrator steals a file with her name from school, implicitly challenging the state's way of defining who she is (ibid., 177–179). The issue of how the working class is represented is broached more generally when the narrator discusses the depiction of precarious and stig-matised working-class people in a TV documentary that makes abundant use of stereotypical images and that the narrator relates to her own experience, an experience that differs from the milieu shown on TV (ibid., 135–138). Late in the novel, moreover, the narrator tells how her father buys two copies of a chroni-cle of their town. In that book, her friend Pikka's family is depicted because his grandfather worked as a manager of a local company (ibid., 209–211). Her own family is absent; they do not belong to the officially recorded history of their home. In the individual form that the poetics of personal authenticity demands of contemporary writing about class, the narrator's story can be read as an intra-diegetic counter-history of her town. At the same time, and due to its play with the autofictional mode, the author's novel functions, to some extent at least, as a possible and plausible counter-history of places like Frankfurt-Sindlingen that foregrounds the diversity of the working class.

The Politics of the Poetics of Personal Authenticity

Streulicht is invested in a poetics that aims at making visible what is not intelligi-ble in the public sphere. The novel functions as a kind of counter-representation that attempts to create awareness for social problems and maybe even tries to intervene in political debates through literary means. While Ohde appears to see her novel in this way, she consciously refrains from using a vocabulary more characteristic of political debate. As she explains, her novel is supposed to work through the affects and the empathy of her readers: "Ich habe diese Begriffe Ras-sismus oder Chancengleichheit nicht verwendet, weil das abstrakte Begriffe sind und nicht besonders literarische. Mir war wichtig, diese Begriffe erlebbar zu machen. Also was sie bedeuten in einer Biografie und wie die sich anfühlen"[15] (Romanowsky 2022). In this respect, Ohde's understanding of the political, or at least educational, use of literature meets that of the editors and contributors of *Klasse und Kampf*. To a varying extent, all of these authors seem to agree that, as Otoo (2021) puts it, "people are much better able to cognitively comprehend an issue [structural discrimination] if it is related through a personal story" (123); and this appears to be a far cry from a Brechtian aesthetics of defamiliarisation and its argument against empathy in the critical reception of art. Indeed, the rela-tive popularity of such texts as *Streulicht*, *Ein Mann seiner Klasse* or *Serpentinen* indicates that the personal is a way of narrating class society that resonates, I would argue, with people under historical conditions characterised by the in-

creasing cultural, social and political importance of subjective ways of life, authentic personal experience, cultural recognition and identity politics since the
1970s (Nachtwey 2018, 184–189). The fact that recent writing about the working
class incorporates and foregrounds such issues appears to be one condition for
the success it has had in enabling a new literary discourse about class society.

The understanding that Ohde, Barankow and Baron, Otoo and others appear
to share of how to spark through literature the creation of aware, even political,
subjects can partially account for why the poetics of personal authenticity is one
preferred means of treating class among contemporary authors.[16] Besides other
possible explanations that concern genre, the prevalence of such ideas about
literature and subject formation also illuminates the relative absence in many
examples of this kind of literature of the necessarily abstract level of sociological
analysis that was so characteristic of *Retour à Reims*. In Eribon's text, the sociological and theoretical dimensions serve as a way to complement, confirm,
correct, theorise and make more objective the subjective experience of an individual. This approach contributes to creating knowledge about class society that
is more multifaceted—both in terms of the methods of knowledge production
and the forms of representation—than what we encounter in the literary writing
that was triggered by the German translation of *Retour à Reims*.

The problem of the place of theory in such literature relates also to the question of how class is thematised in these texts. In this writing, class appears overwhelmingly as an issue of recognition and democratic participation—who is represented and in what way? Who is allowed to participate in society, culture and
politics?—and also as an issue of redistribution and socio-economic equality,
such as demands for a fairer distribution of social wealth, equal access to education, better working and less precarious living conditions, etc. Yet what is largely
absent from this literature is a thematisation of class in the context of a critique
of capitalism as "an institutionalized societal order" (Fraser 2022, 19). This would
be a systemic critique that went beyond questions of recognition and redistribution to engage with such issues as the mode of production, exploitation, the commodity form, systemic crisis or impersonal rule that have long occupied Marxist
theorists (Fraser 2003, 20). On the one hand, this may be too much to ask of
a burgeoning literature about class society in the first place.[17] On the other, it
seems relevant to point out that a form of literary writing concerned with making class society palpable and understandable through personal experience and
in the form of first-person narratives may likely have its epistemic and representational limitations with respect to those levels of capitalist society that are only
accessible through abstraction and theory (see also Spoerhase 2017, 36–37).

Yet with respect to debates about diversity in a post-migrant and increasingly
more class-aware German society, the poetics of personal authenticity serves as a

powerful foundation for literary intervention because it ties in simultaneously with two paradigms in the discourse of diversity. In a study on the history of the term, Georg Toepfer (2020) demonstrates that diversity encompasses the "paradigm of self-fulfilment [*Selbstentfaltungsparadigma*]" that foregrounds "the individual and the actualization of their authentic, in each case specific, desires and characteristics." The second paradigm the term diversity relates to is the "paradigm of justice," that is, the "recognition of social heterogeneity as an integral moment of modern societies," which entails the political demand that such heterogeneity needs to be represented in social institutions (139; 140–141). To the extent that new writing about class narrates intersectional working-class stories as simultaneously socially formed and typical *as well as* individual and personal, it articulates both paradigms. It does so through a poetics of personal authenticity that authors mobilise to legitimate their claims about class society and their demands for recognition, justice and equality for both the individuals and the socio-cultural groups that these individuals may not embody, but nevertheless belong to.

Because the collective dimension of the individual experience is also always explored in these writings, these texts point beyond an exclusive "emancipation of the individual" (Spoerhase 2017, 36) and simultaneously address "collective problems and solutions" (ibid., 37). They do so, even if they do not foreground this aspect, and may not be able to, because they revolve around the upward mobility of an autodiegetic narrator. Read individually and as an emerging corpus, these texts appear to articulate the desire of people socialised in the working class to move out of a subordinated socio-cultural position. They put centre stage their aspiration to make their own the economic, social and cultural resources and opportunities that hegemonic social groups and the existing class structure do not allow working-class subjects to possess: such as being a legitimate voice in the public sphere, something that the people of the "unheard half" (Friedrichs 2021, 17) are denied both as individuals and as parts of a social group.

Notes

1. Unless otherwise noted, all translations from German are mine.
2. A major reason for the success of Eribon's book was that its publication coincided with questions about the role of the working class and of growing social inequality in the context of the ascendancy of the Alternative für Deutschland party, Brexit and the election of Donald Trump. These questions occupied the German public in 2016, and Eribon appeared as someone who had already addressed them with respect to the French working class and the Front National.
3. "The voices collected here are as diverse as our society is."

4. "Our title *Class and Struggle* appears to promise a programme, a manifesto, an accusa-
   tion. This anthology is none of that, and somehow it is still all of it."
5. "[T]hey do not make themselves the megaphone of a group, a political party, or a current."
6. "We want to use personal perspectives to make grievances palpable and invite empathy."
7. "With respect to structural discrimination it is the case that people are much better
   able to cognitively comprehend an issue if it is related through a personal story."
8. Between 2005 and 2022, the lower of two tiers of unemployment benefits was called *Hartz
   IV*, or *Arbeitslosengeld II*; it was subsequently renamed *Bürgergeld*, or 'citizen's money.'
9. "I refer to my class background as poverty class. We were rich in education and poor
   in income and social recognition. The group of people that lives in material poverty is
   diverse [...] The reality of my class of origin proves wrong all the clichés about people
   on *Hartz IV* and 'the workers.'"
10. "What is there to romanticise? There was also misery in our neighbourhood. Before
    the fall of the wall, after the fall of the wall. Drunks, the sick [*Kranke*], the socially
    neglected [*Verwahrloste*], salvagers [...]."
11. "While people from mainstream society are allowed to have individual biographies,
    people with a so-called migration background are denied one. Our function seems to
    be to serve as a *pars pro toto* for a group."
12. "On the one hand, my father's biography is a very classical and ordinary guestworker-
    biography. On the other, it often reminds me of *Catch Me If You Can*—unfortunately
    without Leonardo DiCaprio and airplanes."
13. "How is a single human being [...] supposed to embody all of Germany's migration
    history?! The beauty of every human being lies in their individuality—and therefore
    also in their individual stories."
14. "For her, it was never about protecting me. Never about exemplifying to me the kind
    of independence that made her secretly eat pork when she was ten or eleven years old."
15. "I did not use the terms 'racism' or 'equal opportunity' [in the novel] because these
    are abstract and not particularly literary terms. It was important to me to make these
    terms palpable. And what they mean for a biography and how they feel."
16. Of course, my argument would need to be differentiated in more detail with respect to
    the specific poetics developed by each of these authors.
17. Still, it is worth pointing out that the lack of a systemic critique that goes beyond rec-
    ognition and redistribution may be a symptomatic absence in a context where debates
    about intersectionality have influenced a lot of the recent writing about class and diver-
    sity. Due to the importance of the category of identity, among other factors, intersec-
    tional approaches appear to have limitations with respect to theorising the social be-
    yond discriminations of, and inequalities between, different socio-cultural groups and
    thus remain largely uninterested in how social groups, such as classes, are positioned ac-
    cording to functional relations or through impersonal forms of social organisation that
    are necessary for production and reproduction in capitalist societies; see Soiland 2008.

References

Axeli-Knapp, Gudrun. 2013. "'Intersectional Invisibility:' Anknüpfungen und Rückfragen an ein Konzept der Intersektionalitätsforschung." In *Fokus Intersektionalität: Bewegungen und Verortungen eines vielschichtigen Konzepts*, edited by Helma Lutz, María Teresa Herrera Vivar, and Linda Supik, 243–264. 2nd ed. Wiesbaden: Springer VS.

Barankow, Maria, and Christian Baron. 2021. "Vorwort." In *Klasse und Kampf*, edited by Maria Barankow and Christian Baron, 7–12. Berlin: Claassen.

Baßler, Moritz. 2022. *Populärer Realismus: Vom Internationalen Style gegenwärtigen Erzählens*. Munich: C. H. Beck.

Becker, Martin. 2021. "Sonnenbrand." In *Klasse und Kampf*, edited by Maria Barankow and Christian Baron, 145–158. Berlin: Claassen.

Bjerg, Bov. 2020. *Serpentinen*. Berlin: Ullstein.

Butler, Martin. 2019. "Authentizität." In *Handbuch Literatur & Pop*, edited by Moritz Baßler and Eckhard Schuhmacher, 267–282. Berlin, Boston: De Gruyter.

Cha, Kyung-Ho. 2023. "The Postmigrant Critique of the Bildungsroman and the Epistemic Injustice of the Education System in Deniz Ohde's *Scattered Light*." In *Epistemic Justice and Creative Agency: Global Perspectives on Literature and Film*, edited by Sarah Colvin and Stephanie Galasso, 131–147. New York, London: Routledge.

Dröscher, Daniela. 2018. *Zeige deine Klasse: Die Geschichte meiner sozialen Herkunft*. Hamburg: Hoffmann und Campe.

Ernst, Christina. 2020. "'Arbeiterkinderliteratur' nach Eribon: Autosoziobiographie in der deutschsprachigen Gegenwartsliteratur." *Lendemains* 180: 77–91.

Frank, Arno. "Bremsklotz." In *Klasse und Kampf*, edited by Maria Barankow and Christian Baron, 13–31. Berlin: Claassen.

Fraser, Nancy. 2003. "Soziale Gerechtigkeit im Zeitalter der Identitätspolitik: Umverteilung, Anerkennung und Beteiligung." In Nancy Fraser and Axel Honneth, *Umverteilung oder Anerkennung? Eine politisch-philosophische Kontroverse*, 13–128. Frankfurt am Main: Suhrkamp.

Fraser, Nancy. 2022. *Cannibal Capitalism: How Our System Is Devouring Democracy, Care, and the Planet—and What We Can Do about It*. London, New York: Verso.

Friedrichs, Julia. 2021. *Working Class: Warum wir Arbeit brauchen, von der wir leben können*. 2nd ed. Berlin, Munich: Berlin Verlag.

Gerk, Andrea. 2020. "Industriepark als Heimat: Deniz Ohde über *Streulicht*." *Deutschlandfunk Kultur*, 16 October 2020. Accessed 14 April 2023. https://www.deutschlandfunkkultur.de/deniz-ohde-ueber-streulicht-industriepark-als-heimat-100.html.

Harvey, David. 2007. *A Brief History of Neoliberalism*. Oxford, New York: Oxford University Press.

hooks, bell. 2000. *Where we Stand: Class Matters*. New York, London: Routledge.

Jaquet, Chantal. 2018. *Zwischen den Klassen: Über die Nicht-Reproduktion sozialer Macht. Mit einem Nachwort von Carlos Spoerhase.* Translated by Horst Brühmann. Konstanz: Konstanz University Press.

Jay, Martin. 2013. "The Weimar Left: Theory and Practice." In *Weimar Thought: A Contested Legacy*, edited by Peter E. Gordon and John P. McCormick, 377–393. Princeton, Oxford: Princeton University Press.

Karabulut, Pinar. "Augenhöhe." In *Klasse und Kampf*, edited by Maria Barankow and Christian Baron, 82–95. Berlin: Claassen.

Kemper, Andreas, and Heike Weinbach. (2007) 2020. *Klassismus: Eine Einführung.* 3rd ed. Münster: UNRAST-Verlag.

Krämer, Sybille. 2012. "Zum Paradoxon von Zeugenschaft im Spannungsfeld von Personalität und Depersonalisierung: Ein Kommentar über Authentizität in fünf Thesen." In *Renaissance der Authentizität? Über die neue Sehnsucht nach dem Ursprünglichen*, edited by Michael Rössner and Heidemarie Uhl, 15–26. Bielefeld: transcript.

Kreknin, Innokentij. 2019. "Autofiktion." In *Handbuch Literatur & Pop*, edited by Moritz Baßler and Eckhard Schuhmacher, 199–213. Berlin, Boston: De Gruyter.

Mayer-Ahuja, Nicole, and Oliver Nachtwey. 2021. "Verkannte Leistungsträger:innen: Berichte aus der Klassengesellschaft." In *Verkannte Leistungsträger:innen: Berichte aus der Klassengesellschaft*, edited by Nicole Mayer-Ahuja and Oliver Nachtwey, 11–44. Berlin: Suhrkamp.

Mayr, Anna. 2020. *Die Elenden: Warum unsere Gesellschaft Arbeitslose verachtet und sie dennoch braucht.* Berlin: Hanser.

Meyer, Clemens. 2021. "Antihelden." In *Klasse und Kampf*, edited by Maria Barankow and Christian Baron, 175–185. Berlin: Claassen.

Meyer, Katrin. 2017. *Theorien der Intersektionalität zur Einführung.* Hamburg: Junius.

Nachtwey, Oliver. (2016) 2018. *Die Abstiegsgesellschaft: Über das Aufbegehren in der regressiven Moderne*, 8th ed. Berlin: Suhrkamp.

Ohde, Deniz. 2020. *Streulicht.* Berlin: Suhrkamp.

Otoo, Sharon Dodua. 2021. "Klassensprecher." In *Klasse und Kampf*, edited by Maria Barankow and Christian Baron, 109–124. Berlin: Claassen.

Romanowsky, Hanna. 2022. "Deniz Ohdes Roman *Streulicht*: Wie bestimmt Herkunft unseren Bidungsweg?" MDR Kultur, 22 July 2022. Accessed 14 April 2023. https://www.mdr.de/kultur/literatur/deniz-ohde-leipzig-interview-ich-wollte-schon-immer-schriftstellerin-sein-100.html.

Schaub, Christoph. 2020. "Autosoziobiografisches und autofiktionales Schreiben über Klasse in Didier Eribons *Retour à Reims*, Daniela Dröschers *Zeige deine Klasse* und Karin Strucks *Klassenliebe*." *Lendemains* 180: 64–76.

Scholz, Leander. 2019. "Arbeiterkinderliteratur." *Texte zur Kunst* 115: 121–133.

Schuhen, Gregor. 2020. "Erfolgsmodell Autosoziobiografie? Didier Eribons literarische Erben in Deutschland (Daniela Dröscher und Christian Baron)." *Lendemains* 180: 51–63.

Seeck, Francis. 2021. "Kohlenkeller." In *Klasse und Kampf*, edited by Maria Barankow and Christian Baron, 65–81. Berlin: Claassen.

Soiland, Tove. 2008. "Die Verhältnisse gingen und die Kategorien kamen. *Intersectionality* oder Vom Unbehagen an der amerikanischen Theorie." *querelles-net* 26. Accessed 14 April 2023. https://www.querelles-net.de/index.php/qn/article/view/694/702.

Spoerhase, Carlos. 2017. "Politik der Form: Autosoziobiografie als Gesellschaftsanalyse." *Merkur* 71, no. 7: 27–37.

Standing, Guy. 2021. *The Precariat: The New Dangerous Class. Covid-19 Edition.* London, New York, Dublin: I. B. Tauris.

Topefer, Georg. 2020. "Diversität: Historische Perspektiven auf einen Schlüsselbegriff der Gegenwart." *Zeithistorische Forschungen / Studies in Contemporary History* 17: 131–144.

Walter, Klaus. 2021. "Die Wurmfortsätze des Postfordismus: Gespräch mit Deniz Ohde über ihren Roman *Streulicht.*" *Jungle World*, 4 February 2020. Accessed 14 April 2023. https://jungle.world/artikel/2021/05/die-wurmfortsaetze-des-fordismus.

2.2
Narrating the Precariat

Social Wounds in Terézia Mora's and Wilhelm Genazino's Novels

OLAF BERWALD

Introduction

This contribution examines how the nexus of class, intersectional (economic, sexual, anti-migrant) violence, marginalisation, (self-)isolation and suicide is worked through in recent novels by Hungarian-born novelist and translator Terézia Mora (b. 1971) and Wilhelm Genazino (1943–2018). Rather than offering a large-scale theoretical commitment, this essay can be read as a dialogic nod to Malte Ibsen's *A Critical Theory of Global Justice* (2023), in which Ibsen reconceptualises the labour of theory "as an inherently *cooperative* effort [...] an open-ended and intercultural platform for the critique of the pathologies and injustices of global capitalist modernity" (Ibsen 2023, 348).

Focusing on Mora's monumental novel *Das Ungeheuer* (2013) and on several of Genazino's short novels that were published between 1977 and 2018, I conduct comparative soundings of Mora's and Genazino's narrative approaches to unflinchingly exploring the dehumanising dimensions of precarity.[1] To what extent do their fictional works respond to a calling that Max Horkheimer laconically summed up, in a notebook entry from 1969, as the "task to lend a voice to unarticulated suffering" ("Aufgabe ist es, dem Sprache verleihen, das leidet und stumm ist") (Horkheimer 1988, 544)? Both Genazino, whose professors in Frankfurt included Adorno, and Mora, whose suicidal protagonist is a voracious reader of social theorists, provide moving and nuanced literary explorations of what Oliver Nachtwey calls "downward mobility" (Nachtwey 2018, 103–161). Nachtwey even explicitly mentions Genazino as a fiction writer from whom social theorists can learn (ibid., 3). For the sake of conceptual clarity, it is of vital importance not to blur the terminological boundaries between precarity, a concept that focuses on concrete socio-economic factors, and precariousness, a rather vague term that runs the risk of being misused to depoliticise concerns about

economic equity and social justice by offering a mere existentialist view of everybody's mortality. Judith Butler (2009) defines precarity as a "politically induced
condition in which certain populations suffer from failing social and economic
networks of support and become differentially exposed to injury, violence, and
death," and she warns against confusing "precarity" with a "postulation of a gen-
eralized precariousness" (25; 33).[2] In the same vein, Marissia Fragkou (2019)
asserts that "[t]he choice of the term 'precarity' rather than 'precariousness'
[…] deliberately serves to foreground the material conditions that facilitate and
maintain the uneven distribution of vulnerability and management of precarious
life" (6). Michiel Rys and Bart Philipsen (2021) also assert that precarity "refers
more specifically to a range of experiences that are all somehow the outcome
of capitalism's neoliberal mutation" (2). Following Butler's, Fragkou's, Rys and
Philipsen's call to embrace the concept of precarity in order to investigate the
concrete realities of social and economic injustice, and their representations in
cultural texts, this chapter examines precarity as a thematic thread and narrative commitment in Genazino's and Mora's prose explorations of the irreversible
damage to which predatory capitalism and its inherent pandemic indifference to
questions of dignity and mental survival subject individual lives.

Internalised Class-Based Marginalisation in Genazino's Novels

Playful aesthetic praxis and the activation of the reader's awareness of class conflict, at times drastic, and sometimes wrapped in melancholic humour, are inextricably interwoven in Genazino's novels. All his slim volumes of prose fiction can
be read as one continuous work of self-replicating episodic freeze-frames without a sequential linear plot, exemplifying Emily Hogg's (2021) observation that
"[p]recarity disrupts the experience of time's passing" (160). In his 2004 Büchner
Prize acceptance speech titled "Der Untrost und die Untröstlichkeit der Literatur"
("The lack of consolation and the inconsolability of literature"), Genazino offers
an outline of a poetics that is informed by a dialectics of Hegelian and Marxian
provenance. Genazino asserts that the experience of reality coerces us to embrace
a way of thinking that is capable of contributing to social change. While a writer
tries to resist this coercion, their fiction "repeats" and "preserves" this conflict,
and the literary work in turn makes it impossible for the reader to ignore existing
social and economic injustice (Genazino 2004). In the same speech, Genazino
maintains that even as isolated individuals, we ought "to fight against the pathology" of the labour and housing market, as well as against "the pathology of aging"
and love. For Genazino, literature is always driven by an acute awareness of so-

cial, economic and emotional "deprivation" ("Mangel"), and he defines literature as "our palliative habitat" ("unsere palliative Heimat") in which the economy of our longing ("unsere Sehnsuchtswirtschaft") still survives (Genazino 2004).

Genazino's posthumously published notebooks, which became available in 2023, include a wide range of observations of and reflections on precarity in the author's immediate urban environment in Frankfurt. In a journal entry from 2004, Genazino notes that many people in his neighbourhood suffer from poverty and mental health challenges without having any access to healthcare (Genazino 2023, 335–336). In notebook entries from 2015 and 2017, Genazino observes that "Die Zahl der Männer, die Mülltonnen öffnen und nach Nahrungsmitteln suchen, ist inzwischen fast so groß wie die Zahl der Männer, die ihr Auto öffnen, einsteigen und dann davonfahren,"[3] and he asserts that "[i]n den Innenstädten hat es nie so viele Obdachlose gegeben, nie so viele Hungernde, die die Papierkörbe durchwühlen, weil sie hoffen müssen, ein weggeworfenes Brot oder eine halbfaule Orange zu finden"[4] (ibid., 414; 426).

The unnamed but outsider, middle-aged, male narrator-protagonists in Genazino's novels are either unemployed or experience dehumanising work environments. They often walk through urban landscapes and observe minute details of the lives of seemingly intact but deeply damaged fellow citizens. Through a socially conscious and empathetic lens that is reminiscent of Büchner's and Baudelaire's works, Genazino's narrators and protagonists, reliable in their attempts to navigate unreliable economic conditions, are diagnostic flaneurs who walk through their unnamed home cities and observe their own and other people's precarious, wounded lives. Analysing 'flaneur' narrators and protagonists in novels by Siri Huvstedt, Ian McEwan and others, Eva Ries (2022) suggests that "contemporary Anglophone flânerie texts negotiate post-sovereign performances of subjectivity" (270). Genazino's narrators inhabit a semi-sovereign status—while walking the margins of society, they purposefully undermine it by not looking away from the victims of class warfare. At once relentless, precise and compassionate, Genazino's narrating voices offer incessant episodic soundings of society's friable foundations.

The protagonist in Genazino's novel *Abschaffel* (1977), a title that evokes negative connotations of being phased out and discontinued for the sake of accumulating money, is an office employee who experiences daily alienation and despair at work where he feels that he does not belong. Quiet, despondent and jumpy, he tries not to let his despair lead him to hate his colleagues, an escalation to which some of his colleagues have already succumbed (Genazino 1977, 122). Feeling completely out of place at work, his persistent state of alienation there takes a psychological toll on him: "Es ist eine ganz tolle Verzweiflung, wenn man merkt, daß man dort, wo man ist, nicht hingehört"[5] (ibid., 112).

Witnessing the normalisation and internalisation of a gradual loss of self-esteem and dignity among employees and the unemployed alike forms a thematic thread throughout Genazino's oeuvre. For example, the narrating wandering researcher of precarity and "observer of suffering" ("Leidbeobachter") in Genazino's novel *Wenn wir Tiere wären* (*If We Were Animals*, 2011) notices a customer in a supermarket who gives a tip to a female cashier during checkout, and seeing her accepting the tip without acting surprised makes him wonder about whether cashiers' salaries are now so much below a living wage that they have to rely on donations in order to secure their basic needs (Genazino 2023, 221; Genazino 2011, 137). The narrator in Genazino's novel *Der Fleck, die Jacke, die Zimmer, der Schmerz* (*The Stain, the Jacket, the Rooms, the Pain*, 1989) witnesses the routine self-commodification of a female cashier who is sticking price tags on her lower arm while frantically operating the register. He feels the urge to take her by the hand and help her quit her job. But realising that insisting on a world where working in dignity is possible would be considered a symptom of insanity, he leaves the supermarket inconspicuously. "Draussen, auf der Strasse, durchreisst mich ein kurzer Schmerz. Dann laufe ich so umher, wie die anderen es von mir erwarten dürfen"[6] (54). This passage alludes to the famous ending of Georg Büchner's novella *Lenz* (1836), whose suicidal protagonist undergoes an irreversible mental crisis and finally resigns to simulating socially accepted basic human etiquette while feeling numb inside: "He seemed quite rational, conversed with people, but a terrible emptiness lay within him, he felt no more anxiety, no desire; he saw his existence as a necessary burden"[7] (79).

While taking a walk in his unnamed city, the protagonist in Genazino's novel *Ein Regenschirm für diesen Tag* (*An Umbrella for Today*, 2001) is approached by a woman who asks him to watch her suitcase for a while. Only when she returns holding a medical prescription in her hand does he realise that she is probably homeless and was too embarrassed to take her suitcase with her to a doctor's waiting room (ibid., 11). Another example of someone quietly hiding their economic difficulties occurs in the same novel when the narrator wonders whether his friend Margot supplements her income with occasional sex work (ibid., 91). Genazino's novels point at the systemic economic cruelty of a seemingly still intact urban society whose state of destitution is quietly increasing. The narrator in one of the episodes in Genazino's novel *Außer uns spricht niemand über uns* (*Except for Ourselves, Nobody Is Talking about Us*, 2016) all of a sudden finds himself among many slightly ragged people, arguably homeless, equipped with backpacks and synthetic mattresses, prepared to sleep outside (20).

There are moments in Genazino's short novels that encapsulate social wounds and psychological injuries with an evocative precision that is rarely matched in contemporary fiction. In stark contrast to most flaneurs in modernist and post-

modern world literatures, Genazino's narrative selves are not self-contained voyeurs who aestheticise destitution and despair. The narrative membrane between
observer and observed always remains permeable in his fiction. The following
passage from his novel *Der Fleck, die Jacke, die Zimmer, der Schmerz* (1989) is a
compelling example of self-critical awareness of poverty and of the constant risk
of becoming cruelly indifferent voyeurs of suffering. Genazino's 'flaneur' does
not fit the conventional role expectations of an indifferent voyeur who consumes
spectacles of suffering. In this regard (of the pain of others), the narrator of the
following scene catches himself in the imminent act of almost labelling another
human. He feels embarrassed for having almost succumbed to forming a fixed
image of a woman who lives in poverty and is possibly homeless:

> Über den Rudolfsplatz geht eine ältere, verwitterte, fast schon herunterge-
> kommene Frau; sie zieht ein vollbeladenes, quetschendes, fahrbares Gestell hinter
> sich her, auf dem (in Beuteln, Paketen und Kartons verpackt) alles verstaut ist,
> was sie zum Leben noch braucht. Eine Minute lang will ich herausfinden, ob die
> Frau noch MITGLIED der Gesellschaft ist oder nicht mehr, welche Zeichen an
> ihr dafür sprechen und welche dagegen, ob sie als JENSEITIGE, als SCHWANK-
> ENDE oder ENDGÜLTIG ABGEGLITTENE zu betrachten ist. [...] [D]ann be-
> merke ich, dass ich mich denkend an der Frau vergangen habe. Ich schäme mich
> ein wenig und versuche, die Frau anerkennend anzuschauen. Aber die Frau lehnt
> meine Blicke ab. Sie geht davon aus, dass sie von niemandem etwas zu erwarten
> hat. Anerkennung schon gar nicht.[8] (Genazino 1989, 97)

The narrator in *Die Obdachlosigkeit der Fische* (*The Homelessness of Fish*, 1994)
observes a homeless woman who appears to be an alcoholic who is standing in
front of a house. A dog is approaching her and the woman starts to talk with the
dog who is looking back at her, "the only living thing that still tolerates being close
to her." The woman appears to be so grateful for being "seen" by the animal that
she tries to stroke it. But she slips and falls to the ground (Genazino 2006, 40).

In the same novel, the narrator, who works as an elementary school teacher,
is haunted by a pedagogically disastrous moment that exemplifies the extent to
which the education system's bureaucratised rigidity violates the psychological
freedom of children:

> Einmal [...] hat das verhaltensgestörte Kind zu mir gesagt: Ich weiss jetzt, daß
> zwei und zwei vier sind, ich will zu meiner Mama. Und als ich antwortete: Das
> geht nicht, du musst warten, bis es läutet, habe ich genau bemerkt, wie das Kind
> von dieser Antwort vergewaltigt wurde. Im Oktober wird die Vergewaltigung
> forgesetzt.[9] (ibid., 31)

The narrator's experience of having grown up very poor as a child in post-war Germany still shapes his resistance to throwing away expired food in *Außer uns spricht niemand über uns* (2016, 20).

When the narrator/protagonist in that novel, an unemployed actor, is offered a role in a local theatre, it turns out that it would be an unpaid engagement, and he turns the offer down (ibid., 99). The narrator in *Kein Geld, keine Uhr, keine Mütze* (2018) asks himself why he never learned any profession and was instead surviving through an unpredictable series of temp jobs while being in constantly dire financial straits (Genazino 2018, 69). He observes that the number of men who open garbage bins searching for food is almost as high as the number of men who are employed to empty them (ibid., 14).

Genazino's novels perform a precise modality of precarity research. In his oeuvre, not even full-time employees lead undamaged lives. The narrating observer of his city's daily life in *Die Obdachlosigkeit der Fische* (1994) observes a leaden psychic numbness among commuters on their bus home from work: "Jetzt fahren sie wieder nach Hause, die armen kleinen Tiere, zu den Schlachtbänken der Einbildung, der Vergeblichkeit und der Hoffnung"[10] (Genazino 2006, 9). Noticing that the inside of the bus is dimly lit, the narrator muses that the burnt-out, tired bus riders whom he perceives as tranquilised animals probably even prefer not to be able to see themselves very well (ibid.).

While at the end of *Das Glück in glücksfernen Zeiten* (2009), Genazino's narrator experiences a brief moment of euphoric happiness, hoping that he will still be able to shape his own future, the thrust of his novels presents a grim outlook on the chances for sustained social change (158). Instead of feeling empowered to move toward a more bearable and breathable level of aliveness, the narrator in *Kein Geld, keine Uhr, keine Mütze* (2018) suffers from extreme indecisiveness that has turned into severe anxiety, of which he believes he could die without anyone noticing (68). Wondering whether he has become inadvertently "frozen inside his stories," the narrator offers a disillusioned self-diagnosis in performative self-imprisonment prose, "a torpor becomes irreversible the moment in which the ossified person gladly tries to fit in with their state of torpor" (ibid.).[11] With an acerbic self-consoling mantra that explicitly alludes to Genazino's university teacher Adorno's volume, *Minima Moralia: Nachrichten aus dem beschädigten Leben* (*Reflections from Damaged Life*, 1951), the narrator in *Mittelmäßiges Heimweh* (2007) concludes, "I am damaged, I have time [*Ich bin beschädigt, ich habe Zeit*]" (189). In his posthumously published poetics lectures, *Die Angst vor der Penetranz des Wirklichen* (*The Fear of Reality's Obtrusiveness*, 2020), Genazino posits that we have all lowered our expectations of society to the most fundamental physical and psychological necessities, uncertain of whether we can even secure these aspirations anymore:

Die Menschen gehen dorthin, wo sie Arbeit, Liebe, Toleranz und dann auch noch eine Wohnung finden, mit anderen Worten: wo sie hoffen dürfen, dass sie von der meist enttäuschenden Wirklichkeit nicht mehr allzu stark vergewaltigt werden können.[12] (33)

Mora's Exploration of Suicide and the Normalisation of Exploitation

In her Frankfurt poetics lectures published as *Nicht sterben* (2014), Terézia Mora explicitly declares her solidarity with Genazino's aesthetic and political goal of "finding verbal images that can shed light" on economic and social issues that are usually rendered scarcely visible, society's "blind spots,"[13] as Mora quotes Genazino (Mora 2014, 146–147). Mora's novel *Das Ungeheuer* (*The Monster*, 2013; French translation 2015, *De rage et de douleur le monstre*, received the German Book Award)—whose pages are literally divided in half, in the tradition of narrative split-screens practiced by Genet, Derrida's *Glas* (1974, one column partially in the voice of Christiane Hegel, the philosopher's sister, who took her own life in 1832), and J. M. Coetzee's *Diary of a Bad Year* (2008)—offers one narrative stream on the upper half of each page, narrating a journey undertaken by Flora's widower Darius, while presenting the reader either with empty space or with the journal entries of Flora, the female protagonist, that Darius found on her laptop after her suicide. While the novel forms a part of a trilogy whose other two volumes focus more on Darius, for the sake of this essay, Flora is by far the more intriguing protagonist because she embodies the lethal irreversibility of precarity (see Mora 2009 and 2019). Like Mora, Flora is Hungarian and im-migrated to Germany. Also like the author, being a translator was one of Flora's career goals. The novel's title evokes associations with Goya's etching *El sueño de la razón produce monstruos* (*The Dream of Reason produces Monsters*, 1799). Delmira Agustini's poem "Visión" (1913) defines sadness as "a monster" ("un monstruo de tristeza") that devours us from within (108–109), and the lyrical "I" in Manfred Peter Hein's poem "Jahr um Jahr" (2006) perceives themselves as their own monster (45; "Ungeheuer meiner selbst"). In her recently published non-fictional volume, *Fleckenverlauf: Ein Tage- und Arbeitsbuch* (*Stain Progression: A Journal and Workbook*, 2021), Mora reminds the reader that Mary Shelley described herself as a "monster" because she felt as if she had been "composed and manipulated by others, just like her sad protagonist [*von anderen zusam-mengesetzt und manipuliert worden sei wie ihr trauriger Held*]" (Mora 2012, 209). Mora draws a clear parallel between Mary Shelley's self-labelling and the state of mind and struggle of Flora in *Das Ungeheuer*.

In her poetics lectures that were published as *Der geheime Text* (*The Secret Text*, 2016), Mora asserts that "Das, was Flora widerfährt, ihre allmähliche Vernichtung durch ihr eigenes Inneres ist etwas, über das man nicht 'flüssig' erzählen kann"[14] (Mora 2016, 102). This realisation must have contributed to Mora's creation of narrative split-screens throughout the novel. The top half of each page presents a road-movie-style journey. Flora's widower Darius is taking her ashes to Italy, driving all the way in a car, accompanied by a young woman. In an intertextual nod to Hölderlin's and Brecht's *Empedocles* texts, which present divergent versions of the Ancient Greek philosopher's suicide, Mora has Darius finally arriving at the Aetna volcano with Flora's ashes, where he presumably spreads them.[15]

Darius' mourning reflections on Flora's long suffering offer an important contextual perspective on "food-insecure" life among Berlin's academic precariat in the early twenty-first century: "Also 20 Jobs, 20 körperlich schwere, geistig unter- und emotionell überfordernde Dienste, eine Fußsoldatin in der Armee der sogenannten Hilfskräfte"[16] (Mora 2013, 48). In her essay on "pathologized femininity and capitalist economy" in Mora's novel, Karin Terborg (2022, 174) highlights the suffocating force of precarity and exploitation in Flora's life. Darius remembers that long before her suicide, Flora had moved out and isolated herself from him and the rest of the world:

> Zuerst ist sie nur aufs Land gezogen, wir hatten gerade unsere Jobs verloren, beide gleichzeitig, und das nicht zum ersten Mal, so was kommt vor, aber sie hat sich einfach verweigert, sie hat sich geweigert, die Stadt jemals wieder zu betreten, sie hat sich geweigert, unsere Wohnung zu betreten, sie hat den ganzen stürmischen Herbst und den ganzen harten Winter in einer Hütte am Waldrand überstanden [...] Sie hat sich erhängt, an einem Baum, abseits des Wegs, anderthalb Tage, bis sie jemand fand, barfuß.[17] (Mora 2013, 39)

Darius hires a Hungarian translator to translate Flora's electronic diary. As Anne Fleig and Caroline Frank assert in recent articles, Darius becomes a compassionate reader of Flora's journal, which helps him with his mourning process (Fleig 2019, 68; Frank 2022, 155). However, Darius's reflections do not reveal any adequate understanding of the depths of Flora's long-term mental and physical suffering at the hands of a cruel social environment.

A foreign student without a work permit, Flora works occasional precarious temp jobs (her first one is ironically a brief stint as an interpreter at a conference on communism) and is exploited in unpaid internships, where she is constantly harassed, humiliated and subjected to physical and psychological sexual and xenophobic violence. In a recent article, Meyer-Gosau summarises Flora's life of day-to-day abuse as "an unbearable humiliation [*eine nicht zu ertragende Kränkung*] from beginning to end" (Meyer-Gosau 2019, 43).

Flora does not make a living wage. In her e-journal, she lists how much money she earns each month. For many months, that number is zero. As an unpaid intern, Flora cannot afford anything beyond rent and food. She cannot even afford public transportation and clings to the hope that neither her bicycle nor her shoes will be in need of repair or replacement in the near future (Mora 2013, 133). When she catches pneumonia and has to spend several days in a hospital, Flora is relieved because at least during her hospital stay she receives free food (ibid., 167). Flora undergoes repeated stays in a psychiatry ward: "3 Tage in der dummen Klinik. Weil ich mir nicht helfen konnte und in Pantoffeln und Top schluchzend draussen in der Kälte herumlief"[18] (ibid., 382). Outlining her sense of loneliness, Flora identifies with her illness: "Niemand ist da. Die Krankheit und du. Du und du"[19] (ibid., 664). Flora is diagnosed with bipolar disorder (ibid., 610–611). This leads her to consider the degree of "hatred" that "those" in society "who have not received any diagnosis" harbour "against those who have been diagnosed"[20] (ibid., 614).

At times in her journal, Flora expresses her fierce wish to live her daily life in dignity, or at least to "reduce the level of being humiliated [*Das Gedemütigt-sein minimieren*]" (ibid., 104). Engaging in a moment of brutal self-loathing, Flora, whose career goal is to work as a translator, tells herself,

> Hör auf zu sagen, du wärst Übersetzerin. Einen Dreck bist du. Die korrekte Antwort lautet: ich jobbe als Kellnerin und Verkäuferin, ansonsten bin ich Hausfrau. Und offensichtlich ist mir das nicht fein genug. Snobistische Schlampe.[21] (ibid., 592)

Flora's first sexual experience results in the cold-blooded lover's (a teacher) demand to "have it removed" (ibid., 105–106). One employer uses Flora's lack of a work permit as leverage against her (ibid., 309–310). She is routinely bullied at work and during lunch (ibid., 295–297). Refusing the sexual advances of one of her bosses, Flora notices "the hatred in his eyes" (ibid., 141). When Flora enters a used bookstore for a job interview, she leaves immediately upon witnessing that the owner is verbally abusing an employee (ibid., 306). A group of men assault Flora on a sidewalk, "Der eine fasst mir zwischen die Beine. [...] Ich werde nicht weinen, nicht fluchen, nicht um Hilfe bitten, wie auch, ich spreche nicht einmal die Sprache anständig"[22] (ibid., 151). Another time, a man on a bicycle pursues her on sidewalk, and firemen pour beer on her (ibid., 187). While Flora is walking on a sidewalk, a man mistakes her for a prostitute and injures her leg, and an ambulance arrives (ibid., 361–362).

When she is beaten up on a sidewalk again, Flora believes that her lack of parental care is noticeable and contributes to her being the target of so many assaults: "Niemandes Kind. Der Mann, der mich auf der Strasse verprügelt hat, konnte es tun, weil er gesehen hat, dass ich ein Niemandskind bin"[23] (ibid., 367). Flora's reflections on the constant bullying and physical attacks perform vertiginous vicious circles: "Die Frage ist nicht, wie konnte das passieren. Die Frage ist, wieso passiert es nicht jeden Tag. *Tut es doch*"[24] (ibid., 362). "[S]ich vertilgen auf Raten Wenigstens benutze ich keine Männer mehr dafür."[25] Flora feels fragmented and thrown away "like a shard [*wie eine Scherbe*]" (ibid., 382). On a regular basis, Flora suffers from nightmares of being physically attacked, raped, tortured and killed (ibid., 271–273; 363–365).

Flora becomes an astute diagnostician of society's systemic ills and their devastating self-silencing impact on individual lives:

> Die Stufen des Schmerzes. Schmerz, den man aushalten kann, ohne einen Ton zu sagen. Schmerz, den man sprechend aushalten kann. Schmerz, den man weinend aushalten kann. Schmerz, den man brüllend aushalten kann. Schmerz, den man winselnd aushalten kann. Und schließlich erneut: Schmerz, den man nur tonlos aushalten kann. [...] Überhaupt, die Leute, die nicht mehr reden können. Die Skala der Verstummung.[26] (ibid., 192, 396)

In disagreement with her psychiatrist, Flora posits that "sein Leid nicht mitteilen, also keine Hilfe erfahren zu können, kann einen umbringen"[27] (ibid., 251). However, in palinodic fear of verbalising her inner thoughts and emotions, Flora admonishes herself: "Rühr dich nicht. Schweig still. Nicht nur außen. Drinnen. Kein Wort. Wenn du es aussprichst, bringt es dich um"[28] (ibid., 675). In the same vein, after having read the medieval German mystic Meister Eckhart, Flora writes in her journal, "Ich traue mich nicht, die Dinge im Grund meiner Seele zu benennen. Wenn ich ihren Namen ausspreche, töten sie mich"[29] (ibid., 380).

At times, Flora uses her e-journal to comfort and encourage herself and to give herself survival technique advice: "Draußen sein zu müssen ist schrecklich. Aber es nicht mehr zu können ist es ebenfalls. Sei draußen, solange du es kannst, und dann sei wieder drinnen, solange du das kannst"[30] (ibid., 582). Flora concedes that one of the major effects of all her traumatising experiences has been being filled with hatred: "Das Problem ist, dass ich keine Angst empfinde, keine Verzweiflung oder Traurigkeit. Kein Beleidigtsein. [...] Sondern: Hass"[31] (ibid., 369–370).

Echoing Arno Gruen's critique of what constitutes "normal," Joyce McDougall's term "normopathy" and Christopher Bollas' concept of "normotic personality," the obsessive pursuit to conform, Flora articulates, and refuses to disappear into, the *mise-en-abime* of "becoming ill from trying to be normal [*Krank werden am Versuch, normal zu sein*]" (ibid., 176; see Bollas 1989, 137–156). Flora is mocking society's systemic psychological violence through relentless demands to conform: "Als wäre ich tauglich. Ein nützliches Glied der Gesellschaft. Als würde dazu gehören, dass man sich konform verhält. Dem anderen nicht durch deine Natur zur Last fallen. Wahre Höflichkeit"[32] (Mora 2013, 441). In another journal entry, Flora lists her marketable skill set with disarming precision and a bit of sarcasm: "Meine Fähigkeiten [...] Meine positiven Eigenschaften sind: Einfühlungsvermögen Fleiss Verlässlichkeit Pünktlichkeit Ehrlichkeit Meine 'negativen' Eigenschaften sind: / Ich habe es gerne, wenn man mich respektvoll behandet, allerdings erwarte ich das nur von Gesunden"[33] (ibid., 600–601).

In rare moments of reprieve from relentless dehumanisation, Flora enjoys brief glimpses into the possibility of trust and inner warmth. For example, in a gynaecologist's waiting room, she has a sympathetic conversation about the lack of empathy in society with an older patient who also suffers from anxiety and anger (ibid., 595–597). The few temporary jobs that Flora enjoys are short lived, including three weeks as a salesperson at a coffee-shop, from which she is let go because the owner does not have the financial resources to continue to employ her, and a six-month job at a bakery that Flora describes as the happiest time of her life, until it is made unbearable by a xenophobic customer (ibid., 307).

In her diary, Flora also notes a momentary experience of happiness when catching a glimpse of indestructible strength and beauty in nature:

> Für einen Moment war es gelungen; ich ging auf der Strasse, die übliche Hölle, sah mich verzweifelt um, was könnte helfen, und erblickte den knorrigen, kahlen Baum im Kirchgarten, und wie ich in seine Krone hineinsah, in diese vollkommene, wunderschöne Schwärze, spürte ich, wie das Glück in meinem Körper anwuchs, ich spürte, jetzt bin ich glücklich. Ich sah sie mir an, die kahle Baumkrone, der Stamm war zerfetzt, überall beschnitten, ein hässlich malträtierter Stamm, aber die Krone, die Krone im Winterregen war perfekt. Sie machte mich glücklich für etwa 5 Sekunden. Danach wirkte es nicht mehr. Ich ging weiter in der Hölle.[34] (ibid., 625)

During another walk in a cemetery, Flora is elated to hear a part-time assistant gardener with a health condition telling her patronising supervisor, "Just leave me alone [...] Can't you see that I'm already sweeping the leaves as well as I can? [...] I saw and heard it and I was happy. I'm sweeping as well as I can. Thank you"[35] (ibid., 429). But her rare glimpses into a bearable life are not enough for Flora to overcome the cruelty of her daily experiences, and her class-conscious self-diagnosis is an unanswered cry for help: "Ich schäme mich dafür, ein Mensch zu sein"[36] (ibid., 273). While most recently, social theorists Christoph Menke, in his *Theorie der Befreiung* (2022, 465), and Fréderic Gros in his volume *La Honte est un Sentiment Révolutionnaire* (2021, 169–170), elaborate on their Marxian hope for a revolutionary potential of "shame," for Genazino's Flora, the onslaught of economic, physical and emotional humiliation remains insurmountable.

Can we overcome interpersonal and systemic numbness and violence under predatory economic conditions? An avid reader of Erich Fromm and Arno Gruen, Flora considers the possibility of "repairing" societies and individuals (Mora 2013, 407). She asks herself whether a non-violent society is possible: "Was für eine Arbeit wäre das, bis man jeden Einzelnen soweit hätte, dass er sich nicht nur dann lebendig fühlt, wenn er etwas zerstört"[37] (ibid., 368). Mora's and Genazino's literary projects invite the reader to social explorations beyond perpetuating split-screens of "the aesthetic" versus "the political."[38] Their vulnerable narrating voices are discomforting and indispensable.

Far from merely thematising structural social injustice, Mora's and Genazino's unsparing novels co-advance the shared labour of reading social wounds by fostering the reader's perceptiveness and productive fury about what the narrator in Genazino's novel *Die Kassiererinnen* (1998) exposes as an unbearable socially imposed discrepancy between "Wie großartig wir denken können und wie armselig wir leben müssen"[39] (Genazino 1998, 12). Mora's 2013 novel and Genazino's fiction from the 1970s to the 2010s conduct narrative examinations of the "monstrosity" of a society that imposes precarity on a growing segment of its population. While their narrative techniques are slightly divergent, Mora's and Genazino's works can be fruitfully read together. One can even imagine a "monstrous" reading of Genazino's fiction as possible parts of passages composed by Mora's e-diary writer Flora. Genazino's and Mora's works that have been briefly discussed here heed Max Horkheimer's warning that theory is a form of aggression ("Theorie ist Aggression") (Horkheimer 1988, 224). "Theorists" of social and economic change solely through the craft of fiction writing and in full awareness of every fixed terminology's tendency toward self-commodification, Mora and Genazino refrain from offering simplistic escape routes. Their protagonists and the people observed by them do not exemplify generic universal crises of the human condition. Instead, they witness and experience the concrete continuous threat that social and economic precarity poses to the mind and body. Mora's and Genazino's works present and perform a partial (and in Flora's case, an irreversible) disintegration of human resilience. In doing so, they cultivate new kinds of readers who are unwilling to accept that precarity, and mediated collective numbness towards it, have the final word.

Notes

1. All translations of quoted passages from Mora's and Genazino's works in this essay are mine.

2. See also Isabell Lorey's affirmative reception of Butler's emphasis on the need to distinguish between precariousness and precarity (2015, 17–22).

3. "[T]he number of men who open trashcans to search for food equals the number of men who open and get into their car and drive away."

4. "[T]he number of the homeless in inner cities has never been this high, there have never been so many starving people who go through the trash, hoping to find bread that someone has thrown away, or a half-rotten orange."

5. "It is a completely insane kind of despair to realise that you do not belong where you are."

6. "Outside, on the street, I am briefly being torn apart by pain. Then I continue to walk around just like the others can justly expect me to."

7. The German original reads: "Er tat alles, wie es die andern taten. Es war aber eine entsetzliche Leere in ihm."

8. "An older, weather-beaten woman is crossing Rudolf Square. She is pulling a fully packed, overly stuffed cart behind her on which (packed in bags, bundles, and cardboard boxes) all her bare necessities are stowed. For a moment I want to find out whether the woman is still a MEMBER of society or not anymore, what about her indicates for or against counting her as being OUTSIDE of society, TEETERING or IRREVOCABLY SLIPPED. [...] [T]hen I realise that my thoughts about her constituted a form of violation. A bit embarrassed, I try to look at the woman appreciatively. But the woman refuses my attempt to make eye contact. She assumes that she cannot expect anything from anyone. Least of all recognition."

9. "Once the child with a behavioural condition told me, 'Now I know that two plus two makes four, I want to go to my mom.' And when I responded, 'That is not possible, you have to wait until the bell rings,' I clearly noticed the child being violated by this kind of answer. The violation will proceed in October."

10. "Now they are on their way home, these poor miserable animals, to the slaughterhouse blocks of the imagination, futility and hope."

11. The German original reads: "Denn eine Erstarrung war erst dann eine Erstarrung, wenn der Erstarrte sich freudig in seine Erstarrung fügte."

12. "Humans move to where they can find work and love, where they are tolerated and can even find an apartment to stay, in other words where they can hope that reality, while mostly bringing disappointments, will not continue to violate them too extremely anymore."

13. Literally, "Die Sprachbilder finden, die das bis dahin Diffuse erhellen können ('Die toten Winkel ausleuchten,' wie Genazino es nannte.)" On the social implications and libidinal economies of the text/image dialectic, see for example Rancière 2009 and 2019.

14. "What Flora is subjected to, her gradual obliteration by her own inner self, is something that cannot be narrated 'fluently.'"
15. The novel's final sentence reads: "Von Catania nach Gravina, von Gravina nach Rifugio Sapienza, von dort aus zu Fuss" (Mora 2013, 681).
16. "20 jobs, 20 physically demanding kinds of service for which she was intellectually overqualified but emotionally unprepared, a foot soldier in the army of so-called temps."
17. "At first she just moved to the countryside, we both had just lost our jobs, both at the same time, not for the first time, it happens, but she simply closed herself off of anybody, she refused to ever return to the city, she refused to set foot in our apartment, she endured the whole stormy fall and the whole hard winter in a cabin at the edge of the forest [...] She hanged herself at a tree, off the path, it took one and a half days until someone found her, barefoot."
18. "3 days in the stupid hospital. Because I was helplessly running outside in the cold in slippers and a top, sobbing."
19. "Nobody is there. The sickness and you. You and you."
20. "Der Hass derer, die keine Diagnose haben, auf die, die eine haben."
21. "[S]top pretending that you are a translator. You are a piece of crap. The correct answer is, I work temp jobs as a waitress and salesperson, otherwise I am a homemaker. And that is obviously not good enough for me. Snobbish slut."
22. "One of them grabs me between my legs. [...] I'm not going to cry or curse of ask for help, how could I, I don't even speak the language properly."
23. "Nobody's child. The man who beat me up on the street was able to do it because he saw that I'm nobody's child."
24. "The question is not how this could happen. The question is why does it not happen every day. *But it does.*"
25. "Obliterating oneself incrementally. At least I don't use men for that anymore."
26. "The levels of pain. Pain that is endurable without making any sound. Pain that you can endure talking. Pain that you can endure crying. Pain that you can endure screaming. Pain that you can endure whimpering. And finally: Pain that you can only endure soundlessly. [...] The people who are not capable of expressing themselves anymore. The degrees of falling silent."
27. "[N]ot being able to communicate one's own suffering can get you killed."
28. "Do not move. Stay quiet. Not only towards the outside world. Inside. Not a word. If you spell it out it will kill you."
29. "I don't dare to spell out the things that I carry deep in my soul. They will kill me when I speak their name."
30. "Leaving one's place is frightful. But so is not being able to do it anymore. Leave your place for as long as you can bear, and then be inside again for as long as you can stand it."
31. "The problem is that I don't feel any fear, despair, or sadness. Not feeling offended. [...] But: full of hate."

32. "As if I were serviceable. A useful member of society. As if acting in conformity were part of it. Not inconveniencing others by being yourself. True politeness."

33. "My positive qualities are: Empathy diligence reliability punctuality honesty My 'negative' qualities are: I like to be treated respectfully, but I only expect that from sane people."

34. "For a moment it worked; I was walking on the street, the usual hell, I look around me in despair, what could help me, and I saw the gnarly leafless tree in the churchyard, and as I looked into its crown, into this perfect, beautiful blackness, I felt happiness grow inside my body, I felt, 'I am happy now.' I took a good look at the leafless treetop, the trunk was torn apart, cut back everywhere, an ugly maltreated trunk, but the crown, the crown in the winter rain was perfect. It made me happy for approximately 5 seconds. After that it did not help anymore. I continued to walk in hell."

35. The German original reads: "Es ist mir gelungen, zum Friedhof zu gehen, um dort zu spazieren – phantastisch. Lass mich bloss in Ruhe, sagte die behinderte Friedhofspflege-Aushilfe zu ihrer sie bevormundenden Kollegin. Ich fege doch schon so gut ich kann! Und fegte und fegte trockene Blätter von der Allee zur Kapelle. Ich sah und hörte das und war glücklich. Ich fege doch schon so gut ich kann! Danke."

36. "I am ashamed of being a human."

37. "What kind of labour would it require to bring each individual to the point of not only feeling truly alive when they destroy something."

38. See my previous contribution to this question: "Do we have a nuanced vocabulary that enables us to discuss the role of contemporary literature in advocating for social justice without reducing the mutual suspicions of the aesthetic and the political to a rigid dichotomy?" (Berwald 2015, 275).

39. "[O]ur magnificent cognitive capabilities and the miserable ways to which we are constrained to live."

References

Adorno, Theodor W. (1951) 2020. *Minima Moralia: Reflections from Damaged Life*. Translated by Edmund F. N. Jephcott. London, New York: Verso.

Agustini, Derlmira. 2003. *Selected Poetry of Delmira Agustini: Poetics of Eros*. Edited by Alejandro Cáceres. Carbondale: Southern Illinois University Press.

Bartl, Andrea, and Friedhelm Marx. 2011. *Verstehensanfänge: Das literarische Werk Wilhelm Genazinos*. Göttingen: Wallstein.

Berwald, Olaf. 2015. "The Ethics of Listening in Dana Ranga's *Wasserbuch* and Terezia Mora's *Das Ungeheuer*." In *Envisioning Social Justice in Contemporary German Culture*, edited by Jill Twark and Axel Hildebrandt, 275–289. Rochester: Camden House.

Bollas, Christopher. 1989. *The Shadow of the Object: Psychoanalysis and the Unthought Known*. New York: Columbia University Press.

Büchner, Georg. 2004. *Lenz*. Translated by Richard Sieburth. Brooklyn: archipelago.

Butler, Judith. 2009. *Frames of War: When Is Life Grievable?* London, New York: Verso.

Coetzee, J. M. 2008. *Diary of a Bad Year*. New York: Viking Penguin.

Derrida, Jacques. 1974. *Glas*. Paris: Éditions Galilée.

Fansa, Jonas. 2007. *Unterwegs im Monolog: Poetologische Konzeptionen in der Prosa Wilhelm Genazinos*. Würzburg: Königshausen & Neumann.

Fleig, Anne. 2019. "Tragödie und Farce: Formen der Mehrstimmigkeit in Terezia Moras Romanen." *Text+Kritik* 221 (January): 55–69.

Fragkou, Marissia. 2019. *Ecologies of Precarity in Twenty-First Century Theatre: Politics, Affect, Responsibility*. London, New York: Methuen Drama.

Frank, Caroline. 2022. "Unter- Nach- und Gegeneinander von Stimmen und Perspektiven in Terézia Moras *Das Ungeheuer*—Roman und Hörbuch." In *Terézia Mora: Kasseler Grimm-Poetikprofessorin 2021*, edited by Stefanie Kreuzer, 151–168. Würzburg: Königshausen & Neumann.

Genazino, Wilhelm. 1977. *Abschaffel*. Reinbek b. Hamburg: Rowohlt.

Genazino, Wilhelm. 1989. *Der Fleck, die Jacke, die Zimmer, der Schmerz*. Reinbek b. Hamburg: Rowohlt.

Genazino, Wilhelm. 1998. *Die Kassiererinnen*. Reinbek b. Hamburg: Rowohlt.

Genazino, Wilhelm. 2001. *Ein Regenschirm für diesen Tag*. Munich, Vienna: Hanser.

Genazino, Wilhelm. 2004. "Der Untrost und die Untröstlichkeit der Literatur: Büchnerpreisrede 2004." Deutsche Akademie für Sprache und Dichtung. Accessed 14 April 2023. https://www.deutscheakademie.de/de/auszeichnungen/georg-buechner-preis/wilhelm-genazino/dankrede.

Genazino, Wilhelm. 2006. *Die Obdachlosigkeit der Fische*. Munich: Hanser; 1st ed. 1994. Reinbek b. Hamburg: Rowohlt.

Genazino, Wilhelm. 2007. *Mittelmäßiges Heimweh*. Munich: Hanser.

Genazino, Wilhelm. 2009. *Das Glück in glücksfernen Zeiten*. Munich: Hanser.

Genazino, Wilhelm. 2011. *Wenn wir Tiere wären*. Munich: Hanser.

Genazino, Wilhelm. 2016. *Außer uns spricht niemand über uns*. Munich: Hanser.

Genazino, Wilhelm. 2018. *Kein Geld, keine Uhr, keine Mütze*. Munich, Vienna: Hanser.

Genazino, Wilhelm. 2020. *Die Angst vor der Penetranz des Wirklichen*. Heidelberg: Winter.

Genazino, Wilhelm. 2023. *Der Traum des Beobachters: Aufzeichnungen 1972–2018*. Edited by Jan Bürger and Friedhelm Marx. Munich: Hanser.

Gros, Fréderic. 2021. *La Honte est un Sentiment Révolutionnaire*. Paris: Albin Michel.

Gruen, Arno. 2000. *Der Fremde in uns*. Stuttgart: Klett-Cotta.

Hammer, Erika. 2020. *Monströse Ordnungen und die Poetik der Liminalität: Terezia Moras Romantrilogie "Der einzige Mann auf dem Kontinent," "Das Ungeheuer" und "Auf dem Seil."* Bielefeld: transcript.

Hein, Manfred Peter. 2008. *Nachtkreis: Gedichte 2005–2007*. Göttingen: Wallstein.

Hogg, Emily J. 2021. "The Future is a Ghost: Precarity, Anticipation and Retrospection in Anneliese Mackintosh's 'Limited Dreamers' and Lee Rourke's *Vulgar Things*." In *Precarity in Contemporary Literature and Culture*, edited by Emily J. Hogg and Peter Simonsen, 160–175. London, New York: Bloomsbury Academic.

Horkheimer, Max. 1988. *Gesammelte Schriften 14: Nachgelassene Schriften 1949–1972*. Frankfurt am Main: Fischer.

Ibsen, Malte F. 2023. *A Critical Theory of Global Justice: The Frankfurt School and World Society*. Oxford: Oxford University Press.

Lehnert, Nils. 2018. *Wilhelm Genazinos Romanfiguren: Erzähltheoretische und (literatur-) psychologische Zugriffe auf Handlungsmotivation und Eindruckssteuerung*. Berlin, Boston: De Gruyter.

Lorey, Isabell. 2015. *State of Insecurity: Government of the Precarious*. Translated by Aileen Derieg. London, New York: Verso.

McDougall, Joyce. (1993) 2015. *Plea for a Measure of Abnormality*. New York, London: Routledge.

Menke, Christoph. 2022. *Theorie der Befreiung*. Berlin: Suhrkamp.

Meyer-Gosau, Frauke. 2019. "Bis ins Innerste vorstoßen: Beim Lesen von Terezia Moras Roman *Das Ungeheuer*." *Text+Kritik* 221 (January): 43–54.

Mora, Terézia. 2009. *Der einzige Mann auf dem Kontinent*. Munich: Luchterhand.

Mora, Terézia. 2013. *Das Ungeheuer*. Munich: Luchterhand.

Mora, Terézia. 2014. *Nicht sterben: Frankfurter Poetik-Vorlesungen*. Munich: Luchterhand.

Mora, Terézia. 2016. *Der geheime Text*. Vienna: Sonderzahl.

Mora, Terézia. 2019. *Auf dem Seil*. Munich: Luchterhand.

Mora, Terézia. 2021. *Fleckenverlauf: Ein Tage- und Arbeitsbuch*. Munich: Luchterhand.

Nachtwey, Oliver. 2018. *Germany's Hidden Crisis: Social Decline in the Heart of Europe*. Translated by David Fernbach and Loren Balhorn. London, New York: Verso.

Rancière, Jacques. 2009. *Le spectateur émancipé*. Paris: La fabrique d'éditions.

Rancière, Jacques. 2019. *Le travail des images: Conversations avec Andrea Soto Calderón*. Dijon: Les Presses du Réel.

Ries, Eva. 2022. *Precarious Flânerie and the Ethics of the Self in Contemporary Anglophone Fiction*. Berlin, Boston: De Gruyter.

Rys, Michiel, and Bart Philipsen. 2021. "Introduction: Poetics and Precarity—Literary Representations of Precarious Work, Past and Present." In *Literary Representations of Precarious Work, 1840 to the Present*, edited by Michiel Rys and Bart Philipsen, 1–19. Cham: Palgrave Macmillan.

Terborg, Karin. 2022. "Pathologisierte Weiblichkeit und kapitalistische Wirtschaft: Die fragile Frau in Terézia Moras Kopp-Roman-Trilogie." In *Terézia Mora: Kasseler Grimm-Poetikprofessorin 2021*, edited by Stefanie Kreuzer, 169–181. Würzburg: Königshausen & Neumann.

2.3
"Know Where to Fish"

Class and Gender Precarity and Project-based Networks in Creative and Cultural Industries

VALERIA PULIGNANO, DEBORAH DEAN, MARKIETA DOMECKA
AND LANDER VERMEERBERGEN

Introduction

In the sociology of work, Kalleberg (2018) describes precarity in the formal economy as "employment that is uncertain, unpredictable, and risky from the point of view of the worker" (1). It is accepted that project work is, to varying degrees, precarious work (Hodgson 2004) and to aid understanding of the complex phenomenon of precarisation across economies, we consider areas of the creative industries, where the project form is predominant (Eikhof and Warhurst 2013). Specifically, we aim at understanding *how* and *why* the facilitating process of the project form, the network, contributes to systemic patterns in project work commodification and to the generation of precarity which is grounded on a class-based understanding of gender. In so doing, we locate the understanding of 'class imaginaries' in contemporary cultural and creative industries (CCIs), and the concept of class in general, at the intersection of ideological and socio-economic dimensions. Accordingly, we use a broader sociological definition of social class which focuses on the inequality of access to resources and refers to a meaningful status characteristic that influences people's perceptions and expectations, as does gender. Grabher (2004) calls networking "the emblematic practice in project ecologies" (1502) and analyses have shown that networks in the creative industries shape organisational outcomes (Antcliff, Saundry and Stuart 2007; Grugulis and Stoyanova 2011; Sydow and Staber 2002); however, the dimensions involved in how and why are less well established. Studies report on networking as the way "to overcome information asymmetries within the project-based political economy of creative production" (Lee 2011, 550) and these asymmetries represent two, linked, aspects of networking—effective protection of insiders and effective exclusion of outsiders—that are important to understanding patterns in precarity. As we shall see, although networking practices differ across countries and sectors, there are strong similarities in how they particularly affect self-employed women's ability to acquire and trade creative and financial gains.

We argue that disadvantaging networking processes derive from commodification in project work, which must be considered as an embedded form within industrial and national contexts (i.e. socio-economic and policy structures) in assessing their effects on unequal outcomes which are naturalised through ideology and cultural normative processes eventually generating inequality. Commodification in project work refers to the employing project organisations shifting risk by "imposing the discipline of market competition on workers" (Greer 2016, 165). Therefore, our attention is directed at an under-researched dimension of precarity: how this type of project work is *organised* (Peticca-Harris, Weststar and McKenna 2015).

This chapter considers creative industry networks as mediating precarious outcomes for aspirant workers through informal, individualised cultural processes. In particular, we contend that understanding how and why networks organise project-based transactions can be achieved through a synthesis of material and non-material lenses. First, we illustrate that the project work dynamics accounting for how creative capacity is commodified in the marketplace involve the industrial logic of risk minimisation and the national regulatory contexts in which they are embedded. Second, in investigating how these dynamics affect project workers, we show the homophilous processes that generate inclusion and exclusion, through classed, gendered 'sorting.' In so doing, we can identify the conditions under which certain outcomes occur and contribute to organisation studies' theorising about project work, and specifically its facilitation of a precarity which is class-based and gendered. We ground our argument within an empirical comparative cross-national study of precarious jobs within CCIs, and use a narrative 'storytelling' approach as a heuristic tool for the analysis of precarity which makes it possible to uncover broader tendencies in the rearticulation of class experiences in relation to race and gender.

We define class in Bourdieusian terms, following Savage et al. (2015), whose work on class has been informed by 'capitals, assets, resources' (1013) and focuses first of all on the relationship between class and inequality. Central to our argument on class and gender precarity in CCI is the structural asymmetry translated into more open or more constrained access to resources. Hence, precarious class-based outcomes are identified as the unequal positioning of workers within and incomplete access to networks of sociability and recognition as detrimental to upward mobility.

Creative Industry Project Work Dynamics and Networks

The output of creative industries is uncertain before and during its 'making,' as is its outcome (Menger 2014), and high degrees of risk are therefore inherent (Caves 2000). Creative organisations utilise project work partly to achieve flexibility within an inherently volatile and unpredictable market for creative products (Hesmondhalgh and Baker 2011). These projects are precarious because they emerge from market-based employer demands, which are intermittent, temporary and unpredictable, and work arrangements that are contingent and casual (McKinlay and Smith 2009).

Recruitment and selection via networks are outcomes of the project-based nature of creative work, which increasingly results from the wider retrenchment and downsizing creative organisations have been undergoing since the 1990s (Baumann 2002). We know that precarious work has been disproportionately done by women across sectors (Fudge and Owens 2006) and in the creative industries patterns of gendered occupational segregation remain distinct (such as higher-status cinematographers being mainly men, and lower-status makeup artists mainly women) (Taylor et al. 2017), and, as our findings clarify, risk is not shifted in gender-neutral ways.

Recruitment, training and quality control are informally fulfilled by networks, mainly consisting of production managers, heads of department and established workers trusted as having knowledge that needs to be passed on. The economic logic underpinning creative organisations influences their capacity to take on or transfer risk in order to minimise costs. This logic, combined with oversupplied labour markets, encourages and enables reliance on trust (Antcliff, Saundry and Stuart 2007) and "reproducing the familiar" (Dean 2008, 169), which entrenches gender segmentation in products, and in how and by whom those products are made.

Work in organisation and employment studies considers power relations (inherent in informal networks) as a key driver of gender inequality (Healy, Kirton and Noon 2010), and Acker's (2000) and others' work on organisations as embedding and expressing gendered differentiation is well known. The career structures within and surrounding creative organisations are similarly gendered (Tuckett 2019) and indicate use of distinctive resources by the (very largely) men dominating them. Organisation and employment studies scholars have pointed to the over-representation of white, male, middle-class gatekeepers, such as film and TV writers and casting directors (Friedman, O'Brien and Laurison 2017) and the significance of gatekeepers and intermediaries in shaping disadvantage (Dean 2008; Delmestri et al. 2020; Grugulis and Stoyanova 2012). US research has evidenced women's disadvantage in US TV and film production (Lauzen

2019), and the ways in which networks operate to facilitate these discriminatory effects (Christopherson 2009). As we will show, the power relationships which underlie concentration of resources nurture "the social processes through which forms of capital can be developed and transformed" (Vincent 2016, 1166), and therefore add understanding of how class-based gendered processes of precarisation unfold.

Theoretical Synthesis

There are many different lenses through which to understand the complex phenomena of unequal access to work in the creative industries. These include: examination of multiple levels producing racist exclusion in film industry performance and production jobs (Hennekam and Syed 2018); social class origin as a barrier for performers (Friedman, O'Brien and Laurison 2017); and access to work as tied to societal positions and conceptions of 'women' (Dean 2008). Whatever their focus, most accounts mention the relevance of networks to access. Notably, Antcliff, Saundry and Stuart (2007) emphasise the importance of power relations in the valuing of social capital in UK television sector networks, as well as for trust and friendship in a fragmented, competitive landscape. In doing so, they concentrate on the significance of forms of network rather than their gendered effects. Grugulis and Stoyanova's (2012) study of UK film and TV does examine racialised, gendered effects of social capital and networks and provides valuable insights into the relationship between 'quality' of networks and 'quality' of jobs (1311). Here, we focus primarily on understanding the relation between networks and class-based gendered precarity, which necessitates integrating several conceptual elements as patterns of inequality in access are generated at country, sector and occupational/individual (network) levels.

In common with Lamont, Beljean and Clair (2014), we recognise the importance of specifying 'cultural processes' in understanding inequalities (here, in access to, and distribution within, creative industry projects). The authors define cultural processes as "ongoing classifying representations/practices that unfold in the context of structures (organizations, institutions) to produce various types of outcomes" (586) and we see the operations of networks as cultural processes fostering commodification mechanisms at industry (and country) levels. We discuss the homophilous nature of these operations linked to the sorting practices in their creation and maintenance of boundaries and hierarchies (Lamont et al. 2014, 598) within these contexts.

Meshing Different Theoretical Conceptualisations

To understand the sorting practices sustaining commodification, we consider Charles Tilly's theoretical conceptualisation of inequality as 'opportunity hoarding,' as refined by Erik Olin Wright, with a gendered reading of Pierre Bourdieu's theory of capital, in particular the concept of 'symbolic capital.' Their connections with industrial and country 'material' contexts is elaborated, to produce an analytical framework that enables us to account for the patterns we observe.

As indicated, creative project networks act as informal recruitment structures in mediating access to work. This informality, and dispersed knowledge, create the need to both *interpret* and *indicate* dimensions of (technical) suitability and (social) acceptability (Jewson and Mason 1986), resulting in fair/unfair discrimination, or sorting. Bourdieu's (1986) concept of symbolic capital, as misrecognition of resources ("unrecognized as capital and recognized as legitimate competence," 18), enables us to begin to account for these processes. Symbolic capital is understood as the ways in which an individual's possession of other capitals is signalled. Possession of these capitals—economic (money, property rights), cultural (embodied dispositions, in an institutionalised form like qualifications) and social (resources linked to group membership, providing credentials)—is represented to 'dominating' others indirectly through legitimised signs of 'recognition.' In our study contexts, examples might include willingness to accept an unpaid job in TV or possession of a white male body in dance. Moi (1991) argues that, despite the lack of gendered awareness in his original theorising, the concepts Bourdieu developed allow for room "to determine what kind of specific consequences" (1019) conceptual claims might have, and thus contribute to a general analysis of social power. Illustrating this point, Vincent (2016) utilises Bourdieusian concepts in his study of self-employed women HR consultants, surfacing the effects of "(patriarchal) structures of time within fields" (1179). There is a significant body of work engaging with Bourdieu's concepts in relation to women's employment. Our own focus is not women workers per se, but on how and why the creative project networks operate so as to promote a class- and gender-based understanding of precarity.

Bourdieu (1986) sees capital in the forms noted above as "what makes the games of society—not least, the economic game—something other than simple games of chance offering at every moment the possibility of a miracle" (15). We see the operation of creative industry projects as a useful example of this argument. Each project (or game) offers opportunity for occupational advancement and creative fulfilment. Each is new, therefore uncertain and ostensibly open to the widest range of talent for the alchemy necessary for transformation into a successful product. Instead, we see similar patterns across industries and countries of over-representation of predominantly white men and middle- and upper-class people in the most rewarded occupations. Moi's (1991) summary of Bourdieu's concept of the field as "a competitive system of social relations which functions according to its own specific logic or rules" (1020) maps directly on to creative project networks. Core to the field is the power to attribute or withhold 'legitimacy' (here, assign competence), through possession of symbolic capital particular to that field and recognised as such by others. This recognition forms part of the habitus (internalised norms and values) of the players in the field and therefore, pertinently for our study, the field "functions as a form of censorship" (ibid., 1022), excluding those without the requisite symbolic capital. As Bourdieu (1989) argues, "agents are distributed in the overall social space [...] according to the overall volume of capital they possess" (17).

This distribution can be explained by Tilly's (1998) argument that structures can underwrite a 'hoarding' of various kinds of opportunities, as the expression of power relationships. Accordingly, 'durable inequalities' are constructed within and through organisations and they are 'social relational' in character. For instance, reputation (symbolic capital, shared recognition) is an intangible sorting mechanism mediated by dominant network figures and used by—ultimately— organisations in access to future work. As Menger (2006) puts it, "the several dimensions of inequality are magnified by the work system in the arts, which builds on networks, reputation, short term contracts, and highly individualized performance ratings" (40).

Tilly (1998) is clear that 'opportunity hoarding' does not necessarily involve exploitation, but that this complementarity can occur, as when "the effort of a favoured minority provides a resource-owning elite with the means to extract surplus from an essential but otherwise unavailable larger population" (154). Thus, in our terms, networks involving dominant gatekeepers to projects do not exploit (or acquire) economic capital from their operations. However, opportunity hoarding via these project-based creative industry networks facilitates exploitation, and thus increases precarity.

Bounding of categories in occupational networks is where the relevance of symbolic capital becomes evident. Wright (1997), conceptualising the interaction of class and gender, argues that there is "an agenda of issues that need to be considered within empirical research and theory construction" (118) and one of the five forms of class/gender interrelations he conceptualises is especially pertinent here, which is gender sorting into class locations. He discusses social science explanations of gender differences in occupational distributions, noting that forms of "inequality, domination and discrimination" can have direct effects on opportunities for access to different types of jobs, or indirect effects on access "by affecting their acquisition of relevant resources" (ibid., 122). This recalls Tilly's opportunity hoarding, which indeed Wright compares to his own concept of "non-exploitative economic oppression" (ibid., 31), where one group is advantaged at the expense of others. However, Wright (2000) critiques Tilly's own criticism of 'individualist' explanations of inequality as misplaced in placing more emphasis on the "organizational bases for exploitation" (458) than on multi-causal explanations involving inequality culture in general. Our consideration of project networks utilises this plural lens.

Contextualising a Class- and Gender-Based Understanding of Precarity

Although the concept of opportunity hoarding is valuable in understanding how the operation of networks takes account of the gendered accrual and recognition of symbolic capitals, nevertheless economic rules of engagement bind individuals within social and industrial contexts (Sydow and Staber 2002). As we shall see in discussion of findings, these practices reflect specificities indicative of the wider economic and social relations of production. This in turn affects the functioning of project networks, whereby opportunities are increased or reduced.

Contexts can be more or less de-commodified (and therefore precarious) in the extent to which industry structures reflect marketisation and state support, and people can still obtain social protections (exposed to more or less risk) regardless of their work arrangement (Kalleberg 2018). Greer, Salamuk and Umney (2019) theorise the need to take account of embeddedness issues in a more actor-centred approach. An informed understanding of our findings requires this approach: here, the state is not a direct transaction organiser, but a 'silent actor' in that it can mitigate commodification. Meardi, Donaghey and Dean (2016) and Pulignano, Dean, Domecka and Vermeerbergen (2023) reiterate the importance of attending to the role of the state in gender relations and employment and thus "understanding [...] state intercession in its nation's class system" (566).

The degree and nature of the endemic risk in creative industries is also affected by incentives emerging from differing country-based market governance regimes, central to the nature of project work (Christopherson 2002). Through exerting downward pressure on costs, they undermine institutional structures which might mitigate precarity instead. Aroles, Hassard and Hyde (2021) discuss precarity in creative institutions as a situation in which "there is almost total cessation in traditional funding," which leaves the organisation "financially powerless and forced to focus on short-term strategies and plans" (14). As Doerflinger, Pulignano and Vallas (2020) further posit, it is important to identify construction of distinct types of economic and social forms of production where commodified labour might have access to structural power if they "hold strategic locations within the labor process or favorable positions in the labor market" (6). This brings us to the precise significance of networks to a class- and gender-based understanding of precarity in project work. Reliance on previously 'tested' people is seen as desirable, if not essential, in time-limited and inherently risky projects. Thus, we see dominant network actors discriminating in their recognition/assignation of competence to those in possession of relevant symbolic capital, their dominant positions enabling them to hoard opportunities. Men's (especially white, middle-class men's) occupation of Doerflinger et al.'s (2020) 'strategic locations' (6) is clear, as is the research showing that men are more likely to benefit from the 'old boys' network than women (Grugulis and Stoyanova 2012).

Recalling the significance of cultural processes (Lamont, Beljean, and Clair 2014) noted above, we argue that what animates the class-based operation of sorting practices by networks is homophily, i.e. individuals' preference for interacting with others similar to themselves in terms of social characteristics such as gender, class and 'race' (Ibarra 1992; 1995), enabled/promoted by the commodification inherent in the project form (Bushell, Hoque, and Dean 2020; Melamed et al. 2020).

Homophily is operationalised through networks' (mis)recognition of symbolic capital. However, as we contend below, the extent of the power of dominant networks to hoard opportunities through such recognition is bounded by industrial (and national) contexts.

Research Design and Methodology

We use autobiographical narrative interviews (Schütze 2008) to contextualise the subjective experiences into class background. Here, we refer to Savage, Warde and Devine's (2005) consideration of resources as both economic (income) and cultural (educational credentials and competences acquired through family which "secure and perpetuate access to economic capital" (Crompton 1998, 149)) to allocate people to a specific class category. We asked each participant to self-identify in class terms (Reay 1998) in light of types of resources possessed, as in Savage et al. (2005). These are economic (income), social (networks) and cultural (educational credentials and competences acquired through the family) resources, and they "secure and perpetuate access to economic capital" (Crompton 1998, 149). We were also able to assess some class-based resources through narrative analysis, such as family's financial support in relation to training, unpaid work and unemployment, parents' occupation and family lifestyle (place of residence, holidays and activities), as well as networks of family and friends.

We selected two industries (TV/film, dance) and four countries (Britain, Germany, Sweden, the Netherlands) where we studied the industries following a two-by-two comparison (TV/film in Britain and Germany and dance in Sweden and the Netherlands). The selection-to-difference along both country and industry dimensions was motivated by our expectation of revealing the relative potency of both contexts affecting patterns and cross-cutting mechanisms. Categories were based on: the prevalence of inherently precarious project work, resulting from significant changes in industries and countries; the higher concentration of women in dance in comparison to TV/film industries; and the under-researched status of dance in comparison to TV/film.

We conducted seventy-seven interviews (fifty-one narrative with project workers and twenty-six semi-structured with experts) (Table 1 for sample description of expert interviews). Twenty-five narrative interviews were conducted in TV/film in Britain and Germany. In the Netherlands and Sweden, in dance, we collected twenty-six narrative interviews across different genres (i.e. ballet, contemporary dance and street dance). Using snowball sampling, we interviewed twenty-seven women (eleven in TV/film and sixteen in dance), twenty-three men (fourteen in TV/film and nine in dance) and one non-binary person (in dance) (Table 2 for sample description of biographical narrative interviews).

Table 1: Participant overview: expert interviews

TV/Film	Position of interviewees and number of interviews
United Kingdom	Academic (N=1), Trade unionist (N=2), Representative of professional association (N=1)
Germany	Academic (N=3), Trade unionist (N=1), Representative of professional association (N=2)
Europe	Trade unionist (N=2), Representative of professional association (N=1)
Dance	
Sweden	Academic (N=2), Trade unionist (N=1), Representative of professional association (N=1), Representative of funding body (N=2), Operative manager (N=1), Representative of public employment service (N=1)
The Netherlands	Academic (N=2), Trade unionist (N=1)
Europe	Trade unionist (N=2), Policy maker (N=1)
Total number of expert interviews	**27**

Table 2: Participant overview: narrative biographical interviews

No.	Code and name	Age	Gender	Majority/ minority ethnicity*	Class background	Profession	
1	DE01_Agnes	30	F	Maj	Lower middle	Junior producer	
2	UK01_Radek	44	M	Maj	Working class	Editor	
3	DE02_Dirk	41		Maj	Working class	Editor	
4	DE03_Amina	30	F	Min	Lower middle	Editor, journalist	
5	DE04_Timo	42	M	Maj	Working class	Sound engineer, camera assistant	
6	UK02_Mike	60	M	Maj	Working class		
7	DE05_Benjamin	50	M	Maj	Lower middle	Camera operator	
8	DE06_Nico	42		Maj			
9	DE07_Sandra	46	F	Maj	Middle class		
10	DE08_Hannah	40	F	Maj	Lower middle	Set decorator	
11	UK03_Jacinta	43	F	Min	Working class		
12	DE04_Penny	46	F	Maj	Working class	Makeup	TV/Film
13	UK05_Liz	35					
14	DE09_Frieder	37					
15	UK06_Sean	51	M	Maj	Lower middle	Location manager	
16	UK07_Jake	60					
17	DE10_Brianna	40	F	Min	Lower middle	Graphic designer	
18	UK08_Zoe	31	F	Maj			
19	DE11_Hanno	52	M	Maj	Middle	Director	
20	UK09_Peter	71					
21	UK10_Chris	59	M	Maj	Middle	Extra (actor)	
22	UK11_Anja	29	F	Maj	Middle class	Camera assistant	
23	UK12_Terrie	40	F	Min	Lower middle		
24	UK13_Niall	36	M	Maj	Lower middle	Location scout	
25	UK14_Sam	53	M	Maj	Working class	Sound technician	

No.	Code and name	Age	Gender	Majority/minority ethnicity*	Class background	Profession
26	NL01_Alba	41	F	Maj	Working class	
27	NL02_Francesco	34	M			
28	SE01_Nadja	30	F	Min		
29	NL03_Anis	30	M		Lower middle	
30	SE02_Anna	39	F	Maj		
31	SE03_Fabiano	50	M			
32	NL04_Jasmin	28	F	Min		
33	SE04_Filip	27	M			
34	SE05_Arianna	28				Dancer
35	SE06_Isabelle	23	F			
36	NL05_Leen	28			Middle	
37	NL06_Jane	38		Maj		
38	NL07_Alessandro	31				Dance
39	SE07_Jaime	32	M			
40	SE08_Elias	29				
41	NL08_Bart	40				
42	NL09_Lisa	23	F	Maj	Upper middle	
43	NL10_Mia	32	F	Maj	Lower middle	
44	SE09_Hiroko	44	F	Min		
45	SE10_Iris	28				
46	SE11_Sandra	32				Dancer/choreographer
47	SE12_Astrid	33	F		Middle	
48	NL11_Dominika	32		Maj		
49	NL12_Sara	36				
50	SE13_Jon	41	M			
51	SE14_Nikola	31	NB			

* Majority (usually White) / Minority (usually non-White) ethnicity

TV/Film in Germany and the UK

Project work in TV and film means a series of temporary jobs all over the world, ranging from a day to a few months, with no 'occupational' income in between. 'Jumping from project to project,' which may significantly differ in type, is often very intensive (i.e. shifts usually up to fifteen hours or more), as several respondents indicate, and is punctuated by periods of no work, where people often suffer the limits independent self-employment status impose when accessing the social security system:

> I'm lucky I don't have a family to feed, so the money [I earn] is used to pay all the tax, pension provision, which many of my colleagues don't do, because they say yes, how am I supposed to pay for it? (DE07_Sandra, 46, F, camera operator)

> Everything shut down [due to Covid]. We were in freefall, it felt a little bit like you were jumping out of a plane, oops. No parachute. And financially already if I don't get a phone call—I don't work. I don't have any unemployment benefit rights built in the contracts that I have. Sometimes I don't even have contracts. (UK06_Sean, 51, M, supervising location manager)

The uncertainty of funding requires the industry to adjust swiftly to the changing environment, without incurring 'fixed' costs. Doing project work means "to make and to sell to be paid" (DE05_Ben), but "if there's a way to not pay you, you won't get paid" (UK13_Niall, 36, M, location scout):

> I did an internship and moved from Berlin to Hamburg. They [company] used volunteers a lot [...]. Thanks to the editor, I started working as a researcher and a soundman. And then I was cameraman for very little [money]. I asked if they had more for me. They said yes and then there was no end to it. I worked from Monday to Friday in Hamburg, and on weekends I was in Berlin and then drove there again. Later they offered me volunteer work again. (DE04_Timo, 42, M, sound engineer and camera assistant)

> Last year I did a prep for a job. And I said: "Look I want money to pay for it, you can just give me a nice contract in the new year and I'm happy." And then I got the job and after three weeks they let me go because someone said that I was too expensive. (UK13_Niall, 36, M, location scout)

Workers report being easily replaced, as the number of people "creating the magic" (DE04_Timo) is always higher than the number of jobs available. Camera operators in Germany report that their fees have not changed since the mid-1990s. Having a low wage and irregular hours in expensive cities like London or Berlin is difficult for those with fewer resources at their disposal. Zoe, a white working-class woman, who cannot rely on family resources, is constrained because of "working in a pub during the weekends" to enable "trying to get either work experience or […] paid work in anything to do with film and TV during the week" (UK08_Zoe). Women and men from a working-class background of all ethnicities struggle to "make ends meet" (DE02_Dirk) and to access high-quality jobs. This contrasts with white middle-class and upper-middle class women and men entering the industry, who often come from "a film family" (DE06_Nico) and therefore have resources and contacts at their disposal (UK10_Chris). Class background can also be relevant in the event of workplace conflict. We inter-viewed Ben (DE05), a white working-class camera operator, who was informally "blacklisted" for filing a court case against a production company paying low rates and insisting on classifying crew as self-employed, despite being depend-ent on the organisation for assignment of tasks and supervision. After the case (which he lost), Ben found it difficult to get hired, having been stigmatised as "a troublemaker," and he did not have any financial buffers.

Having contacts with the right directors and producers "who run the show" (UK07_Jake) is crucial, since they place people in project departments. Terrie, a working-class woman of mixed African-Caribbean heritage, identified the "in-ner circles" of power in the industry:

> It's like concentric rings, so in the middle you have family members and then it goes out, friends, acquaintances. A lot of people that sort of sit within those circles tend to be private or public school educated, they tend to be male, white Anglo-Saxon Protestants. They tend to be out of a particular type of mould, which is quite identifiable, it's a type [laughing]. (UK12_Terrie, 41, F, camera assistant)

Terrie's narrative reflects the industry structure in Britain, where, in contrast to state-backed policy aimed at "promoting a more diverse workforce" (Of-com 2019), representation of Black, Asian and minority ethnic people fell from 12% in 2009 to 5.3% in 2012 (Creative Skillset 2013) and 4.2% in 2018 (Brook, O'Brien and Taylor 2018). Moreover, high-status creative roles are mainly white, middle-class and male-dominated (ScreenSkills 2019). Between 1999 and 2003, fewer than 15% of films were credited to a female screenwriter (Sinclair, Pol-lard and Wolfe 2006), and only 14% of directors and screenwriters in 2012/2013 were women (Newsinger and Presence 2018). Similarly, in Germany between 2009 and 2013, women directed 22% of films, fewer than 9% were produced by women and only 14% of scripts were written solely by women (Loist and

Prommer 2019). Illustrating Wright's (1997) gender sorting into class locations, the UK film industry largely consists of "women in hair, makeup, costume and props, and men in camera, sound and directing" (UK12_Terrie), and similarly in Germany:

> In the camera department, there's one woman to ten men. Maybe even one in twenty. Because you move many kilos a day [...] That's a woman's constitution, you have to be on your toes, you have to be fast and for many it is simply too much [...] I have always enjoyed working with female colleagues. Well, not as camer-awomen. In other areas such as equipment, props, decoration. (DE11_Hanno, 52, M, head of camera department)

'A Culture of Recommendations'

Networks decide "who works, how, where, and the pay" (UK11_Anja). Thus, project workers are recruited, tried and tested by networks, and if the (individualised, unmonitored) assessment is positive, they are recommended for new projects. Interviewees refer to it as "a culture of recommendations" (UK12_Terrie) or "referral marketing" (DE11_Hanno). This was confirmed by our expert interviewees and summarised by a white lower-middle class female camera assistant: "it's all about who you know, not really what you know. It's all about contacts" (UK11_Anja).

As lack of access to networks means less access to jobs, those different from the usual members of 'instrumental' networks (women, working-class and minority ethnic people) struggle. They usually have "a mountain to climb" (UK02_Mike). "It is important the network knows in advance who you are [...] [I]t is crucial within an industry where people need to know who they can trust and rely upon" (UK07_Jake). The network bears the risk as it is "primarily responsible for the accomplishment of the project's goals, in accordance with broadcasting funders' requests" (UK07_Jake), so seeks to counterbalance the risk of "having to do a lot with not much" typical of an industry featuring fragmentation and uncertainty (UK07_Jake). Network gatekeepers are aware their reputation (symbolic capital) is at stake and that they are expected to help police quality and deadlines. Networks become like "a family and once you are part of the family, you get called [for jobs] because you're one of them" (DE09_Frieder).

The privilege of particular in-groups is reinforced and maintained over time through active (direct) and effective (indirect) discrimination. This particularly applies to access to productions where symbolic capital is the highest—feature films and high-end TV series, which can compete for industry rewards (Academy Awards, BAFTAs).

> I couldn't enter these large feature films because I wasn't in those circles. Every time I asked and they didn't directly know me, nothing would come back and one time I even got an e-mail back saying: "Thanks very much but I will be going with my tried and tested team." (UK11_Anja, 29, F, camera assistant)

"Those circles" (UK11_Anja) are virtually closed for outsiders as there are active strategies to secure the privilege of insiders. Several interviewees referred to precarious, often unpaid, positions within the industry as frequently allocated to women in 'assistant' positions. In Germany, female interviewees from a working-class and lower-middle-class background spoke about being put into the role of "*Mädchen für alles*" (a girl doing everything). In Britain, female interviewees reported unequal treatment on the job; white, middle-class, better-connected men have more opportunities to learn, while working-class and minority ethnic women are hampered by auxiliary tasks in 'service' roles:

> There were two of us but I had done three years of training so I was more experienced [...] and I was tasked with looking after the DOP, the cinematographer. [...] He refused to eat the catering that was provided. So, every day I had to go out and get him his lunch with his driver and sometimes even prepare it for him [...] And there were several other things I had to do, like buying him socks because he forgot to put socks on one day [...] I basically felt like a waitress [...] And, of course, the other trainee was where I wanted to sit really, right next to the camera. (UK11_Anja, 29, F, camera assistant)

Even if women manage to reach parallel positions to those of men, their comments and requests are frequently ignored or rejected, which "makes it difficult to do well the work they are supposed to do" (DE01_Agnes). They often encounter mistrust of their capacities, which hinders their performance:

> The DOP [director of photography] was very reluctant to let me do certain types of things. And because he didn't have a lot of trust in me, I became more nervous around him. And as you perform worse, it justifies their opinion of you. (UK11_Anja, 29, F, camera assistant)

Highlighting the homophilous nature of networks, women often only discover structural inequalities when they start talking to men working in other, male-dominated, departments:

> Men hang out more with men, and women with women. [...] [W]omen are quite open about their rates, so we discuss what we're earning, seeing quite similar

amounts. And only men who are my very close friends can say: "I'm earning this." And I'm like "What? How are you earning that much money?," and they are like "Oh all the guys are," "What?!" (UK08_Zoe, 31, F, graphic designer)

However, network processes are sometimes mediated at other levels. In German public broadcasting, project workers are offered an 'employee-like freelancer' (*feste Freie Mitarbeiter*) employment status, regulated by collective bargaining. Accordingly, project workers enjoy social benefits (i.e. annual and sick leave and pension schemes) (Herkel 2019) and longer-term contracts provide more regular work and remuneration. The *feste Freie* status provides a path, from standard freelancing to more protected freelancing to permanent employment, without over-reliance on homophilous networks. This enables female workers in Germany to reduce their dependence and thus potentially change the composition of networks in core jobs. Amina, a working-class woman of Moroccan origin, has worked for several years as *feste Freie'* for a public broadcaster in Germany:

> Next year I'll have an open-ended contract. After ten years [of *feste Freie*] you are automatically a permanent employee. […] [B]y being a *feste Freie* you have social security and discretion. (DE03_Amina, 30, F, editor)

There is no comparable employment security for freelancers in the UK and no British female interviewees reported any such discretion, which may also help explain why and how the domination of white middle-class men in core positions is reproduced.

Dance in Sweden and the Netherlands

Dancers construct careers as a patchwork of projects, following their passion for "a beautiful art, which is awfully structured" (NL12_Sara). Respondents describe project work as "doing gigs here and there" (NL10_Mia), ranging from music videos, through corporate or cultural events, to working in clubs, where the work is informal and pay is difficult to negotiate. "Body work"—as Anis (NL03) describes dance—requires "a long and ongoing investment in physical capital," which is the result of "discipline, ongoing exercise and continuous diet you learn since you are a child" (NL03_Anis). Our respondents told us that working-class children normally do not enter ballet schools due to the investment needed, in fees and costs related to specialist clothing. In the exceptional cases when they do become dancers, they recognise the extent of family effort it required: "I remember my parents counting every cent to pay for the school" (NL01_Alba, 41, F, dancer). Further, after graduation, entry to the core labour market involves participating in numerous workshops, often led by well-known coaches (dominant network gatekeepers), and multiple auditions, with family covering fees and travel costs. Thus, while middle-class dancers are given many opportunities to sell 'body work', working-class dancers may only have one chance or may be pushed away from dancing altogether: "We stayed in London, which was great, but it cost a ton of money" (NL06_Jane, 38, F, dancer).

However, there are national context mediators. Both countries have publicly funded dance organisations, offering a mix of permanent and dependent project work employment. In Sweden, "competitive commodification"—as Laermans (2015) describes it—is ameliorated on acceptance by this type of organisation as dancers get a public grant, providing regular income. Places are limited; there is fierce competition to enter the "protected dance shells" (NLEX02) and applicants cannot easily reach these desirable positions (cf. "thousand for one place only," SE12_Astrid). Unlike the Netherlands, however, in Sweden an equal number of male and female dancers are recruited annually to publicly funded dance organisations, which stems from the state's gender equality policy and the need to have enough female and male dancers to fill the roles in classical ballet. This appears equitable, yet the population of women applicants is far greater. In both countries, male dancers are "still seen as holy grails" (SE10_Iris) and a larger proportion of female dancers are cut off from potential stable employment.

Those who do not enter compete for project work, largely in private organisations. In the Netherlands, competitive commodification fosters "permanent rivalry" (NL01_Alba). Dancers constantly need to prove themselves, as "even after 20 years, when a new choreographer comes in, I still have to audition" (NL01_Alba, 41, F, dancer). Economic capital allows capacity to cope with these employment conditions: in Sweden almost 52% of those entering the industry have parents with high-level education, and family resources can make all the differences to survival and progress. It includes both the family of origin—"my parents had a lot of money saved for me, which I used" (SE09_Hiroko, 44, F, dancer/choreographer)—and partners—"I was lucky I met my husband, financially it was a huge relief" (NL06_Jane, 38, F, dancer). People who cannot rely on family or a partner's wealth must do extensive 'side' jobs, which hinders vital daily training and, longer term, prevents self-promotion in the artistic field, hindering crucial access to networking: "Dance jobs are not good for class travellers" (SEEX01).

'An Economy of Invitations'

To participate in auditions, dancers need to register by paying a fee and they also need to travel. Mitigation of precarity is available in Sweden, where the Public Employment Service (*Arbetsförmed*) offers "reimbursement for travel costs associated to the participation of auditions" (SEEX03). There is no equivalent support from the Dutch state authorities and working-class project workers reported being pushed towards exhausting work patterns, "applying for everything there is" (NL10_Mia, 32, F, dancer/choreographer) and often unable to afford attendance at auditions. Further, dancers need to be invited to audition. Those who get invited via networks have higher chances of audition success. SEEX08 describes networks as the "economy of invitation." All parties are aware of this process, including the dancers themselves: "you can always go to auditions, but your chances are very small if you don't know anybody there" (NL03_Anis, 30, F, dancer). In the Netherlands, white middle- and upper-class male choreographers and directors occupy key positions in networks and several respondents reported that in ballet, these gatekeepers decide who to admit in accordance with the narrowly defined "ideal of the bodily beauty," that is "white female and male dancers" (NL01_Alba). Thus, minority-ethnic dancers are often excluded because they are associated with a devalued form of embodiment. In Swedish ballet, although being a white middle- and upper-class man can also be an advantage, almost 70% of choreographers in key positions in networks are women (Konstnärsnamnden 2016). Moreover, the number of lower-middle-class dancers and choreographers in Sweden has increased from 841 in 2007 to 1,032 in 2014 (Flisbäck 2014; Konstnärsnamnden 2016). Both minority-ethnic and white working-class female dancers usually rely on them for being invited to audition, which potentially implies broadening of the 'economy of invitations' to other social groups:

> We have one member whose mother works at the opera, so she helped us sew some costumes […] [M]y boyfriend's is a photographer, so we've collected favours here and there. (SE06_Isabelle, 23, F, dancer)

The dominant pattern, however, is of pressure for quick and reliable selection, meaning that invited dancers are "tried and tested" or have strong recommendations coming from "trusted" colleagues. According to dancers, networks "know where to fish" and therefore they can "make and break careers" (NL09_Lisa, 23, F, dancer). Starting from schools and dance academies, being well connected provides visibility in a large pool, and being connected to established figures offers special treatment:

> My parents come from the dance world. So I had a huge advantage and opportunity to have some private auditions […] My parents worked here in the theatre, so I had access to the physiotherapist and to the workout studio. And so many choreographers already knew me since I was a kid. (NL09_Lisa, 23, F, dancer)

> One of my friends was chosen to be a choreographer and I remember him choos-
> ing me. That was just like really manipulative but it ended up happening that I had
> the job. (NL06_Jane, 38, F, dancer)

Project work relies on such homophilous networks. Entering, leaving and re-en-
tering the industry necessitates reliance on networks for access: "you get jobs because people know they can rely on you and therefore they keep recommending
you" (SE13_Jon). Active networking includes participation in workshops led by
renowned coaches and in international dance competitions, as well as attendance
at festivals and galas, which presupposes invitation by someone already 'inside':

> You learn you always have to network, always talk to people or go to shows and
> always talk to your colleagues and invite them to what you do. And go to shows,
> talk to the choreographers, go to workshops, you need to do it all. (NL03_Anis)

The embedded transfer of risk—from ultimate employing organisation to individual worker—is evident.

Networks are homophilous because they actively rely on those they 'recognise' (symbolic capital), while actively excluding those not in possession of the
right (gendered, racialised) symbolic capital. They also exclude inactively, in not
being able to 'see' others whose lack of capital means they do not even make
it into the orbit of the network. The result is effective discrimination through
sorting practices, reinforcing gendered, racialised, classed precarity. This is because working-class women, who engage early in second jobs, are those who
are primarily unrecognised by networks—partly because women comprise the
majority of dancers and partly because they combine irregular dance gigs with
other sources of income in their side jobs (e.g. in retail, hospitality, care work,
cleaning). This leads to overwork and underpay, as 60–80 hour working weeks
still barely exceed the minimum wage. More generally, male advantage was also
acknowledged by middle- and upper-class men:

> If you are a good and a well-resourced male dancer you are definitely luckier than
> if you are a good female well-resourced dancer, being a man in the dance world is
> always like you're more important. (NL07_Alessandro, 31, M, dancer)

Discussion and Conclusions

We developed a theoretical approach to precarity based on the practices of project networks, which constitute the organising principles of project work within

creative industries. In doing so, we also complement current understanding of classed and gendered processes of precarity within creative industries (Dean 2008; Friedman, O'Brien and Laurison 2017) by suggesting that contemporary class perceptions which emerge through the experience of precarity rely fundamentally on the feeling of not being connected—palpable in the case of performing artists, and this may be extrapolated to representations of class in the arts. We reveal all this by examining how and under which conditions project networks can affect discriminatory dynamics in worker precarity. Our approach is distinctive and it adds to the contributions in Part 2 of this volume on "Personalising Class: Individuals and Collectives" in two ways.

First, it reveals in the capital–labour relationship the core of the tension between the more individual experiences of discrimination and the shared socio-economic relations and interests that underpin collective class identities. It does so by pointing to commodification in project work as a key driver for the discriminatory dynamics we observe. Our findings provide further insight into how networks seek to manage the risk exerted by (de)commodification pressures within industry (and country) contexts. In so doing, our analysis also extends existing studies in the field of the sociology of work and employment (e.g. Greer, Salamuk and Umney 2019) by indicating networks, with their dominant gatekeepers, as the crucial form of 'transaction organiser' in creative industries. As we empirically show, this contributes to shaping precarity in that risks are not only transferred from employing organisations to workers, but that networks function as agents of capital in allocation of resources, and maintain the gendered, racialised inequalities that shape employing organisations. Thus, we explain how networks become precarity organisers by specifying the homophilic (mis)recognition of symbolic capital in their practices. These practices underpin commodification in project work, which homophily shapes. Hence, our results reveal the importance of commodification in project work for understanding how precarity is generated and sustained by the homophilic nature of networks' cultural processes. We argue that how, and how far, project networks contribute to enhancing or reducing *opportunities* (Tilly 1998) that people derive from 'possession' of resources ('symbolic capital': Bourdieu 1986), depends on relationships embedded into industry (and country) structures (facilitating *gendered sorting into class locations*: Wright 1997). Sydow, Lindkvist and DeFillippi (2014) pointed to embeddedness as relevant to project-based organisations and our study confirms and extends this significance in illustrating how embeddedness accounts for project networks sustaining advantages through creating opportunities for some, while reducing them for others, who will likely do more irregular, poor-quality project work and over shorter careers. In particular, we explain how commodification results from project networks pragmatically retaining control over economic and symbolic resources (e.g. public subsidies and early bodily investment) available within the industry (and country) to enable the project. Thus responsibility and control properties are concentrated within the network operating in accordance with the requirements of powerful funding agents.

Recalling our discussion of Tilly (1998) and Wright (1997) above—and this is the second way we see distinctiveness in our work—our findings point to the practice of 'sorting' as accounting for how the operations of project networks reproduce advantage and disadvantage by opening and closing opportunities at the intersection of gender and class within different industries and countries. We identify the homophilic nature of project network practices and show they work for the networks' internal purposes, creating and maintaining these networks as effective and powerful. In particular, we contend that structures are critical to shaping the risks which in turn account for the greater or lesser importance of the homophilous networks in generating precarity. Varieties of industry- and country-based industrial funding arrangements, de-regulation and broader access to social security provision are all relevant to how risk is redistributed. As such, these arrangements reflect the role of the state as 'silent actor' contributing to or mitigating (the 'power' of) homophily. This is because disadvantage is perpetuated at the point of assessment by homophilous networks but also beforehand, in that many creative workers do not even become visible to networks: the risk shifted onto them is too great a constraint.

Our comparative analysis shows that sorting can take different forms depending on industry structure. It can channel people on entrance to the industry (primarily TV/film) or it can make or break opportunities and careers for people within the industry (primarily dance). First, within TV/film, where 'learning while doing' is prevalent: in UK TV/film, the presence of private capital as a primary source of financing within vertically disintegrated systems of production account for the powerful role of project networks; in Germany, the organising of content production within a 'dual system' distributes power to networks. In both cases, recruitment practices follow the 'culture of recommendations' to ensure projects can deliver in accordance with the artistic and economic expectations of commissioning broadcasters. Homophily in networks produces outcomes that meet these expectations and maintains them as powerful. Accordingly, women tend to be concentrated in jobs traditionally associated with expectations of their gender (Alvesson and Billing 2009), unless they resemble the same racialised attributes of class (usually white and middle- and upper-class) of those of the network. Thus, their symbolic capital reflects the male elite. However, in German public broadcasting, employment protection can mitigate the effects of homophily in networks. The stability deriving from the 'employee-like freelancer' (*feste Freie Mitarbeiter*) contract provides more regular work and remuneration, which reduces dependency on networks for access to jobs. At the same time, under less pressure for cost-efficiency, and (de-)commodification in project work through relatively generous public resources, the capacity of networks to open or close opportunities is—slightly—reduced. The possession of economic capital, necessary to teach children how to keep the body ready to work at any time, is the condition underpinning entrance to dance and then maintaining that readiness. Findings showed that dancers construct their careers as a 'patchwork' by moving between organisations, countries and choreographers, and between dance techniques and styles. At the same time, resources are linked to personal connections. Networks organise accomplishment of the project's goals by establishing relationships with dancers who can be 'trusted' because they possess the greatest economic resources to guarantee long-term, ongoing investment in physical capital, or who are recommended by a dominant actor in the field (such as a relative who has already worked in dance). Economic capital and the trust it generates nurture an 'economy of invitation' which privileges upper- and middle-class people in audition participation in both Sweden and the Netherlands. We noted an increase in participation by non-privileged groups in Sweden, working on projects with gatekeepers from similar backgrounds, confirming that networks operate in a homophilic way, in that different network members can provide different types of access to resources. Conversely, white middle- and upper-class male choreographers and artistic directors dominate key positions in networks in the Netherlands and largely decide who to admit in accordance with possession of cultural capital: the narrowly defined bodily idea of white female and male dancers. Overall, this reveals some difference in how project networks function as a device for gendered precarity within dance organisations in both countries. As we saw, notwithstanding gender-equal numbers admitted to some Swedish dance companies, a far greater proportion of women are disadvantaged. However, for those who do enter, public grants in Sweden (dis)embed project work from the market-based relationships of production by providing less unstable social conditions within the industry. In contrast, in the Netherlands, both female and male lower-middle-class and working-class dancers report regular exclusion from auditions by project networks who do not consider them as meeting their preferences (see Figure 1).

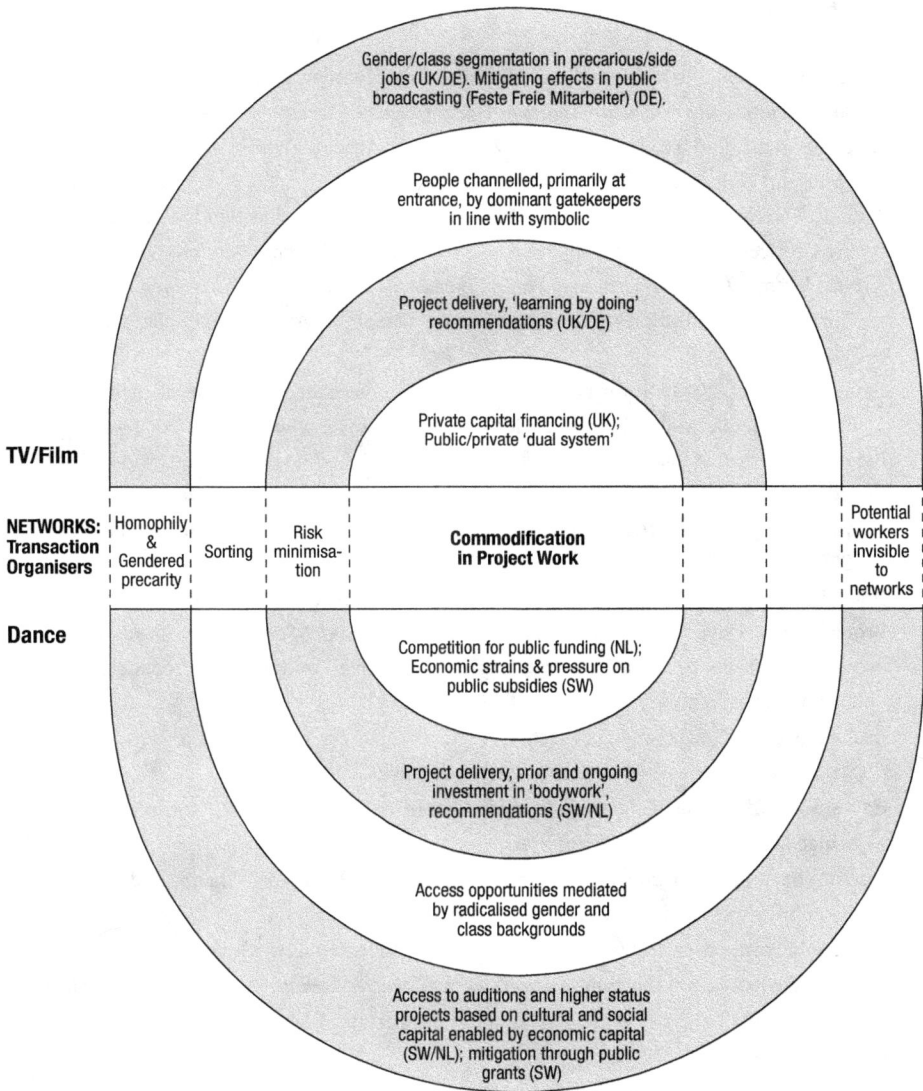

Gender/class segmentation in precarious/side jobs (UK/DE). Mitigating effects in public broadcasting (Feste Freie Mitarbeiter) (DE).

People channelled, primarily at entrance, by dominant gatekeepers in line with symbolic

Project delivery, 'learning by doing' recommendations (UK/DE)

Private capital financing (UK); Public/private 'dual system'

TV/Film

NETWORKS: Homophily | | | | | Potential
Transaction & | Sorting | Risk | **Commodification** | | workers
Organisers Gendered | | minimisa- | **in Project Work** | | invisible
precarity | | tion | | | to
| | | | | networks

Dance

Competition for public funding (NL); Economic strains & pressure on public subsidies (SW)

Project delivery, prior and ongoing investment in 'bodywork', recommendations (SW/NL)

Access opportunities mediated by radicalised gender and class backgrounds

Access to auditions and higher status projects based on cultural and social capital enabled by economic capital (SW/NL); mitigation through public grants (SW)

Figure 1: Commodification of project work and networks as 'transaction organisers' generating class and gender precarity

References

Acker, Joan. 2000. "Revisiting Class: Thinking from Gender, Race, and Organizations." *Social Politics: International Studies in Gender, State & Society* 7: 192–214.

Alvesson, Mats, and Yvonne D. Billing. 2009. *Understanding Gender and Organizations.* Thousand Oaks: Sage.

Antcliff, Valerie, Richard Saundry, and Mark Stuart. 2007. "Networks and social capital in the UK television industry: The weakness of weak ties." *Human Relations* 60: 371–393.

Aroles, Jeremy, John Hassard, and Paula Hyde. 2021. "'Culture for Sale': The Effects of Corporate Colonization on the UK Museum Sector." *Organization Studies* 43, no. 4: 347–368.

Baumann, Arne. 2002. "Informal Labour Market Governance: the Case of British and German Media Production Industries." *Work, Employment and Society* 16: 27–46.

Berauer, Wilfried. 2020. *Filmstatistisches Jahrbuch 2020.* Baden-Baden: Nomos.

Bourdieu, Pierre. 1986. "The Forms of Capital." In *Handbook of Theory and Research for the Sociology of Education*, edited by John G. Richardson, 241–258. Greenwood: Abc-Clio.

Bourdieu, Pierre. 1989. "Social Space and Symbolic Power." *Sociological Theory* 7: 14–25.

Brook, Orian, Dave O'Brien, and Mark Taylor. 2018. *Panic! Social Class, Taste and Inequalities in the Creative Industries.* London: Creative London. https://createlondon. org/event/panic-paper.

Bushell, Meryl, Kim Hoque, and Deborah Dean. 2020. *The Network Trap: Why Women Struggle to Get into the Boardroom.* Berlin: Springer.

Caves, Richard E. 2000. *Creative Industries: Contracts Between Art and Commerce.* Cambridge MA: Harvard University Press.

Christopherson, Susan. 2002. "Project Work in Context: Regulatory Change and the New Geography of Media." *Environment and Planning A* 34: 2003–2015.

Christopherson, Susan. 2009. "Working in the Creative Economy: Risk, Adaptation and the Persistence of Exclusionary Networks." In *Creative Labour: Working in the Creative Industries*, edited by Alan McKinlay and Chris Smith, 72–90. Basingstoke: Palgrave Macmillan.

Creative Skillset. 2013. *Classifying, Measuring the Creative Industries.* London: ScreenSkills.

Crompton, Rosemary. 1998. *Class and Stratification.* Cambridge: Polity Press.

Dean, Deborah. 2008. "No Human Resource is an Island: Gendered, Racialized Access to Work as a Performer." *Gender, Work & Organization* 15: 1–21.

Delmestri, Guiseppe, Filippo C. Wezel, Elizabeth Goodrick, and Marvin Washington. 2020. "The Hidden Paths of Category Research: Climbing new heights and slippery slopes." *Organization Studies* 41, no. 7: 909–920.

Doerflinger, Nadja, Valeria Pulignano, and Steven P. Vallas. 2020. "Production Regimes and Class Compromise among European Warehouse Workers." *Work and Occupations* 48, no. 2: 111–145.

Eikhof, Doris R., and Chris Warhurst. 2013. "The Promised Land? Why Social Inequalities Are Systemic in the Creative Industries." *Employee Relations* 32, no. 5: 495–508.

Flisbäck, Marita. 2014. *A Survey of Artists' Income from a Gender Perspective—Economy, Work, and Family Life.* Stockholm: Konstnärsnämnden.

Friedman, Sam, Dave O'Brian, and Daniel Laurison. 2017. "'Like Skydiving without a Parachute': How Class Origin Shapes Occupational Trajectories in British Acting." *Sociology* 51: 992–1010.

Fudge, Judy, and Rosemary Owens. 2006. *Precarious Work, Women, and the New Economy: The Challenge to Legal Norms.* Oxford: Hart Publishing.

Grabher, Gernot. 2004. "Temporary Architectures of Learning: Knowledge Governance in Project Ecologies." *Organization Studies* 25: 1491–1514.

Greer, Ian. 2016. "Welfare reform, precarity and the re-commodification of labour." *Work, Employment and Society* 30: 162–173.

Greer, Ian, Barbara Samaluk, and Charles Umney. 2019. "Toward a Precarious Projectariat? Project dynamics in Slovenian and French social services." *Organization Studies* 40: 1873–1895.

Grugulis, Irena, and Dimitrinka Stoyanova Russell. 2012. "Tournament careers: Working in UK television." In *Careers in Creative Industries*, edited by Chris Mathieu, 88–106. London: Routledge.

Healy, Geraldine, Gill Kirton, and Mike Noon, eds. 2010. *Equality, Inequalities and Diversity: Contemporary Challenges and Strategies.* London: Macmillan International Higher Education.

Hennekam, Sophie, and Jawad Syed. 2018. "Institutional racism in the film industry: a multilevel perspective." *Equality, Diversity and Inclusion: An International Journal* 37: 551–565.

Herkel, Günter. 2019. "Mehr Rechte für Freie bei ARD und ZDF." Menschen Machen Medien. Accessed 15 April 2023. https://mmm.verdi.de/tarife-und-honorare/mehr-rechte-fuer-freie-bei-ard-und-zdf-62031.

Hesmondhalgh, David, and Sarah Baker. 2015. "Sex, Gender and Work Segregation in the Cultural Industries." *The Sociological Review* 63: 23–36.

Hodgson, Damian E. 2004. "Project Work: The Legacy of Bureaucratic Control in the Post-Bureaucratic Organization." *Organization* 11: 81–100.

Huppatz, Kate. 2009. "Reworking Bourdieu's 'Capital': Feminine and Female Capitals in the Field of Paid Caring Work." *Sociology* 43: 45–66.

Ibarra, Herminia. 1992. "Homophily and Differential Returns: Sex Differences in Network Structure and Access in an Advertising Firm." *Administrative Science Quarterly* 37: 422–447.

Ibarra, Herminia. 1995. "Race, Opportunity, and Diversity of Social Circles in Managerial Networks." *Academy of Management Journal* 38: 673–703.

Jewson, Nick, and David Mason. 1986. "Modes of Discrimination in the Recruitment Process: Formalisation, Fairness and Efficiency." *Sociology* 20: 43–63.

Kalleberg, Arne L. 2018. *Precarious Lives: Job Insecurity and Well-Being in Rich Democracies*. Hoboken: John Wiley & Sons.

Konstnärsnamnden. 2016. *Konstnärernas demografi, inkomster och sociala villkor*. Stockholm: Konstnärsnamnden.

Laermans, Rudi. 2015. *Moving Together: Making and Theorizing Contemporary Dance*. Amsterdam: Valiz.

Lahaut, Dimitri. 2019. *Kunst als gunst. Beloning van ZZP'ers in de sector kunst*. Amsterdam: Bureau Lahaut.

Lamont, Michèle, Stefan Beljean, and Matthew Clair. 2014. "What is missing? Cultural processes and causal pathways to inequality." *Socio-Economic Review* 12: 573–608.

Lauzen, Martha M. 2020. "Boxed In 2019–20: Women On Screen and Behind the Scenes In Television." San Diego: Center for the Study of Women in Television and Film, San Diego State University. Accessed 15 April 2023. https://womenintvfilm.sdsu.edu/wp-content/uploads/2020/09/2019-2020_Boxed_In_Report.pdf.

Lee, David. 2011. "Networks, cultural capital and creative labour in the British independent television industry." *Media, Culture & Society* 33: 549–565.

Loist, Skadi, and Elizabeth Prommer. 2019. "Gendered Production Culture in the German Film Industry." *Media Industries* 6: 95–115.

Manning, Stephan, and Jörg Sydow. 2007. "Transforming Creative Potential in Project Networks: How TV Movies Are Produced under Network-Based Control." *Critical Sociology* 33: 19–42.

McKinlay, Alan, and Chris Smith, eds. 2009. *Creative Labour: Working in the Creative Industries*. Basingstoke: Palgrave Macmillan.

Meardi, Guglielmo, Jimmy Donaghey, and Deborah Dean. 2016. "The strange non-retreat of the state: implications for the sociology of work." *Work, Employment and Society* 30: 559–572.

Melamed, David, Matthew Sweitzer, Brent Simpson, Jered Z. Abernathy, Ashley Harrell, and Christopher W. Munn. 2020. "Homophily and Segregation in Cooperative Networks." *American Journal of Sociology* 125: 1084–1127.

Menger, Pierre-Michel. 2006. "Artistic Labor Markets: Contingent Work, Excess Supply and Occupational Risk Management." In *Handbook of the Economics of Art and Culture*, edited by Victor A. Ginsburgh and David Throsby, 765–811. Amsterdam: Elsevier.

Menger, Pierre-Michel. 2014. *The Economics of Creativity: Art and Achievement under Uncertainty*. Cambridge MA: Harvard University Press.

Moi, Toril. 1991. "Appropriating Bourdieu: Feminist Theory and Pierre Bourdieu's Sociology of Culture." *New Literary History* 22: 1017–1049.

Myndigheten för Kulturanalys. 2017. *Dramatiska villkor: Länsteatrarnas ekonomiska handlingsutrymme 1980–2015*. Stockholm: Myndigheten för Kulturanalys.

Newsinger, Jack, and Steve Presence. 2018. "United Kingdom: Film Funding, the 'Corporate Welfare System' and Its Discontents." In *Handbook of State Aid for Film: Finance, Industries and Regulation*, edited by Paul C. Murschetz, Roland Teichmann, and Matthias Karmasin, 447–462. London: Springer.

Ofcom. 2019. *Diversity And Equal Opportunities in Television: Monitoring report on the UK-based broadcasting industry*. London: Ofcom.

Peirce, Charles S. 1997. *Pragmatism As a Principle and Method of Right Thinking: The 1903 Harvard Lectures on Pragmatism*. Albany: SUNY Press.

Peticca-Harris, Amanda, Johanna Weststar, and Steve McKenna. 2015. "The perils of project-based work: Attempting resistance to extreme work practices in video game development." *Organization* 22: 570–587.

Pots, Roel. 2000. *Cultuur, koningen en democraten: Overheid & cultuur in Nederland*. Nijmegen: Sun.

Pulignano, Valeria, Deborah Dean, Markieta Domecka, and Lander Vermeerbergen. 2023. "How state influence on project work organization both drives and mitigates gendered precarity in cultural and creative industries." *British Journal of Industrial Relations* 61, no. 2: 313–335.

Reay, Diane. 1998. *Class Work: Mothers' Involvement In Their Children's Primary Schooling*. Oxfordshire: Taylor & Francis.

Salmons, Janet E. 2015. *Doing Qualitative Research Online*. Thousand Oaks: Sage.

Savage, Mike, Alan Warde, and Fiona Devine. 2005. "Capitals, assets and resources: some critical issues." *British Journal of Sociology* 56: 31–47.

Savage, Mike, Fiona Devine, Niall Cunningham, Sam Friedman, Daniel Laurison, Andrew Miles, Helene Snee, and Mark Taylor. 2015. "On Social Class, Anno 2014." *Sociology* 49, no. 6: 1011–1030.

Schütze, Fritz. 2008. "Biography Analysis on the Empirical Base of Autobiographical Narratives: How to Analyse Autobiographical Narrative Interviews—Part One and Two." *European Studies on Inequalities and Social Cohesion* 2: 153–242.

ScreenSkills. 2019. *Annual ScreenSkills Assessment*. London: ScreenSkills.

Sinclair, Alice, Emma Pollard, and Helen Wolfe. 2006. *Scoping Study into the Lack of Women Screenwriters in the UK*. Brighton: Institute of Employment Studies for the UK Film Council.

Sydow, Jörg, and Udo Staber. 2002. "The Institutional Embeddedness of Project Networks: The Case of Content Production in German Television." *Regional Studies* 36: 215–227.

Taylor, Matthew, Greg Marsh, Diane Nicol, and Paul Broadbent. 2017. *Good work: The Taylor review of modern working practices*. London: Department for Business, Energy & Industrial Strategy.

Tilly, Charles. 1998. *Durable Inequality*. California: University of California Press.

Tuckett, J. 2019. *What Share of the Cake?* Accessed 15 April 2023. https://jennifertuckett.com/.

Vincent, Steve. 2016. "Bourdieu and the gendered social structure of working time: A study of self-employed human resources professionals." *Human Relations* 69: 1163–1184.

Windeler, Arnold, and Jörg Sydow. 2001. "Project Networks and Changing Industry Practices Collaborative Content Production in the German Television Industry." *Organization Studies* 22: 1035–1060.

Wright, Erik O. 1997. *Class Counts: Comparative Studies in Class Analysis*. Cambridge: Cambridge University Press.

Wright, Erik O. 2000. "Metatheoretical Foundations of Charles Tilly's Durable Inequality." *Comparative Studies in Society and History* 42: 458–474.

PART 3

NARRATING CLASS: VOICE AND BELONGING

3.1

Double(ing) Voices

Narrating Precarious Class Status and Class Identities

SULA TEXTOR

> You said it would be better here.
> I know.
> It's not.
> No.
> Megan Gail Coles (2019, 83–84)

Canadian author Megan Gail Coles' novel *Small Game Hunting at the Local Coward Gun Club* (2019) narrates one day in the lives of its characters, who are all connected by one place: the restaurant where most of them work and others come to enjoy lunch or dinner. At the centre of this net of characters is Iris. She is a twenty-nine-year-old art graduate with an underprivileged background; she had hopes for a better future when, together with her childhood friend Olive, she left her rural home to come to the city; she hoped to escape the social world of her upbringing, a world marked by poverty and violence. But: "No," nothing "is better here," she remembers admitting to Olive. After what looked like the promising start of an upward social journey, she now works as a waitress with no means to improve her situation and is more vulnerable than ever.

It would be easy to imagine Iris being the first-person narrator of her own story, had her social journey been successful. She seems to be well read in sociology, among other things, and might be able to write an insightful autobiographical text about her authentic (although, of course, fictitious) experience of the mechanisms of social reproduction from the perspective of one who escaped, the exception to the rule. But Iris is no exception. Her situation is one of precarity; after work she does not have the energy to work on her paintings anymore, and we can hardly imagine her writing anything at all, let alone a novel.

And thus, the novel in which her story is told is nothing like the sociologically informed autobiographical texts which, following the success of Édouard Louis' debut novel *En finir avec Eddy Bellegueule* (2014) and the widespread reception of Didier Eribon's *Retour à Reims* (2009), have served as catalysts for the re-emergence of 'class' as a category in literary as well as socio-political discourses (see e.g. Schaub 2020, 64) and, by providing a set of recurring narratives and narrative strategies, have been giving shape to these discourses since then—mostly in France and Germany, but also internationally.

Small Game Hunting is not an autobiographical text; it does not have a first-person narrator, nor even a tangible narrator-figure at all, but a mere narrating voice voicing the characters' thoughts, fluidly shifting from one perspective to another. The novel is not narrated in retrospective, but in the present tense, and 'class' as a concept is almost completely absent from the characters' minds. Yet it is equally precise and insightful, although less explicit, in its analysis of class relations, social inequality, of precarity and the multiple ways in which forms of domination and discrimination intersect. By not focusing on one perspective but lending a voice to all the characters without reinstating a sovereign omniscient or first-person narrator, the heterogeneity of what could at first glance be perceived as a coherent social class is made apparent: their respective roles in the intricately intersectional structure of relations of power, domination and violence become tangible as these structures are perpetually being (re)produced in their interaction. My analysis of Coles' novel will focus on its narrative voice, which, I will argue, offers in many respects a more adequate—aesthetically and politically—way of narrating forms of precarious class positions and 'class struggle' in contemporary neoliberal capitalism, or at least a narrative countermodel to what is probably no longer merely a "genre-in-the-making": autosociobiography (Ernst 2020, 80; Blome, Lammers and Seidel 2022, 1).

As my analysis of Coles' novel stems from and is shaped by an uneasiness with the dominance of autosociobiographical narratives in and beyond literary discourse, it is embedded in some reflections on this uneasiness and the questions that arise from it. This somewhat unorthodox juxtaposition of the paradigmatic mode of narrating class identity in the twenty-first century with a recent example of a different narrative approach to many similar questions shows that different narrative modes have pervasive implications for the representation of class-related experiences, which, whether they are labelled as fiction or not, comment on contemporary conditions. Nevertheless, a common aspect of narrating precarious class status and identity also emerges from this juxtaposition: forms of narrative hybridity.

Potentials and Pitfalls of Autosociobiographical Transclasse Narratives

Who Speaks? In Whose Language? And to Whom?

The texts which belong to what is about to or already has become *the* genre for talking about class share: (a) an interest in the analysis and depiction of class relations, classist discrimination and the role of socio-economic factors in multilayered forms of domination; (b) the theme of the social climber; (c) the combination of literary forms of writing with sociological or sociologically informed analyses; and (d) a set of specific "narrative patterns"[1] (Blome 2020, 545)—a first-person narrator who looks back on their working-class origins and retrospectively tells the story of their economic and social advancement. By drawing on sociological knowledge (Bourdieu's concepts of the 'social space', 'social reproduction' and '(split) habitus', etc. seem to be almost omnipresent), the narrators of autosociobiographical texts objectify and validate their individual experience as a transindividual phenomenon (cf. Blome, Lammers and Seidel 2022, 3f.), while at the same time claiming its authenticity[2] by choosing an autobiographical or at least autofictional mode of writing.

As more and more autosociobiographical texts are being written and read, the genre contributes to the increasing visibility and an increasingly heterogenous representation of working-class positions and identities (cf. for example Schaub in this volume). But it also prevents other forms of narrative reconsiderations of class structures from gaining attention as such; in the case of *Small Game Hunting*, for instance, class-related aspects are often absent from discussions of the novel, even though they are one of the novel's central themes. The immense popularity of the genre also raises questions about the "adequacy" of these narratives with regard to their "Sprecher:innenposition," the position from which they speak (Blome 2020, 567; Blome, Lammers and Seidel 2022, 6): their narrators look back at their working-class origin from a privileged position and are able to publicly write about their experience only because of the access to language and discourse this position provides them with (cf. Blome 2020, 569–570). Furthermore, these texts mainly address an equally privileged readership and often also perform a legitimisation of their authors' acquired class status. Many authors of autosociobiographical texts are aware of those questions. Annie Ernaux for example famously said in an interview with sociologist Isabelle Charpentier (2005):

> J'ai réfléchi alors à ma position d'écrivain-narratrice transfuge, issue du monde
> dominé mais appartenant maintenant au monde dominant, [...] alors que les
> lecteurs appartiennent, eux, au monde dominant [...] C'est vrai que c'est toute

l'ambiguïté de la posture des autobiographies littéraires "d'en bas"… puisque précisément, elles émanent de gens qui en sont sortis. Alors que la langue, l'écriture, le langage, ce sont les ressources et les instruments de la culture dominante.[3] (167–168)

In answer to this "ambiguity," Ernaux develops what she calls "l'écriture de la distance" ("writing of the distance"), an objectifying writing style without any form of judgement, she claims, in which she amalgamates the language spoken by her parents and grandparents as she remembers it with "classic" syntax and vocabulary (ibid.; cf. ibid., 167–169). There is an element of hybridisation in this technique, on which other authors of autosociobiographical texts draw in their writing as well. However, this form of hybridity remains rudimentary in first-person narration, as the narrative discourse is stabilised and integrated by the voice of the narrator. Different worlds may resonate in the words we read, but the narration is that of one voice only.

Transclasse Narratives and Working-Class Nostalgia

As is implicit in this quotation from Ernaux, autosociobiographical narratives of the lives of the social climbers, the *transfuges de classe* ("class defectors"), rely on (the assumption of) clear-cut class divisions and—the common French term to designate subjects of upward social mobility speaks for itself in this respect—an essentialist concept of class identity with moral undertones. This might seem little surprising given the fact that autosociobiographies narrate "class relations in terms of the relations between generations" (Blome 2020, 545). Still, it may seem nostalgic that prototypical imaginings of the working class of past generations serve as a constant point of reference when narrating *transclasse* experience of the mechanics of social reproduction and the loss of stable class identities, of being caught in a sort of social 'in-between space' (cf. Blome, Lammers and Seidel 2022, 10; Jaquet 2018, 138–139).

A nostalgia for prototypical working-class subjects and realities is not only perceivable in recent literary and in fact other cultural spheres of production, but also in political rhetoric, as well as political and economic theory. Referring to an essay by Angela McRobbie, Emily Hogg (2021) argues for example that "[c]entring class identity and the site of the workplace as the foundations of a new radical politics […] indicates a nostalgia for older forms of masculinized industry and obscures other locations for the development of political consciousness and collective struggle" (6). McRobbie (2010) herself calls for a "different kind of thinking about class, one which focuses on this twilight status" (61), and similarly, Guy Standing (2011) argues that while past generations "could describe themselves in class terms, and others would recognize them in those terms," today those terms "are little more than evocative labels" (8). Emily Hogg (2021) analyses different "aesthetic strategies" of literary texts dealing with precarity in the neoliberal present and observes that in these texts, "it is formal and aesthetic undecidability, the resistance to conventional categories, that allows artistic work to challenge established norms" (13). In Megan Gail Coles' novel *Small Game Hunting*, these aesthetic strategies centre around forms of hybridisation, a much more dynamic form of narrative hybridity than can be perceived in autosociobiographical first-person narrative: a hybrid narrating voice that is corrosive to the narratological category of voice itself and allows for the novel to depict precarity, unstable class identities and social injustice not from a stable, omniscient or first-person perspective, but as it is produced and reproduced in the structural relations between and interactions of the characters themselves.

Transclasse Narratives and Meritocratic Ideology

In order to avoid the pejorative term *transfuge de classe* to designate the figure of the social climber in autosociobiographical narratives, that is, these texts' narrators, Chantal Jaquet has coined the term *transclasse*. In her book *Les transclasses ou la non-reproduction* she sketches a theory of social non-reproduction from a socio-philosophical perspective, analysing the causes and the political, economic, social and emotional preconditions of *transclasse* biographies (Part I) as well as what she calls the "complexion" of *transclasse* subjects (Part II). Her analysis relies heavily on readings of literary texts, that is, fictional or autobiographical narrativisations of *transclasse* experiences, from Stendhal's *Le Rouge et le noir* (1830) to Annie Ernaux's *La Place* (1983) and *La Honte* (1987), and Didier Eribon's *Retour à Reims*. Interestingly, it is not entirely clear why. She says that she makes use of these literary texts as "instruments of thought" (2018, 24–25). However, there is a blind spot in her approach, as she completely overlooks the specifically literary and aesthetic qualities of these text and offers a merely thematic reading.

Still, her discussion of these texts provides some interesting insights. From her reading of Stendhal and Ernaux she concludes that "non-reproduction is the continuation of reproduction by other means. The social order is preserved by the expulsion of an element that threatens it, that introduces disorder" (ibid., 80). That is, *transclasse* narratives do not challenge the mechanisms of domination along the lines of class hierarchies, they even prove to be indicative of "ideological constructs of a society that wants to see itself as fundamentally democratic, in which individual ambition above all determines social mobility" (Spoerhase 2018, 233). This arouses the suspicion that these narratives' success might in part be due to the fact that they appeal to meritocratic ideas, which subverts the genre's potential for shedding a critical light on the mechanisms of meritocracy itself.

Class-Passing, Hybridity and Mimicry

In the second part of her essay, Jaquet analyses what she refers to as the "complexion" of *transclasse* subjects, using this term to criticise the socio-philosophical concept of the 'person' (cf. Spoerhase 2018, 235). The *transclasse* is, Jaquet claims

> un être de métamorphose, de sorte que l'on peut non seulement se demander ce qui subsiste du moi ancien mais si l'idée d'un moi identique à lui-même malgré les changements ne perd pas toute pertinence.[4] (2014, 106)

At first, she refers to the *transclasses'* social transformation as a "mimesis" (ibid., 40). Later on, however, she describes the transition from one class position to another as an act of "*passing*," that is, to *pass as* "a member of a social group other than his or her own" (ibid., 122). I would suggest that this "passing" is in fact more an act of *mimicry* than a simple *mimesis*. It is a subaltern subject's imitation, or mimicking, of a hegemonic subject position—her class position.

In reference to colonial discourses, Homi K. Bhabha (1984) analyses mimicry as an ambiguous discursive figure destabilising symbolic-hierarchical relations. Effective colonial authority, he argues, depends upon a "reformed, recognizable Other, as *a subject of a difference that is almost the same, but not quite*" (126). The colonised subject's imitation of the coloniser seems to confirm the coloniser's authority. However, as the imitation is always only partially unsuccessful, it remains recognisable as an imitation—which is where Bhabha locates a subversive potential:

> mimicry stricken by an indeterminacy: mimicry emerges as the representation of a difference that is itself a process of disavowal. Mimicry is, thus, the sign of a *double articulation*; a complex strategy of reform, regulation, and discipline, which "appropriates" the Other as it visualizes power. (ibid.; emphasis added)

The same holds true for the passing of *transclasse* subjects. Jaquet (2018) remarks that there remains a slight "delay" in their reactions, in their observations of "the codes" of their surroundings (144) and thus their imperfect metamorphosis potentially uncovers or hints at the class-based hierarchies of social discourse. Both Bhabha and Jaquet stress that the respective mimicry they describe is accompanied by a "hybridization" (ibid., 137) of the 'mimicking' subject: "Mimicry conceals no presence or identity behind its mask," it "rearticulates the whole notion of *identity* and alienates it from essence" (Bhabha 1984, 129).

Now to come back to the methodological blind spot in Jaquet's essay: why literature? Why would literary texts prove to be productive for her reflections, not merely as examples of *transclasse* biographical experience, but as aesthetic textures? Because they are—potentially—capable of depicting precisely this process of hybridisation and hybrid identities, I would suggest. *Transclasse* subjects have become not only socially and culturally, but also linguistically alienated from their origins. And neither the language of their social origins nor the language of literature and of academic discourses alone can be adequate to tell their story. They are caught in an in-between space also linguistically, as can be seen in the quotation from Annie Ernaux above. Critics have commented upon narrative techniques of navigating this linguistic, cultural and social in-betweenness. Alex Demeulenaere (2021), in his analysis of "mechanisms of indirect speech" (149) in texts by Eribon, Louis and Nicolas Matthieu for example, has described "a fusion, a polyphonic clash between an elaborate writing style [...] and a common, precarious voice in working-class speech" (ibid., 147). In these moments of polyphony, "two [...] perspectives open up" and start to drift apart; "a position of double belonging" is articulated (ibid.). Demeulenaere remarks that Eribon, Louis and Mathieu "want to give a voice to those who are barely audible in public space" by "integrating working-class speech" into the "written, codified French language" of literature (ibid.). However, as this intention of "giving a voice" and the act of imitation itself remain perceivable in the narrative and thus hierarchise the voices of the polyphony created, it does not come as a surprise that others read the same aspects of the same texts (here Louis' debut novel) as representing the working class in a stereotypical way, that is, as a form of othering (cf. Lenz 2019).

The narrativisation of hybridity remains rudimentary in first-person narratives with claims to autobiographical authenticity, as—Spoerhase stresses exactly this in his concluding remarks on Jaquet's essay—these texts' perspectives "often remain obsessed with notions of identity that seek to substitute a harmonious and closed self for the hybrid individual" (Spoerhase 2018, 252). Consequently, he reads Jaquet's essay as "a vehement plea not to pursue the identity imaginaries that fuel th[e] fear" of the hybridisation of identities (ibid., 253). But since, as I have argued, *transclasse* narratives in the autosociobiographical mode are in themselves a limiting factor for the hybridity of narrative representations of precarious class status and class identities, we need to look beyond examples of this popular 'genre-in-the-making'—which brings me to my reading of Megan Gale Coles' *Small Game Hunting*.

Megan Gail Coles' *Small Game Hunting at the Local Coward Gun Club* (2019)

No, it is true, nothing is better for Iris and her childhood friend Olive in the medium-sized coastal town of St. John than it was in their rural homes in the impoverished Bay Area of Newfoundland. Iris, who my reading will focus on, grew up with her mother after her father left them, she "played pretend-poorer as a child to lessen the bleakness by comparison" (Coles 2019, 17). She is now in her late twenties, has studied Art in Ontario but then was neither admitted to graduate school, nor could she find an adequate position in a gallery (ibid., 21). Still, she needs to pay off her student loan, which is why she works as a waitress at the Hazel, "a faux downhome cottage restaurant" (Trnka 2021, 141), but what she has left at the end of the month is barely enough to pay her phone and electricity bill. She is having an affair with the restaurant's cook, John, whose socio-economical background is quite similar to hers, but who is married to George, daughter of one of the most influential men in town and owner of the Hazel, and John will not leave her for Iris. Even though working with him becomes more and more unbearable for her as he is taking advantage of the power he has over her, emotionally and as her superior at work, she is acutely aware that she must not lose this job.

Iris is at the centre of the novel's net of characters, who are all connected through one place: the Hazel. Over the course of the day on which the narrated events take place, they all meet there, some as guests but most as staff members.[5] It is Tuesday, a rather ordinary day, except for the fact that a blizzard is drawing in and immobilises the city of St. John in the afternoon. All the characters, guests as well as staff, are stuck at the Hazel, causing the usual conflicts between the characters to boil over—those between the employees and their superior, those between male customers and the waitresses, between John and Iris, etc. For a moment it seems as if the situation will escalate into a fist-fight, but the arrival of the most influential man in St. John, who is at the top of all the hierarchies at play, prevents anything from happening. The staff will not have stood up for themselves, they will not have acted as a group, her male co-workers will not have defended Iris against the misogynist insults she has suffered, and this Tuesday, Valentine's Day, ironically, will remain a rather normal, although abnormally depressing, day at work. Collective formation fails in the microcosm of the Hazel, because, in short, "[i]n a social world of intersecting axes of oppression, […] precariousness is […] not something we all experience to the same extent or in the same way" and precarity serves as "a means of control […] that systematically undermines workers' capacity to rebel" (Hogg 2021, 7). This becomes very tangible in the intricately structured narration of Megan Gail Coles' novel, both for its characters and readers.

In the course of the events of the day, the narrative voice moves between the characters' perspectives; we see them through the eyes of others as well as through their own perception and thoughts. No 'narrator' emerges; everything is narrated by a voice only perceivable as the voicing of other voices, the characters' or those in their heads. We as readers are put "in the uncomfortable position of occupying the minds of difficult characters, characters who are either being exploited and abused due to their marginalized social positions, or in turn, the perspectives of their abusers" (Trnka 2021, 141). Thus, power relations become tangible in a very material experience of a division into 'us' and 'them.' But what makes our position as readers even more uncomfortable is that these categories remain fluid; two characters who are on one side in one situation will be divided by different interests and positions in another.

Narrating the Precariat

Still, the focus is mainly on 'us' the staff, who (except for John) can all be described as belonging to what Guy Standing and others have termed the precariat: they lack, among other things, "employment security" or "occupational security," they almost all have "a higher level of formal schooling than the level of the job they are expected to perform" requires (Standing 2011, ix), and are humiliated by the fact that their employer seems to want "undying thanks for just above minimum wage" as she lectures them "while a pair of thousand-dollar dogs sleep at her feet" (Coles 2019, 58). Standing stresses that "what distinguishes the precariat more than labour status is the lack of an occupational identity or narrative they can give themselves" (Standing 2011, ix). This is poignantly illustrated when a woman at Iris' table bluntly tells her:

> You shouldn't be a server.
> I'm not.
> Well. … but you are.
> No. I'm not.
> My dear girl, you are serving us right now.
> I am.
> Which means you are a server.
> […]
> Iris doesn't even know how she has come to serve.
> Was it John? Or George? Her father? The past? Was it something lacking in herself? (Coles 2019, 223)

Iris works as a waitress because she sees no other option, and she does not identify with her work. Her educational background and the hopes she had for her future prevent her from having a stable professional identity working as a waitress and thus she does not feel like she is part of a coherent social group with her co-workers.

In addition to this, Iris' perspective is especially illustrative of the fact that 'us' and 'them' in the microcosm of the Hazel are not stable categories. Although it is 'us' serving 'them,' 'us' responsible for 'their' emotional well-being,[6] 'us' who are perceived to stand at the socio-cultural periphery by 'them,' who consider themselves as the centre[7]—none of these 'us's or 'them's form a homogenous group, and none of them overlap completely, especially because of the unequally vulnerable, intersectional position of each individual within different ones of those groups. For instance, Iris' male co-workers are just as unaware of Iris' vulnerability to sexist discrimination and forms of sexual violence as is her boss, who, although a woman herself, is in an independent position economically and has never worked for anybody else; and while her colleagues might want to defend her in some situations, they let her down in others for fear of losing their jobs.

Iris' lack of occupational identity as well as the vulnerability and precarity of her position at work are expressed by the use of theatrical metaphors. Her interaction with customers is repeatedly referred to as acting a part (cf. e.g. ibid., 223, 225), which is corrosive to her sense of self, especially as she is aware of the fact that her part is written and attributed to her by others who are better off:

> But baygirls make great waitresses.
> They've the ideal upbringing for the whole undertaking. Efficiency bred out of necessity centuries ago, refined by capital and industry. Taking too long resulting in sickness and/or death. (ibid., 18)

While Iris does not identify as belonging to a specific social class, others who are well above her in class terms do not hesitate to let her know where they think she belongs. In the course of the plot, Iris repeatedly faces such attitudes, and as she does, the narration exposes the (ideo)logical contradiction inherent in this form of discrimination—that is, deterministically ascribing a certain position to someone while at the same time holding them responsible for their social and financial success. It is the novel's narrative layering of different perspectives that exposes self-righteous meritocratic attitudes like these where *transclasse* first-person narrators are faced with an almost unavoidable, at least potential, complicity with meritocratic ideas. And by presenting these different perspectives it also exposes the workings of social stereotypes and prevents stereotypical representations of its characters itself.

Double(ing) Voices: The Subversive Potential of Narrative Mimicry

The passage quoted here is narrated via Iris' perspective. The bitter irony with which her thoughts are related in a form of free indirect discourse vents her desperate powerlessness and her anger, which she cannot actually articulate in her position, because the consequences she would face are severe. What we hear/read is the narrator's voice, who mimics the (unspoken) voices of the characters. As the perspective shifts from one character's mind to another, their perceptions as well as their thoughts and their memories are amalgamated into a constant stream of free indirect discourse. That is, we always hear at least two voices at once: that of the narrator and that of one of the characters. In this double voice, the proportion of the narrating voice varies. Sometimes, although rarely, it comments on the action in ways that seem almost entirely her own; sometimes it is barely perceivable, for example when reporting dialogue between the characters.

As an effect of this narrative technique, different temporal layers, that is, the (characters' perception of and thoughts on) events of the narrative present and musings on past events and flashbacks triggered by the present, overlap. This is the case in the passage quoted above. Iris, in the first of the novel's three parts ("Prep," "Lunch" and "Dinner") is on her way to work, and the train of her thoughts runs on:

> Hey misses! Hey girl! Hey Iris! Smile sure while you're at it.
> Would it kill Iris to smile while she hands them their food?
> Put on a dress, look pretty, eat nothing, have no feelings, never complain. What else can Iris do? Mississauga is calling. Welcome to the National Student Loan Service Centre–
> Ring! Ring! When her phone is actually connected.
> The government wants their money back now!
> Newfoundland has run out of fish/wood/oil and patience, again. Where did it all go?
> Spent on coke and hookers no doubt. (ibid., 19)

Here, her memory of being bullied as a teenager and her anticipation of thoughts about what customers will say/have said to her at work overlap, make her internally rage about what society expects of her, which then reminds her of the pressure to pay back her student loan. This overlapping is in part due to the fact that the novel as a whole is narrated in the present tense (except where characters remember past events). The narrative dynamic this creates is exemplary of what Liam Connell (2021) considers "[t]he characteristic form of" what he calls "the precarity novel": "a novel that presents a seemingly permanent condition of anticipation of unrealized crisis" (28). Similarly, Michiel Rys and Bart Philipsen (2021) note that "the experience of being trapped in the present, as a temporal intermediary between a lost stable past and an uncertainly fluctuating future, is an intrinsic part of precarious phenomenology and hence also of its literary representations" (8). Both Connell and Rys and Philipsen mention anxiety as (one of) the central affect(s) linked to this experience. This anxiety is linked to a "heightened risk of social regression," as—contrary to what I have argued above in reference to *transclasse* narratives with a focus on the past and stable working-class identities—"precarity [...] foregrounds the idea that the boundaries between social strata have to be imagined as permeable" (Rys and Philipsen 2021, 6).

In this example of an exceptionally flexible form of free indirect discourse from Iris' thoughts on her way to work, echoes of a multitude of conflicting voices can be heard: boys from Iris' school, men in the street, customers at the restaurant, her parents or other relatives, 'society' in general, employees of the National Student Loan Service—all blended with the angry snarling voice of the narrator. Or is it Iris' voice that, in her head, adds the aggressive, sarcastic tone? "Would it kill Iris to smile while she hands them their food?" It is the narrator who transforms a potential 'It wouldn't kill you to smile while...' uttered by a customer or maybe John or George into this biting comment by rendering it in indirect speech, of course. As the narrator accesses the sentence via Iris' memory, we are dealing with a double form of indirect speech here, but to what degree Iris' version already contained a biting undertone remains uncertain.

If we try to locate Iris' voice between this polyphony of other voices, between the power they have over her and her will to rebel, it keeps slipping away. When her train of thought comes back to rude comments by customers, we read: "She could talk back but has been socialized against it" (*SGH*, 20). Is this her own thought? Or a comment by the narrator? Here too, as in many other cases, the question remains unresolvable. We can never be quite sure in what proportion Iris is 'talking back' silently, and in what proportion the narrator is talking back for her. Both voices are present, Iris' mimicking the voices of those who have some kind of power over her, thus exposing these underlying power structures, as well as the narrator's voice mimicking Iris' thoughts. What we read is a double voice at least.

This indeterminacy creates a tension that will build up in the course of the second part of the novel, when Iris is waiting on a table where the town's mayor—ironically referred to not as Mayor, but "Major David" by the characters—is having lunch with a couple of colleagues and friends, including "Big George," as the Hazel's staff call him, George's father. The mayor arrives earlier than the rest of the group, and when he does, we get his perspective first:

Major David bets his skinny waitress does drugs. She's certainly thin enough. Her hollowed-out eyeballs suggest something quick. Cocaine. Probably buys a ball of the coke and then complains about being paid minimum wage.

That's why Major David doesn't tip. (ibid., 128)

Iris is upset and exhausted after having a fight with John the night before and again just after arriving at the Hazel. She needs to be on her guard, however, as the mayor projects onto her all that he despises. He feels that Iris is neglecting him while he waits for his company, he starts complaining and threatens to "bring this up with management" (ibid., 167). When the rest of the party has arrived, they join him in complaining about Iris and condescendingly theorising about "Baymen," knowing that this also includes Iris, who is standing at their table. Iris knows who they are, she has waited on them before, but they do not remember her, and while she is getting angry, the focalisation subtly shifts to her perspective.

Baymen, the Mayor says, giving them further permission to forge on.

[...]

Why is the rural Newfoundlander [insert anything here]?

The answer is poverty.

Why is the rural Newfoundlander [insert anything here]?

Still poverty.

Why is the rural Newfoundlander [insert anything here]?

POVERTY. POVERTY. POVERTY, FUCK!

And Iris will not discuss the shit her people buy. Buying lots of shit is not an argument against the kind of poverty they face but proof positive that they face it.

[...]

Fuck my life, Iris thinks [...]. Just nod and pretend ignorance, baygirl.

Smile. Smile for your money. Or starve. (ibid., 206f.)

That she integrates fragments of the discourse that patronises her and stigmatises her people underlines how powerless she is in this situation, and why. Her position is one that prevents her from speaking up for herself, from having a voice of her own; whatever she might say will be considered 'talking back' from the dominant perspective. She is well educated, she understands the sociological dimensions of her situation fully and precisely and would be able to explain them accurately, were she the first-person narrator of her own story. It is crucial for the intricate representation of her socio-economical position and all its consequences that the novel offers that she is not.

Conclusion

Reading Megan Cail Coles' *Small Game Hunting at the Local Coward Gun Club* in the context of autosociobiographical accounts of class relations allows for a critical reflection on contemporary narrativisation of *transclasse* identities and the mechanisms of social reproduction. The novel's narrative technique of fluidly voicing and hybridising the characters' perspectives allows for the intricate representation of a social web structured along lines of class where everyone's identity and ability to voice their perspective depends on those of others, especially for individuals with precarious class status and identity. From this vantage point, it becomes visible how autosociobiographical narratives with their single voice holding authority over narrative discourse conceal dependency and precarity on the level of form. On the plot level, the fact that the protagonist does not escape her social background and is unable to make a better life for herself sheds light on the limitations of stories told by social climbers. Their narratives carry the risk of overemphasising upward social mobility, forgetting about the risk of falling in between the rungs of the social ladder.

Notes

1. Unless otherwise indicated, all translations into English are mine.
2. Cf. Blome 2020, 545 and Christoph Schaub's contribution in this volume for his concept of a "poetics of authenticity."
3. "I then thought about my position of a *transfuge* writer-narrator who is originally from the world of the dominated, but now belongs to the world of the dominant, [...] whereas the readers belong to the dominant word [...] It's true, this is all the ambiguity of the position of literary autobiographies 'from below'... precisely because they are the biographies of those who have left this world. Whereas language, writing, speaking are the resources and instruments of the dominant culture."
4. "[S]o much a metamorphic being that one cannot only ask oneself what remains of the old Self, but also whether the idea of a Self remaining identical with itself despite all changes does not lose its plausibility altogether."
5. The Hazel thus functions as a sort of "microcosm," just like the hotel in Maria Leitner's novel *Hotel Amerika* discussed by Stephanie Marx (2021). Both novels analyse the political realities of their time in a specific context (Leitner's novel is set in New York in the 1920s) and make use of the microcosm of the hotel and the restaurant respectively to show how precarious working conditions function to prevent effective protest.
6. In his essay on James Kelman's fiction, Mathies Aarhus (2021) analyses what he calls "the affects of class," that is, the (narrative representation of) affective structures characteristic of the precariat. He points out that especially in the service industry, "marketing and

speculation in emotions" result in a commodification of what can be called 'emotional labour', thus turning "emotional life" into "a domain of inequality and stratification" (43).

7. There is a quite literal dimension to the concepts of 'centre'/'periphery' in the context of Newfoundland society. In the 1950s to the 1970s, the federal government, in an attempt "to diversify, industrialize and modernize the provincial economy" by, among other things, providing "health care, education, electricity and transportation to all residents of the province," urged the population of remote areas along the Bays into larger, more accessible 'growth areas', which resulted in the abandonment of many communities (Martin 2006a). They were promised "employment on the offshore draggers and trawlers, in the new fish plants, or in spin-off industries," which "was to be the fishery of the future, with good wages and secure employment" (Martin 2006b). However, the reality was that many families were economically worse off after resettlement and the experience of dislocation, the necessity to adopt to a new lifestyle and the loss of cultural identity caused much distress. The novel threatens to reverse this socio-cultural centre-periphery relation, especially in the sections focalised on Iris (cf. e.g. Coles 2019, 205).

References

Aarhus, Mathies G. 2021. "Anxiety in the Precariat: The Affects of Class in James Kelman's Fiction." In *Precarity in Contemporary Literature and Culture*, edited by Peter Simonsen and Emily J. Hogg, 42–55. London: Bloomsbury Academic.

Bhabha, Homi K. 1984. "Of Mimicry and Man: The Ambivalence of Colonial Discourse." *October* 28: 125–133.

Blome, Eva. 2020. "Rückkehr zur Herkunft: Autosoziobiografien erzählen von der Klassengesellschaft." *Deutsche Vierteljahrsschrift für Literaturwissenschaft und Geistesgeschichte* 94: 541–571.

Blome, Eva, Philipp Lammers, and Sarah Seidel. 2022. *Autosoziobiographie: Poetik und Politik*. Berlin, Heidelberg: J. B. Metzler.

Coles, Megan Gail. 2019. *Small Game Hunting at the Local Coward Gun Club*. Toronto: House of Anansi Press.

Connell, Liam. 2021. "Anxious Reading: The Precarity Novel and the Affective Class." In *Precarity in Contemporary Literature and Culture*, edited by Peter Simonsen and Emily J. Hogg, 27–41. London: Bloomsbury Academic.

Demeulenaere, Alex. 2021. "Writing the Voices of Precarity in Contemporary French Literature." In *Literary Representations of Precarious Work, 1840 to the Present*, edited by Michiel Rys and Bart Philipsen, 145–158. Cham: Palgrave Macmillan.

Ernaux, Annie, and Isabelle Charpentier. 2005. "La littérature est une arme de combat...." In *Rencontres avec Pierre Bourdieu*, edited by Gérard Mauger, 159–175. Broissieux: Éditions du Croquant.

Ernst, Christina. 2020. "'Arbeiterkindliteratur' nach Eribon: Autosoziobiographie in der deutschsprachigen Gegenwartsliteratur." *Lendemain* 180: 77–91.

Hogg, Emily J. 2021. "Introduction." In *Precarity in Contemporary Literature and Culture*, edited by Peter Simonsen and Emily J. Hogg, 1–24. London: Bloomsbury Academic.

Jaquet, Chantal. 2014. *Les transclasses ou la non-reproduction.* Paris: PUF.

Jaquet, Chantal. 2018. *Zwischen den Klassen: Über die Nicht-Reproduktion sozialer Macht. Mit einem Nachwort von Carlos Spoerhase.* Translated by Horst Brühmann. Göttingen: Konstanz University Press.

Lenz, Markus A. 2019. "'Parallelgesellschaft' der Retrospektive oder Klassenbewusstsein des Außenseiters? Didier Eribons *Retour à Reims* und Édouard Louis' *En finir avec Eddy Belleguele." Romanische Studien Beihefte* 8: 163–177.

Lorey, Isabell. 2015. *State of Insecurity: Government of the Precarious.* Translated by Aileen Derieg. London, New York: Verso.

Martin, Melanie. 2006a. "Centralization." Newfoundland and Labrador Heritage. Accessed 6 December 2022. https://www.heritage.nf.ca/articles/politics/centralization. php.

Martin, Melanie. 2006b. "Was Resettlement Justified?" Newfoundland and Labrador Heritage. Accessed 6 December 2022. https://www.heritage.nf.ca/articles/politics/resettlement-analysis.php.

Marx, Stephanie. 2021. "The Impossibility of Protest: Precarity in Maria Leitner's Reportage Novel *Hotel Amerika*." In *Literary Representations of Precarious Work, 1840 to the Present*, edited by Michiel Rys and Bart Philipsen, 73–87. Cham: Palgrave Macmillan.

McRobbie, Angela. 2010. "Reflections on Feminism, Immaterial Labour and the Post-Fordist Regime." *New Formations* 70 (Autumn): 60–76.

Rys, Michiel, and Bart Philipsen. 2021. "Introduction: Poetics and Precarity: Literary Representations of Precarious Work, Past and Present." In *Literary Representations of Precarious Work, 1840 to the Present*, edited by Michiel Rys and Bart Philipsen, 1–19. Cham: Palgrave Macmillan.

Schaub, Christoph. 2020. "Autosoziobiografisches und autofiktionales Schreiben über Klasse in Didier Eribons *Retour à Reims*, Daniela Dröschers *Zeige deine Klasse* und Karin Strucks *Klassenliebe." Lendemain* 180: 64–76.

Spoerhase, Carlos. 2018. "Aufstiegsangst: Zur Autosoziobiographie des Klassenübergängers." In Chantal Jaquet, *Zwischen den Klassen: Über die Nicht-Reproduktion sozialer Macht*, 231–253. Göttingen: Konstanz University Press.

Standing, Guy. 2011. *The Precariat: The New Dangerous Class.* London: Bloomsbury Academic.

Trnka, Alexandra. 2021. "Megan Gail Coles: *Small Game Hunting at the Local Coward Gun Club." Newfoundland and Labrador Studies* 31, no. 1: 141–144.

3.2

Obstacles to Leaving, Problems of Arriving

Gender and Genealogy in Contemporary German Narratives
of the Social Climber (Christian Baron, Bov Bjerg,
Deniz Ohde, Anke Stelling)

IRENE HUSSER

Over the last years, social problems and questions of class have gained importance in German literature; literary scholar Leonhard Herrmann (2021) even
diagnoses a "social turn" in texts of authors like Sybille Berg, Deniz Ohde, and
Marlene Streeruwitz. There are various literary and non-literary reasons for this
new-found interest. After the rise of neoliberalism in the 1980s and 1990s and
its large-scale enforcement in the 2000s (for instance, the German 'Hartz IV'
agenda was launched in 2005), the 2010s showed the consequences of neoliberal
social politics in Western societies: the increasing divide between rich and poor,
the erosion of the middle class, the rising number of social upheavals, the up-
surge of right-wing populism. These shifts in social reality resonated with a literary field that is dominated by realist poetics, at the heart of which lies the ambition to convey socially representative and relevant content and to make societal
contributions (Tommek 2015). Influenced by the international success of French
authors Annie Ernaux, Didier Eribon, and Édouard Louis, who have shaped
the genre of autosociobiography (Spoerhase 2017; Blome, Lammers and Seidel
2022) and popularised class narratives in contemporary literature, the German
literary and cultural field in the late 2010s/early 2020s has become intensely invested in themes of class and social inequality.

Nevertheless, certain methodical challenges have arisen together with problems faced by literary scholars when dealing with contemporary fiction and
autofiction that revolve around the themes of class society and social mobility.
These sociologically informed texts operate with and sometimes openly reflect
on theoretical concepts of class, milieu, habitus, field and so forth, so that the
literary scholar is apparently left with identifying these concepts and confirming

that the texts are sociologically well-informed. These epistemological troubles are aggravated by the realist mode of the texts. Moritz Baßler (2013; 2021) argues in a structuralist tradition that texts applying realist techniques engage in world-building by adopting collective cultural frames and scripts and thereby tend to rather affirm than challenge the readers' (e.g. sociological) knowledge and worldview. Analyses that dwell on the thematic concept are therefore prone to reproduce what has already been reproduced by popular realism.

A way out of this interpretative deadlock is to focus on narrative strategies and devices that construct and convey meaning by following some and dismissing other literary traditions, tropes, and socio-cultural scripts: these are concepts of freedom and determinism, autonomy and heteronomy, individual and society that have defined the discourse of social climbing since the eighteenth and nineteenth century. An enormous part of contemporary fiction and autofiction on class still explores upward social movement. This narrative preference cannot, therefore, be only attributed to the authors' biographical contexts.[1] The experience of social transgression also proves the existence of classes and class borders, legitimises the act of exposing the world of the underprivileged and gives occasion to reflect on questions of social justice in the twenty-first century. Contemporary narratives of the social climber take the protagonists back to their biographical starting points and showcase their estrangement together with their emotional and/or political involvement with their milieu of origin. By following this plot structure, contemporary class (auto)fiction focuses on the determining role of family and descent for social mobility, and in doing so, also explores the influence of gender and gender images on disengaging from one's social upbringing. In this chapter, I will argue that this link between genealogy and gender serves to express an ambivalent view on the possibilities of upward social movement, reflecting the narrators' disidentification from, yet bond to, their milieu of descent and its gender norms, as well as their remaining discomfort with the milieu of arrival and its rejection of working-class life.

Class, Gender and (Anti-)Genealogy: A Historical Sketch

The figure of the social climber can be traced back to ancient and Christian sources, reappearing in literary modernity in the eighteenth century, since then taking many masks as picaresque hero, parvenu or self-made man. In German literature of the eighteenth century, this figure is closely linked to the idea of *Bildung* and the genre of the *Bildungsroman* (for example, Karl Philipp Moritz's *Anton Reiser*), whereas nineteenth- and early twentieth-century literature—meaning Realist novels by Gustav Freytag, Fanny Lewald or Friedrich Spielhagen, (fictional as well as non-fictional) self-made narratives from the turn of the century and Weimar literature—instead focuses on aspects of wealth and success that are presented as the drive for and purpose of the characters' development.[2] The recurrence of this figure underlies the social climber as a paradigmatic modern subject who represents individual autonomy instead of social determinism, the future instead of the past, and discontinuity instead of tradition. From philosophers of the Enlightenment to French Revolutionists, bourgeois culture in the eighteenth century opposes the heredity of offices and rights, "futurizing the concept of generation" (Parnes, Vedder and Willer 2008, 82–119; see also Moretti 2000, 3–6); Benjamin Brückner (2019) argues that this shift from genealogy to descendance is popularised and radicalised in the nineteenth-century life sciences with biological, psychiatric, hygienic, and other discourses underlining the dangers of heritage and heredity for future generations (77–128). It is only under these historical circumstances that the social climber becomes a mirror for anti-genealogical phantasies of self-production and self-efficacy. The occurrence of this figure usually coincides with times of change and crisis when modern societies need to bolster or question meritocratic values.

Scholars like James V. Catano (1990; 2001) and Jana Vijayakumaran (2022) have pointed out that anti-genealogical narratives of social advancement are generally male narratives that promote certain gender norms and ideals—for example, the late nineteenth- and early twentieth-century narrative of the self-made man is a narrative of self-creation that presents the image of a potent, virile, individualistic, and strong-minded masculinity. This masculinity is resolutely defined

> against the feminine by presenting two negative arguments. The most specific negative appeal in a myth concerned with origins alludes to escape from the mother. A second, more subtle appeal encourages departure from the realm of the feminine, with its daily interpersonal concerns, and a subsequent movement into the mythical realm of individual and corporate battle. (Catano 1995, 426)

The self-made man is origin-free in terms of his maternal origins and female influence in general, his virile agility and vigorousness serving as a discursive counterpoint to cultural diagnoses of modern decadence, decay, and exhaustion (Vijayakumaran 2022, 48–49).

Nevertheless, there are also female narratives of social transgression that in the nineteenth century often build upon a heteronomous structure with the heroines marrying into the upper class. This plot predestines female class narratives to promote values of compromise and social reconciliation, though Gunhild Kübler (1982) shows that realist writers as Wilhelm Raabe and Theodor Fontane

likewise explore failed social advancement and, in doing so, criticise the meritocratic ideology and materialism of bourgeois society.[3] Female social climbers in
nineteenth-century literature are thereby not only more likely to fail, but also require other qualities than their male counterparts: Kübler argues that, particularly in fiction by popular female authors like Eugenie Marlitt and Minna Kautsky,
successful social advancement is reserved for heroines who embody the ideal of
the innocent woman, that is to say, who affirm bourgeois gender-specific morals
instead of performing the materialistic, economic principles of bourgeois society.

In modern bourgeois society, masculinity and femininity function as metaphors for rather abstract social relations and structural conflicts (Koschorke
2000), enabling the description and management of these problems—with systems of hetero-reference being encoded as female and self-referentiality being
viewed a male principle (Kucklick 2008, 209–236). By regarding femininity and
masculinity as cultural codes, it is possible to differentiate between narratives
with male/female characters, on the one hand, and gendered cultural codes that
are applied to these characters to narrate class society, on the other. Considering this, when it comes to social mobility, narratives with male protagonists
historically promote values of individualism, self-efficacy, and autogenesis that
are presented as male virtues. Narratives with female characters tend to apply a
heteronomous plot structure, conveying the image of the dependent, yet morally impeccable woman, and focus more on limitations and borders of class society. Literature can perpetuate these concepts, but also explore conflicts that
arise from gender binarism and even defy the notion of "Geschlechtscharaktere"
(natural gender dispositions) (Hausen 1976). Social advancement of male characters can be displayed within a female narrative and vice versa—as, for example,
texts on the New Woman in Weimar literature do: the character Gilgi in Irmgard
Keun's novel of the same name (1931) must adapt to the modern working world
and its values of individualism, self-control, and self-reliance to economically
survive, sacrificing her romantic, giving, sensual self that is encoded as female.

On that basis this chapter sets out to explore the themes of genealogy and gender in contemporary novels of class advancement. On the one hand, it examines
the gendered cultural scripts and codes of social mobility to which the narratives
adhere, and on the other, it elicits how these scripts are employed to voice gender
troubles that come up in the process of social transgression in the twenty-first
century. On that note, I will take a closer look at the texts of Christian Baron, Bov
Bjerg, Deniz Ohde, and Anke Stelling, and analyse different gender–genealogical
constellations. This approach helps to contextualise the novels in their relation
to historical cultural perceptions of class and gender and understand their socio-
political agendas that build on these patterns while also challenging them.

Fathers: Objects of Patricide and Pity

Since the eighteenth century, with thinkers like John Locke and Immanuel Kant, the patriarch (in the political as well as in the familial sense), who rules despotically over his household/country and demands obedience from his family members/subjects, becomes a suspect figure, contradicting the new enlightened ideals of the autonomous, rational, mature individual (Thomä 2008, 28–47). Nevertheless, modernity is still haunted by the patriarchal nightmare: the image of the cruel, imperious, unforgiving father and his claim to absolute power. The fear of this atavistic figure is also why—from Johann Wolfgang Goethe's early works to those of Franz Kafka and literary modernism—German literature has extensively fantasised about (real or metaphorical) patricide: the patriarch not only represents asymmetrical (familial, social and political) power relations but also embodies tradition and genealogy.

In the same way, adjacent disciplines employ the trope of patricide to reflect on modernity's relation to authority and tradition. For Sigmund Freud, the murder of the forefather and the sons' guilt over their patricide lie at the origin of religion and morality. In sociology, Pierre Bourdieu (1999) argues that social reproduction in modern meritocratic societies *requires* patricide: the "successful inheritance is a murder of the father accomplished at the father's injunction, a going beyond the father that will preserve him and preserve as well his own 'project' of going beyond" (508). Bourdieu thereby denies patricide to be an exclusively anti-genealogical act when the process of succession implies the idea of advancement that can only be achieved through extending the father's achievements. Bourdieu indicates that this structure of inheritance is characteristic of middle-class ideology; upper and lower classes, on the other hand, tend to reproduce themselves through preservation. Provided that the "son's identification with the father's desire as a desire for preservation produces an unproblematic inheritor" (ibid., 508), the most radical form of patricide can be attributed to a person who, in an anti-genealogical manner, refuses the father's desire for mere preservation.

This radical gesture is topical for contemporary narratives of the social climber. The fathers in texts by Bjerg, Baron, and Ohde represent repetition and stagnation. In Bjerg's *Serpetinen* (*Serpentines*, 2020),[4] the male protagonist, a professor of sociology from a rural working-class family, comes from a line of suicidal fathers: his own father killed himself when the protagonist was a teenager. The father in Baron's *Ein Mann seiner Klasse* (*A Man of His Class,* 2020) is a copy of his own brutal, abusive, and aggressive father, the narrator's grandfather, who is at the centre of Baron's latest novel *Schön ist die Nacht* (*Beautiful is the Night,* 2022). In Ohde's *Streulicht* (*Scattered Light,* 2020), the daughter returns to her hometown and her father's house. The novel captures the paralysing, almost *post-histoire* atmosphere of a post-industrial city that is embodied in the father and his living arrangements. His apartment is flooded with wastepaper and other old, useless things, reflecting his adherence to the past and his milieu of origin. This trait of nostalgia and the fear of change are presented as a paternal heritage: "Mein Großvater und mein Vater waren vom selben Schlage: Sie hassten Veränderungen, schon das Reden darüber ihnen zuwider"[5] (Ohde 2020, 24). Though given the chance to attend a school for higher education, the narrator's father chooses the life of his paternal ancestors, serving in the military and completing an apprenticeship in the same company as his father did.

All three texts suggest that breaking the vicious circle of paternal inheritance is a necessity. This process is usually initiated by establishing a physical (leaving the hometown) and, by this, emotional distance that allows the protagonists to dissociate from the fathers' values as well as their fears of failure. The texts of Baron and Bjerg furthermore demonstrate that, for the male protagonists, patricide first and foremost aims at the gender norms of the working-class milieu. The first-person narrators in *Ein Mann seiner Klasse* and *Serpentinen* revolt against concepts of masculinity identified with dominance, virility, and physical strength. The texts expose this masculinity as toxic since it enables misogyny, homophobia, racism, and violence, as well as self-destructive behaviours. Since the fathers' identities are essentially based on the exclusion of the—female, queer, foreign, and so forth—other, for the male characters, patricide comes along with revoking these exclusions and identifying with the excluded: the protagonist in Bjerg's novel takes his wife's last name; the narrator in Baron's *Ein Mann seiner Klasse* befriends a boy with a migrant background and later in life chooses a career in writing, when in his childhood he had to be careful about showing interest in poetry and other things his father considered feminine.

Nevertheless, the texts do not simply present strong-minded subjects who, in enacting patricide, move on from their milieu of origin, but rather explore the powers of genealogy and class descent. The protagonist in Bjerg's *Serpentinen* feels haunted by the male curse of destruction and self-destruction. At the beginning of the novel, the narrator likewise finds himself considering suicide; he admits to reproducing the alcoholism and toxic male behaviour he has desperately tried to get away from. Similarly, the first-person narrator in Baron's autosociobiography (2020) reflects on struggling with a violent temper in his teenage years that he ascribes to his upbringing in a culture of male violence: "In wenigen Jahren, so hoffte ich, würden Kneipenschlägereien für mich normal warden, ich würde zur Bundeswehr gehen und dort trinkfest werden"[6] (160), the narrator focalises his younger self who regarded his father as a role model. Ohde's novel ends with the father's comforting as well as resigning message to his daughter:

"Wenn's nichts wird, kommst wieder heim"[7] (ibid., 285), indicating that the social transgression is not completed yet, that there is still a chance of failing, that
the milieu's self-sabotaging ways might prevail in the end.

This focus on the powers of genealogy shows that contemporary class narratives are particularly interested in the struggles and obstacles of class advancement and disagree with the (neo-)liberal idea of the fully autonomous, origin-
free subject. Though the narrators succeed in climbing the social ladder, the
texts explore what ties them to their social origin and show the impossibility of
a clean break. The irreducibility of genealogy is forcefully illustrated by a plot
structure that most contemporary narratives of social transgression employ: in
the narrative present, the protagonists deal with absent, that is, already deceased
or physically ill and mentally broken patriarchs. This narrative construction, on
the one hand, evades a direct confrontation with the imperious, virile patriarch
and affirms his paralysing impact; on the other, his absence stands in the way of
an ultimate break from the past. The protagonist in Bjerg's novel (2020) regrets
not having a father to kill and free himself from: "Den Vater umzubringen oder
den Stiefvater, das war die Befreiung. Doch was sollte einer tun, wenn der Vater
sich selbst umbrachte? Wie konnte einer sich befreien?"[8] (71) The text argues
that the symbolic patricide is insufficient, that it implies the danger of self-denial
and self-hatred when not accompanied by introspection and—as Didier Eribon
(2017, 73–97), following Bourdieu, calls it—a critical "re-appropriation" of the
paternal tradition.

For the narrators, this re-appropriation inevitably raises the question of
whether there was ever a consummate patriarch to begin with. Baron's text presents the father as a divided self, as his abrasive, brutal side is contrasted with his
damaged body and resigned spirit. Baron's autosociobiography bears a resemblance to Édouard Louis' *Qui a tué mon père* (*Who Killed My Father*, 2018), directly alluding to the French title: "Wer oder was hat meinen Vater umgebracht?
Sein Kummer? Seine Krankheit? Sein Körper? Seine Arbeit? Seine Armut? Seine
Klasse? Sein Sohn?"[9] (Baron 2020, 279). In his text, Louis contrasts the patriarchal nightmare from his childhood with the present-day father who suffers from
many illnesses and physical ailments that are considered to be the result of the
government's social and labour policy. The father's damaged and disabled body
is highly politicised. It arouses pity and is a sign of social injustice that calls for
systemic change, the text culminating in a demand for revolution. Baron's text is
less explicit. Where Louis enumerates social policy measures in France's recent
history and explores their impacts on the male working-class body, Baron relies
more on showing rather than telling a link between the macro- and microcosm,
building on the readers' cultural knowledge about class and society. Nonetheless,
both texts aim at reconciling the son with the father and politically connecting

the narrators with their milieus of origin. The absence of the patriarch allows the reader to see the vulnerable man behind the violent, authoritarian mask and understand (not excuse) his toxic behaviour as a form of compensation and re-production.

Contemporary narratives of the social climber therefore participate in the modern deconstruction of patriarchy—by, on the one hand, employing the trope of patricide and, on the other, exposing the patriarch as a vulnerable, divided and pitiful self. This dialectics of disidentification[10] and critical re-appropriation of the paternal tradition aims at exploring the injustices of class society. The narrators struggle with disentangling themselves from their roots, but they also find new ways of declaring their solidarity with their class origin. In confronting their fathers, the protagonists explore their (voluntary and involuntary) ties to their social origin and explain their departure negatively—as a desire for distinction: the male narrators reject constituent aspects of their fathers' gender identities, Ohde's female character disidentifies with her father's self-sufficiency. Still, the texts also explore positive reasons for social advancement by focusing on the mother figures.

Mothers: Anti-Genealogy and its Pitfalls

Every narrative of social advancement struggles with the question of why people feel the need to leave (or rather, in most cases, escape) their origins and how they manage to do so. Contemporary narratives show the working-class milieu, embodied by the father, as depressing, suffocating, and toxic, yet the narrators not only explore their alienation from it, but also detect a maternal tradition of not-belonging. The mother in Bjerg's novel, who was born in former eastern territories of Germany, has always remained a stranger in the Swabian Alps, her husband's homeland. Whereas the father of the first-person narrator was a life-long Nazi, the protagonist remembers a scene at the kitchen table, in which the mother, a simple working-class woman, quotes from Paul Celan's poem "Todes-fuge" ("Deathfugue"). In Baron's *Ein Mann seiner Klasse*, the narrator remembers his late mother as an artistically gifted, sensitive, warm-hearted woman who is destroyed by patriarchal physical and psychological violence and dies an early death from ovarian cancer. After his mother's death, he is raised by his two aunts who also—each in her own way—do not conform to their milieu of origin and its gender roles: his aunt Juli takes up the role of the "Familienoberhaupt" ("head of the family") (Baron 2020, 226) that is usually designated to the patriarch, while his Aunt Ela has married into the "Bildungsbürgertum" (ibid., 233) and intro-duces the narrator to high culture and art.

In both texts, the mothers (and mother-like characters) are constructed as not fully adjusted to their class of origin, thereby serving as a mirror to the sons' non- and disidentification with their social backgrounds. Because the working-class milieu is shown to perpetuate a patriarchal system in which the female is othered and excluded, male narrators, in their rejection of working-class masculinity, solidarise and identify with the other. Interestingly, the mothers and female relatives rarely succeed in overcoming their social origin—exceptions are Baron's Aunt Ela and, in non-German literature, the mother in Édouard Louis' *Combats et Metamorphoses d'une femme* (*A Woman's Battles and Transformations*, 2021). In other cases, the mothers have neither the will nor the means to leave tradition behind, but they do pass the sense of not-belonging on to their children, who accomplish what their mothers were not capable of: the narrator in Baron's text becomes a novelist and journalist—a career path that was closed to his mother who also wrote poems, but was ignored and even ridiculed for it by her teachers.

In male narratives of the social climber, the identification with the mother is told without significant ambivalence. The socially deviant mother offers a matrilineal explanation for the capability to transgress. Daughter narratives, on the other hand, struggle with the mother figures, questioning not only their gender identity, but also their social nonconformism. Like Baron's and Louis' texts, Ohde's novel explores the mother's road to independence: She emigrated from her home country of Turkey on her own, refusing to subordinate herself to strict religious rules, and even left her husband for a short period of time. The novel encodes the yearning for freedom as female—not only in the mother's and daughter's biographies, but also in a short neighbourly scene witnessed by the narrator: a woman on a balcony opposite tells her lover that they "müssen hier weg" ("need to get away from here") (Ohde 2020, 216), while her male counterpart remains silent and, so the narrator assumes, refuses to see the oppressiveness of their town.

Despite this female transgressive potential, Ohde's narrator recognises a "Bigotterie" ("bigotry") (2020, 226) in her mother's self-identification as a strong-minded woman. The daughter takes umbrage at her mother's view on womanhood, regarding her husband, and men in general, as a "Naturgewalt" ("force of nature") (ibid., 229) that women need to face. The narrator deconstructs this image of the confident female who bears her husband's outbursts of rage with serenity as resignation and holds it against her mother that she did not resist her husband, passing this self-sufficiency on to her daughter: "Man konnte nicht davon ausgehen, dass es auf der Welt etwas Besseres gab, man konnte es nicht einfach so einfordern. Das habe ich von ihr gelernt"[11] (ibid., 226). The mother cannot serve as a role model for liberation because she abandoned the road to female independence,[12] yet the narrator at the same time takes up this unfinished project that logically results in class transgression: independence, self-actualisation and emancipation, which until the nineteenth and early twentieth century were seen as a bourgeois male project, have become values of the individualistic upper-middle-class milieu (Koppetsch 2001) in the second half of the twentieth century. The mother could have never indulged in her heretical impulses in the working class, so it is left to the daughter to follow in her footsteps.

Ohde's narrative illustrates Bourdieu's (1999) concept of the social climber's "habitus divided against itself, in constant negotiation with itself and with its ambivalence" (511), but instead of murdering the father in order to "preserve him and preserve as well his own 'project' of going beyond" (ibid., 508), the narrator in *Streulicht* inherits her mother's impulse to 'go beyond' and must commit matricide in order to accomplish the project of female independence. The narrator counteracts her mother's bigotry by revoking the "Unwissenheit" ("ignorance" or "lack of knowledge") (Ohde 2020, 41) she was exposed to as a child and addressing controversial socio-political issues that the parent tried to protect her from. Growing up as the daughter of a Turkish mother, the narrator witnessed racism and became a victim of a racist assault, which the mother regarded as an accident and a misunderstanding: "Aber du kannst nicht gemeint sein. Du bist Deutsche"[13] (ibid., 49). The text presents this inability to address obvious problems as a working-class mentality, a self-protective mechanism which defines the mother's and father's social roles, all of which constitutes exactly what the narrator needs to overcome—implying that the novel, on a self-referential level, can be seen as a manifestation of this process.

In Anke Stelling's *Schäfchen im Trockenen*[14] (2018), the female narrator, a mother herself, likewise attributes her social advancement to a maternal inheritance, but she dismantles the female "Hoffnung auf Neuanfang, auf Unschuld"[15] (Stelling 2019, 141) as naïve and socially affirmative. Whereas Ohde's protagonist identifies with the bourgeois individualistic claim for female self-liberation and accuses her mother of having failed to accomplish it, Stelling's narrator accuses mothers like hers of passing their dreams of freedom on to their daughters—"ohne Idee davon oder Hinweis darauf, wie sie vielleicht zu verwirklichen wären"[16] (ibid., 8). Stelling rejects the idea of liberation put forth from an unenlightened point of view, i.e. one which disregards socio-economic realities and social power relations. In her adult life, the narrator recognises distinctions between herself as a social climber and her friends who come from an upper-middle-class social background—distinctions that lead to a break. The narrator must learn that genealogy matters in terms of material inheritance and struggles with addressing these issues in a meritocratic society that is ruled by the neoliberal idea that anybody can economically succeed if they have the will to do so.

Unlike Baron's or Ohde's text, Stelling's novel is written from the standpoint of a person who has lived among the bourgeois establishment for decades and wonders how she could not see the difference. The search for explanations leads her to her mother's self-delusion and again "Unwissenheit"[17] ("ignorance" or "lack of knowledge") (ibid., 56), for which the narrator tries to compensate. The novel is addressed to the narrator's eldest daughter, whom she tries to save from the misconceptions she has been exposed to all her life:

> Anders als meine Mutter werde ich nicht davon ausgehen, dass sie mit der Zeit schon erfährt, was sie wissen muss; anders als Renate und ihre Freundinnen werde ich nichts zurückhalten in der Vorstellung, dass meine Erzählung die Kinder negativ beeinflussen, entmutigen oder in ihrer Entfaltung behindern könnte. Im Gegenteil, ich stelle mir vor, dass ich sie ausrüste mit Wissen und Geschichten. Dass ich sie nicht naiv und leichten Mutes, sondern beladen mit Erkenntnissen und Interpretationen losschicke—Rüstung und Waffen wiegen nun mal.[18] (ibid., 12)

In all four examples, the narrators' estrangement from their milieus of origin is not only traced back to their mothers, but this narrative arrangement also constructs a tradition of not-belonging or of a longing to leave which inherently refuses the idea of autogenesis. At the beginning of this chapter, I argued that masculinity and femininity in bourgeois society function as metaphors for rather abstract social relations, with systems of hetero-reference being traditionally encoded as female and systems of self-referentiality being described as male. Though not every text is as outspoken in its critique of neoliberalism as Stelling's novel, contemporary narratives of the social climber contradict the idea of a socially permeable, meritocratic society and, in (among other things)[19] constructing a maternal tradition of anti-genealogy, display a heteronomous, historically female-associated structure.

Despite this common ground, male and female narrators show a different degree of identification with their mothers, which implies that the references to the parents also serve to express conflicts of gender identity that come with social advancement. For male characters, class transgression requires a critique of working-class masculinity, which is enacted through identification with the female other, whereas female narrators reject the patriarchal tradition, but also address female failure to break with this tradition. Therefore, Stelling's and Ohde's narratives, more than Baron's and Bjerg's texts, reflect on the idea of emancipation, exploring its conditions and constraints, but also—with Stelling's narrator redefining motherhood—looking for ways of accomplishing it.

Concluding Remarks

This chapter set out to explore ways in which modern class societies employ binary gender codes as a mode of self-description and self-critique and to illuminate the role of literature in these negotiations. Comparing contemporary narratives of the social climber with narratives of the late nineteenth and early twentieth centuries, one can see that many twenty-first century literary works reject of idea of autogenesis and autonomy by, on the one hand, embedding the impulse to leave in a female tradition of not-belonging, while, on the other, presenting characters who fail to fully break with the paternal genealogy. This focus on genealogy voices doubts about the idea of absolute freedom and individualism, though the texts at the same time do not renounce the project of social climbing but explore structural obstacles as well as challenges and rebounds that come with it.

Regarding class narratives in terms of gender also makes clear that in bourgeois society gender additionally bears a distinctive quality. Contemporary bourgeois culture promotes an anti-patriarchal set of values—a mindset that can be traced to eighteenth-century literature, which attempted to redefine the patriarch as a loving, forgiving father, while working-class masculinity, with its stress on physical strength and dissociation from the feminine, is nowadays viewed as outdated and toxic. Contemporary narratives of the social climber reproduce this discourse of toxic masculinity, yet the texts do not simply condemn traditional working-class masculinity but depict, and in some cases declare their political solidarity with the disabled, emotionally suffering, and insecure individuals that the protagonists' violent fathers equally are.

Literature is not only capable of exposing that modern societies rely on binary gender codes but can also explore the effects of these structures on individuals and their gender identities. The texts broach the issue of gender troubles that come with social transgression. Male narrators are required to break with the norms of working-class masculinity and identify with the other of the patriarchal system, the female-encoded tradition of not-belonging and individualism, whereas female narrators struggle with finding a female role model, refusing their mothers' self-delusional habits, but also not coming to terms with upper-middle-class femininity (embodied by the narrator's best friend Sophia in Ohde's *Streulicht*). By alienating their protagonists from the gender norms they were raised by, applying historically female narratives to male characters and vice versa (female longing for emancipation), but also by showing the destructive effects of working-class masculinity and femininity on the parent generation, all texts participate in the contemporary deconstruction of gender binaries and thereby show their alignment with bourgeois culture.

Nevertheless, this deconstruction does not mean full adjustment and uncritical identification, and the texts also indicate problems of arriving in the middle- to upper-class individualist milieu. Stelling in particular voices discomfort and accuses her bourgeois friends of hypocrisy, but Ohde and Bjerg also depict the not-fully-belonging of their narrators to their milieu of arrival. Just as the protagonists are incapable of leaving their descent behind, the texts display an ambivalence regarding the narrators' attitude to the upper-middle-class set of values: they, on the one hand, identify (or have identified) with its emancipatory, individualistic promises and, on the other, become aware of the exclusion that comes with it.

Notes

1. Many of the texts can be counted among the genre of autosociobiography or rather autofiction: they are written by authors who themselves come from an underprivileged social background and blur the line between autobiography and fiction. For the role of this authenticity-suggesting genre in contemporary popular realism, cf. Baßler 2022.
2. For a comparison of the two genres *Bildungsroman* and *Aufstiegsroman*, cf. Vijayakumaran 2022, 119–150.
3. On economic criticism in realist literature of the nineteenth century, see Breyer and Thanner 2019; and Schößler and Blaschke 2019.
4. The titles' translations as well as the following translations of passages from Baron's, Bjerg's, Ohde's and Stelling's novels are my own.
5. "My grandfather and father were of the same kind: they hated change, were repulsed by the mere mentioning of it."
6. "In a few years, so I hoped, bar fights would become a part of my everyday life, I would join the army and be able to hold my drink."
7. "If this does not work out, you'll just come back home."
8. "Murdering the father or stepfather, that was liberation. But what should one do if the father killed himself? How could one liberate oneself?"
9. "Who or what killed my father? His grief? His illness? His body? His work? His poverty? His class? His son?"
10. For this aspect see also Jaquet 2018, 106–134.
11. "One could not assume that there was something better in the world, one could not simply claim something. That I learned from her."
12. Cf. "Nie war es ihr darum gegangen, mir diese Unabhängigkeit vorzuleben, die sie erfasst hatte, als sie mit zehn oder elf Jahren heimlich Schweinefleisch aß" ("She was never about setting an example of that independence that had gripped her when she decided to eat pork at the age of ten or eleven") (Ohde 2020, 229).

13. "They don't mean you. You're German."
14. There is no literal translation for this title; it builds on the German saying "seine Schäf-chen ins Trockene bringen," which is equivalent to the English idiom "to feather one's own nest."
15. "[H]ope for a fresh start, for innocence."
16. "[W]ithout having an idea or giving a clue on how to achieve them."
17. The same term is used in Ohde's novel, as discussed above.
18. "Unlike my mother, I will not assume that she will learn with time what she needs to know; unlike Renate and her friends, I will not hold back thinking that my story might have a negative influence on the children, discourage them or interfere with their de-velopment. On the contrary, I imagine that I supply them with knowledge and stories. That I send them off burdened with insight and interpretation—armour and weapons are a heavy weight."
19. Baron and Ohde also focus on the role of the educational system and other public institutions that usually thwart, but in some rare cases (for example, with dedicated teachers) enable, upward social mobility.

References

Baßler, Moritz. 2013. "Die Unendlichkeit des realistischen Erzählens: Eine kurze Ge-schichte moderner Textverfahren und die narrativen Optionen der Gegenwart." In *Die Unendlichkeit des Erzählens: Der Roman in der deutschen Gegenwartsliteratur seit 1989*, edited by Carsten Rohde and Hansgeorg Schmidt-Bergmann, 27–45. Bielefeld: Aisthesis.
Baßler, Moritz. 2021. "Der neue Midcult." *POP. Kultur und Kritik* 18 (Spring): 132–149.
Baßler, Moritz. 2022. *Populärer Realismus: Von International Style gegenwärtigen Er-zählens*. Munich: Beck.
Baron, Christian. 2020. *Ein Mann seiner Klasse*. 3rd ed. Berlin: Ullstein.
Bjerg, Bov. 2020. *Serpetinen*. 3rd ed. Berlin: Ullstein.
Blome, Eva, Phillip Lammers, and Sarah Seidel, eds. 2022. *Autosoziographie: Poetik und Politik*. Berlin, Heidelberg: Metzler.
Bourdieu, Pierre. 1999. "The Contradictions of Inheritance." In *The Weight of the World: Social Suffering in Contemporary Society*, edited by Pierre Bourdieu, 507–513. Stan-ford: Stanford University Press.
Breyer, Till, and Veronika Thanner. 2019. "Geld- und Kreditverhältnisse im Realismus." In *Handbuch Literatur und Ökonomie*, edited by Joseph Vogl and Burkhardt Wolf, 536–550. Berlin, Boston: De Gruyter.
Brückner, Benjamin. 2019. *Familie erzählen: Vererbung in Literatur und Wissenschaft, 1860–1900*. Freiburg im Breisgau, Berlin, Vienna: Rombach.

Catano, James V. 1990. "The Rhetoric of Masculinity: Origins, Institutions, and the Myth of the Self-Made Man." *College English* 52, no. 4 (April): 421–436.

Catano, James V. 2001. *Ragged Dicks: Masculinity, Steel, and the Rhetoric of the Self-Made Man.* Carbondale: Southern Illinois University Press.

Eribon, Didier. 2017. *Gesellschaft als Urteil.* Berlin: Suhrkamp.

Hausen, Karin. 1976. "Die Polarisierung der 'Geschlechtscharaktere'. Eine Spiegelung der Dissoziation von Erwerbs- und Familienleben." In *Sozialgeschichte der Familie in der Neuzeit Europas. Neue Forschungen,* edited by Werner Conze, 363–393, Stuttgart: Klett.

Herrmann, Leonhard. 2021. "Nach dem Populismus: Komplexität, Polyvalenz und der 'Social Turn' in Büchern von Deniz Ohde, Marlene Streeruwitz und Sibylle Berg." *Gegenwartsliteratur: A German Studies Yearbook* 20: 315–342.

Jaquet, Chantal. 2018. *Zwischen den Klassen: Über die Nicht-Reproduktion sozialer Macht.* Göttingen: Konstanz University Press.

Koppetsch, Cornelia. 2001. "Milieu und Geschlecht: Eine kontextspezifische Perspektive." In *Klasse und Klassifikation: Die symbolische Dimension sozialer Ungleichheit,* edited by Anja Weiß, Cornelia Koppetsch, Albert Scharenberg, and Oliver Schmidtke, 109–137. Wiesbaden: Westdeutscher Verlag.

Koschorke, Albrecht. 2000. "Die Männer und die Moderne." In *Der Blick vom Wolkenkratzer: Avantgarde—Avantgardekritik—Avantgardeforschung,* edited by Wolfgang Asholt and Walter Fähnders, 141–162. Amsterdam, Atlanta: Rodopi.

Kübler, Gunhild. 1982. *Die soziale Aufsteigerin: Wandlungen einer geschlechtsspezifischen Rollenzuschreibung im deutschen Roman 1870–1900.* Bonn: Bouvier.

Kucklick, Christoph. 2008. *Das unmoralische Geschlecht: Zur Genese der negativen Andrologie.* Berlin: Suhrkamp.

Louis, Édouard. 2019. *Who Killed My Father.* Translated by Lorin Stein. London: Harvill Secker.

Louis, Édouard. 2021. *A Woman's Battles and Transformations.* Translated by Tash Aw. New York: Farrar, Straus and Giroux.

Moretti, Franco. 1987. *The Way of the World. The* Bildungsroman *in European Culture.* London: Verso.

Ohde, Deniz. 2020. *Streulicht.* 3rd ed. Berlin: Suhrkamp.

Parnes, Ohad, Ulrike Vedder, and Stefan Willer. 2008. *Das Konzept der Generation: Eine Wissens- und Kulturgeschichte.* Frankfurt am Main: Suhrkamp.

Schößler, Franziska, and Bernd Blaschke. 2019. "Die Entdeckung der Ware." In *Handbuch Literatur und Ökonomie,* edited by Joseph Vogl and Burkhardt Wolf, 523–535. Berlin, Boston: De Gruyter.

Spoerhase, Carlos. 2017. "Politik der Form: Autosoziobiografie als Gesellschaftsanalyse." *Merkur* 71: 27–37.

Stelling, Anke. 2019. *Schäfchen im Trockenen.* 3rd ed. Berlin: Verbrecher Verlag.

Thomä, Dieter. 2008. *Väter: Eine moderne Heldengeschichte.* Munich: Hanser.

Tommek, Heribert. 2015. *Der lange Weg in die Gegenwartsliteratur: Studien zur Geschichte des literarischen Feldes in Deutschland 1960–2000*. Berlin, Boston: De Gruyter.

Vijayakumaran, Jana. 2022. *Der Selfmademan in der deutschsprachigen Erzählliteratur der Moderne: Zur Imaginationsgeschichte einer Schlüsselfigur*. Berlin, Boston: De Gruyter.

3.3

Narrating Class and Classlessness in Contemporary British Novels of Black Women's Social Climbing

KATRIN BECKER

Introduction: British (Post-)Migrant Fiction, Intersectionality and Upward Mobility

A marked frequency of narratives of successful upward mobility seems to distinguish British post-migrant literature in the late twentieth and early twenty-first century from migrant fiction rooted in the post-war Windrush era.[1] Canonised examples of the latter, such as Sam Selvon's *The Lonely Londoners* (1956), narrate experiences of economic precarity and social marginalisation of black migrants from the crumbling British Empire, evoking their disappointed hopes for a good or better life in the 'mother country' (Bentley 2003, 41). In addition, Selvon's sequel titled *Moses Ascending* (1975) mocks "the upwardly mobile pretensions of the immigrant black" (Sigal 1988, 134). By contrast, the 1990s saw the publication of a wave of post-migrant *Bildungsromane* that frequently figure black social climbers of working-class origin seemingly fulfilling the hopes of their parental migrant generation. Mark Stein (1998; 2004) has influentially argued that these 'Black British' texts, centred on post-migrant subjectivities attaining 'new' positions of wealth and power, portray and purvey the social transformation of Britain.[2] Following Joseph R. Slaughter (2006), we may also characterise these post-migrant novels of trans-/formation as "perform[ing] a certain kind of incorporative literary social work" (1411), building on the genre's historical function as a "conventionalized [...] narrative pattern for participation in the egalitarian imaginary of the new bourgeois nation-state, a plot for incorporation of previously marginalized people" (ibid., 1410). Although post-millennial "black writing of Britain" (McLeod 2010, 46) certainly goes beyond "the affective and political concerns of black Britons" (ibid., 51), fiction centred on post-migrant, black subjectivities of working-class origin negotiating the incorporative-transformative promise of upward mobility remains prominent.

For instance, Natasha Brown's debut *Assembly* (2021a) has been reviewed as "a novel about the kind of person the UK government's recent commission on race would have wanted to profile in their report" (Collins 2021), as an example of "the success of those minority groups that have been surging forward into the middle class and the elite" (Commission on Race and Ethnic Disparities 2021, 234). Like much public debate on inequality and intersectionality, this report understands 'class' as "socio-economic background" that 'intersects' with "ethnicity" as "causes holding back equality of opportunity" (ibid., 10); a similar perspective seems to underlie Bernardine Evaristo's (2021) contention that "the triple intersections of colour, class and gender inform and complicate the battle to achieve in our society" (viii). My own analytical perspective draws on the recent reappraisal of class within the field of British sociology, particularly by scholars such as Imogen Tyler (2015), who insists on an understanding of class as the persistent socio-historical problematic of "structural conditions of inequality" (496) that necessitate 'the battle to achieve' in the first place. Tyler connects the conceptual erosion of class in this sense to the political formation of New Labour, whose "attempt to 'decouple' inequality from class" (ibid., 497) introduced a neoliberal notion of classlessness, as epitomised by Tony Blair's speech "on taking office, announc[ing] the dawn of a new meritocratic and 'classless' society" (Tyler 2013, 7). Mike Savage (2015) critically connects these and subsequent re-investments in social mobility back to Michael Young's satirical dystopia *The Rise of the Meritocracy* (1958), arguing that: "A more competitive, ruthless and indeed meritocratic system can nonetheless generate high levels of inequality in life chances which go hand-in-hand with very unequal processes" (Savage 2015, 189). And yet, as Jo Littler (2018) adds, despite its in-built tautology, ideological wear and empirical evidence to the contrary in our own contemporary moment, "meritocratic hope" (11) retains its "cultural pull" (ibid., 220); meritocracy, Littler (2020) writes, still "functions as the core legitimating ideological principle for the inequalities of contemporary capitalism" (17).

In this chapter, I trace variations of the dominant "master plot" (Abbott 2002, 43) of individual upward mobility across a selection of novels that narrate black female achievement against all intersectional and structural odds, beginning with Nicola Williams' *Without Prejudice* ([1997] 2021), and moving on to Zadie Smith's *NW* ([2012] 2013), Bernardine Evaristo's *Girl, Woman, Other* ([2019] 2020), and Natasha Brown's *Assembly* (2021a). With a particular focus on aesthetic and narrative strategies, my analyses tease out how these (at times semi-autobiographical) novels negotiate neoliberal claims of classlessness related to the meritocratic master plot of social climbing that is still offered as an (individualising) remedy for (structural) inequality in the social imaginary of contemporary Britain, to second-generation 'migrants' in particular. Much like the cross-class fiction analysed by Sula Textor in this volume, the novels discussed below construct in-between voices and perspectives of 'transclass' individuals (Jaquet 2014, 13) who are both adapted and unadapted to the social contexts they navigate (ibid., 125). However, this chapter departs from Chantal Jaquet's approach by reading transclass novels against the backdrop of the ideologically charged imperative of upward mobility, a 'valorising' discourse decidedly factored out by Jaquet (ibid., 10–12). Taken together, the texts discussed in this chapter are conspicuously concerned with such valorisations, and they juxtapose the individual transclass trajectories they narrate with glimpses of the kinds of collective modes of alleviating socio-economic inequality that Jaquet, once again, appears to sideline (ibid., 10).[3]

Narrating the Careers Talk: Towards a Metanarrative Deconstruction of the Master Plot

A recurrent episode narrated in contemporary British fiction centred on upwardly mobile black women of working-class origin is them giving motivational speeches to potential social climbers in schools or similar educational or community institutions. A good starting point for tracing this key episode across a range of texts is Nicola Williams' *Without Prejudice*, originally published in 1997 and reissued in 2021 as part of the Penguin series *Black Britain: Writing Back,* curated by Bernardine Evaristo. Just before giving a careers talk at her former school, we witness the protagonist, criminal-law barrister Leanne (Lee) Mitchell, successfully negotiating a difficult brief (chapter one and two); we are also filled in about the particulars of her post-migrant, intergenerational success story, and have seen her being celebrated as a truly self-made lawyer by a titled colleague (chapter three). As Evaristo (2021) notes in her introduction to *Without Prejudice*, "[i]n these first pages, Lee has been revealed to us as a plucky protagonist who understands what it takes to succeed" (vii). Centred on "a black female barrister who is succeeding against the odds" (ibid., vi), Evaristo further contends, the legal thriller "offers us a vision of black female achievement that is essential to attaining and inspiring a more meritocratic nation" (ibid., ix).

This is indeed an adequate description of the novel's political stance as mapped onto the character's careers talk, a foil that is reworked in later novels of black female achievement and thus deserves critical analysis. We may start by considering how the character describes her two-fold motivation to her colleague. Firstly, she wants to "rub" Mrs Cox's "face in it" (*WP*, 28)[4]—i.e. in her successful entry into the legal profession despite all the *dis*couragement she received from her former careers teacher (see also ibid., 20). When Lee arrives at Fordyce, her former school, an undercurrent of symbolic distinction in her critique of her former educators is more fully expressed when the character's gaze proudly registers the "marked contrast" between her black Saab and "the most dilapidated cars [that] belonged to the teachers" (ibid., 31). Secondly, Lee "want[s] to tell them [the students] that there is an alternative to getting pregnant or working at Woollies" (ibid., 28), which resonates with New Labour's vision of the social, dominant at the time of publication of *Without Prejudice*. Imogen Tyler (2013) has characterised this social imaginary as a renewed "*culturalization* of poverty and disadvantage" through which socio-economic privations "would come to be unshackled symbolically from economic inequalities and reframed as a psycho-cultural problem" (162). Central to this reframing of the problem of structural inequality in New Labour's Britain, Tyler remarks in this context, was the rekindled notion of meritocracy on the one hand, and a new stigmatising 'underclass' discourse on the other.

This, I would argue, constitutes the "ideological *subtext*" (Jameson 1982, 81) of *Without Prejudice* and of Lee's speech addressing a student body "as ethnically mixed as ever" (*WP*, 31) in the school's assembly hall:

> Lee turned to Mrs Cox. "[...] You've given the school a ringing endorsement for its part in my success. Unfortunately," she turned back to the audience, "none of that part is true. [...] [W]hen I was a pupil here, the only work experience we could get was shop work; the highest aim we could have, even the brightest of us, was to become someone's office clerk. You were never, never encouraged to aim for anything higher. [...] This is not about revenge, or ingratitude, or causing embarrassment to the school. But I promised myself that if I was ever invited to address students at Fordyce, I would tell the truth about my experiences here. [...] Don't let anyone put you off, or put you down. Just plan to be a better version of what you already are." (ibid., 34–35)

Lee's critique of her former teachers' low expectations and biases here turns into a critique of their failure to ignite meritocratic hope in their students, a task Lee seeks to accomplish by an emphatic sense of voluntarist self-making in that final, mantra-like 'instruction' for how to succeed. What is—on the level of character and implied author—intended as encouragement can also be read as "an ideological act [...] with the function of inventing [...] formal 'solutions' to [...] social contradictions" (Jameson 1982, 79) as crystallised linguistically in that 'just.'

That contradictory motif of individual success against all structural odds also informs Evaristo's own novelistic depictions of black female achievement, most recently in *Girl, Woman, Other* (2019). However, the latter to some extent rewrites the fiercely individualist sense of self-reliance that *Without Prejudice* propagates by adding a plot twist to one of its post-migrant success stories. One of the sub-chapters is centred on Carole, who—born to Nigerian academics 'downclassed' to manual labour after migration to the UK—overachieves her parents' ambitions for her by becoming one of the high-earning vice presidents of an investment bank in the City. Carole's retrospective *Bildungsroman* narrative includes an invective against her former teacher Mrs King—herself a black female social climber—that seems to hark back to *Without Prejudice*. Carole remembers

> Mrs King [giving] a speech in assembly on the last day of
> Carole's schooling that her protégé, after much dedicated and hard
> work on Mrs King's part, was the first child in the school's history to
> make it to such a prestigious university [Oxford]
> robbing Carole of her moment of glory. (*GWO*, 130)

Girl, Woman, Other revisits this narrative strand in a later sub-chapter with an awkward encounter between adult Carole and a much-aged Mrs King, the latter passive aggressively asking for recognition. Carole eventually breaks the discomforting silence between the two by dutifully thanking Mrs King for her help but the episode—and this narrative strand—ends with Carole actually changing her mind: "it dawns / on her that Mrs King really did help her when nobody else could or / would, how could she have not realized this until now?" (ibid., 422). In sum, then, the final chapter of *Girl, Woman, Other* challenges all-too-absolute notions of self-making at the centre of the master plot of upward mobility by reinscribing the social climber's teacher in the function of a *Bildungsroman* helper figure.[5]

Much like Evaristo's *Girl, Woman, Other,* Zadie Smith's *NW* embeds a 'Black British' *Bildungsroman* narrative along the lines theorised by Stein in a larger entity that has been characterised as a "composite novel" (D'hoker 2018, 28; 18). The novel's third and longest part narrates how Keisha Blake, daughter of Caribbean working-class migrants, becomes Natalie de Angelis, a high-earning commercial barrister, in a highly fragmented prose that can be read as a trope evoking the self-*un*-making experienced by upwardly mobile subjectivities (see Becker 2024).[6] Towards the end of this part, Natalie is invited to give a careers talk that begins as conventionally as may be expected. However, the way in which *NW* constructs this episode soon destabilises the character's attempted reiteration of the master plot of upward mobility: "She gave a speech about time management, identifying goals, working hard, respecting oneself and one's partner, and the importance of a good education. 'Anything purely based on physicality is doomed to failure,' she read" (*NW*, 291). This evocation of physical desire triggers a thought about her "[p]oor" low-achieving childhood friend Leah, which eventually turns into a daydream that resonates with the title of this fragment, i.e. "Envy," with this paratextual marker functioning as a metafictional comment on the inventedness of Natalie's motivational story:[7]

> In between the top of page two and the beginning of page three she must have been reading out loud and making sense, there must have appeared to be an unbroken continuity—no one in the audience was looking at her like she was crazy—yet she found her mind travelling to obscene tableaux. She wondered what Leah and Michel, who always seemed to have their hands on each other, did in the privacy of their bedroom. Orifices, positions, climaxes. (ibid., 291)

Natalie's envious daydream about Leah and her partner Michel's otherwise disinterested bond transports readers back to an earlier fragment signifying Natalie's awareness of the extent of self-interest involved in her marriage to Frank de Angelis:

> Female individual seeks male individual for loving relationship. And vice versa. Low-status person with intellectual capital but no surplus wealth seeks high-status person of substantial surplus wealth for enjoyment of mutual advantages, including longer life expectancy, better nutrition, fewer working hours and earlier retirement, among other benefits. (ibid., 230)

Significantly, this fragment immediately follows Frank's offer to have his wealthy family pay for Natalie's pupillage, the final unpaid stage of her training as a barrister, "[t]his last gap [that] was almost too wide to jump" (ibid., 228). Hence, as readers, we know that Frank is a crucial helper figure in the extra-diegetic, post-migrant *Bildungsroman* narrative that makes up the third part of *NW*. However, this is unknown to the fictional addressees of Natalie's intradiegetic narration of her success story against all intersectional odds that ends as follows: "'And it was by refusing to set myself artificial limits,' explained Natalie Blake to the collective of young black women, 'that I was able to reach my full potential'" (ibid., 291). Overall, the way in which *NW* presents this episode clearly undermines the ideological script of self-reliance and self-entrepreneurship that the character is shown to reproduce; it also serves a metanarrative function, reminding readers of this third part of *NW* that this is in fact not as straightforward a success story as Natalie would have her fictional addressees believe. The narratorial strategy also gestures towards a latent generic shift within this third part of *NW*, from incorporative 'Black British' *Bildungsroman* to novel of adultery, a long-standing vehicle for women's disaffection with an exclusionary bourgeois social order, as Fredric Jameson (2010, 282–283) notes.

Contrary to the nineteenth-century novel of adultery that Jameson discusses, however, novels like *NW* in fact narrate individual black women's disaffection *despite* being incorporated into bourgeois society; it is in this sense, I would argue, that Natasha Brown's novella *Assembly* (2021a) can be described, as the author herself does in an interview, as a "dissatisfaction story" (Brown 2021b). Going beyond the identity-political framework Brown delineates in said interview, I read the dissatisfaction at the heart of *Assembly* as an uncompliant 'structure of feeling' that challenges the master plot of individual upward mobility from the perspective of an unnamed black woman of working-class origin who has climbed her way up and into the financial sector.[8] Crucially, the careers talk episode opens the novella's simultaneously narrated main arch:

> It's a story. There are challenges. There's hard work, pulling up laces, rolling up shirtsleeves, and forcing yourself. Up. Overcoming, transcending, et cetera. You've heard it before. It's not my life, but it's illuminated two metres tall behind me and I'm speaking into the soft, malleable faces tilted forwards on uniformed shoulders. I recite my old lines like new secrets. Click to the next slide. Giant, diverse, smiling faces in grey suits point at charts, shake hands and wave behind me. The projector whirrs and their faces morph into the bank's roaring logo. (*Assembly*, 9)

This passage highlights the autodiegetic narrator's troubled and troubling inner awareness of the false forms and formulas in which she casts her life story. The imagery resonates with Plato's allegory of the cave in that the narrator presents herself as an object that projects images "two metres tall behind" her, whilst she is fully aware that this is a manipulated and manipulative representation of her life story, received as truthful by the assembled "malleable faces" (ibid.). With the explicit second-person address, narratee and implied reader are reminded how often they have encountered the neoliberal mantra of individual achievement as the narrator showcases its endless repetition of the same stock imagery— "pulling up laces, rolling up shirtsleeves"—and dismisses its worn-out storyline with the satirising phrase "[o]vercoming, transcending, et cetera."

On the next page, the narrator explicitly reflects on the complicity in the reproduction and distribution of the master plot of individual achievement that is expected of her:

> I do these talks—schools and universities, women's panels, recruiting fairs—every few weeks. It's an expectation of the job. The diversity must be seen. How many women and girls have I lied to? How many have seen my grinning face advocating for this or that firm, or this industry, or that university, this life? (ibid., 10)

The narrator's self-ironising image brings to mind Frantz Fanon's (2021) analysis of "the grinning stereotype *Y a bon Banania*," one of "liver[ies] the white man has fabricated" (17). That 'grin' recurs in Fanon's own argument and the sources he consults (see 32; 92; 152–154; 177), and is analysed as a figuration of obedience in the face of colonial oppression and/or continued cultural and economic exclusion. Conjuring such an 'Y a bon' figuration at the intersection of racism and class, *Assembly* invites readers to critically reflect on the narrator's giving herself up as a grinning object used to sell the alleged meritocratic diversity of the institutions and companies she advocates. Her highly analytical narrating self thus voices her concern with the ideological pitfalls of presenting her life story as a black woman's successful struggle for a good life against all intersectional odds. What is more, the title of this first chapter—"ASSEMBLY"—not only names the setting of the character-narrator's careers talk, but as a paratextual marker it also signposts the significance of this passage for the novella as a whole. The initial phrase "[i]t's a story" further introduces a sustained self-reflexive trope of storytelling that—in this instance—serves to highlight the constructedness of the master plot of upward mobility against all odds—and also signals a metanarrative concern with the kind of story *Assembly* tries not to tell. This narratorial strategy appears to be central to Brown's deconstructive agenda, who, in writing *Assembly*, "was concerned with the construction of myth," inspired by Roland Barthes (Brown 2021c). The character-narrator's running self-reflexive commentary on her careers talk can indeed be read as a Barthesian mythology "deciphering" (Barthes 2013, 234) "ideas-in-form" (ibid., 221).

Assembly further harks back to Barthes' mention of a demythifying strategy deployed by literature, namely the "murder of literature": "it is well known that some went as far as the pure and simple scuttling of the discourse, silence—whether real or transposed—appearing as the only weapon against the major power of myth: its recurrence" (ibid., 246). The narrator indeed considers silence as "the least harmful choice" (*Assembly*, 23) when asked to reiterate the master plot of individual achievement against all odds. At the same time, the passage from Barthes can also be connected with the narrator's decision to renounce her company's medical treatment for her recently diagnosed breast cancer, which she regards as "an opportunity [...] [t]o stop the endless ascent" (ibid., 57). As cultural anthropologist S. Lochlann Jain (2010) notes, what dominates the cultural imaginary of cancer are narratives of survivorship that overemphasise individual agency (174). These success stories, Jain writes, "propagate[] the myth that everyone has the potential to be a survivor—even as, ironically, survivorship against the odds requires the deaths of others" (ibid., 175). The heroic figure of the individual fighter against all statistical and structural odds is where the neoliberal imaginaries of cancer survivorship and classlessness intersect, a discursive overlap that *Assembly* builds on. Just before we learn about the narrator's refusal of treatment, her doctor hails her as a "fighter" (*Assembly*, 44). We may connect her refusal of this interpellation with the passage that first explicitly discloses her death wish:

> Generations of sacrifice; hard work and harder living. So much suffered, so much forfeited, so much—for this opportunity. For my life. And I've tried, tried living up to it. But after years of struggling, fighting against the current, I'm ready to slow my arms. Stop kicking. Breathe the water in. I'm exhausted. Perhaps it's time to end this story. (ibid., 13)

It seems that the metanarrative trope of storytelling that runs through *Assembly* migrates onto the level of plot, yet another aesthetic strategy to deconstruct the master plot of upward mobility against all intersectional odds by projecting the narrator's death from cancer as a renunciation of incorporation.

I have thus far neglected the level of story: the main narrative arch progresses towards a garden party at the illustrious family estate of the narrator's likewise unnamed boyfriend, to celebrate his parents' wedding anniversary and to be engaged to him, it seems. Although there is barely any plot-like causality in the conventional sense, the highly fragmented present-tense narrative is shaped by an overarching question, namely whether the narrator can "bring herself to want […] a complete melding with the class that enslaved her" (Biggs 2021, 31). What is more, the character-narrator's self-advancement is repeatedly shown to necessitate traversing political as much as economic lines of division, such as crossing the "divide" separating her from Occupy protestors when she first begins working in the City (*Assembly*, 46). The evening before said garden party, her prospective father-in-law checks her political affiliations: "'Tell me how you ended up in finance. Why aren't you shaking up change in the Labour Party?' He winks. 'Ushering in a new world order.'" (ibid., 62). Tellingly, "the son" assures his "intrigued" father that his wife-to-be is associated with the Blairite faction of the Labour Party, while the character-narrator remains silent (ibid.). The father's half-serious but nonetheless piercing question thus remains unanswered and continues to hover in the narrative, as a reference to the 'Corbyn revolution' feared by the wealthy in 2019, about a structural redistribution of wealth and power from top to bottom.[9] *Assembly* can thus be read as novel(la) of black female achievement that critically reflects on the ideological pitfalls of being incorporated into the higher echelons of British society, of joining those holding most political and economic power in post-imperial Britain (in matrimony), a union more readily embraced by Natalie in *NW* and Carole in *Girl, Woman, Other*.

Narrating the Odds and Alternatives: Destabilising the Master Plot Through Novelistic/Narrative Structure

Contrary to the open-endedness of *Assembly*, the final part of Zadie Smith's *NW* reinstates Natalie as *Bildungshero* as she "return[s] to the fold" (Stein 2004, 23) of her domestic middle-class life. However, as I have elaborated elsewhere (Becker 2021; Becker 2024), the novel's overall composite structure articulates a dialectic of life chances and lack thereof that fundamentally unsettles the master plot of upward mobility, foregrounding the structurally contingent social costs of an individual's 'battle to achieve.' At the same time, Nick Hubble (2016) has convincingly argued that *NW* speaks to the "fall of working-class agency" (202), "the collapse of collective working-class culture" (ibid., 206) in the late twentieth century. Hubble locates that decline in an encounter between two male characters, "white working-class socialist Phil Barnes" (ibid., 205), a sixty-year-old unionised postal worker, and Felix Cooper, a black thirty-two-year-old car mechanic precariously employed at a small garage. While Felix "is happy to listen to Barnes," his "values no longer have much purchase in the contemporary London" that Felix navigates (ibid., 206). Although this is certainly the case on the level of character perspective, the novel as a whole seems to offer a different evaluation, as is implied by Felix's response to Barnes' attempted agitation: "'I'm more about the day-to-day'" (*NW*, 117). Given that the part centred on Felix is a one-day narrative that ends with his death, *NW* seems to suggest both the difficulty *and* the need to renew Barnes' 'traditional' class politics in a twenty-first-century Britain marked by precarious working and living conditions.

Although *Girl, Woman, Other* is less radical in its approach to the master plot of individual achievement against all odds, the cultural pull of neoliberal meritocracy is nonetheless destabilised through the novel's composite form. We 'meet' twelve protagonists in quasi-stand-alone narrative strands mediated in twelve consecutive sub-chapters bearing the respective character's first name as title, grouped into sets of three that make up four chapters (a fifth chapter brings together characters of each set of three and is followed by an epilogue). Accordingly, *Girl, Woman, Other* certainly "resembles the genre of the short story cycle" in that the sub-chapters "can be read independently but are expanded and revised in other stories/subchapters" (Carrera-Suárez and Rodríguez-González 2021, 94). Of particular relevance for my purposes here is the sequencing of textually distinct yet intratextually connected storylines that pulls black female achievement against all intersectional odds into contiguity with the respective social climbers' daughter or mother, former teacher or peer.[10] Building on Wolfgang Iser's (1972) classical theorisation of reading as "the process of anticipation and retrospection, the consequent unfolding of the text" (296), I argue that

Girl, Woman, Other pre-structures marked "retrospective effect[s] on what has already been read" (Iser 1972, 283), calling on readers to 'concretise' (ibid., 279) a recursive aesthetic. Hence, although the novel prominently features "characters [who] achieve individual success through tactics of social mobility that leverage hard-won class-based inclusion against racial dispossession," "[w]inning within the capitalist system, rather than overturning it" (Photopoulos 2022, 201), the recursive interplay of perspectives works towards exposing the ideological underpinnings and pitfalls, the structural contingencies and personal costs of this logic.

The following analysis mainly focuses on two sub-chapters that offer recursive perspectives on the novel's most high-flying achiever, Carole. Beforehand, it is worth revisiting Photopoulos' (2022) thesis—that *Girl, Woman, Other* "valoriz[es] property acquisition" (202) as a means of alleviating 'racial dispossession'—with a view to the interplay of two other characters' perspectives/sub-chapters: Amma, a successful black-feminist playwright and theatre director (*GWO*, 1–40), and her daughter Yazz, a nineteen-year-old student of English literature (ibid., 41–74). To begin with, Amma's eventual "grateful" home-ownership (ibid., 34) is retrospectively refracted through Yazz's critique of her mother's complicity in the gentrification she complains about "as if she herself wasn't a frequenter of the artsy hotspots" (ibid., 44). Amma's "hopeful" entry into the "mainstream" with a production at the National Theatre in London (ibid., 2) in turn resurfaces, in Yazz's perspective, as condescension: "ever since she landed the National gig she's got very snooty about / struggling theatre mates, as if she alone has discovered the secret to / being successful (ibid., 43). Finally, the vision of black-feminist empowerment through individual achievement as staged in Amma's play and narrated in her sub-chapter contrasts with Yazz's emergent awareness of an economic divide within her group of 'sistahs' or "brown girls" at university, with "super-rich" Nenet refusing to "play by / the rules" of the 'battle to achieve,' buying rather than earning her degree (ibid., 72–73). At the same time, Yazz is shown to be equally aware of her own dependence on living rent-free with Amma when she leaves university "with a huge debt and crazy com- / petition for jobs and the outrageous rental prices out there" (ibid., 42).

Moving on to Carole, it is noteworthy that her wish to "be gone" from the economic precarity of her childhood (ibid., 128) is reflected in the eventual erasure of several black female characters associated with these conditions in her sub-chapter. Her former school friend LaTisha is reduced to an 'underclass' caricature in Carole's imagination (ibid., 145); her former teacher Mrs King is last mentioned when Carole remembers entering Oxford University to study maths (ibid., 130); her mother Bummi last occurs when Carole recalls her encouragement to carve out space for herself at Oxford (ibid., 133–134).[11] However, these characters are not 'gone' from the novel; instead, the following sub-chapters essentially narrate these characters' life stories and thus fill readers in on their at times divergent perspectives. I have already commented on how the novel's final chapter reinstates Mrs King as a helper figure for Carole's surging ascent; the sub-chapter that immediately follows the one centred on Carole delves into her mother's perspective (ibid., 150–188) and reinscribes her as yet another crucial helper figure for Carole's transformative-incorporative *Bildungsroman* narrative. Hinted at in Carole's sub-chapter in a vignette showing how Bummi nurtured her daughter's interest in and comprehension of maths (ibid., 121), Bummi, we learn in the subsequent sub-chapter, in fact holds a "first / class [maths] degree from a Third World Country [...] mean[ing] nothing in her / new country," where she only finds work as a cleaner (ibid., 167). In Pierre Bourdieu's terms (2002), even if Bummi's academic credentials cannot be converted into economic capital, Bummi's embodied cultural capital is a crucial condition for Carole's educational trajectory.

In addition, when her husband's death turns her into a single mother, Bummi decides she must "become someone who employed others, rather / than someone waiting to be employed" (*GWO*, 170). In order to raise the initial economic capital, she turns to the only person in her social circle not "living hand / to mouth," namely the bishop of her church (ibid., 172). Her "first transaction" as "a businesswoman" is sex offered in exchange for "an envelope of cash / [...] a low-interest loan to be repaid over two years," knowing that "it would have taken twice as long to save a quarter of it on her / salary" (ibid., 173). This episode and character construction of course evokes the neoliberal subject figure of the entrepreneurial self (Bröckling 2016) and might be read as an embrace of the ensuing mantra of individual responsibility. However, the episode underlines the brutally limited means at Bummi's disposal as a migrant and single mother dependent on low-paid wage labour wishing to "rise above my station in order to / raise my child as the sole wage-earner in a parenting situation of one" (*GWO*, 170). That this escape from precarity is predicated on what is essentially an act of prostitution—depicted, from Bummi's perspective, as both violating and degrading, but nonetheless necessary "to elevate her- / self and her daughter" (ibid., 174)—can be read along the lines of Jane Elliott's critical notion of neoliberal 'suffering agency.' That is, the 'choices' open to Bummi—precarity or prostitution—evoke the "imprisoning nature of suffering agency, the way in which choices made for oneself and according to one's own interests can still feel both imposed and appalling" (Elliott 2013, 84), rather than an emphatic sense of opportunity. What is more, the character's perspective explicitly ironises the notion of 'equal opportunity' when she imagines her future as "proprietor of her own cleaning com- /pany, which would be an Equal Opportunities Employer, like all / other cleaning companies," wishing her late husband were around "to share the joke" (*GWO*, 170). Overall, then, the sub-chapter draws attention to the social contingencies and personal costs of Carole and Bummi's intergenerational narrative of incorporation into the bourgeois socio-economic order.

The interplay of Carole and Bummi's perspectives further teases out an intergenerational pattern of symbolic violence as theorised by Bourdieu. In the symbolic hierarchy of cultural practices that serves to legitimate socio-economic inequalities, Bourdieu (1998) argues, "dominated lifestyles are almost always perceived, even by those who live them, from the destructive and reductive point of view of the dominant aesthetic" (9). Initially feeling out of place as a black woman of working-class origin at Oxford—"crushed, worthless and a nobody" (*GWO*, 132), Carole ventures on a path to acquire 'legitimate'—i.e. recognisably middle-class English—ways of speaking, eating, dressing one's body and furnishing one's home (ibid., 136–138). However, Carole's continued process of self-making after university is—much like in the third part of Zadie Smith's *NW*—presented in less-than-celebratory terms: "and if she has to cripple herself to signal her education, talent, / intellect, skills and leadership potential, so be it" (ibid., 140). What is more, Carole's makeover, refracted through Bummi's perspective at the beginning of the subsequent sub-chapter, is shown to reproduce the symbolic violence she felt subjected to at university. For instance, Carole begins "looking haughtily around their cosy little / flat like it was a fleapit," refrains from eating with her hands, "side-glancing her mama for doing so, as if she was a savage from the jungle" and uses words—highlighted in italics or scare quotes—sounding not only alien but "ironical" to Bummi (ibid., 151). Hence, in this case, the recursive interplay of Carole and Bummi's perspectives and sub-chapters brings to the fore both the personal costs and the ideological pitfalls of self-(re)making.

Finally, the sub-chapter centred on Carole's former teacher Mrs King—i.e. Shirley—offers yet another angle on Carole's success story, narrating the character's professional and personal trajectory from the 1980s to the 2010s, with a sustained focus on her shifting work ethos and teaching philosophy (ibid., 217–248). It opens by presenting a young Shirley as the first black teacher in a 'multicultural' state comprehensive school, dedicated to "the principle of social mobility" (ibid., 229) through education and helping "those who are disadvantaged" (ibid., 228), imagining that "every step she takes will raise these children up, she will leave no / child behind" (ibid., 220). The sub-chapter ends with a view of a disillusioned, overworked teacher clinging to "mentoring projects" for "a few promising children [...] of obvious intelligence" with "variable" results, which "makes teaching slightly more bearable" (ibid., 248). The narrative arch connecting these two 'Shirleys' maps developments in the public educational sector from the 1980s onwards onto the narrative. Beginning with "large classes / and lack of resources" (ibid., 234), "it was bad and got worse when the Thatcher government began to / implement its Master Plan for Education" including league tables and the national curriculum (ibid., 235). Shirley's social history then fast-forwards to the 1990s and 2000s, recording rising rates of utmost poverty among the children's families as well as juvenile delinquency (ibid., 236–237). Although Shirley begins adopting the 'underclass' rhetoric propagated by New Labour, she is also shown to be increasingly aware of the "the great middle- / class scam": "parents 'helped' them [their children] so much with their / homework they appeared to be child prodigies" (ibid., 240). Ironically, this would also pertain to Carole, Shirley's "first and greatest achievement" (ibid., 248), and her "exceptional grasp of maths" (ibid., 245). Overall, then, Shirley's teacher perspective renders visible the social and (politically made) institutional contingencies that form the backdrop of 'the battle to achieve' in/via education, foregrounding that except for her own individual commitment to "giving these kids a fighting chance / [...] everything else was against them" (ibid., 234). Carole's success story against all institutional odds is thus recontextualised as an utter exception to the rule, rather than a hope-inducing model to be emulated.

Thus, *Girl, Woman, Other*, much like *NW* and *Assembly*, narrates intersectional transclass experience in a way that problematises the master plot of upward mobility. The novel likewise juxtaposes that experience with glimpses of collective modes of class-based agency aimed at alleviating socio-economic inequality on a larger scale. As Sonya Andermahr (2021) notes, "the only characters involved in [such] class politics are men" who are "almost always seen through critical or mocking eyes" of the female protagonists, while black women's experiences of class-related inequalities never seem to trigger any political alliances on that basis (2–3); hence, "it is class politics that ends up being othered" (ibid., 4). Indeed, (both black and white) male figural bearers of socialist class politics are frequently othered from the perspectives of black female character-focalisers but the most sustained instance of such othering is also the most politically fraught one, namely the ambivalent portrayal of Sylvester, an old friend of Amma's who "still ran his socialist theatre company, The 97%" (*GWO*, 32). The rendition of Amma's perspective juxtaposes her ridicule of Sylvester's "revolutionary zeal" (ibid.) with her own sense of entitlement (and desire) to enter 'the mainstream' and reform it from within (ibid., 33), yet this outlook is also ironically refracted through the elitist perspective of Roland, yet another social climber and Yazz's biological father. The only passage throughout *Girl, Woman, Other* that enters the mind of a (black) male character ends with a quoted interior monologue (Cohn 1978, 12–13) in which Roland addresses Sylvester: "you can keep your social conscience, Comrade, because he / Roland, has something far more powerful up his sleeve and it's called / CULTURAL CAPITAL!!!" (*GWO*, 410). Thus, while Sylvester mainly functions as a vehicle for other characters' self-assurances, he may also be read as a socialist spectre that haunts the novel's social climbers.

Outlook: The (Im)Possibility of Intersectional Class Politics for Below?

In sum, the post-millennial British novels of black female achievement discussed above approach the master plot of individual upward mobility in aesthetically productive ways that allow us to reflect on the ideological underpinnings and pitfalls, as well as the social contingencies and personal costs, of individual advancement against all intersectional and structural odds. These novels are thus resistant to all-too-affirmative readings of the success stories they tell. At the same time, these narratives of individual advancement are to some extent contrasted with glimpses of collectively organised struggles for economic redistribution. Such political perspectives are all the more relevant for the study of literary representations of socio-economic inequality in neoliberal Britain if we follow David Harvey (2007). Neoliberalism, he argued, is a "political project to achieve the restoration of class power" (ibid., 16) to "economic elites" (15) who pushed back against "working-class institutions such as labour unions and political parties of the left" (ibid., 11–12). As Magnus Nilsson argues in this volume, literature may work towards (re)making class-conscious collectivities, as a basis for restoring class power for below, by presenting common experiences of socio-economic conditions. In contrast to the literary representations of precarity that Nilsson investigates, the novels surveyed in this chapter imply a more ambiguous political outlook. While the transclass experience certainly emerges, in and across these texts, as the singular yet shared condition defined by Jaquet (2014, 19), individual striving for socio-economic betterment is shown to be in tension with more collective modes of agency to that end. *NW* seems to lament the decline of the latter since the late twentieth century, whereas *Assembly* remotely registers attempts to renew class politics aimed at socio-economic redistribution from top to bottom in the 2010s. *Girl, Woman, Other* in turn reinstates doubts about the gendered omissions of 'traditional' socialist class politics but also appears to be (almost literally) in two minds about the identity-political strategy to change 'the establishment' from within by joining it. And yet, given that all three novels—unlike *Without Prejudice*—undermine ideologically charged valorisations of individual transclass trajectories, they may also educate desire for the extraliterary possibility of an intergenerational, intersectional class politics that pushes back against those holding most political and economic power in a more sustained fashion.

Notes

1. Literary-historical accounts of British migration literature usually begin with the "immigrant writers" of the so-called 'Windrush generation' (Vadde 2015, 61), which "takes its name from the Empire Windrush, a German troop-ship commandeered by the British during the war, which arrived in Tilbury in 1948 carrying about 500 West Indian migrants" (ibid., 62).

2. For an overview and discussion of more recent scholarship on the Black-British *Bildungsroman*, see Becker 2024.

3. And yet, it is worth pointing out that Jaquet's more recent contribution to the debate is more attuned to the ideological function of transclass narratives that I am interested in here. For instance, Jaquet (2023) speaks of transclass trajectories as part of "a society that generates its own deviations and oppositions while remaining fundamentally identical to itself" through a "dialectic of reproduction and non-reproduction in which classes are perpetuated through a transclass flow," "a movement that maintains immobility in the guise of change" (182).

4. For in-text citations referring to the literary texts I analyse, I use the novels' titles (i.e. *NW* and *Assembly* instead of Smith 2013 and Brown 2021a) or abbreviated versions (i.e. *WP* for Williams 2021 and *GWO* for Evaristo 2020).

5. The conception of Carole's character links with Jaquet's (2014) emphasis on the social constitution of transclass individuals (99–102). Much like the autosociobiographical novels discussed by Jaquet, *Girl, Woman, Other* narrates Carole's transclass trajectory with a sustained focus on her childhood, her familial and social background, her affects, and romantic attachments (see Jaquet 2014, 220), some of which I shall elucidate in the following section.

6. This again provides a link with Jaquet (2014), i.e. her comment on the idea of the self-made individual: "rien ne se fait à partir de rien, mais toujours à partir d'une histoire. [...] [I]l s'agit tout autant de se défaire que de se faire" (182).

7. My use of the term 'metafictional' here and 'metanarrative' below is based on Fludernik (2003). In addition, the character's 'narrated monologue' (see Cohn 1978, 13) may also be considered as an example of double-voicing in transclass novels (see Textor in this volume), in this case communicating both the character's ideological investment in and cynicism towards neoliberal classlessness as well as signalling the implied author's ironic distance.

8. According to Raymond Williams (2015), a 'structure of feeling' stems from the "experience of the work of art itself," as "a pattern of impulses, restraints, tones" that can be traced in its literary form and language, and related to "the material life, the social organization, and [...] the dominant ideas" of its historical moment (159). In fact, Williams argues that, a 'structure of feeling' arises from the "interaction" between the dominant ideas of a time and "the whole process of actually living [the] consequences" (ibid.).

9. In early September 2019, three months prior to the general election, the *Financial Times* ran a series of articles titled "The Corbyn Revolution" that detailed (and essentially warned against) the consequences of Jeremy Corbyn's election manifesto for economic and financial elites (Financial Times 2019).

10. My wording here is indebted to Caroline Edwards' (2019) theorisation of the "networked novel" (15).

11. The phrase 'to carve out space' is indebted to Stein (2004, 30) where it signifies black Britons' transformative-incorporative entry into the British public sphere.

References

Abbott, H. Porter. 2002. *The Cambridge Introduction to Narrative*. Cambridge: Cambridge University Press.

Andermahr, Sonya. 2021. "Race, Sex and Class in Bernadine Evaristo's *Girl, Woman, Other*." Paper presented at *Working-class Women Write! A One-Day Conference Celebrating Working-class Women Writers,* online, 5 March 2021. https://pure.northampton.ac.uk/ws/portalfiles/portal/32233152/Race_sex_and_class_in_Evaristo_s_Girl_Woman_Other.pdf.

Barthes, Roland. (1957) 2013. *Mythologies*. Translated by Richard Howard and Annette Lavers. New York: Hill and Wang.

Becker, Katrin. 2021. "Intersections of Class and Narrative Discourse: Forms at Work in Zadie Smith's *NW*." In *Forms at Work: New Formalist Approaches in the Study of Literature, Culture, and Media*, edited by Elisabeth Kovach, Imke Polland, and Ansgar Nünning, 167–184. Trier: Wissenschaftlicher Verlag Trier.

Becker, Katrin. 2024. "Voyage Out, Voyage Up? Subjectivities of Post-Migration and Cruel Optimism in the (Un)Making of the Black-British *Bildungsroman*." *Interventions: International Journal of Postcolonial Studies*, online, 8 January 2024. https://doi.org/10.1080/1369801X.2023.2290561

Bentley, Nick. 2003. "Black London: The Politics of Representation in Sam Selvon's *The Lonely Londoners*." *Wasafiri* 18, no. 39: 41–45.

Biggs, Joanna. 2021. "Pure, Fucking Profit." *London Review of Books* 43, no. 14 (15 July 2021): 31.

Bourdieu, Pierre. 1998. *Practical Reason: On the Theory of Action*. Stanford: Stanford University Press.

Bourdieu, Pierre. (1986) 2002. "The Forms of Capital." In *Reading in Economic Sociology*, edited by Nicole Wolsey Biggart, 280–291. Malden: Blackwell.

Bröckling, Ulrich. 2016. *The Entrepreneurial Self: Fabricating a New Type of Subject*. Translated by Steven Black. London: Sage.

Brown, Natasha. 2021a. *Assembly*. London: Hamish Hamilton.

Brown, Natasha. 2021b. "Author Natasha Brown On Writing The Debut Novel Of The Summer." Interview by Zing Tsjeng. *Vogue*, 18 May 2021. Accessed 14 April 2023. https://www.vogue.co.uk/arts-and-lifestyle/article/assembly-natasha-brown.

Brown, Natasha. 2021c. "An Interview with Natasha Brown By Nataliya Deleva." Interview by Nataliya Deleva. *Ex/Post*, 5 July 2021. Accessed 14 April 2023. https://www.expostmag.com/post/an-interview-with-natasha-brown-by-nataliya-deleva.

Carrera-Suárez, Isabel, and Carla Rodríguez-González. 2021. "Growing Up Multiply: British Women Write the Ampersand Experience." In *Postcolonial Youth in Contemporary British Fiction*, edited by Laura María Lojo-Rodríguez, Jorge Sacido-Romero, and Noemí Pereira-Ares, 81–99. Leiden: Brill.

Cohn, Dorrit. 1978. *Transparent Minds: Narrative Modes for Presenting Consciousness in Fiction*. Princeton: Princeton University Press.

Collins, Sara. 2021. "*Assembly* by Natasha Brown review—a modern Mrs Dalloway." *The Guardian*, 12 June 2021. Accessed 14 April 2023. https://www.theguardian.com/books/2021/jun/12/assembly-by-natasha-brown-review-a-modern-mrs-dalloway.

Commission on Race and Ethnic Disparities. 2021. "Commission on Race and Ethnic Disparities: The Report." GOV.UK, 31 March 2021. Accessed 14 April 2023. https://assets.publishing.service.gov.uk/government/uploads/system/uploads/attachment_data/file/974507/20210331_-_CRED_Report_-_FINAL_-_Web_Accessible.pdf.

D'hoker, Elke. 2018. "A Continuum of Fragmentation Distinguishing the Short Story Cycle from the Composite Novel." In *Constructing Coherence in the British Short Story Cycle*, edited by Patrick Gill and Florian Kläger, 17–31. London, New York: Routledge.

Edwards, Caroline. 2019. "Networked Novel." In *The Routledge Companion to Twenty-First Century Literary Fiction*, edited by Daniel O'Gorman and Robert Eaglestone, 13–24. Abingdon: Routledge.

Elliott, Jane. 2013. "Suffering Agency: Imagining Neoliberal Personhood in North America and Britain." *Social Text* 31, no. 2: 83–101.

Evaristo, Bernardine. (2019) 2020. *Girl, Woman, Other*. London: Penguin.

Evaristo, Bernardine. 2021. "Introduction." In Nicola Williams, *Without Prejudice*, v–ix. London: Penguin.

Fanon, Frantz. (1952) 2021. *Black Skin, White Masks*. Translated by Richard Philcox. London: Penguin.

Financial Times. 2019. "FT Series: The Corbyn Revolution. Should business be worried about Jeremy Corbyn becoming prime minister?" *Financial Times*, 1 September 2019. Accessed 15 November 2023. https://www.ft.com/content/db9a1fbe-c8d4-11e9-af46-b09e8bfe60c0.

Fludernik, Monika. 2003. "Metanarrative and Metafictional Commentary: From Metadiscursivity to Metanarration and Metafiction." *Poetics* 35, no. 1–2: 1–39.

Harvey, David. (2005) 2007. *A Brief History of Neoliberalism*. Oxford: Oxford University Press.

Hubble, Nick. 2016. "Common People: Class, Gender and Social Change in the London Fiction of Virginia Woolf, John Sommerfield and Zadie Smith." In *London in Contemporary British Fiction: The City Beyond the City*, edited by Nick Hubble and Philip Tew, 195–210. London: Bloomsbury.

Iser, Wolfgang. 1972. "The Reading Process: A Phenomenological Approach." *New Literary History* 3, no. 2: 279–299.

Jain, S. Lochlann. 2010. "Be Prepared." In *Against Health: How Health Became the New Morality*, edited by Jonathan M. Metzl and Anna Kirkland, 170–182. New York: New York University Press.

Jameson, Fredric. 1982. *The Political Unconscious: Narrative as a Socially Symbolic Act.* Ithaca NY: Cornell University Press.

Jameson, Fredric. 2010. "Afterword: A Note on Literary Realism." In *A Concise Companion to Realism*, edited by Matthew Beaumont, 279–289. Chichester: Wiley-Blackwell.

Jaquet, Chantal. 2014. *Les transclasses ou la non-reproduction*. Paris: PUF.

Jaquet, Chantal. 2023. "Classes and Transclasses." *Crisis & Critique* 10, no. 1: 162–183.

Littler, Jo. 2018. *Against Meritocracy: Culture, Power and Myths of Mobility*. London: Routledge.

Littler, Jo. 2020. "Neoliberal Meritocracy, Racialization and Transnationalism." In *Forward, Upward, Onward? Narratives of Achievement in African and Afroeuropean Contexts*, edited by Eva Ulrike Pirker, Katja Hericks, and Mandisa Mbali, 17–20. Düsseldorf: hhu books.

McLeod, John. 2010. "Extra Dimensions, New Routines. Contemporary Black Writing of Britain." *Wasafiri* 25, no. 4: 45–52.

Photopoulos, Cornelia. 2022. "'Be Gone.' Escaping Racialized Working-Class Space in Bernardine Evaristo's *Mr. Loverman* and *Girl, Woman, Other*." In *Locating Classed Subjectivities. Intersections of Space and Working-Class Life in Nineteenth-, Twentieth-, and Twenty-First-Century British Writing*, edited by Simon Lee, 183–205. New York: Routledge.

Savage, Mike. 2015. *Social Class in the 21st Century*. London: Penguin.

Selvon, Samuel. 1956. *The Lonely Londoners*. London: Alan Wingate.

Selvon, Samuel. 1975. *Moses Ascending*. London: Davis-Poynter.

Sigal, Clancy. 1988. "Bourgeois Black." In *Critical Perspectives on Sam Selvon*, edited by Susheila Nasta, 134. Washington: Three Continents Press.

Slaughter, Joseph R. 2006. "Enabling Fictions and Novel Subjects: The *Bildungsroman* and International Human Rights Law." *PMLA* 121, no. 5: 1405–1423.

Smith, Zadie. (2012) 2013. *NW*. London: Penguin.

Stein, Mark. 1998. "The Black British Bildungsroman and the Transformation of Britain: Connectedness Across Difference." In *Unity in Diversity Revisited? British Literature and Culture in the 1990s*, edited by Barbara Korte and Klaus Peter Müller, 89–105. Tübingen: Gunter Narr Verlag.

Stein, Mark. 2004. *Black British Literature: Novels of Transformation.* Columbus: Ohio State University Press.

Tyler, Imogen. 2013. *Revolting Subjects: Social Abjection and Resistance in Neoliberal Britain.* London, New York: Zed Books.

Tyler, Imogen. 2015. "Classificatory Struggles: Class, Culture and Inequality in Neoliberal Times." *The Sociological Review* 63: 493–511.

Vadde, Aarthi. 2015. "Narratives of Migration, Immigration, and Interconnection." In *The Cambridge Companion to British Fiction since 1945*, edited by David James, 61–75. Cambridge: Cambridge University Press.

Williams, Nicola. (1997) 2021. *Without Prejudice.* London: Penguin.

Williams, Raymond. (1979) 2015. *Politics and Letters: Interviews with the New Left Review.* London: Verso.

Young, Michael. 1958. *The Rise of the Meritocracy: 1870–2033.* London: Thames & Hudson.

PART 4

PERFORMING CLASS: MATERIALITY AND AFFECT

4.1

Affected by Discomfort

Class and Precarity in Twenty-First Century Theatre

MARISSIA FRAGKOU

Introduction

In her introduction to the edited collection *Smashing It: Working Class Artists on Life, Art and Making It Happen*, working-class playwright, poet and activist Sabrina Mahfouz (2019) writes:

> Today more than ever, let's celebrate the genre-shifting, world-changing art being made by working class [sic] artists in the UK. Let's remind ourselves that for every crucial article detailing the depressing lack of working-class representation across the creative industries, we need to celebrate the working-class artists leading the way in their fields, telling their stories the way they need to be told. (9)

Notwithstanding Mahfouz's optimistic and celebratory assessment of the current work produced by working-class artists in the UK, her statement articulates a deep concern regarding the difficulties and barriers they continue to face within the cultural industries. Following Mahfouz, this essay examines current theatre work created by working-class performance makers in the UK through a detailed discussion of particular dramaturgical approaches whilst also considering the material conditions for artists and creatives in relation to precarity, class and neoliberalism.

Celebrating the multiple class identities that compose twenty-first century British theatre necessitates intersectional and decolonial approaches which seek to question regimes of knowledge production (Bala 2017). Such approaches build on the significant work carried out by feminist and post-colonial thinking and their intersectional perspectives towards social inequalities (Tyler 2013, 157; Collins 2019, 1). "Class inequality," Katie Beswick (2020) suggests, "is inherently intersectional, always entangled with injustices related to race, gender, sexuality and disability, to the extent that it is difficult to understand the lived experiences and stigmas produced by distinct identity positions as separate from class" (266).

Contemporary examinations of class identities also require further attention to how class is experienced as a felt reality or, following Raymond Williams (1977), as "structures of feeling." Current sociological class analysis focuses on class's affective dimension; this either concerns feelings experienced by persons identifying as working class or the negative feelings projected towards them and how these operate as additional mechanisms of stigmatisation and marginalisation (Skeggs 2012). Affective approaches to class also traverse the study of the "precariat," Guy Standing's (2011) neologism congealing a class formation based on insecure and hyperflexible labour conditions which "experiences the four A's—anxiety, anger, anomie and alienation" (33). "Class feeling" is also, as Beswick (2020) argues, "an important dimension of understanding how barriers to access and participation operate in theatre contexts," and thus it is significant to view "class as a structure of feeling through which theatres operate—one that exists beyond socio-economic measures" (267). Viewing class in the theatre affectively further implicates audiences who are invited to engage with class issues as *representation* and ponder on their own positions of privilege.

In attending to the above questions and need for expanding methodological approaches when discussing class in twenty-first century theatre, I will be specifically focusing on two examples of autobiographical work by UK-based performance makers Scottee and Travis Alabanza. Drawing on feminist affect theory as a key methodological tool of analysis, the chosen examples will be examined through the lens of 'discomfort' as an affective strategy adopted to question normative orthodoxies about class identities and to explore its 'felt realities' and intersections with gender, sexuality and race. Departing from a Massumian approach which considers affect as different from emotion, I am here adopting Sara Ahmed's understanding of emotion as both physiological and socially determined and thus inseparable from affect. In *The Cultural Politics of Emotion*, Ahmed (2004) argues how normativity is by definition exclusionary, as it "is comfortable for those who can inhabit it" (148). More specifically, heteronormativity, she argues, "functions as a form of public comfort by allowing bodies to extend into spaces that have already taken their shape" (ibid.). I would like to extend this analogy by considering middle-class sensibility as a normative space to specifically think about theatre institutions as well as theatre audiences and the spaces of comfort they occupy. In doing so, I will be exploring how Scottee and Travis Alabanza tackle their own vulnerability and precarity to capture the affects of working-class identities and pose important questions about class privilege and care.

Precarity, Class and Theatre

After some years of apparent obsolescence, class has resurfaced as a legitimate category of analysis. In the UK in particular, the assumed redundancy of class was largely buttressed by New Labour's rhetoric of "we are all middle class now," or the need to eradicate "class divisions" promoted by New Labour leader Tony Blair, which has further intensified the stigmatisation of people who might receive state benefits or live in council estates as a "workless class" minority (Blair qtd. in Tyler 2013, 159) or "an underclass" who exist outside of the social system as "social abjects" (Tyler 2013).

Contemporary considerations of class examine the implications of global insecurities in the context of neoliberalism; such implications can be read as conditions of precarity. A wealth of publications across several disciplinary fields, from economics, sociology to literature and performance studies, examine precarity as a nexus of material conditions of injustice shaping contemporary identities. Judith Butler (2009) describes precarity as "that politically induced condition in which certain populations suffer from failing social and economic networks of support and become differentially exposed to injury, violence and death" (25). Drawing on Butler, Isabell Lorey (2015) also distinguishes between precariousness, an existential and a "socio-ontological dimension of lives and bodies" (11), and precarity, which connotes the conditions of inequality and "processes of othering" distributing precariousness (ibid., 12). For Lauren Berlant, precarity refers to "proletarian labor-related subjectivity," which has now extended to the bourgeoisie and is "a rallying cry for a thriving new world of interdependency and care that's not just private, but it is also an idiom for describing a loss of faith in a fantasy world to which generations have become accustomed" (Puar 2012, 166).

The above discussions regarding existing inequalities within the field of work and labour, the differential distribution of vulnerability and the quest for care and interdependency against the backdrop of neoliberalism have become chief concerns in the fields of performance studies. Precarity is discussed with regard to the material and affective labour and lived realities of performers and creatives (Ridout and Schneider 2012, 6); others have approached it as a representational trope that speaks to the ethical dimensions of encountering precarious identities on stage (Pewny 2011) whilst capturing the intersections of vulnerabilities and risks shaping identities in the contemporary world (Fragkou 2018). In staging precarious identities, that is, identities that have been marginalised or subjected to social injustices in the context of contemporary neoliberal capitalism, one has to think about the various affective devices mobilised through processes of theatrical framing. Arguably, theatre concerned with precarity seeks to cultivate ethical spectatorial engagement vis-à-vis social injustices and distant human suffering

(Pewny 2011); it brings audiences closer to those 'other' worlds through eliciting emotions such as sympathy, empathy, pity, anger and compassion. Such an ethical engagement with precarious identities might also be fraught with complexity. On the one hand, "[c]ompassion, like other forms of caring, may also reinforce the very patterns of economic and political subordination responsible for such suffering" (Spelman qtd. in Ahmed 2004, 22). On the other, the bombardment of images of suffering which are widely consumed by the public might lead to compassion's de-politicisation manifest as "compassion fatigue" (Mestrovic 1997, 56). In this conundrum, representations of the working class can promote voyeurism, encouraging "poverty porn" (Savage 2015, 353), or a false empathy that keeps middle-class audiences within their own comfort zones, thus re-affirming their biases without necessarily troubling the very structures that produce those class inequalities.

As a cultural form, the British theatre industry is largely dominated by creatives who occupy certain positions of privilege in terms of gender, race, ethnicity and class and shape how and for whom theatre is made. Recent studies into inclusion and diversity in the UK's arts sector demonstrate concerns over the consistent barriers preventing workforce and audience diversity in terms of ethnicity, race and class (Consilium 2016). As Madani Younis, the former artistic director of London's Southbank Centre, argues, there is an urgent need to

> challenge how cultural institutions see themselves and who they see themselves serving. Let's be honest: if cultural value is dictated by an entrenched elite, is it any surprise that we have such a narrow understanding of what and who we are? (Gardner 2015)

In recent years, there have been clear efforts to disrupt such pathologies entrenched in the theatre sector through the promotion of agendas of diversity and inclusion. In 2014, the Arts Council of England, the most important source of arts funding in the country, warned arts organisations that their funding will be cut unless they commit to "making audiences, programmes and their workforce more diverse" (Brown 2014).[1] Further independent initiatives such as Tonic Theatre, an organisation that closely works with arts organisations on developing their gender equality and diversity agendas, and the trans-casting statement signed by several theatres committing to avoid casting cisgender actors in trans, non-binary and gender-non-conforming roles (Trans Casting Statement n.d.), have seen flagship institutions such as the National Theatre pledging to increase the visibility of creatives who identify as female, black and Asian and improve audience demographics (National Theatre n.d.).

Despite such initiatives, perennial issues still plague the realities of artists from less privileged backgrounds, raising questions regarding institutional equality and diversity agendas. In her important study on institutional processes of committing to diversity and inclusion, Ahmed (2012) has shown that institutions might well seem to be making advances towards diversity and inclusion through the creation of statements of commitment. Yet these remain "non-performatives: they do not bring into effect what they name" (119). Selina Thompson (2017), a Leeds-based performance artist who identifies as Black, female, working class and disabled, speaks about the tokenism that often underpins such institutional initiatives, which fail to ensure the viability of artists from socially disadvantaged backgrounds who continue to feel excluded:

> This system/industry cries out, in a loud, and performative way for people from marginalised communities to become a part of it—but does not value their health and wellbeing and the potential realities of their backgrounds enough to make the changes that would make their presence in that system tenable.

Furthermore, class as an identity marker of inequality continues to remain largely invisible or unspoken within cultural institutions' agendas for widening participation in the arts. According to Elaine Aston (2020),

> barriers to social mobility within the arts have strengthened rather than weakened [...]. Unlike gender which is a protected characteristic, there is no protection against social class discrimination. Hence, discriminatory practices perpetuated by the middle-class bias of the profession go unchecked. (21)

In addition, Aston continues, the lack of an intersectional approach in evaluating privilege creates further exclusions (ibid.). This is justified by the fact that "arts organisations are still frequently run by cultural elites tethered to old-fashioned notions of cultural and class identities" (Lola Young qtd. in Arts Council England 2016, 102). For this reason, as Liz Tomlin (2020) stipulates in her study on class barriers in the theatre industry, "[i]t is vital to keep talking about it [class] if the socio-economic inequities that are deeply rooted in the theatre-making ecology are ever to be contested or overturned" (252).

The above concerns about class barriers and the lack of intersectional understandings of class further interlace with the identity of the artist as precarious worker whose labour is not always valued as work (Jackson 2012, 23). This is coupled with current models of arts sustainability, which largely adopt a neoliberal ethos and further deepen precarisation and inequalities: theatre in the UK follows a business model of entrepreneurship, which fundamentally changes the relationship between the artist and the state. Since the beginning of the twenty-first century, UK arts funding has been considered to be "public investment," thus transforming arts organisations into "small businesses that could support the economy, the education of the young people and the social fabric of a mul-ticultural society" (Tomlin 2015, 34). The growth of the cultural industries as an important economic sector in the UK forces artists to become "artpreneurs" who internalise and perform the ideological values of market economy, that is, self-interest, individualism, growth and profit (Harvie 2013, 63). Following post-2010 funding cuts implemented by the various Conservative governments, the ideal of the less state-dependent artist has been further enhanced and is cel-ebrated in the guises of "resilience" and "sustainability" (Arts Council England 2013, 31). This rhetoric poses numerous challenges to theatre makers, particu-larly those working within small-scale alternative theatre (Field 2013), who are asked to perform their value by often having to meet market demands while be-ing unable to achieve financial independence and stability and thus being forced to self-finance their work.

In addition to questions around class and precarity in terms of artistic repre-sentation and policy, another significant aspect concerns the politics in repre-senting class identities on stage. After a rich post-war theatre production fuelled by class issues, in the early 1990s class seemed to slowly disappear from British theatre—a symptom of a wider decline of identity politics during this period. Nevertheless, since the 2008 financial crisis, the British stage has been inundated with plays that explicitly deal with processes of precarisation and exclusion.[2] This return can be attributed to wider socio-cultural shifts within the context of twen-ty-first century Britain and the practices of precarisation that exacerbate existing social inequalities. With reference to Imogen Tyler's notion of the "social abject," Nadine Holdsworth (2021) describes how in the twenty-first century

> the English nation is blighted by a number of internal rifts and fissures that pit people against each other in ways that cast particular groups as threats to the na-tion, as unruly or demeaned citizens that need to be contained or expelled. (3)

Such "threats to the nation" also appear in the guise of "the precariat" (Stand-ing 2011), a class category which resists clichéd representations of people liv-ing within precarity, whilst also drawing attention to how their vulnerability "is linked to their structural location in society" (Savage 2015, 353).

Drawing on Standing's neologism, theatre scholars Peter Simonsen and Mathies Aarhus (2020) have coined the term "theatre of the precariat" to de-scribe this resurgence of class on the contemporary British stage:

> The plays constituting the theater of the precariat most obviously share thematic features and a concern with characters who belong to the precariat. They are also

marked by an interest in developing different techniques for activating and engaging with the audience's sense of ethics, both indirectly by staging an everyday lifeworld that is insecure or falling apart and more directly by addressing the audience as audience, by interacting physically with the audience through theater space and dramaturgy. (336)

Simonsen and Aarhus' definition can be applied to autobiographical performance, which "can engage with the pressing matters of the present which relate to equality, to justice, to citizenship, to human rights" (Heddon 2008, 2) and acknowledges the audience's presence. Although the notion of the 'precariat' can be criticised for not taking into consideration the intersections of inequalities within contemporary conditions of precarity, the examples that follow could be classed as part of the "theatre of the precariat" in that they stage insecure and hostile worlds and interact directly with their audience, and by doing so, they bring to the fore vulnerabilities and a social commentary about the differential allocation of vulnerability and processes of othering.

Scottee's *Bravado* (2017) and *Class* (2019)

Scottee is a prolific working-class, queer and neurodivergent artist who has worked across different performance styles that predominantly explore queer and working-class identities in contemporary Britain. Scottee has been particularly vocal about access and class agency in the theatre; growing up on a council estate in Kentish Town in North London in the 1990s, he left school at fourteen without gaining any qualifications or attending art school. He is committed to "making stuff that emotionally disrupts people for better or worse to think a little bit differently about the world in which we operate" and his work revisits identity politics from an intersectional point of view (SavidgeReads 2019). This "emotional disruption" of the audience is pursued in his two autobiographical shows *Bravado* and *Class* where he tackles disturbing personal material by examining the intersections of class, gender and sexuality.

Bravado is "a memoir of working-class masculinity" (Scottee 2017) covering the period 1991–1999 which focuses on the performer's own experience of bullying, abuse and sexual exploitation by his male peers on the council estate he grew up in. The piece was performed in conventional theatres as well as non-theatre spaces, typically male spaces such as "pubs, garages, changing rooms" (Scottee 2017, 20) and asked the audience to engage with Scottee's story by means of a proxy, a volunteer from the audience who is invited to read the script in his place.

The piece focuses on "the complexities of feelings, particularly male feelings" (Harvie 2017, 13). In his foreword, Scottee (2017) discusses his own feelings about working-class men as a mixture of fear and love:

> I don't like being on a train or bus, or waiting in public when groups of working-class blokes are present, I fear encountering football supporters, stag dos and lads on a night out—I worry what they might do to me, what they might say, what might happen—I fear potential. [...] [T]his fear is not one-sided, it's a mutual fear. They fear me and my effeminacy. [...] To complicate matters, I also love working-class men. I love their familiarity. (9)

Fear acts as a catalyst in *Bravado,* enabling Scottee to create his performance material about the toxicity of working-class heteronormativity: "this is how maleness and misogyny succeed: they live off our fear and off their potential—it's time to relinquish it" (ibid., 10). In dealing with his own fears, Scottee uses his vulnerability as his own act of "bravado," offering a testimony of the discomfort that working-class and queer bodies experience.

Ahmed (2014) describes discomfort as "a feeling of disorientation: one's body feels out of place, awkward, unsettled" (148). In *Bravado*, Scottee (2017) shares different stories from his childhood to his teenage years on the council estate which made his body feel "out of place": during the Sunday family pub gatherings where the parents would "encourage us to call each other girlfriend and boyfriend" (25); the same gatherings would transform into battlegrounds of toxic masculinities ending up in blood. Other scenarios of "compulsory heterosexuality" (Butler 1988, 524) concern Scottee's failure to rehearse a "masculine" identity, which would make him the object of bullying and banter and impress a "dose of shame" upon him (Scottee 2017, 31). As Ahmed (2004) argues, shame is a complex emotion "associated as much with cover and concealment, as it is with exposure, vulnerability and wounding. [...] Shame involves the intensification not only of the bodily surface, but also of the subject's relation to itself" (104). In one of the sections, entitled "Tears," the performer narrates a story of when Scottee's drunken father would physically assault him and he had to hide in his parents' room with his little brother. The tears that follow acts of violence reveal, as he explains, not remorse but shame and embarrassment, which is intensely felt by the whole family: "[We are embarrassed] that yet again we're sweeping broken glass or boarding up smashed windows. That yet again the neighbours will know" (Scottee 2017, 37).

In the context of the performance, Scottee's feelings of shame as exposure transform into an empowering gesture. Scottee (2017) explains that he wanted to "remove the comfort" of him sharing his trauma as something that has been

resolved, as this would encourage audience complacency (10). Sharing graphic
stories of toxic masculinity becomes an act of vulnerability and an ethical call
to empathise and care for working-class queer identities. The onus is primarily
placed on the volunteer, who has so far been "a bloke" (ibid.) and who stands
in for the men who have induced such trauma. By mediating his own experiences of discomfort and "feeling out of place" in spaces where toxic masculinity
is rife through the voice of another male body, he resists becoming an object
of scrutiny and of the "wound fetishism" that underpins "testimonial culture"
and spectacularises stories of pain and suffering (Ahmed 2004, 32). In so doing,
he returns the experience of discomfort back to the audience and particularly
the male volunteer who represents his abusers on the estate. At the end of the
performance, Scottee (2017) narrates the last time he accidentally crossed paths
with his childhood male peers and the subsequent feelings of anger this brief
encounter yielded:

> I want them to acknowledge I exist,
> ....that I survived scathed, bruised, battered, bleeding. [...]
> I want their confidence to be in crisis,
> to feel they are not good enough
> and that they do not belong. [...]
> I want their sexuality to be informed by the violent acts I force upon them. [...]
> I want them to be sorry. [...]
> I want them to love me. (44–46)

One of the volunteers who took part in *Bravado* describes this experience of
voicing Scottee's story to a live audience as a way of sharing another's pain and
taking responsibility for it: "I'd accidentally stumbled into somebody's pain and
shared it with strangers by making it my own" (Stewart Who? 2017, 19).

Discomfort as dramaturgical strategy also underpins Scottee's subsequent
performance *Class*, where he returns to his personal autobiography to impress
upon the audience feelings of working-class identities. The diegetic space of the
performance is once more the council estate, which, as Tyler (2013) argues, mobilises the figure of the "chav," a "pejorative and ubiquitous term of abuse of and
abhorrence at Britain's poor" who are the subject of "mockery, contempt and
disgust" (ibid., 162; 165). The "chav," Tyler proposes, as a racialised denominator
needs to be treated as

> a figure through which ideological beliefs (the underclass), economic interests
> (the erosion of the welfare state) and a series of governmental technologies (me-
> dia, politics, policy, law) converge to mystify neoliberal governmentality by natu-

ralizing poverty in ways that legitimize the social abjection of the most socially
and economically disadvantaged citizens within the state. (ibid., 170–171)

As mentioned above, such practices of social abjection are symptomatic of the
wider fissures currently dividing the British nation, which promulgate the logic
of an "us" and "them."

Scottee (2020) purposefully mirrors the above processes of stigmatisation
and division to problematise their affective dimensions. Drawing on the semi-
otic iconography of the "chav," he evokes the ways in which the working class are
often perceived by contemporary Britain's cultural hegemony as "social abjects":
he wears a "red tracksuit, gold earrings, necklaces and rings and a pair of new,
white trainers" (1) and puts on a "mock cockney accent" (ibid., 2).

Scottee also directly addresses the audience, reminding them of their own
privilege and spaces of comfort: he specifically draws attention to external features that define middle-class identities or their consumer habits, creating a division between "us" and "them." As director Sam Curtis Lindsay (2020) notes,
the performance space itself toyed with notions of comfort and discomfort: "the
space would be 'soft' using a carpet—like the nicest room in your house you have
to take your shoes off […]. In that softness, we found the danger and the joy in
this story and tried to make it a conversation" (ix). This false feeling of comfort that would allow middle-class spectating bodies to "take up space" quickly
evaporates as Scottee makes them feel conscious of their class identity. In order
to foreground contemporary forms of depoliticisation inherent in narratives of
"responsible capitalism" promoted by everyday acts of charity, the audience are
given supermarket tokens to put in a box that is labelled: "Working-class communities need? Money OR Love" (Scottee 2020, 1).

The piece also draws attention to the middle-class composition of the audience and their theatre-going habits:

> Good, just seventeen more hours of this shit to go before you are free to grab a
> glass of Rosé and tell each what good people you are for coming to see this show
> by someone you probably wouldn't invite to a dinner party. (ibid., 4–5)

His provocative tone evokes the feelings of anger which characterise the precariat. Further the mobilisation of discomfort in *Class* reminds us of the precariat's
feelings towards its media representations; as theatre critic Ben Walters (2019)
observes, what he names as Scottee's "theatres of discomfort" place emphasis on
the audience's privileged position: "If you are middle class you might prefer to
avoid a situation in which you will be caricatured, patronised or judged; not everyone, of course, has that luxury."

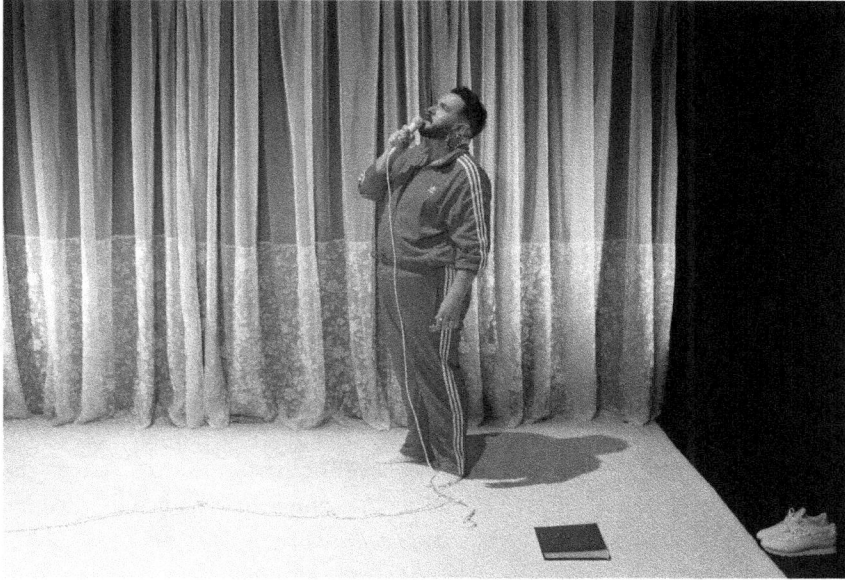

Scottee performing in *Class* at HOME theatre, Manchester, 2019.
Reproduced with permission © Holly Revell

Echoing *Bravado*, in *Class* (2020) Scottee confesses how his feelings of inadequacy and shame have shaped his identity and shares some "trauma-fuelled memories" regarding his and the rest of the council estate's abject and precarious living conditions, such as how the black mould in his bedroom contributed to "childhood asthma attacks" (27) or his fear of "leaving the house at fourteen because there were threats against my life for being queer" (ibid., 31). It similarly makes use of discomfort as an act of resisting "wound fetishism." This is achieved here through a different reversal of the gaze: at the end of the performance, Scottee reveals two mirrors that point at the audience whilst saying: "I am not doing this to hurt you. [...] I want us to see each other properly without defence. I want us to acknowledge why we're here, why we came" (ibid., 33).

Class also reminds us of the precarious position of a working-class artist who is trying to survive in the context of the neoliberal cultural industries. When the piece was performed at the Edinburgh Fringe, a festival circuit that relies on artists who self-fund their work in the hope that they can gain traction, theatre critic Kate Wyver (2019) pointed out that: "*Class* may not be an easy watch, but at the fringe, a space that continues to shut people out as it gets more and more expensive, it is an important one." As Scottee reminds the audience of their privilege, he also uses them as representatives of "the overwhelmingly middle-class British culture industry" (Walters 2019).

Travis Alabanza's *Burgerz* (2018)

> I am young, black, common, trans, grew up on an estate, didn't go to art school and
> suddenly, I am in your meeting room, I am your artist in your gallery taking up
> space in the media and writing and selling out debut shows. (Mahfouz 2019, 22)

Non-binary performer and writer Travis Alabanza reminds us of the power
structures that determine the rules of accessibility to the arts and the invisible
affective labour of claiming space in an elite and exclusionary artistic terrain that
requires cultural, financial and social capital. Alabanza is one of the very few
trans artists who have gained recognition in the UK and internationally: they
were the youngest person to secure a residency at London's Tate Modern at the
age of twenty-one and have written two plays that have toured internationally:
Burgerz (2018) and *Overflow* (2020). They have also performed in Scottee's *Putting Words in Your Mouth* (2016), exploring the complexities and contradictions
within the LGBTQ+ community in contemporary Britain.

Alabanza's autobiographical piece *Burgerz* explores discomfort emerging from
the violence of "compulsory heterosexuality" (Butler 1988, 524), which dehumanis-
es and punishes bodies that resist a binary logic. *Burgerz* examines the intersections
of gender, sexuality and race; its starting point is a transphobic incident Alabanza
experienced while walking across Westminster Bridge in London in which someone threw a burger at them and called them "tranny." The incident was witnessed by
a few people but no one intervened or asked Alabanza if they were feeling alright.

Burgerz was staged at a time when trans and gender-non-conforming persons
have achieved visibility and recognition; following the Gender Equality Act 2010,
gender reassignment is recognised as a protected characteristic which safeguards
transgender persons in England, Wales and Scotland from harassment. At the
same time, trans and non-binary people continue to experience transphobia,
which has risen dramatically in recent years.[3] During the making of the piece,
Alabanza's research showed that trans persons often experience transphobia in the
form of having food thrown at them (Affan 2021, 99). For this reason, *Burgerz* reflects a collective experience of hostility and transphobia, which victimises bodies
not conforming to "stereotypical social norms" and negatively affects their mental
health and well-being (Ellis, Bailey and McNeil 2016, 213). As Alabanza (2018) explains, "*Burgerz* has become an emblem for so many other incidents, deaths, acts
of violence and harm, that the trans and gender-nonconforming community have
to face every single day. *Burgerz*, for me, is about archiving the pain in our reality."

As an emotion, pain is "continually evoked in public discourse, as that which
demands a collective as well as individual response," particularly regarding oth-

Travis Alabanza performing in *Burgerz* at Hackney Empire, London, 2018.
Reproduced with permission © Holly Revell

ers (Ahmed 2004, 20). Although pain fuels compassion, it might also serve to re-affirm relations of power; in the case of *Burgerz*, Alabanza's own traumatic experience of discomfort caused by transphobia is tackled with humour. During the performance, Alabanza uses the burger as a device to re-assemble their memory of this particular and other transphobic events and to ask questions about the violence of heteronormativity; in doing so, the burger becomes a symbol of gender-based and racial violence which fills the lives of trans and gender non-conforming people with precarity.

Alabanza (2018) invites a cis white male audience member to help them make the burger as a way of reassuring them that they can do this on their own (20). The first instruction that the volunteer is asked to repeat intimates how taxonomies and definitions of identity create comfort zones for normative bodies whilst generating violence for bodies that fall outside the binary: "Travis, before you can make the burger, it is important you decide the type of box the burger would go in" (ibid., 21). Alabanza also shifts the discussion to race, reminding us that gender carries its own repertoire of "correct performances," which have been particularly buttressed by colonialism (ibid., 33).

Here the explicitness of the autobiographical material and the direct audience address remind us that whilst the visibility afforded to trans lives in the theatre means it might operate as a "safe space," this does not necessarily guarantee safety outside of it:

> If I walk out of this room right now, leave you and leave like this, like how I want to be, in these clothes, in this gender, I will be beaten, I will be bashed, I will be shouted at, I will be hurt. And you will go home. (ibid., 46)

This confession brings into sharp focus the violence of heteronormativity (and whiteness), which allocates differential levels of comfort to bodies, thus limiting the spaces that gender non-conforming bodies occupy in public (Butler 1988, 522).

Alabanza further emphasises the responsibility of witnessing such acts of violence by drawing attention to the privileged position of the witness. They ask a woman to join them on stage, who is handed the burger. Alabanza (2018) then tells the audience that when they were attacked, their gaze met that of a woman, who then turned away. The female volunteer reads a text that pledges commitment to solidarity, inviting the audience to consider the significance of allyship and unity in difference, as well as the spaces of comfort they occupy.

> I vow to protect you, as in the plural, as in more than just you. I vow to realise that in my safety, in my comfort, in my silence, comes your danger, hurt and entrapment. I vow to know that I cannot possibly be free, whilst you the plural are still hurt. [...] When I throw this burger I will throw it, not to hurt you again, but to acknowledge that I have hurt you before. [...] An action born out of violence with a hope to turn to a promise. A promise to do better. (59–60)

Conclusion: Towards an Ethics of Care

What can we learn from contemporary theatre and performance focusing on class identities? The so-called "theatre of the precariat" is concerned with "class feeling" (Beswick 2020), which emanates from the conditions of precarity and dispossession affecting twenty-first century marginalised identities. In exploring the complexities of class affects in the twenty-first century, it also draws attention to how class, gender and race interlace as ecologies of precarity. Further, it takes issue with the audience's privileges and, for this reason, "the theatres of the precariat" explored in this chapter primarily address middle-class audiences through strategies that create discomfort.

Although both Scottee and Alabanza confess that they do not have the answers to the questions they pose, their intention to publicly share their private experiences of being at risk allows them to "take up space" in public discourse in order to mobilise allyship and solidarity and "a new world of interdependency and care that's not just private" (Puar 2012, 166). This emphasis on care is particularly significant at a time when "care has been—and continues to be—overshadowed by totalitarian, nationalistic and authoritarian logics that rearticulate and reorient our caring inclinations towards 'people like us'" (Care Collective 2020, 15). In other words, to "put care centre stage means recognising and embracing our interdependencies" (ibid., 22); for Scottee and Alabanza, care is mobilised through difference, as they are asking their middle-class audiences to consider both their privilege and the possibility for interconnectedness. As shown, their performances unsettle normative spaces of comfort which historically belong to the middle class and, by extension, also expose the complicity of theatre structures to the violence of excluding working-class experience. This temporary affective displacement of privilege mobilised in the examples discussed in this chapter might work to question how spaces of privilege are created and maintained and to what extent our own practices of care disturb these. In the words of theatre critic Lyn Gardner (2020), they ask us to question our own ethics of care: "who cares, and do we care enough? Do we care in a way that genuinely makes a difference? Or do we care in theory but not when it really affects us?" (v).

Notes

1. The Arts Council have since expanded their understanding of diversity to also include gender reassignment (including transgender) and sexual orientation in addition to gender, disability, race and ethnicity.

2. Some examples include Jez Butterworth, *Jerusalem* (2009), Stan's Cafe, *The Just Price of Flowers* (2012), Simon Stephens, *Port* (2013), Alexander Zeldin, *Beyond Caring* (2014) and *Love* (2016), Gary Owen, *Iphigenia in Splott* (2016), and The Paper Birds, *Broke* (2014) and *Mobile* (2016).

3. According to official statistics published by the UK's Home Office, the rate of hate crimes against transgender people increases every year. In 2021-2022 the number of offences against transgender people saw a 56% increase in comparison to the previous year (Home Office 2022).

References

Affan, Erkan. 2021. "Erkan Affan in Conversation with Travis Alabanza and Malik Nashad Sharpe." *QED: A Journal in GLBTQ Worldmaking* 8, no. 1: 98–103.

Ahmed, Sara. 2004. *The Cultural Politics of Emotion*. Edinburgh: Edinburgh University Press.

Ahmed, Sara. 2012. *On Being Included: Race and Diversity in Institutional Life*. Durham: Duke University Press.

Alabanza, Travis. 2019. "Resolutions for the Common, Black, Queer, Young Kid (and anyone else who may need it)." In *Smashing It: Working Class Artists on Life, Art and Making it Happen*, edited by Sabrina Mahfouz, 20–23. London: The Westbourne Press.

Alabanza, Travis. 2021. *Burgerz*. London: Methuen.

Arts Council England. 2013. *Great Art and Culture for Everyone: 10-Year Strategic Framework: 2010–2020*. 2nd ed. Accessed 7 April 2023. https://www.artscouncil.org.uk/sites/default/files/download-file/Great_art_and_culture_for_everyone.pdf.

Arts Council England. 2016. *Analysis of Theatre in England*. Accessed 7 April 2023. https://www.artscouncil.org.uk/sites/default/files/download-file/Analysis%20of%20Theatre%20in%20England%20-%20Final%20Report.pdf.

Aston, Elaine. 2020. *Restaging Feminisms*. Cham: Palgrave Macmillan.

Bala, Sruti. 2017. "Decolonising Theatre and Performance Studies." *Tijdschrift voor Genderstudies* 20, no. 3: 333–345.

Beswick, Kate. 2020. "Feeling Working Class: Affective Class Identification and its Implications for Overcoming Inequality." *Studies in Theatre and Performance* 40, no. 3: 265–274.

Brown, Mark. 2014. "Arts in England told to make progress with diversity or have funding axed." *The Guardian*, 8 December 2015. Accessed 7 April 2023. https://www.theguardian.com/uk-news/2014/dec/08/arts-council-england-make-progress-diversity-funding-axed-bazalgette.

Butler, Judith. 1988. "Performative Acts and Gender Constitution: An Essay in Phenomenology and Feminist Theory." *Theatre Journal* 40, no. 4: 519–531.

Butler, Judith. 2009. *Frames of War: When is Life Grievable?* London: Verso.

Care Collective. 2020. *The Care Manifesto: The Politics of Interdependence*. London: Verso.

Consilium Research & Consultancy. 2016. *Equality and diversity within the arts and cultural sector in England 2013-2016*. Arts Council England.

Curtis, Sam Lyndsay. 2020. "Director's Note." In Scottee, *Class*, ix. London: Salamander.

Ellis, Sonja J., Louis Bailey, and Jay McNeil. 2016. "Transphobic victimisation and perceptions of future risk: a large-scale study of the experiences of trans people in the UK." *Psychology & Sexuality* 7, no. 3: 211–224.

Field, Andy. 2013. "Two Ideas Towards Transparency," *Ephemerous*, 24 November 2013. Accessed 7 April 2023. https://andytfield.wordpress.com/2013/11/24/transparency/.

Fragkou, Marissia. 2018. *Ecologies of Precarity in Twenty-First Century Theatre: Politics, Affect, Responsibility*. London: Bloomsbury Methuen.

Gardner, Lyn. 2015. "Diversity is key to creativity—and British theatre's challenge for 2015." *The Guardian*, 6 January 2015. Accessed 7 April 2023. https://www.theguardian.com/stage/theatreblog/2015/jan/06/diversity-creativity-british-theatre-2015.

Harvie, Jen. 2013. *Fair Play: Art, Performance and Neo-liberalism*. Basingstoke: Palgrave Macmillan.

Harvie, Jen. 2017. "Bold Love." In Scottee, *Bravado*, 11–15. London: Salamander.

Heddon, Deirdre. 2008. *Autobiography and Performance*. Basingstoke, New York: Palgrave Macmillan.

Hill Collins, Patricia. 2019. *Intersectionality as Critical Social Theory*. Durham: Duke University Press.

Holdsworth, Nadine. 2020. *English Theatre and Social Abjection: A Divided Nation*. Cham: Palgrave Macmillan.

Home Office. 2022. "Hate Crime, England and Wales, 2021 to 2022." GOV.UK, 6 October 2022. Accessed 7 April 2023. https://www.gov.uk/government/statistics/hate-crime-england-and-wales-2021-to-2022/hate-crime-england-and-wales-2021-to-2022.

Jackson, Shannon. 2012. "'Just in Time': Performance and the Aesthetics of Precarity." *TDR: The Drama Review* 5, no. 4: 10–31.

Lorey, Isabell. 2015. *State of Insecurity: Government of the Precarious*. Translated by Aileen Derieg. London: Verso.

Mahfouz, Sabrina, ed. 2019. *Smashing It: Working Class Artists on Life, Art and Making it Happen*. London: The Westbourne Press.

Mestrovic, Stjepan. 1997. *Postemotional Society*. London: Sage.

National Theatre. n.d. "Diversity in our Audience." National Theatre. Accessed 7 April 2023. https://www.nationaltheatre.org.uk/about-the-national-theatre/diversity/in-our-audiences.

Pewny, Katharina. 2011. *Das Drama des Prekären: Über die Wiederkehr der Ethik in Theater und Performance*. Bielefeld: transcript.

Puar, Jasbir. 2012. "Precarity Talk: A Virtual Roundtable with Lauren Berlant, Judith Butler, Bojana Cvejic, Isabell Lorey, Jasbir Puar, and Ana Vujanovic." *TDR: The Drama Review* 56, no. 4: 163–177.

Ridout, Nick, and Rebecca Schneider. 2012. "Precarity and Performance: An Introduction." *TDR: The Drama Review* 56, no. 4: 5–9.

Savage, Mike. 2015. *Social Class in the 21st Century*. London: Pelican.

SavidgeReads. 2019. "Class, Books, Bodies, Creativity & Queerness with Scottee." 5 February 2019. Conversation, 22:22. Accessed 7 April 2023. https://www.youtube.com/watch?v=cbQkNPS4pog.

Scottee. 2017. *Bravado: Written and Lived by Scottee*. London: Oberon.

Scottee. 2020. *Class*. London: Salamander.

Simmonsen, Peter, and Mathias Aarhus. 2020. "Theater of the Precariat: Staging Precarity in Alexander Zeldin's *Love*." *Contemporary Literature* 61, no. 3: 335–361.

Skeggs, Beverley. 2012. "Feeling Class: Affect and Culture in the Meaning of Class Relations." In *The Wiley-Blackwell Companion to Sociology*, edited by George Ritzer, 269–286. London: Blackwell.

Standing, Guy. 2011. *The Precariat: The New Dangerous Class*. London: Bloomsbury Academic.

Stewart Who? 2017. "Foreword: Bravado, a Perspective." In Scottee, *Bravado: Written and Lived by Scottee*. London: Oberon.

Thompson, Selina. 2017. "Theatre, Performance and Employment Provocation: QMUL." Accessed 7 April 2023. https://selinathompson.co.uk/blog/theatre-performance-and-employment-provocation-qmul/.

Tomlin, Liz. 2015. *British Theatre Companies: 1995–2014*. London: Bloomsbury.

Tomlin, Liz. 2020. "Why we still need to talk about class." *Studies in Theatre and Performance* 40, no. 3: 251–264.

Trans Casting Statement. n.d. Accessed 7 April 2023. http://www.transcastingstatement.com/.

Tyler, Imogen. 2013. *Revolting Subjects: Social Abjection and Resistance in Neoliberal Britain*. London, New York: Zed Books.

Walters, Ben. 2019. "Theatre review: Scottee, *Class*: Assembly Roxy, Edinburgh." *The Scotsman*, 15 August 2019. Accessed 7 April 2023. https://www.scotsman.com/arts-and-culture/edinburgh-festivals/theatre-and-stage/theatre-review-scottee-class-assembly-roxy-edinburgh-1410528.

Williams, Raymond. 1977. *Marxism and Literature*. Oxford: Oxford University Press.

Wyver, Kate. 2019. "Scottee: Class review—check your privilege, row A." *The Guardian*, 8 August 2019. Accessed 7 April 2023. https://www.theguardian.com/stage/2019/aug/08/scottee-class-review-check-your-privilege.

4.2
The Redundancy

Playing Production in Academic Capitalism

SARAH POGODA

The Socialist Production Play: Redundant?

In 1956/7 GDR playwright Heiner Müller completed his socialist production play *Der Lohndrücker* (lit. *The Wage Squeezer*).[1] Production play is a theatre genre mainly known in the former Socialist Bloc, as these plays dealt with the problems and challenges the socialist societies in-their-making faced in the industrial production sector, for example scarcity of resources and skilled workers. In most cases, these plays presented so-called *Helden der Arbeit* (Heroes of Labour), workers whose unprecedented work ethics benefited the socialist economy, usually by increasing factory output. They were meant to act as role models. The cast for staging the production plays were often recruited from factory workers and the plays were performed to an industrial workforce as the audience.

Der Lohndrücker was based on the historical case of Hans Garbe, who in the very beginnings of the GDR rebuilt a furnace under the most adverse conditions—namely while the furnace was in use. Putting his life at risk, Garbe secured productivity and production goals. In Müller's text Garbe is named Balke, a word play on *Balken,* which is German for 'beam,' and by also referencing the historical moment of socialism-in-the-making, Balke's name indicates the central role of hardworking workers, as a beam is one of the principal horizontal structural members of a building. Similarly to Garbe, Balke also opts to rebuild a furnace while production is in process, but in so doing he faces a number of challenges, from red tape to existing conflicts within his team. The workers mistrust Balke and sabotage his endeavour, as his operation raised production norms, causing his co-workers' wages to be reduced in relation to the level of productivity expected from them, while Balke is rewarded with a substantial bonus, hence the title of the play. In a sense, Balke is both a hero and an enemy of the working class for whom the GDR was meant to be built, and to whom the state was meant to belong. In this ambiguity Müller brings ideological and class conflicts pre-

dominant in the early GDR to stage and adds a critical dimension that is rather
unusual in the traditional production play. Müller's play was initially quite popular, but quickly fell out of fashion, as the political developments in the GDR of
the 1960s reframed existing conflicts and made the production play redundant.
Only in 1988 did Müller himself bring it back to stage for the Deutsche Theater
in Berlin, at the same time admitting that it was actually "not the most up-to-
date play at the moment" (Suschke n.d.; translated by me).

Today, more than 30 years later, the years of building up socialism and the
conflicts in industrial production in the early GDR seem more distant than ever.
Still, when reading *Der Lohndrücker* with students in 2018, I felt reading a precise description of the working conditions and conflicts to which I was exposed
to as an employee of a British university. Was I misapprehending Müller's play or
my working conditions? Müller once suggested that reality might never change
to such an extent that certain plays could not be written or staged anymore.[2]
Moreover, in his seminal study on *Der Lohndrücker*, Falk Strehlow attributes
Balke not exclusively to the early GDR but reads him "as a phenomenon of col-
lective/social/historical working conditions or liminal experiences" (Strehlow
2006, 66; translated by me). Was it possible that the socialist production play was
relevant beyond its immediate GDR context? Bewildered, I commenced a creative research process for staging *Der Lohndrücker*. About nine months later, on a
sunny Sunday afternoon in Bangor, North Wales, a group of about 20 people followed my invitation to see the resulting multi-media site-specific performance,
entitled *The Redundancy*.[3]

Welcomed in the foyer of the New Main Arts Building of Bangor University,
the audience was introduced to the proceedings of the day and equipped with a
comprehensive programme[4] as well as MP3 players and headphones. The words
of welcome and the event's programme guided the audience through fifteen stations at three different locations, announced the timing for live performances
and contained instructions for a playlist.[5]

The audience was encouraged to navigate through buildings, rooms and out-
door sites on their own terms, pause and observe, listen to songs and audio files,
pass some time or move on, gather or split apart. In the first location, Bangor
University's Main Arts Building, the audience would find the building devoid of
people—typical for a Sunday afternoon, particularly during the semester break.
The absence of staff and students created an eerie atmosphere increased by the
haunting media installations: the audience walked through corridors in which
incorporeal voices were lamenting strategy papers on how the university would
focus on 'blue chip' grant income, on how an increasingly competitive higher
education (HE) market sets imperatives to prioritise curriculum developments
in subject areas with large and/or growing demand, or on how best to claim a

Remains of the old Britannia Bridge
Structure, staging Balke calling
colleagues to increase productivity
(Bangor, 2019).
Reproduced with permission © Huw
Jones

market advantage. At the same time, the title of the performance, *The Redundancy*, suggested a fatalistic premonition, given that academic life was marked by the absence of those who usually embody it. The suggested incorporeality of the academic workforce paradoxically made it possible to focus on the material conditions of academia, instead of supporting the assumption of academia as an intellectual occupation or immaterial vocation. The university building was staged as an installation of academic work, with some rooms and offices in their everyday shape, and with others re-arranged to host films or performance, or functioning as topical installations. Depending on how audiences engaged with the installations on offer, they would have seen embodied variations of working conditions, such as people shovelling horse manure in the pouring rain,[6] young academics running back and forth between their offices and the department's printer, the installation of a standing desk, or a theatre director physically agitated and angrily smashing his mobile phone on the ground. This arrangement linked pre-industrial forms of labour with the digital age and marked academia as a still relevant site of labour whose material conditions are performed and thus are sewn into the fabric of academic bodies and subjectivities.

The second location connected the knowledge economy to the history of the local industrial economy and the haunting past of the British Empire. Britannia Bridge was completed in 1850 and provided the necessary rail link for convenient travel to and from Ireland/Wales. Its construction employed stonemasons, clerks, brick makers, sailors, contractors, engineers, riveters, foundry workers and carpenters from the local area and beyond. That sunny day in June 2019, its remains provided the stage for one performer who called on to his co-workers to work extra hours to ensure that all production targets were met. Later, only moments after the audience listened to the anthem *The Internationale*, they would learn about how those very co-workers physically attacked the performer for his enforcement of changes and increased productivity targets at their workplace.

The third location was private accommodation. Upon entering, the audience walked through the projection of a film showing individuals reading parts of Müller's *Hamletmaschine*. Walking further down the corridor, they could turn into the left-hand bedroom re-arranged as an archival installation with documents, props and films, allowing engagement with the research process of the performance, and at the same time staging the invisible mental workload that troubles academics' sleep. The right-hand bedroom on the corridor was shut, only showing a note on its doors saying: "Scene 12 had to be cancelled due to sick leave." The corridor finally led into an open-plan kitchen, where free food and drinks were served. The audience stayed for hours to discuss the four-hour performance and how it related to their own working conditions.

The Redundancy blends immersive theatre, installation art and site-specific performance, and used multi-media tools (e.g. audio, music, film, online tools and apps, a printed programme). It did not stage a theatre production of the play *Der Lohndrücker*, but rather assembled loosely related stations to make visible working conditions in UK HE. In its beginnings, the project was not planned to take this form—nor this title. Indeed, these were the outcomes of a nine-month-long research process that was determined by the very working conditions in question. The following essay will thus focus on the conditions of the research process and the form of the performance.

Beginnings

UK universities are responsible for the academic standards of all awards granted in their names, and the quality of students' teaching and learning. Universities have generated processes for top-down management and monitoring of academic quality and standards. Academic, professional and support staff are obliged to review and apply frameworks, policies and procedures which universities want to use to foster a culture of continuous improvement—a culture, it should to be noted, which is one of auditing excess, not even sparing students, and which has expanded vastly since the so-called "quality revolution" (Newton 2002) in the 1990s. This was further spurred by the Further and Higher Education Act 1992, which pushed massive changes in UK HE, including a diversification and rise in student cohorts, which resulted in a demand to align and monitor standards across HE institutions (Laughton 2003, 310f). Particularly for pre-1992 universities, the growing advance of internal quality monitoring arrangements that align with monitoring activities through external quality bodies meant a severe shift from rather *laissez-faire* organisation to explicit management (Deem 1998, 48).

Moreover, the substantial increase of tuition fees in 2011 and the shift to students as customers (GOV.UK 2011), representation, consultation and feedback mechanisms turned the question of academic standards into that of student satisfaction. For teaching and learning, the so-called 'Quality Assurance Agency in Higher Education' sets subject benchmark statements and regularly checks on universities' Quality Assurance procedures. Peer-based validation and revalidation, annual programme monitoring, external examiners, school, college and university committees, module evaluation and staff–student liaison committees are instruments most universities use.

Student feedback on one of my modules, entitled "Divided Germany," suggested that students felt the length of the core readings for the module difficult to manage. Responding to this, I changed my syllabus and introduced Heiner Müller's play *Der Lohndrücker,* replacing a 200-page novel. *Der Lohndrücker* is a play of only nineteen scenes, most of minimal length. It allowed me to still discuss the complex interdependencies of economy, politics and culture in the early years of the GDR, without asking students to read a text that was felt to be too time-consuming. Thus, my engagement with Müller's text is a result only of the shifts in academic production, in this case towards the prioritisation of customer satisfaction. Though replacing the novel was not imposed by academic authorities, I felt a rather intangible pressure to respond to students' evaluation. This pressure was fed firstly by the increased dependency of my job on student numbers, which seem to improve with better student satisfaction and student experience rankings, and secondly by the implicit imperatives of the quality assurance forms academics are made to complete at the end of each academic year and which are of course part of the customer satisfaction regime in British HE. The GDR module is thus perceived as a commodity, designed and delivered by an academic worker.

The Neoliberal University as a Socialist Production Play?

Discussing the play with students, I started to talk explicitly about the very working conditions to which I was exposed to as an employee at a British university— in my case, a university that was in the process of restructuring due to financial woes. But how could it be that a play dealing with issues of production in early

Socialism (as in the case of *Der Lohndrücker*) reverberated with neoliberal realities at British universities?

Recent theories on neoliberal capitalism identify the close entanglement between HE, universities and capitalism, whether in political, economic or cultural terms (Allmer and Bulut 2018). Academic labour is based on and shaped by information and communication (Fuchs and Sevignani 2013, 257), which renders universities agents in information capitalism or the knowledge economy. 'Academic capitalism' (Slaughter and Leslie 1997; Slaughter and Rhoades 2004) thus has prominent features such as marketisation, growing managerial governance and increasing competitive pressure. In a very short time, competition in academia has come to be defined in terms of economic instead of intellectual prestige.[7] This is not only a result of enforced New Public Management (NPM), but also of the marketisation of HE under New Labour, when Britain imposed tuition fees, which now stand at £9,000. At the same time, government grants to universities continued to decline. Today universities are 70% funded by tuition fees.[8] Universities compete for paying customers, customers who pay for education as an informational commodity, a commodity created by universities. This means universities operate not only on the intersection between public sector and productive industries, but also as conduit to the service sector. The justification for promoting competition in education and research is based on the belief that education and research excel only when they obey market dynamics that apply in productive industries or the service sector.

As Mark Fisher (2009) explains in his seminal essay *Capitalist Realism*, the restructuring of HE has created a quasi-market and implemented a culture of competition and auditing,[9] on all aspects of research (REF, PURE),[10] teaching (TEF, QA) and administration.[11] British universities delight in competition, indeed celebrate it: students and institutionally nominated committees create annual awards and prizes for outstanding achievers among university staff (Student-Led Teaching Award, Equality Role Model Award, Career and Employability Award), which later can be used as mandatory evidence when applying for promotion. That being said, in the UK, universities are not private companies but charities. The means of production are therefore not owned by private capitalists, and academics do not generate surplus value. This seems to exclude the HE sector from the class debate. And surely, isn't academia a vocation rather than labour as a productive force (Weber 1946)? But maybe the romantic perception of academia as a vocation obstructs the true material reality of working in academia in the UK?

Indeed, in recent years, the UK government has further enabled universities to access private investments (McGettigan 2013, 128), and to act similarly to private companies (e.g. investing on the stock market, outsourcing, etc.). As such, universities operate in real estate, tech industries or hospitality, and thus often bind themselves in fixed performance agreements with creditor banks. False investments, high levels of debt and interest obligations have caused financial strain in many universities.

From Lohndrücker to Redundancy

This was also the case for my employer, which carried out two rounds of so-called restructuring measures in 2017/18 and 2018/19—in the meantime, a third was added in 2020/21. This included suspension of promotions, cancellation of automatic wage increases, research budget cuts, sale of estates, closure of entire departments and finally job cuts. The latter had priority and enforced a trauma-tising deep-cut restructuring of the whole university—at this point, three times in a row. The resulting loss of more than 300 jobs in three years has always been referred to in technical jargon as 'redundancies.' Redundancy is a labour law term defined on the UK government's official website as follows:

> Redundancy is when you dismiss an employee because you no longer need any-one to do their job. This might be because the business is:
> • changing what it does
> • doing things in a different way, for example using new machinery
> • changing location or closing down
> For a redundancy to be genuine, you must demonstrate that the employee's job will no longer exist. (GOV.UK. n.d.)

In the UK, traditional modes of academic self-governance have almost fully been replaced by top-down management practices (Park 2013). This came with new expectations about the role of academic workers (Deem 2004), particularly as regards budgetary responsibility in times of enhanced resource dependency (Slaughter and Leslie 1997). In this climate, university management often del-egate the burden of justifying redundancies to faculties or schools themselves, via so-called budgetary responsibility. Faculties and schools must write their own business plans, in which they identify any so-called 'redundant staff' (not by name, but in the job description and FTE).[12] As a result, colleagues—mostly involved in the writing up of these three-year plans themselves—become com-petitors.[13] We write the business plans, of course trying to save all members of staff, but at the same time we try to distinguish ourselves from other colleagues as indispensable by taking on additional tasks despite the already unmanage-able workload. With universities in dire financial straits and recruitment freezes, the "reserve army" (Marx and Engels 1968, 661) of unemployed academics is growing (Lin and Chiu 2016), increasing pressure on high performance for the employed academic wage earner—the threat of being made redundant results in willingness to accept unbearable working conditions. According to a 2021 survey run by the University College Union (2021), "staff in higher education are working an average of 50.4 FTE hours per week—more than 2 unpaid days each week" (26). The regulation, teaching technologies and research funding in the UK today increased academics' dependence, as they do not own the means of HE production (libraries, certification, rooms, technology). And without employment academics risk not being able to afford the means of their livelihood— putting them in the same position of dependency as the traditional proletariat. However, as it was redundancy that university management used as leverage to silence staff regarding increased workloads, and not the falling in wages suggested by the title of Heiner Müller's play, I changed the name of the artistic research from *Der Lohndrücker* to *The Redundancy*. At Bangor, staff work more than their contracted hours, and are thus paid less, the implicit reward being the hope that they may pass on the cup of redundancy.[14] In the end, our willingness to accept increased workloads provided the means to justify redundancies.

Engaging with Müller's play made me question the dialectics of my own role—at the same time compromising and compromised—within the conditions of academic labour more openly than—but alongside—union actions.

Horseshit Jobs

Most of the tasks filling up the two days of unpaid labour are of an administrative nature and feed the auditing processes or customer satisfaction priorities (UCU 2021, 33), directly or indirectly delivering the neoliberal university under which my colleagues and I suffer. Such tasks are experienced as detrimental to performance, job satisfaction or mental health, as they have little to do with research or teaching. I therefore started to wonder why my colleagues and I were still delivering these tasks, which were reinforcing the neoliberal mode of HE. What is our relationship to labour? Why do we continue to act as overachievers similar to Balke (Allmer 2018b)? Do we consider our unpaid labour heroic?

In his play *Herakles 5*, Heiner Müller refers to the fifth labour of Herakles, the cleaning of the stable of Augeas. But different to the Greek myth, Müller's play shows Herakles and the cleansing not as a heroic action, but as trivial work. Herakles is thus not a heroic god-like figure, but simply willing to work.[15] The text inspired me to invite colleagues and friends to a farm on Anglesey where they were asked to shovel horseshit from one end to the other end of a manure heap. Partly accompanied by workers' songs, partly without music, we explored our willingness to work, our perception of 'horseshit jobs,' and whether the point-less repositioning of the manure heap could gain any heroic notion or mean-ingfulness. Involving a physically strenuous task, at times in the pouring rain, *Herakles 5* made visible all the participants' almost unconditional willingness to work—labour as an end in itself. Despite our best efforts, however, there was no notion of heroism to it, rather that of an existential fatalism. The increase in the norm—after about an hour a second wheelbarrow was fetched and the group asked to find ways to increase the efficiency of the work—changed little in this willingness; instead participants started discussions about improvements. The strong physicality of the experiment furthermore highlighted the reciprocity of subjectivity and work. Considering David Graeber's pamphlet against so-called *Bullshit Jobs* (2019), we see how *Herakles 5* simultaneously questions simple di-chotomies or devaluations of certain forms of work and work ethics. If work is indeed an anthropological force, labour disputes need to include an inquiry into meaningful and meaningless work.

Efficiency, Efficiency at Any Price

With this fatalistic willingness to work in mind, I felt that I wanted to create a space for colleagues to start conversations and explorations on working condi-tions at Bangor University, and our roles within these conditions. The accelerat-ed pace of the restructuring and the increased workload that came with it hardly allowed any critical engagement with the redundancy process.

Initially, I envisioned a Brechtian 'Lehrstück'[16] stage production of *Der Lohn-drücker* with my colleagues as the cast to bring together the concrete historical-economic constellations of the two realities, that of a furnace in the GDR in its early years and that of Bangor University in 2019 in the UK. However, my first call out did not elicit any expressions of interest. One colleague merely pointed out that it would be helpful to know about the required time commitment—providing yet another example of the shortage of spare time due to an excessive workload. I therefore started to experiment with forms of performativity which would enable participation as part of daily working routines or outside of work-ing hours but with minimal commitment. Here, the line "Efficiency, efficiency at any price" from Scene 5 of *Der Lohndrücker* became the project's catchphrase. Scene 5 caught my eye more than any other scene, as it presents a precise de-scription of the plant's situation, and correspondingly, with only slightly tweaked wording, the scene would contain the working conditions of Bangor University under restructuring, and thus the difficulties I encountered in staging the play. In a nutshell, these were: no budget, no staff, no resources, and heavy workloads.

Second call out to colleagues for *The Redundancy project*, then still titled *The Scab* (Bangor 2019). Reproduced with permission © Huw Jones

As such, the scene offered an excellent exposition of the conflicts of the play—as well as insight into the production conditions which would inform its staging.

After work, four temporarily employed colleagues joined me in the beautiful evening sun for a stroll along the shores of the Menai Strait, but instead of recreational activities, we were there to film the slightly reworded Scene 5. By doing so, we embodied academic subjectivities who invest leisure time in pursuing their vocational passion for their research (Gill 2010; Jaffe 2021).

Following the catchphrase, we ran the scene on the spot, without rehearsal, in single shots only, and the cast had not spent any time preparing their lines, as I handed out the script only minutes before shooting.

> **Actor 1**: I'd only like to tell you, Sir, this won't work. A schedule that's based on the assumption that colleagues and friends will be available over 2 months of production is irresponsible, if not absurd, with the workload everybody is in. One dropping out, and the performance will face chaos!
>
> **Actor 2**: *(Looking into playwrights, not very attentive)* We are facing chaos, Mister. We're restructuring an institution. That spells: Efficiency, efficiency at any price.
>
> **Actor 1**: Maybe efficiency will be the price. I'm washing my hands of it, I'd only like to have pointed that out.
>
> [...]
>
> **Director**: *(enters, talking on mobile phone)* Listen, Schurek, I need them. Am I supposed to work with my bare body? *(pauses, listens to the person on the phone)* What does that mean, all our cast has been allocated? I have not received anyone. *(pauses, listens to the person on the phone)* I know that we are supposed to generate academic research, impact and students and not art and stuff. I am not asking anyone to break rules. *(pauses)* No, I am not willing to make sacrifices. *(stops the phone conversation and throws the phone on the floor. Director turns to the 2 actors)*

We are supposed to do a 21 person play with three actors. Our production play will be a chamber play. *(exit)*

Actor 3: *(enters, with smart phone in hands)* I need something on production outputs for my PURE Profile.[17]

Actor 1: That will be tough.

Actor 3: How are we doing with the performance?

Actor 1: No boot walks by itself alone.

Actor 3: What's that?

Actor 1: First somebody's got to put it on the foot.

Actor 2 (to Actor 3): I've got something for you, colleague. Wait here, I'll get the director. *(Actor 1 exits. Silence. Actor 2 comes back with Producer)*

Director: Do you know what a production play is?

Actor 3: A theatre genre mainly known in the former Socialist Bloc, as these plays dealt with the problems and challenges the socialist societies in-their-making faced in industrial production sector. Often, the cast of these plays were recruited from factory workers, and performed at relevant production sites.

Actor 1 to Actor 2: Well, maybe she knows all theatre history by note?

Director: We are short of workers, after the redundancies. We'll have to cancel our performance, if further people bail on us. The scenes we were recently rehearsing will need reediting as actors had left.

Actor 3: Sabotage.

Director: Redundancies! Workloads!

Actor 3: I see. Objective obstacles.

Actor 1: *(to the director)* So, you say, it is impossible to do the performance with those left?

Director: I was saying, the play requires 14 actors. That is the norm, the script sets you. The producer has just told me, we will do it with what we have. What remains to be done then: outsourcing, pre-recording, digitisation and blue sky thinking. He said. *(All exit in different directions)*

The scene focuses on the conflict constellation between academic duties and artistic commitment, but also provides the viewer with necessary explanations (genre: production play; background: redundancies, PURE, etc.) and introduces the threat that the production play might be cancelled. Conditions would only allow a chamber play, since a chamber play usually consists of four characters. However, though the scene might appear like a chamber play—as only four actors performed—it was rewritten into this form (the original scene requires nine actors) due to the conditions of production, and thus truly remained a production play. Via re-entry, the production piece would not turn into a chamber play. And this applied for *The Redundancy* as a whole, as its form reflected the conditions of its production. Indeed, *The Redundancy* applied the very means of production that the tweaked script for Scene 5 had anticipated: "outsourcing, pre-recording, digitization." In this manner, the video recording of Scene 5 was used as exposition for the performance of *The Redundancy* and was shown to the whole of the audience only shortly after the welcome. In the following I will discuss example applications of outsourcing, pre-recording and digitisation in the production of *The Redundancy.*

Experiment I: Subdivision and Pre-fabrication of Scene 5

As a matter of redundancy, I decided to perform Scene 5 once more, but in its original script. Via email, I asked nine of my colleagues for help. Each of them received only the text of one of the characters in Scene 5. I instructed them to record their text with their smartphones and send the recording to me for editing.[18] In this way, I could have reduced their mental load, since engagement, even understanding, of the conflict in Scene 5 was neither possible nor necessary, but I reproduced the sense of 'alienated labour' that is intrinsic to most processes of auditing students[19] and ourselves.[20] Furthermore, I was able to reduce my colleagues' time investment to a minimum. However, during the time-consuming editing of the audio files, it became apparent that I had to invest time later in the process that I believed I had saved earlier. The reduction of the time investment for my colleagues led to a maximisation of the time investment for me. For the performance, the audio recording was played in the Bangor University Council Chamber, a representative meeting room in the historic wing of the Main Arts Building, often in use for meetings of the Executive Committee.

Experiment II: Outsourcing and Digitisation of Scene 8a

Another experiment consisted of outsourcing production and mobilising invisible labour resources, thereby creating a network, which is a typical form of production in the post-Fordist economy, especially in the information sector (Castells 1996). Instead of working with colleagues in Bangor, I asked friends outside of Wales (Germany, USA, England, Sweden) to help with a digital performance of Scene 8a. I created a Google account for each character, and sent the account details and the text of the whole scene to each volunteering friend. Using Doodle Poll, we decided on a one-hour appointment (14 May 2019, 10 pm CET) to log in with the characters' profiles in a Google Docs document. I was registered as the stage director, so I worked in italics and also recorded the digital live performance as a desktop film with QuickTime. Step-by-step, each character typed out their lines when it was their turn. As Google Docs displays the account name of the person typing, the flickering account name in the document thus embodied the character in real time. This digital live performance lasted twenty-seven minutes and six seconds. Some friends reported stage fright.

For the performance, I compressed the desktop film to five minutes and twenty-five seconds by speeding it up by 400%.[21] I added a soundtrack, composed by a local musician. Using various industrial noises, the soundtrack created a link between the industrial reality of the GDR play and the knowledge industry of the university, whose reality of digital mediation in teaching and research was applied using Google Docs. Adding to this, I uploaded the video file to a Blackboard course—the virtual learning environment in use at Bangor University—that I created specifically for the project. On the day of the presentation, the audience gathered in a group and watched the video on the central screen in the Multi-Media Lab after witnessing how I opened the Blackboard application beforehand in order to play the clip.

Experiment III: Who is Speaking?

Another experiment resulted from my observation that I increasingly heard variations of statements from the play in meetings, or that I could read them in the strategy papers disseminated by university management for review by staff. I decided to exaggerate this observation and selected phrases from the play, and handed one each to my colleagues, including those who never responded to my call to participate in the *Lohndrücker* experiment. I asked everyone to use their phrase as often as possible in any situation over the course of a week. Some colleagues replied that they often wondered whether the other person was saying a phrase from the play or making an authentic statement, since they could easily place their phrase afterwards as if it were part of the written dialogue of the play. The superimposition of fiction and reality made both ambiguous. This was further supported by feeding results of the experiments back into the system. For instance, we put out three issues of a fictional newspaper called *The Daily Worker.* Similar to the character of the journalist in *Der Lohndrücker, The Daily Worker* reported on heroic work achievements but also events (e.g. disappearances of workers) from Heiner Müller's play as well as from Bangor University. Each issue was distributed to my co-workers' pigeonholes[22] in order to blur the boundaries between the fiction of Müller's *Der Lohndrücker* and everyday academic working reality. This way reality regains its potentiality, as its fictionalisation challenges the imperative of necessity of how things are. Such potentiality enables us to imagine a transformed reality, which in the case of Bangor University at that time was often perceived to have no alternative (see also Fisher 2009).

Production, Play and Class Consciousness

The Redundancy emerged from the consecutive loop of redundancies, increasing workload and efficiency regimes, further informed by the means of production in academia—means which differ significantly from those depicted in the original version of *Der Lohndrücker*. Müller's text was marked by their absence, most profoundly in the installation for Scene 12, in which Balke's co-worker Krüger is incapable of continuing his work on the furnace due to severe health concerns. *The Redundancy* did not show this scene, neither in the performance, nor film or audio, but simply displayed a note on a closed bedroom door in the private accommodation, saying: "Scene 12 had to be cancelled due to sick leave." By the re-entry of the means and conditions of production, the artistic form of *The Redundancy* showed the economic, cultural and institutional framework of HE in the UK.

The choice of the genre of the production play enabled me and my colleagues to explore our vocational mindset, which has been co-opted by mechanisms of academic capitalism to become a means of self-exploitation. Our idealisation of work (McRobbie 2015) is exploited by HE employers, particularly to justify and enable redundancies. Though Angela McRobbie's argument in her monograph *Be Creative* primarily dissects the ideology of creativity outside of the academic labour market, applying it to the mindset of academics shines a light on how the neoliberal governmental regimes of self-entrepreneurship and creativity suspiciously converge with the vocational mindset of the autonomous academic intellectual. The romantic idea of academia as a passionate and rewarding vocation offers fertile ground for exploitation. A young hardworking person in precarity settles for the promise of successfully obtaining a permanent contract, which again holds the false promise of middle-class status. Similar to the creative industries parsed by McRobbie, academic reality is that of portfolio careers, project culture, multi-tasking and uncertainty.

Instead of reproducing the trajectory of the autonomous and individual overachiever, *The Redundancy* clearly enabled the participating colleagues to explore and experience new forms of communal solidarity and co-creation without necessarily reprogramming their mindsets. In this sense, did *The Redundancy* also generate class consciousness? In the process of restructuring, the then vice chancellor visited schools and departments as a cynical exercise in staff culture. Those colleagues who had been involved in *The Redundancy* welcomed the vice chancellor by papering the corridor with posters showing lines from the play or quotes from activists. A futile gesture, sure, but one which would not have happened if it had not been for *The Redundancy*. The vice chancellor noticed and decided to visit the school a second time, as he felt it had shown the most unease with the changes brought about by the restructuring. His visit coincided with the ongoing national unionised industrial action in UK HE. The national dispute was initially only on changes to pensions, but later expanded to pay gaps, casualisation and precarity, workloads, and falling pay. *The Redundancy* enabled staff and union members to translate the macro-activism and its campaign into practices of micro-activism in their immediate daily experience and by doing so tailoring the campaign to the specificities of their locality.

But what is the role and position of *The Redundancy* within academic capitalism? On the one hand, *The Redundancy* is a product of academic capitalism and emerged as such by deploying its means and mechanism. On the other hand, *The Redundancy* re-appropriated these elements and generated a space and time for micro-activism. For example, I might have used university resources (facilities, printers, camera equipment, digital tools, software and working hours) but not to directly benefit the university's productivity and more in the notion of what Michel de Certeau (2014) terms "faire la perruque" (13ff.). In a similar vein, Sarah Bernstein and Patricia Malone (2021) refer to punk-feminist DIY in terms of appropriating 'resources' of the university to explore the resistive and liberatory possibilities in existing within the institution but as a non-institutionalised subjectivity (130ff.).

However, this essay adds one further twist to *The Redundancy*. The insights and knowledge generated in the course of the micro-activist process is re-entered into capitalist valuation when I presented a paper on the project at a conference in Berlin and when I present *The Redundancy* as a research project, its performance as a research output, papers as research activities and, last but not least, this essay as a research output to potentially be considered for the next REF. Now, my colleagues' and my own undoubtedly meaningful activities in and outside of our working hours are rendered as unpaid academic research. My drive to create a space of lived academic vocation is rendered *ex post facto* academic labour.

Notes

1. The English translation by Carl Weber uses the title *The Scab*, which is misleading, as it suggests a different conflict to be negotiated in the play (Müller 1990, 23–56).
2. In *Mülheimer Rede*, Müller was sharing the hope for a world in which plays such as *GERMANIA TOD IN BERLIN* could not be written anymore simply because a changed reality would not provide for it (Müller 1989).
3. The trailer can be viewed here: https://lfbrecht.de/wp-content/uploads/2020/11/01-Trailer-Redundancy-Save-The-Date_comp.m4v.
4. Programme can be viewed here: https://lfbrecht.de/wp-content/uploads/2020/11/07_Programmheft.pdf.
5. The playlist included audio performances of scenes from *Der Lohndrücker*, a soundtrack composed by Alan Holmes for the project, as well as a number of workers'

protest songs and songs varying themes from the play, e.g. *Sabotage* (by Beastie Boys) or Joseph Beuys' *JajajaNenene* performance from 1968.

6. A video clip can be viewed here: https://lfbrecht.de/wp-content/uploads/2020/11/09-Herakles-01-comp.m4v.

7. For a discussion of the concept of academic capitalism, see Schulze-Cleven et al. 2017.

8. In England, the situation for arts courses is even bleaker, as they experienced further 50% cuts in government grants for teaching (Weale 2021).

9. On this see also Mark Fisher in conversation with Mark Fuller (Fuller 2009).

10. REF = Research Excellence Framework. The REF is a process of expert review, carried out by expert panels for 34 subject-based units of assessment, to provide accountability for public investment in research or to inform selective allocation of funding for research, i.e. the REF is an instrument to increase competition and performance pressure in academia: https://www.ref.ac.uk/about-the-ref/what-is-the-ref/. PURE is a Research Information Management System that enables ongoing auditing and surveillance of academic performance in respect to research activities. It is public facing but offers increased data capture for internal purposes: https://www.elsevier.com/en-gb/solutions/pure.

11. In particular, the latter implemented the absurdity of an auditing of the auditing, particularly in surveilling students' engagement in classes or communication with tutors.

12. FTE = full-time equivalent, which refers to the number of hours considered full-time.

13. A conflict we reflected in a video clip, entitled "Academic Cannibalism," appropriating a scene from Heiner Müller's play *Die Schlacht*. An excerpt can be viewed here: https://lfbrecht.de/wp-content/uploads/2020/11/02-Video-Academic-Cannibalism-Ausschnitt_comp.m4v.

14. Similar mechanisms are in place for precariously employed staff who work extra hours in the hope to gain secure employment in the future (Allmer 2018a, 60).

15. See Müller (2000), and for insightful essays on *Herakles 5*, see Riedel (1997) and Lehmann (1996).

16. Brecht envisioned the genre *Lehrstück* as an experimental form of modernist theatre for exploring the possibilities of learning through acting, including but not limited to playing roles, adopting postures and attitudes.

17. PURE is a Research Information Management System that allows all research activities to be efficiently managed and thus monitored. All university employees whose employment contracts include a research component must enter all their activities into the system in a timely manner. The information posted there is transferred to the university's website. The publications entered there are evaluated for their suitability every seven years in the national REF (Research Excellence Framework). Depending on their ranking in the REF, universities receive state research grants. The PURE profile is also crucial for promotions. See also: https://www.bangor.ac.uk/research-innovation-and-impact-office/pure.php.en.

18. An excerpt can be accessed here: https://lfbrecht.de/wp-content/uploads/2020/11/06_ Audio-Szene-5_Ausschnitt.mp3.

19. An electronic surveillance tool records all contacts with students in and outside of class. Students submit extension requests or report circumstances affecting their academic performance electronically via a so-called Request Center, generating transparent metrics for analysing student experience.

20. The university must report its annual financial costs to the Higher Education Funding Council for Wales and these costs have to be split between teaching, research and other using a methodology called Transparent Approach to Costing. Staff must fill in an online form on how they spend their time between teaching, research and other, on a percentage basis rather than numbers of hours or days, thus the survey does not allow any data on real working hours.

21. I wanted the real working hours not to be visible in the final product. It was not entirely successful, since the unusually fast blinking cursor in the Google document made the acceleration of real time visible, but an exact determination of the acceleration (by four times) remained intuitively impossible. This disruption prompts the viewer to question the relationship between product and working time. To watch an excerpt, visit: https://lfbrecht.de/wp-content/uploads/2020/11/08-Szene-8A-Ausschnitt_comp.m4v.

22. See the issues here:
Daily Worker 1: https://lfbrecht.de/wp-content/uploads/2020/11/03_Daily-Worker.pdf.
Daily Worker 2: https://lfbrecht.de/wp-content/uploads/2020/11/04_Daily-Worker.pdf.
Daily Worker 3: https://lfbrecht.de/wp-content/uploads/2020/11/05_Daily-Worker.pdf.

References

Allmer, Thomas. 2018a. "Theorising and Analysing Academic Labour." In "Academic Labour, Digital Media and Capitalism," edited by Thomas Allmer and Ergin Bulut, special issue, *tripleC: Communication, Capitalism & Critique* 16, no. 1: 49–77.

Allmer, Thomas. 2018b. "Precarious, always-on and flexible: A case study of academics as information workers." *European Journal of Communication* 33, no. 4: 381–395.

Allmer, Thomas, and Ergin Bulut. 2018. "Introduction: Academic Labour, Digital Media and Capitalism." In "Academic Labour, Digital Media and Capitalism," edited by Thomas Allmer and Ergin Bulut, special issue, *tripleC: Communication, Capitalism & Critique* 16, no. 1: 44–48.

Bernstein, Sarah, and Patricia Malone. 2022. "Common Language: Academics Against Networking and the Poetics of Precarity." In *Literary Representations of Precarious Work, 1840 to the Present*, edited by Michiel Rys and Bart Philipsen, 129–143. Cham: Palgrave Macmillan.

Castells, Manuel. 1996. *The Rise of the Network Society.* Vol. 1, The Information Age: Economy, Society and Culture. Oxford: Blackwell.

de Certeau, Michel. 2014. *Kunst des Handelns.* Berlin: Merve.

Deem, Rosemary. 1998. "'New managerialism' and higher education: The management of performances and cultures in universities in the United Kingdom." *International Studies in Sociology of Education* 8, no. 1: 47–70.

Deem, Rosemary. 2004. "The Knowledge Worker, the Manager-academic and the Contemporary UK University: New and Old Forms of Public Management?" *Financial Accountability & Management* 20, no. 2: 107–128.

Fisher, Mark. 2009. *Capitalist Realism: Is There No Alternative?* Winchester: Zero Books.

Fuchs, Christian, and Sebastian Sevignani. 2013. "What Is Digital Labour? What Is Digital Work? What's Their Difference? And Why Do These Questions Matter for Understanding Social Media?" *tripleC: Communication, Capitalism & Critique* 11, no. 2: 237–293.

Fuller, Matthew. 2009. "Questioning Capitalist Realism: An Interview with Mark Fisher." *MROnline,* 27 December 2009. Accessed 20 December 2022. https://mronline.org/2009/12/27/questioning-capitalist-realism-an-interview-with-mark-fisher/.

Gill, Rosalind. 2010. "Breaking the Silence: The Hidden Injuries of the Neoliberal University." In *Secrecy and Silence in the Research Process: Feminist Reflections,* edited by Róisín Ryan-Flood and Rosalind Gill, 228–244. London: Routledge.

GOV.UK. n.d. "Making staff redundant." GOV.UK. Accessed 20 December 2022. https://www.gov.uk/staff-redundant.

GOV.UK. 2011. "Consultation outcome: Higher education White Paper—students at the heart of the system." GOV.UK, 28 June 2011. Accessed 20 December 2022. https://www.gov.uk/government/consultations/higher-education-white-paper-students-at-the-heart-of-the-system.

Graeber, David. 2019. *Bullshit Jobs: The Rise of Pointless Work and What We Can Do About It.* London: Penguin Books.

Jaffe, Sarah. 2021. *Work Won't Love You Back: How Devotion to Our Jobs Keeps Us Exploited, Exhausted and Alone.* New York: Bold Type Books.

Laughton, David. 2003. "Why was the QAA Approach to Teaching Quality Assessment Rejected by Academics in UK HE?" *Assessment & Evaluation in Higher Education* 28, no. 3: 309–321.

Lehmann, Hans-Thies. 1996. "Über Heiner Müllers Arbeit." *Merkur* 50: 542–548.

Lin, Eric S., and Shih-Yung Chiu. 2016. "Does Holding a Postdoctoral Position Bring Benefits for Advancing to Academia?" *Research in Higher Education* 57, no. 3: 335–362.

Marx, Karl, and Friedrich Engels. 1968. *Das Kapital: Kritik der politischen Ökonomie.* Vol. 23, Werke. Berlin (GDR): Dietz Verlag, 640–677.

McGettigan, Andrew. 2013. *The Great University Gamble: Money, Markets and the Future of Higher Education.* London: Pluto Press.

McRobbie, Angela. 2015. *Be Creative: Making a Living in the New Culture Industries*. London: Polity Press.

Müller, Heiner. 1989. "Mühlheimer Rede." In *Heiner Müller Material*, edited by Frank Hörnigk, 101. Leipzig: Steidl.

Müller, Heiner. 1990. "The Scab." In *The Battle: Plays, Prose, Poems by Heiner Müller*, translated and edited by Carl Weber, 23–56. New York: PAJ Publications.

Müller, Heiner. 2000. "Herakles 5." In *Werke III: Die Stücke 1*, edited by Frank Hörnigk, 397–409. Frankfurt am Main: Suhrkamp.

Newton, Jethro. 2002. "Views from Below: Academics coping with quality." *Quality in Higher Education* 8, no. 1: 39–61.

Park, Elke. 2013. "From Academic Self-Governance to Executive University Management: Institutional Governance in the Eyes of Academics in Europe." In *The Work Situation of the Academic Profession in Europe: Findings of a Survey in Twelve Countries. The Changing Academy*, edited by Ulrich Teichler and Ester Ava Höhle, 183–203. Vol. 8, The Changing Academic Profession in International Comparative Perspective. Dordrecht: Springer.

Riedel, Volker. 1994. "Im Zeichen der Ambivalenz: Zur Herakles-Rezeption in der deutschen Literatur seit 1960." In *Herakles/Herkules I*, edited by Ralph Kray, Stephan Oettermann, and Karl Riha, 263–271. Basel: Stroemfeld.

Schulze-Cleven, Tobias, Tilman Reitz, Jens Maesse, and Johannes Angermuller. 2017. "The new political economy of higher education: between distributional conflicts and discursive stratification." *Higher Education*, no. 73: 795–812.

Slaughter, Sheila, and Larry L. Leslie. 1997. *Academic Capitalism: Politics, Policies, and the Entrepreneurial University*. Baltimore: John Hopkins University Press.

Slaughter, Sheila, and Gary S. Rhoades. 2004. *Academic Capitalism and the New Economy: Markets, State and Higher Education*. Baltimore: Johns Hopkins University Press.

Strehlow, Falk. 2006. *Balke: Heiner Müllers „Der Lohndrücker" und seine intertextuellen Verwandtschaftsverhältnisse*. Stuttgart: ibidem.

Suschke, Stephan. n.d. "Chronologie der Inszenierung, 10. September 1987." *dossier ID 703a*. Berlin: Archiv der Akademie der Künste.

University and College Union. 2021. "UCU Workload Survey 2021: Data Report." Accessed 20 December 2022. https://www.ucu.org.uk/media/12905/UCU-workload-survey-2021-data-report/pdf/WorkloadReportJune22.pdf.

Weale, Sally. 2021. "Funding cuts to go ahead for university arts courses in England despite opposition." *The Guardian*, 20 July 2021. Accessed 20 December 2022. https://www.theguardian.com/education/2021/jul/20/funding-cuts-to-go-ahead-for-university-arts-courses-in-england-despite-opposition.

Weber, Max. 1946. "Science as Vocation." In *Essays in Sociology*, edited and translated by Hans H. Gerth and C. Wright Mills, 129–156. New York: Oxford University Press.

4.3

"The View Is Nice,
but You Can't Eat It"

A Poetics of Precarity in *Bait* (2019, Dir: Mark Jenkin)

DANIEL BROOKES

Introduction

The title of this essay is taken from the advertising material for *Bait*, which, in turn, was appropriated from UK charity Church Action on Poverty in their campaign to create food banks in Cornwall. The phrase sets the metaphysical and the material as related but curiously counterposed. For England's southern- and westernmost county, "still a land apart" (Beacham and Pevsner 2014, 1) owing to its unique admixture of industries and ancestries as much as its geographical composition and extremity, this relationship between person, culture and place was not always so fraught. Across Cornwall, the remnants of ancient populations (in the form of megaliths) and extractive industries are visible, indicating the intertwining of labour and community practice extending from the Stone and Bronze Ages, through the Christian annexation of this corner of the island, and into the era of a place dependent upon fishing and leisure. *Bait*, the first feature by Cornish director Mark Jenkin, suggests that the visitation of rentier capitalism, described by Guy Standing (2016) as the situation in which rentiers "derive income from possession of assets that are scarce or artificially made scarce," is a force which alters this long-standing relationship between place and people. 'The view' is that fetishised and idealised component of a place, separated out by commodity form, obviating the difficulties of the longstanding social order: the need for cultural practice, the need to maintain social formation, and the need to eat.

Local people disenfranchised by an 'affordability gap,' in which median salary falls beneath the requirement for a mortgage, has contributed to rising tensions in conurbations deriving income from rural tourism across England and Wales. According to a November 2022 study by the University of Exeter, only six Cornish postcodes featured 'positive affordability' (Williams and Lawlor 2022) for residents, while a quadrennial study of multiple deprivation in Cornwall published in 2019 showed that "primary types of deprivation in Cornwall's worse affected neighbourhoods relates to income, employment, education, skills and training and health and disability" (Cornwall Council 2019).

It is this reality that frames *Bait* (2019) and constitutes its central tension. Martin, a fisherman, has sold the family home to the Leighs, a London-based couple who use much of the property for seasonal leisure and generate passive rental income from a converted loft previously used for storing nets. Now living in social housing on the outskirts of town, Martin commutes by car to the harbour, where the parking space typically reserved for fishermen is given over to tourists. The boat from which Martin and his estranged brother Steven fished with their father (who appears as a ghostly presence throughout the film) has been converted for pleasure cruises, creating a familial schism. Cultural practice (fishing) and the necessities of food are shown to be interrelated, but the alienation from labour and losing traditional footholds in a particular place that Martin experiences further reifies through fractures in the social formation. The village pub, ornamented with remnants of its association with the nautical, closes in winter and is filled with teenagers from out of town in summer. The sociology of the everyday of Henri Lefebrve, be it his analysis of the production of space ("social spaces interpenetrate one another and/or superimpose themselves on one another" (1991, 86)) or on the role of modern man and leisure (on the role of the café: "where the regulars can find a certain luxury…where they can speak *freely…where they play*" (2002, 234)), is reflected throughout *Bait* in a way that activates its *mise-en-scène* above the level of mere backdrop, suggesting the vitality of its inhabitants and determining the historical procedure of its social form.

At three crucial layers of culture, place and work, Martin is alienated. British cinematic drama in the post-Thatcher era is not short of these triply alienated and situationally trapped figures; they populate the works of Ken Loach and Mike Leigh. These figures account for dimensions of women's suffering in works such as *Naked* (1993) and *Nil by Mouth* (1997), underline emasculation and rage in *Dead Man's Shoes* (2004) and *This is England* (2006), and are rendered comedic by the unlikely acts undertaken to find a way forward (*Brassed Off* (1996) and *The Full Monty* (1997)). These works are not just thematically and politically bound but are also broadly operative in the mode of social realism that has driven a great deal of British visual narrative drama across television and film since the 1950s. This connection has several implications for its cinema, but the two I shall utilise in order suggest how *Bait* differs are these: (a) British social realism is typically concerned with an "anti-poetic" and "secular" (Williams 1977, 64) aesthetic notionally divested of mythos that attempts to show reality 'as is'; and (b) the understanding of social hierarchies derives, via a complex lineage, from the descriptions of Karl Marx: the aristocracy, the *bourgeoisie* and the proletariat.

As a counterpoint, British cinema has also featured works which show broadly non-realist approaches to the effects of Thatcherite politics and social class (in Peter Greenaway's *The Cook, the Thief, his Wife, and her Lover* (1989), and the bawdy escapism of *Shopping* (1994) and *Trainspotting* (1996)). Though there is intersectionality in Greenaway, these works do not reflect the ways in which class dynamics have shifted in the broad aspects of Conservatism they attack, heightening their polemic quality by invoking mythic and historic structures of class rather than mapping their new contours. Guy Standing's taxonomy of social classes in Western economies attempts to sharpen distinctions. Middle earners are no longer automatically a homogenous *bourgeoisie*, but a combination of the salariat, proficians, technical workers, and a shrunken form of the former working class that has the greatest social utility (e.g. lorry drivers, builders, electricians). Beneath those, but above the underclass or lumpen proletariat, is the precariat:

> The precariat has *class* characteristics. It consists of people who have minimal trust relationships with capital or the state, making it quite unlike the salariat. And it has none of the social contract relationships of the proletariat, whereby labour securities were provided in exchange for subordination and contingent loyalty, the unwritten deal underpinning welfare states. Without a bargain of trust or security in exchange for subordination, the precariat is distinctive in class terms. It also has a peculiar *status* position, in not mapping neatly onto high-status professional or middle-status craft occupations. (2011, 8)

Bait differs from much British class-conscious production in non-trivial ways. It is both experimental in technique, non-linear in narrative, and aware of how the old certainties of class have stratified in the manner outlined by Standing. It is the ways in which these formal categories of narrative and form explicate the dimension of class that I wish to build on, though firstly I shall explore the ways in which precarity makes itself known throughout *Bait* in order to demonstrate how experimental technique and narrative form serve as both poetic and critique of this precarity.

Precarity and the Pastoral

Precarity in *Bait* takes multiple forms. Protagonist Martin is the avatar of a declining trade, the general collapsed into the individual: he does not have enough work beyond subsistence and does not know what tomorrow will bring. Attempts to save for a boat to restore the scale of his labour to a sustaining degree are routinely dashed by happenstance. Standing may disagree with this essay's conception of Martin's position as a precarious one, suggesting that "it is not right

to equate the precariat with the working poor or with just insecure employment
[…] [T]he precariousness also implies a lack of a secure work-based identity,
whereas workers in some low-income jobs may be building a career" (ibid., 9).
Martin's work-based identity is clear to the viewer and non-seasonal village residents, but it is clearly disappearing and disrespected within a seasonal community ("you're a fisherman? Then where's your boat?" says rentier Tim to Martin)
that includes different class relationships that historically would have been more
closely bonded (pub landlord and community member) before the incursions of
neoliberal economics. Martin also closely corresponds with Standing's suggestion
that the absence of subordination can be bought by job security, with Martin's
apprentice and nephew Neil arguably positioned even further down the ladder,
lacking the memory of the village as social formation around fisheries that shape
(male) labour identity. As viewers we hear freighted discussions of post-Brexit
disputes between Britain and the European Union emerging from diegetic radios,
giving political reality to these suggestions drawn in character building.

In a 2022 paper given on the relationship between *Bait* and class aesthetics,
Andrew Jarvis states that attachment to specific political issues is not what is at
stake inasmuch as the film comprises "a hauntological neorealism that unsettles
any reference to a punctual political issue, Brexit or otherwise, and instead medi-
ates the sensation of historical crisis." Jarvis, in his examination of Jenkin's use of
audio/visual disjuncture, echoes Mark Fisher to underscore a persuasive broader
point about the film revealing capitalist realism as political decision. Non-realist
aesthetics make such modal readings workable and account for the film's liminal
and spectral presences in a satisfying manner. Nonetheless, the intertwining of
several ungeneralised aspects of life contemporary to late-2010s rural tourist-
afflicted Britain prevents *Bait* from serving as a general model for, for example,
post-industrial northern England or the Scottish central belt or indeed western
late-stage capitalism writ large.

Nor would these latter regions be well served by the pastoral. The pastoral, even when the social order introduced is rigorous in its mimesis, operates
through a closed system of distilled mythic conventions that resists attempts to
transpose itself onto other situations. *Bait* may or may not, depending on your
view, meet the strictest historical literary view on the pastoral when considering Leo Marx's "no shepherds, no pastoral" (1986, 8) edict. Terry Gifford's views
on what constitutes the pastoral are more accommodating; themes of return,
the function of idyll, and the exaltation of the rural as "providing an implicit
or explicit contrast to the urban" (2020, 2) are apparent in *Bait*, though their
execution may be rendered as anti-pastoral because of the way in which Jenkin
"attacks the very idealising role inherent in poetry about the English countryside" (in Westling 2014, 22). William Empson's mobilisation of notions of class

in the pastoral, whilst not Marxist in conclusion, acknowledge the relationship between an overtly politicised 'proletarian art' (which he deems "covert pastoral" (1974, 6)) and the focalisation of social address from below which inheres in the pastoral mode. Colin Burrow, whilst worrying about the lack of animals in many of the texts Empson considered pastoral, felt that this structural view of the pastoral had some merit, suggesting that "literary representation necessarily includes a range of entities beyond the particular, and top-down and bottom-up views of the world are structurally as well as generically distinct" (2021, 8).

It is this 'from below' but not necessarily Marxist perspective that may offer more nuance in considering Standing's conception of new social classes and how we might observe connections that operate intersectionally. The social sphere in *Bait* is populated with instantiations of precarity beyond Martin. Neighbour Wenna is reliant on seasonal labour owing to the village pub's closure in the winter months, which she loses. Meanwhile, nephew Neil chooses between forms of precarity, opting to apprentice in the local fishing industry rather than work seasonally on his father's pleasure cruiser. Standing suggests that some members of the precariat have found a "liberating side" (2011, vii) to this economic arrangement and, indeed, not all precariously employed people in *Bait* enter into precarity as a form of social victimhood. The character of the taxi driver, whose sole scene relays in analepsis his previous employment as a fisherman, can survive in precarity owing to his ability to exploit infrastructural and social gaps. His introduction in the narrative comes when he returns Wenna in his taxi from the nearest police station at a cost of £100. In a county whose median wage is approximately £600 per week, with low rail availability and continued bus cuts, precarity equates to entrepreneurial spirit.

Jenkin's inclusion of this character speaks to the ongoing difficulty of traditional solidarity in this new socio-economic arrangement. *Bait* shows several examples of 'looking sideways,' from peer-to-peer, in order to highlight the ongoing separation in labour conditions and how they inscribe emotional states of separateness which increase as the generations become younger. Through ghostly visions of village elders, Martin's generation and the teenagers, *Bait* offers a vision of Cornish village life that has clearly modified in three successive generations, with a constant set of values or feelings shared by all hard to pin down. In its developed form, in *The Long Revolution*, "structure of feeling" (Williams 1992, 48) counters and extends the Gramscian conception of hegemony by suggesting that, alongside the dominant thought forms and cultural practices that exist within a place and people, there must also be room for new feelings, thoughts, practices and ways of life that accounts for the eventual accretion of social change. On these changes, Williams writes "one generation may train its successor [...] but the new generation will have its own structure of feeling, which will not appear to have come 'from' anywhere" (ibid., 49).

Jenkin suggests that the first half of Williams' ideas here holds fast, but considers it in order to identify exactly the particular epoch of British capitalism, with its spirit of encouragement toward Big Tech-powered speculative investors and property developers, that accounts for this change. For Jenkin, conceptions of community dynamics in this Williamsian mode, idealised and naturalised through the juxtaposition of village elders, adults and youths in a harmonious and symbiotic relationship, have become rather a quaint and outdated notion. Structures of feeling are imported from elsewhere and, in this case a nebulous idea of the city-dweller's values, take precedence over resident structures and debates. Furthermore, Jenkin highlights the ways in which lessons descended through generations have become distorted and misunderstood in this new paradigm. The presence of tourists in Cornwall, as acknowledged by *Bait*, is not a new phenomenon. Among the traditional residents of the village, particularly the older and ghostlier presences, the phrase 'fleece them for all them's worth' is deployed in a way that defines the historical and present attitude toward the tourist visitors and acts as shibboleth between residents. However, there are scant or no examples of 'fleecing,' of exploitation without recrimination, performed in *Bait* by its residents to the tourists. The lesson, learned less as serious parable and more as performance of self-identity, has begun to inform interactions between the different forms of lower class.

Framing *Bait* as pastoral allows us to critique ways in which the shared feeling of an unnameable change across disparate characters inhabiting approximately the same social status, particular to an idealised rural scene, is presented in text and/or film. Terry Eagleton suggests that the pastoral entails a complex arrangement in which "the rich are poorer as well as richer than the common people, and that even the intellectual [...] shares a common humanity with others, which ultimately overrides whatever demarcates him or her from them" (1985, 160). *Bait*, along with several British works that have suggested an authentic sharedness and vitality to working-class culture that is either sniffed at or appropriated by a wealthier *bourgeoisie*, presents this arrangement in a broken state that is partially repaired by the film's conclusion. The ongoing separateness between dramatic content and descriptions of its display in film means that there must also be an accounting of other dimensions which shape and complicate interpretation.

Sounds / Aesthetics

Within the chapters of *Some Versions of Pastoral*, Empson chiefly bases his thesis on the poetry and the novel prior to the twentieth century. However, there is one remarkable aside that references cinema:

The Englishman who seems to me nearest to a proletarian artist (of those I know anything about) is Grierson the film producer; *Drifters* gave very vividly the feeling of actually living on a herring trawler and (by the beauty of shapes and water and net and fish, and subtleties of timing and so forth) what I should call a pastoral feeling about the dignity of that form of labour. (1974, 8)

John Grierson's nationality aside (he was Scottish), Empson's recounting of one of *Bait*'s topical and aesthetic forebears articulates a complex positionality within the genre. For Empson, the pastoral is typically employed as a narratological method which focalises social address from the lower parts of its hierarchy in order to tease out alternative senses from textual ambiguities. In this section Empson begins to suggest that a "pastoral feeling" can be evoked by visual but non-narrative means; that an associative flow of images in montage can build a sense-world that connects questions of work and rural environment to suggest abstract subjective states such as 'dignity', which Empson renders elsewhere as "a sense of glory" (ibid., 282) that may render this interpretation as a veiled piece of theology.

At a secular and material level, the visual references to *Drifters* in *Bait* are those which both requisition from history an ongoing connection between practice and place; that is to say that Jenkin suggests *Bait* is of the same world as *Drifters*, save for the modification of the base–superstructure relationship in the intervening ninety years. Nonetheless, there is a metaphysical aspect to *Bait*, an 'inner layer' or embedded romanticism which attempts to communicate this 'dignity' or 'glory', or at least how it faces an uncertain future. Jenkin's references to *Drifters* imbue Grierson's pro-filmic actuality with spectral presences implied by film grain, texture, noise, leakage, damage and flickering light levels. Hand-developed, unevenly exposed, and prone to occasionally scratching the acetate, Jenkin is suggested to have "embraced these artefacts in the visual aesthetic of the film" (British Cinematographer, n.d.), resulting in a restless visual field even in the most static of shots.

My contention is that, by foregrounding method and the artefact not as unwanted but as the presence of the human, Jenkin forges several interesting connections between film and exterior discourses. Firstly, Jenkin connects the external and necessarily physical aspects of people and place with the shared internal dimension that accounts for the dominant 'structure of feeling' that presides within it. Secondly, Jenkin connects the actions of these smaller-scale precariat fishermen with his own physical and fragile artistic practice. Two indicative minutes of montage (Jenkin 2019, 17:49) speak to this. Martin and Neil crouch on a stony beach framed against the tide, cutting caught fish from a net. The longer shots of the sequence show Neil working patiently to loosen a fish, with the ending of this sequence being a wordless smile exchanged between uncle and nephew as the trade continues through the bloodline. The connection between tactility and the production of useful material, and between physical labour and the maintenance of dignity and connectivity, is established.

In the montage at the beginning of the film (Jenkin 2019, 3:38) which announces the arrival of seasonal homeowners and holidaymakers, there is a cutting between two separate spaces: Martin is ritualistically preparing a net to fish whilst the Leighs and their fellow seasonal homeowners exit their bulky cars and complain about the length of the drive before entering their parodically 'nautical' home spaces. The visual clash established in this sequence mobilises several binaries that operate throughout the film: between work and leisure, between poor and rich, between rural and city, and between extractive and derivative labour. Martin is seen with nets, fraying ropes, and digging stony sand to prepare his work, emphasising the texture and connection with objects—whilst Sandra is later seen putting the accoutrements of the globalised middle-class home about the Leigh family's holiday let—prosecco, fresh yogurt—to prepare their work of selling a lifestyle.

What is interesting to note here is not just a visual clash but a sonic clash that operates with a psychological and intertextual component that diverges from the use of objects as signifiers. The images that correspond with shots of Martin working are freighted with machinic noises, bird cries, scrapes and involuntary bodily sounds. The images that correspond with the families arriving are eerily silent and frictionless; they perhaps recall the final triumph of the title characters in *The Birds*, where invaders triumph by numbers, impervious to reason or previous 'ways.' This sonic contrast is not an act of happenstance. Jenkin, who also edited the film, shot the film silently and dubbed on all dialogue and 'diegetic' and 'non-diegetic' sound. These sounds remind us that the social arrangement in this place prior to the invasion of the gentrifiers was tactile, frictional and man-made, and is being replaced by one of internet purchases, modernisations and convenience, characterised by a shared delusion of the rural way of life as organic. The abruptness and foregrounded nature of Jenkin's contrasts underscores the impact that the rapid onset of precarity in the face of rentier capitalism has had within the lifetime of Martin and his generation.

Bait contains a number of ironic visual signs based within local material practices that remind the viewer of a long history of place and economics. Some are flagged up for the viewer to join in the mockery, such as the Leigh family's insertion of a porthole as part of the modernisation of their home. Other such signs do not immediately call attention to themselves: for instance, Martin stores the money for the boat he hopes to buy in a tin while his brother clears up discarded drinks 'tins' from the shell of a former fishing boat. These small and subtle reminders of Cornwall's other major and dying industry, and how its ghostly remnants appear to linger in a mocking and form, stud the *mise-en-scène* of *Bait*. What makes *Bait* particularly interesting in this regard is that Jenkin's protectionist critiques lie not just within the dramatic content but filter through the striking effects created by artisanal techniques and the consequences of an aleatory approach to handling celluloid. The scratches and flickers render important objects such as fish incredibly present, the image demanding extra levels of attention to itself as material. And yet, the objects become spectral as the focus, blur and artefacts partially obscure and prevent clarity. What life has defamiliarised for Martin, Jenkin's techniques defamiliarise for the viewer.

Double Plotting and Intersectionality

The clearest view of the convergence of aesthetic, narrative form and a new understanding of social class as a means of outlining a 'new poetics' of precarity in *Bait* is afforded in three distinct moments. These three sections foreground montage in such a method so forceful as to deliberately reveal the 'double plot' operating as a system of narrative contrasts. Of double plots as a narrative strategy, Empson writes that "the interaction of the two plots gives a particularly clear setting for, or machine for imposing, the social and metaphysical ideas on which pastoral depends" (1974, 30).

This plot interaction is clear throughout *Bait*. What Martin, as symbol of the resident community, endures is mirrored and refracted across the range of his tourist counterparts. Sometimes this is detailed as comedic inversion (the scene that immediately follows Martin and Neil hauling in their net is tourist son Hugo preparing to snorkel with a harpoon in a dilettantish fashion) and sometimes this device operates with a note of tragic irony.

Empson's descriptor 'machine for imposing,' quite without foresight, is a good description of the intensified cinematic method by which Jenkin makes this double plot apparent through montage. In a sequence (Jenkin 2019, 33:58) that combines two separate places in a unified montage sequence, utterances from parallel conversations that turn into arguments from separate rooms of the village pub are joined together as if they were all part of one conversation. The two conversations are on the topic of a new generation of wealth changing the established conventions of village life; the teenagers argue about pool table etiquette while Martin and the landlady argue about the pub's closure in winter. The shot lengths in the scene gradually reduce as the tensions in the disparate conversations rise, accelerating the tempo. In each conversation, financial rationale is given for the change in procedure, but it is the experimental and comical montage that highlights their connections. Though this scene broadly continues the theme of separation between villagers and visitors, and the precariat and the secure, it is apparent that this scene is also at the heart of Jenkin's appraisal of new class intersectionality by creating an energetic set piece out of their fusion.

In establishing thematic connection in such a determined method, Jenkin suggests how ideas that seemed more straightforward under a Marxist conception of class, in this case solidarity and class consciousness, may have become more complicated and diffuse in the social reality Standing describes. The two conversations taking place divide themselves on generational lines; middle-aged workers talking to each other and younger people talking to each other. Jenkin's creative montage reveals an all-encompassing dynamic of powerlessness of precarity that has no respect for distinctions previously given to gender, professional experience and age. Martin and Wenna, representing the underemployed and unemployed respectively, are powerless in their conversations with the landlady and the tourists precisely because they cannot assert the supremacy of their needs or factors of tradition over economic reason and the whip-hand of bourgeois domination of the public sphere. The experimental use of montage binds together for the viewer what appears to have been understood extra-textually by the characters inhabiting this social position. I would like to call this an example of a 'precariat consciousness,' a visual representation of the intersectional understanding that asserts itself between cultural similars, in this case those within the economic struggle recognising those who are set to inherit the same problems.

Raymond Williams argues that, in the reconstitution of what comprises social class as positions within economies change, this recognition is increasingly unlikely given that "traditional definitions have broken down, and that the resulting confusion is a serious diminution of consciousness" (1992, 325). This ability to perceive class-based needs in *Bait* only appears to be a skill possessed by other people who share in these specific needs of certainty and self-identity. Martin gives over one of his freshly caught fish to his unnamed elderly neighbour every day, which, given the scale of his operations, amounts to a significant proportion. Jenkin inserts no subtext that positions Martin and Wenna romantically or even as surrogate or alternative family; their sympathies extend beyond their skillsets and traumas and emerge as the real examples of solidarity within the film. The other example is the relationship between Martin and Neil, which represents a narratological attempt to indicate the futility of proletarian labour bonds as a point of resistance against forces which attempt to diminish them. In *Bait,* and in the fisheries of Cornwall and Wales, the traditional working class as locus of solidarity and labour identity is not present. Rather, Jenkin presents master and apprentice as the rural equivalent of Deliveroo cyclists huddling outside of a city-centre McDonalds.

Jenkin's intensified thematic paralleling through montage returns twice more. The next iteration switches between scenes of cookery (Jenkin 2019, 56:28) in a triple contrast. Sandra and Tim prepare and eat the lobster stolen by their son

Hugo from Martin's lobster pot, while Hugo eats lobster on the beach with his teenage tourist friends. These actions are determinedly contrasted with Neil making a cheap meal of pasta and sauce. The montage binds together the authentic, fresh, local and expensive produce given over to gentrifiers while the locals eat meals from a different part of the chain of globalisation.

The worried expression worn by Sandra during this montage appears to communicate an emerging recognition of and guilt about her role in the changing face of the village. *Bait* suggests that the only successful weapon that the precariat have, especially after Wenna's physical violence toward Tim Leigh fails, in provoking the Leigh family is to arouse a dormant guilt within Sandra, the Leigh family mother. Sandra is frequently framed in shots and montage sequences with various signs indicative of success—the car, the prosecco, the modernised home, the Apple laptop which we see her moving invisible money about with—and frequently espouses rhetoric with a finance-focused politics. However, Sandra is also painted as a modern liberal: allowing her daughter to stop out all night with a rueful grin, siding with the villagers as their tenant complains about the noise, and engaging with Britain's own liberal discourse on the radio.

This incremental guilt, seeded throughout the narrative, feeds into the final intensified double plot section that brings *Bait* to coda (Jenkin 2019, 1:04:09). Sandra visits Martin's home when he is away and, after examining the sparse interior space of the home, puts money in his boat tin to assuage her guilt. As Empson remarks, "the 'bourgeois' themselves do not like literature to have too much 'bourgeois ideology'" (1974, 5). The accumulated value of these class-attached signs is realised by Sandra to have a latent political dimension that affects questions of place. Indeed, it is in the very montage that pairs the Leighs eating lobster miserably as Neil happily eats a terrible-looking pasta dish that this becomes fatefully apparent. The cloistering of 'too much' bourgeois ideology and the accumulation of loaded signs have revealed to Sandra a schism that outlines her own predatory position in local economics. The contradictions of her position in new economic realities become impossible to adequately resolve, hence Sandra's guilt.

But this attempt at restitution is only the one part of the film's closure of its double plot. The subplot, adjoined by more traditional means in the montage, shows a final confrontation between Neil, who has been sleeping with Katie, the daughter of the Leigh family, and the Leigh family son, Hugo (Jenkin 2019, 1:11:08). Hugo baits Neil and Katie out of the fishing hut by audibly dragging Martin's lobster pots, again indicating tourist entitlement. After a quarrel, Neil, tracked by Katie, walks toward Hugo and is stopped by Hugo's hand around his throat. Neil attempts to throw a punch but Katie, in attempting to prevent the punch, teams with Hugo to push Neil from the quayside to his death in his father's boat.

The mirroring of the two plots reminds the viewer that reverse 'exploitation' by the precarious of the settled, and that the mantra of 'fleecing them for all them's worth,' is simply not possible. There may, with upwardly applied pressure and internalised guilt, be a simple form of financial restitution that sees the higher orders (Sandra) giving the lower caste (Martin) what they are owed all along. But parity also comes with a price, in this case blood. The death of Neil, which in Jenkin's edit has been foreshadowed from the commencement of the film, is both an actual and a symbolic one: the actual death is the focus on blood dripping from his temple like the life that is draining from these places. Liberal guilt, restitution and philanthropy can mend the small fissures, but the position of precarity for Jenkin is synonymous with death: by hunger, by danger, by being trapped and by being unable to move forward.

The symbolic death returns us, finally, to Empson and the pastoral. In death, Neil is both at one with the environment and its new martyr. In his analysis of Andrew Marvell's *The Garden*, Empson notes the pastoralist fantasy of wishing to be chained by brambles and nailed by thorns as one in which the narrator "becomes Christ" (1974, 123). Here, Jenkin, framing the narrative with the image of Neil's face in the moment of the realisation of his death, imputes the Christ-myth into Neil, which, in the coda which sees Martin return to sea, appears to have restored the moral conditions that allows for the idealised social order to exist.

Conclusion

The coda to *Bait* presents going backward—reverting the pleasure cruiser back to its former state as a fishing vessel, with the remaining precariat returning to sea as a unified proletarian force—as a way forward. For Martin and Steven, coached in the ways of the sea and bound by the memory of a class-consciousness before neoliberalism, this has emotional realism as it represents the repair of their personal separation. It would be remiss to ignore the occasional strategies such as these in *Bait* which lapse into sentimentalism and protectionism as a double measure. Standing writes of "the nostalgics," those forlorn proletarian workers who are "angry and bitter" at inequality but are drawn to "populist neo-fascism" (2011, 156), and find themselves looking into the past for a political programme that addresses the now.

For Wenna, who makes up the third member of the crew, the film's closure appears incongruous. Standing writes that the youth that make up the largest section of the precariat do "not look back fondly to the labourist employment security of the pre-globalisation era" (ibid.). A promise of solidarity that emerges from a brief triumph of the 'precariat consciousness' appears to have gripped

Wenna, whose expression is ambiguous as she goes out to sea. The latter half of 2022 and early part of 2023 has seen increasing industrial action taken across the traditionally employed parts of the sector (salariat, proletariat) but organisation between various precarities has been poor until now: what role does locality play in precariat solidarity, and does Jenkin imbue Cornwall or the rural honeypots with a mythic quality of their own that allows a fantasy of solidarity that obviates gender and generational belonging to flourish?

Though the pastoral allows the critic to approach the structurally and generically distinct aspects of class-focused examinations of the particularities of place, a further Empsonian reading of *Bait* would need to account in a more sustained fashion for the mythic quality contained therein, and for the extent to which it affects the text. I have conveniently ignored, save for the occasional mention, a stratum of older villagers—an elderly neighbour, the ghost of Martin's father—who appear to wink knowingly whenever trouble is afoot as if to give faith in the old ways. A further excavation of *Bait* must account for their inclusion.

In his combination of experimental aesthetics and narrative flow, Jenkin has explored heretofore unexplained emotional tonalities of precariat experience. The shot-to-shot connective transitions of *Bait* chime against established conventions of 'truthful' capture in British depictions of precarious labour and poverty. Even if we narrow our focus to the 2010s and works such as *The Selfish Giant* (2013) and *I, Daniel Blake* (2016), *Bait* does not share the aforementioned works' anti-poetic style and discourse of sobriety. *Bait* contains sequences which refuse smooth narrative transition that neatly organises time and connects space. In spite of these transitions and disruptions that evoke art cinema's essential "ambiguity" (Bordwell 1979, 60), *Bait* is not a work that attempts to transmit the forces of alienation by the creation of viewer alienation within narrative or character construction. Rather, the presence of this ambiguity appears to be the ongoing unfolding of uncertainties and the demands that this places on both the material and the metaphysical.

References

Beacham, Peter, and Niklaus Pevsner. 2014. *The Buildings of England: Cornwall.* New Haven, London: Yale University Press.

Bordwell, David. 1979. "The Art Cinema as a Mode of Film Practice." *Film Criticism* 4, no. 1 (Fall): 56–64.

British Cinematographer. n.d. "Hooked! Mark Jenkin / *Bait.*" British Cinematographer. Accessed 9 April 2023. https://britishcinematographer.co.uk/mark-jenkin-bait/.

Burrow, Colin. 2021. "The Terrifying Vroom." *London Review of Books* 43, no. 14 (July): 7–10.

Cornwall Council. 2019. "Index of Multiple Deprivation 2019." Together Network. Accessed 9 April 2023. https://togethernetwork.org.uk/uploads/shared/IMD.-2019.-Cornwall.pdf.

Eagleton, Terry. 1986. "The Critic as Clown." In Terry Eagleton, *Against the Grain: Essays 1975–1985*. London: Verso.

Empson, William. 1974. *Some Versions of Pastoral*. New York: New Directions.

Gifford, Terry. 2014. "Pastoral, Anti-Pastoral, and Post-Pastoral." In *The Cambridge Companion to Literature and the Environment*, edited by Louise Westling, 17–30. Cambridge: Cambridge University Press.

Gifford, Terry. 2020. *Pastoral: The New Critical Idiom*. 2nd ed. London, New York: Routledge.

Grierson, John, director. 1929. *Drifters*. New Era Films / Empire Marketing Board. 49 min. DVD.

Jarvis, Andrew. 2022. "The violence of finance in *Bait* (Mark Jenkin, 2019)." Paper presented at *Class and Contemporary UK Film and Television*, online, 7 July 2022.

Jenkin, Mark, director. 2019. *Bait*. Early Day Films / BFI. 1 hr., 29 min. DVD.

Lefebrve, Henri. 1991. *The Production of Space*. Translated by Donald Nicholson-Smith. New York: Blackwell.

Lefebrve, Henri. 2002. "Work and Leisure in Everyday Life." In *The Everyday Life Reader*, edited by Ben Highmore, 225–236. Abingdon, New York: Routledge.

Marx, Leo. 1986. "Pastoralism in America." In *Ideology and Classic American Literature*, edited by Sacvan Bercovitch and Myra Jehlen, 36–39. Cambridge: Cambridge University Press.

Standing, Guy. 2011. *The Precariat: The New Dangerous Class*. London, New York: Bloomsbury Academic.

Standing, Guy. 2016. "The Five Lies Of Rentier Capitalism." Social Europe, 27 October 2016. Accessed 9 April 2023. https://www.socialeurope.eu/five-lies-rentier-capitalism.

Williams, Malcolm and Phoebe Lawlor. 2022. "Local Housing Affordability in Cornwall." University of Exeter. Accessed 9 April 2023. https://www.cornwallalc.org.uk/uploads/uoe-housing-affordability-report.pdf?v=1669736952.

Williams, Raymond. 1977. "A Lecture on Realism." *Screen* 18, no. 1: 61–74.

Williams, Raymond. 1992. *The Long Revolution*. Chatham: Hogarth Press.

PART 5

CLASS BEYOND THE HUMAN: WORK EXPERIENCES AND THE ANTHROPOCENE

5.1
Bare Land

Alienation as Deracination in
Anna Tsing and John Steinbeck

TIM CHRISTIAENS

> Certainly, man thrives best (or has at least) in a state of semianarchy. Then he
> has been strong, inventive, reliant, moving. But cage him with rules, feed him
> and make him healthy and I think he will die as surely as a caged wolf dies.
> I should not be surprised to see a cared for, thought for, planned nation disinte-
> grate, while a ragged, hungry, lustful nation survived.
> —John Steinbeck (1975, 221)

Towards an Ecological Class Politics

In the Anthropocene, life on Earth is increasingly precarious. With every new
heatwave, cataclysmic storm or viral pandemic, we slowly realise that we are living on a damaged planet. According to Bruno Latour, this predicament redraws
the foundations of class conflict (2018, 61). Marx focused on the conflict between capital and labour over who owned the means of production, but today's
ecological conflict pits those who control *the means of reproduction* against those
who have to fend for themselves in increasingly hostile environments. The rich
can reproduce their socio-cultural conditions of existence by hiding away in gated communities, while the poor are stuck on degraded soil. Some own the means
to recreate the environmental background conditions for their way of life, while
others do not. Marx would abhor such a loose utilisation of the vocabulary of
class, but Latour convincingly argues that politics in the Anthropocene revolves
around the *reproduction* of life rather than merely the relations of *production*.
Marx distinguished modes of production from their conditions of reproduction, but this becomes untenable once the economy directly affects its own background conditions (Fraser 2022).[1] When economic expansion is actively cutting
the branch it is sitting on, class analysis must pay attention to the environmental

conditions of possibility of life on Earth. At that stage, "it is a matter of broadening the definitions of class by pursuing an exhaustive search for everything that makes subsistence possible" (Latour 2018, 96).

In the context of unsustainable modernisation, the ecological class is the collective whose livelihood is at risk. They suffer the collateral damage of infinite economic expansion and the reproduction of their ways of being alive is rendered disposable in the name of continued economic growth (ibid., 53). But unsustainable capitalist expansion also harms non-human life. As Baptiste Morizot argues, "the human way of being alive only makes sense if it is entangled in thousands of other ways of being alive conducted by the animals, plants, bacteria, and ecosystems around us" (2020, 35–36, own translation). The ecological class hence consists of *all* living beings deprived of the means of reproduction. With a nod to Giorgio Agamben, I propose to call this human and non-human subject of ecological class politics 'bare land.' Agamben claims that specifically human life reproduces itself not only biologically as 'natural life' (*zōē*), but also culturally as 'socio-political life' (*bios*) (Agamben 1998, 9). However, human beings deprived of the means for reproducing a life worthy of being lived do not simply return to natural life. They become 'bare life' (*nuda vita*), a kind of zero degree of socio-political life. They are human and still appear as human *bios*, yet their subjectivity is bereft of all qualities that make them human. They are torn from community relations and their lifeworld until nothing remains but empty shells of human life. Agamben's examples are inmates of concentration camps treated so violently they turn mute or refugees forcefully impeded from creating a new life in their country of residence. Bare life is a life unable to form long-term relations with any type of human community. It is a mere isolated individual detached from a nurturing collective.

Climate refugees, deprived of the means of subsistence amidst environmental collapse, constitute bare life in Agamben's classical sense of the term. But the unravelling of the biosphere extends beyond the destitution of human life; it affects the non-human web of life as well.[2] Hence why I suggest using the term 'bare land' to describe the denudement of relations among both human and non-human beings. Unsustainable capitalist expansion undermines the livelihoods of entire ecosystems until nothing but barren wasteland is left. Afterwards, there is no other option but to abandon these dead lands (Sassen 2014, 149). Just like Agamben's bare life refers to human subjects stripped of the means to reproduce meaningful lives, bare land is a collective subject consisting of human and non-human living beings who have lost the relational capacity to form meaningful ecosystems. Bare land denotes an ecosystem reduced to its zero degree. Nothing remains but lifeless dust. It is 'collateral damage' (Agamben 2011, 119–120), the waste economic expansion generates to reproduce the *bios* of the more fortunate classes (Nixon 2013; Lessenich 2019).

In *The Mushroom at the End of the World: On the Possibility of Life in Capitalist Ruins*, Anna Lowenhaupt Tsing explains how bare land is formed. Capitalism produces 'ruins' by stripping living beings of the capacity to form their own ecological relations, a necessary condition for the reproduction of life. Contemporary capitalism *alienates* living beings from ecological relations, i.e. capitalism generates "the ability to stand alone, as if the entanglements of living did not matter. Through alienation, people and things become mobile assets; they can be removed from their lifeworlds in distance-defying transport to be exchanged with other assets from other life worlds, elsewhere" (Tsing 2021, 5). Cutting the threads of the web of life through capitalist alienation, however, produces bare land as a side effect, infertile waste deprived of the means to reproduce itself without capitalist support. Alienation is the deracination of living beings from their lifeworld, transforming them into passive cogs for capitalist accumulation. However, Tsing upholds matsutake mushrooms, rare fungi popular among Japanese foodies, as exemplars of the resilience of ecological relations. Even amidst ruins, matsutakes successfully form beneficial relations with other living beings, like pine trees, other fungi and human beings. The insistent capacity to regenerate ecological relations is the ineluctable means of reproduction for the matsutake mushroom. Even at the end of the world, the matsutake persists by perpetually co-producing new lifeworlds for itself and fellow living beings (see also Haraway 2016).

I claim that Tsing's approach to capitalist alienation is descriptively convincing but lacks the affective force for ecological class consciousness. Tsing surveys the web of life from the perspective of living beings quite distant from humankind, articulating a theoretical diagnosis rather than a political exhortation. On an affective level, it is challenging to generate ecological class consciousness among the (presumably) human readers of my chapter if they are presented with only the biographies of mushrooms growing far beyond my home. As Chantal Mouffe (2018, 72) argues, the construction of an emphatically political identity requires an appeal to the affects, like hope, indignation or compassion. Latour and Schultz also stress that ecological politics currently suffers from an affective misalignment, with people failing to identify with the fate of their increasingly inhospitable environments (2022, 47). Why would European humans care about these unknown fungi? The reproduction of our CO_2-intensive livelihoods largely depends on the emission of bare land elsewhere, so in the short run, we stand to benefit more from putting our heads in the sand. I employ Chakrabarty's (2021) suggestion of grounding post-humanist politics first in strategic anthropocentrism to subsequently push for a post-humanist expansion of our human understanding. One must first feel personally interpellated by the crisis of the global means of reproduction before one can grasp the need for an ecological class politics beyond human confines. I turn to John Steinbeck's 1939 novel *The Grapes of Wrath* as a kindred spirit with more mobilising potential. Steinbeck tells the story of a family of impoverished farmers from Oklahoma, the Joads, travelling to California in pursuit of a better life, yet only encountering more poverty, exploitation and anti-immigrant racism. Steinbeck describes in detail the environmental and social devastation, but he focuses on the commodified labour power of migrant farmers rather than commodified mushrooms. Steinbeck's main characters are also uprooted from their entangled histories in the land and community of rural Oklahoma, but they present a more familiar face of the ecological class deprived of the means of reproduction. Steinbeck's outcry against alienation-as-deracination is clear, but the shift in perspective facilitates the empathetic outrage required for building ecological class consciousness. Steinbeck's strategic anthropocentrism helps human readers understand why alienation-as-deracination is a concern.

Alienation-as-Deracination

Tsing's alienation diagnosis should be firmly distinguished from more traditional theories of alienation. The latter usually presuppose some metaphysically anchored essential nature that living beings are supposed to enact. Capitalism then 'alienates' beings by perverting these attempts to actualise their nature. The young Marx, for instance, posits a human species-being (*Gattungswesen*), from which workers are subsequently alienated under industrial capitalism (Marx 2005). Factory conditions are unnatural, according to Marx, because they hinder people from actualising their human nature. But as a post-humanist, Tsing rejects essentialist narratives about human nature. Post-humanism suspects the discourse of human nature to be an oppressive apparatus that normalises human beings that fail to conform to pre-established 'humanity' (Braidotti 2013, 26–27). 'Natures' in the plural, on the other hand, have no pre-established metaphysical essences but are the products of collaborative interweavings between multiple living beings. According to Donna Haraway, "critters—human and not—become-with each other, compose and decompose each other, in every scale and register of time and stuff in sympoietic tangling, in ecological evolutionary developmental earthly worlding and unwordling" (2016, 97). In other words, living beings' natures are not metaphysical givens awaiting actualisation, but the contingent outcome of interactions with other living beings. Existence is an open-ended and non-teleological process of constructing, deconstructing and reconstructing one's nature in collaboration with others. That is why most post-humanists either reject the terminology of alienation or even embrace it as a positive ideal for constructing cyborg futures without an inherent teleology (Braidotti 2013, 88; see also Haraway 1998; Laboria Cuboniks 2018).

Tsing's choice of 'alienation' to formulate her critical theory of capitalism is hence curious. Rather than basing her critique on natural essentialism, she takes a relational perspective on alienation (Haraway 2016, 37).

> I find myself surrounded by patchiness, that is, a mosaic of open-ended assemblages of entangled ways of life, with each further opening into a mosaic of temporal rhythms and spatial arcs. I argue that only an appreciation of current precarity as an earthwide condition allows us to notice this—the situation of our world. (Tsing 2021, 4)

Living beings are constitutively vulnerable and open to the impact of others. If they possess the capacity to relationally affect other organisms, they also have the correlative capacity to be affected by those relations. Instead of identifying independent, autarkic entities with their own essential natures, Tsing proposes a relational ontology that embeds individual organisms in ever-changing living networks. Living beings are always already entangled in heterogenous assemblages lacking a pre-determined teleology. For Tsing, "precarity is the condition of being vulnerable to others. Unpredictable encounters transform us; we are not in control, even of ourselves. Unable to rely on a stable structure of community, we are thrown into shifting assemblages, which remake us as well as our others" (ibid., 20). The matsutake is an excellent example of this ontology; not only is it deeply intertwined with shifting forest ecosystems, but even its own individuality as a specimen is relative. What laymen observe with the naked eye as a single matsutake, biologists have proven to consist of different DNA strains from multiple matsutake individuals (ibid., 237–238). Even a single matsutake is, in fact, an assemblage of several individuals working together to increase their chances of collective survival.

Tsing distinguishes these ecological relations characteristic of the web of life from commodified relations of capitalist networks of exchange. Ecological relations derive from living beings' own capacity to co-produce lifeworlds (ibid., 28). By slowly affecting and being affected by each other, they learn to perceive each other's sensibilities and cooperatively co-engineer ecosystems in which they can collectively thrive. This is a subtle back-and-forth calibration of multiple organisms that, over time, constitutes a smoothly operating web of living beings continually affecting and re-affecting each other.[3] This is an almost imperceptibly slow process taking place in supra-human deep time (Chakrabarty 2021, 190). A rainforest, for example, does not emerge overnight, but slowly materialises, across centuries, by fauna and flora immanently coordinating their conduct with

each other. Ultimately, a wilderness of living beings forms a relatively stable ecosystem without the need for top-down design or coordination. They have collectively established a network of horizontal relations that together produce a
vibrant and flexible ecosystem.

Opposed to such ecological relations are commodified relations of capitalist exchange. Among the different world-forming activities in the web of life,
one creature, 'Modern Man,' supports a peculiar form of ecosystem engineering
that disavows the species' own dependency on the web of life (Tsing 2021, 21).
It represents 'Nature' as a monolithic, passive and external background to its
own socio-economic expansion. 'Nature' appears as an available instrumental
resource for a supposedly independent human civilisation. Capitalism is one
such growth regime that exploits the fecundity of the web of life to further economic expansion (ibid., 5). To this purpose, capital has to subject living beings to
grand-scale efficient methods of production and exchange. Capitalism replaces
the slow horizontal entanglements of the web of life with the faster rhythm of
top-down coordinated capital accumulation. Singular ecological relations developed through mutual affectation across centuries are subjected to the uniform
laws of economic equivalence to speed up the circulation of beings (Moore 2015,
235). This means dissolving the direct ecological relations living beings form
among each other in favour of top-down managed relations of production and
exchange, mediated by capital. The latter takes control over relations between
living beings to synchronise all elements of its supply chain and simplify the
process of capital accumulation (Tsing 2021, 132; see also Morizot 2020, 31).

Tsing stays close to standard Marxist political economy, even if she uses post-
humanist terminology. In *Capital: Volume I*, Marx describes how living labour
is the force to affect and be affected by the world through labour, but capitalism forces workers to sell their living labour as interchangeable commodified
units of 'labour power,' which capital puts to work in a factory system in order
to accumulate surplus value. According to Marx, capital asserts its power over
the labour process by concentrating the power to coordinate the labour process
in the hands of managers and machinery.[4] Artisanal craftsmen in pre-industri-
alised workshops were collectively and autonomously in control of their own
labour. They coordinated the labour process directly with each other, without
the mediation of a boss. Machine-operated factories and assembly-lines, on the
other hand, dispossess workers of the power to form horizontal relations of cooperation. Workers still have to collaborate to produce valuable commodities,
but this process is subsumed under managerial control. Capital sets the terms
for workers' interactions. If assembly-line workers even wanted to take autonomous control of the labour process, they would no longer know how, as the moment of conception of the labour process has been thoroughly separated from

its concrete execution. The knowledge required to run the factory system is entirely concentrated in the managerial echelon, on which workers have become dependent. Factory labour expresses not the immanent vibrancy of living labour and social cooperation, but the commands of capital in pursuit of economic expansion. Individual workers are, in this process, only mere 'living accessories', interchangeable cogs of a centrally planned machine (Marx 2005b, 693).

Tsing agrees with this analysis, but argues that the colonial plantation showcased the dispossession of living cooperation long before the industrial revolution (Tsing 2021, 38–39; see also Tsing 2011). The plantation destroys the back-and-forth rhythm of the web of life typical of, for example, rainforests with a single meticulously managed monoculture that scales up and accelerates the productivity of the land. The living labour of beings forming ecological relations is thereby instrumentalised in a system of top-down commands in service of capital accumulation. The coordination of crops development is concentrated in the hands of capital. Through its mediation, plants are made to grow as fast and cost-efficiently as possible in order to maximise capital expansion. Living beings are reduced to an abstract resource to be maximally exploited. Jason Moore sums it up succinctly:

> In capitalism, the crucial divide is not between Humanity and Nature—it is between capitalisation and the web of life. Capitalism's arrogance is to assign value to life-activity within the commodity-system (and an alienating value at that) while de-valuing, and simultaneously drawing its life-blood from, uncommodified life-activity within reach of capitalist power. (2015, 100)

Tsing locates alienation in the transition from the web of life to capitalist relations of production and exchange.[5] "In capitalist logics of commodification, things are torn from their lifeworlds to become objects of exchange. This is the process I am calling 'alienation'" (Tsing 2021, 121). Alienation occurs when living beings are subsumed under capitalist growth regimes as stand-alone abstract resources. The moving force of life is then no longer the immanent interaction between living beings, but the instrumental logic of capital aiming to accumulate itself. Living beings are, as it were, mere vehicles for capital accumulation moved by an alien power (Marx 2005b, 693). Capitalist subsumption uproots living beings from their ecological relations and refurbishes them as uniform commodities mobile enough to be coordinated independently of the web of life that formed them. The web of life is unwoven and turned into a collection of stand-alone commodities that obey the laws of capital accumulation. For the matsutake, this is a literal process of deracination: they are cut off by the roots and integrated into global supply chains. For the companies investing in the matsutake trade, the mushrooms are simply a shape their capital takes on its trajectory toward self-accumulation. By separating beings from their roots in the web of life, they appear as something alien to themselves. Value is determined extraneously in terms of beings' instrumentality to capital accumulation; whatever is deemed useless is discarded as waste.

In the long run, alienation-as-deracination produces a barren, unlively web of life. By dismantling ecological relations, it undercuts living beings' means of reproduction. Once living beings are dispossessed of the force to guarantee their own thriving via ecological relations, they become dependent on capital reproducing them for profit. The crops grown in a monoculture field cannot survive independently without the interference of capitalist management. If these living beings stop being useful to capital, the latter emits them as bare land. By cutting living beings loose from the webs that shape their nature, the long-term effect is a loss of overall vitality. The colonial plantation, for example, must destroy lush rainforests in order to concentrate the management of plant growth in the hands of agricultural experts. The continued reproduction of life is henceforth conditional on its utility to capital expansion. The resulting monoculture can maximise the productivity of profitable crops, but it undermines the land's long-term resilience. Single-crop fields are dependent on the continued investments of capital for their survival (Moore 2015, 112). They are more vulnerable to environmental deprivation or infectious disease because they fail to ensure their reproduction through ecological relations. By concentrating the coordination of relations among living beings under capitalist management, the crops become unable to flexibly react to outside influences. They have become too dependent on the co-ordinating, alien power of capital (Morizot 2020, 185). Just like Marx's deskilled factory workers become dependent on the coordinating power of capital, living beings that have lost their potential to form ecological relations helplessly depend on the whims of capital to survive. Monoculture farming is subsequently faced with a dilemma: either it must attempt to immunise plantations from external contaminations from the web of life—by spraying pesticides, importing super-fertilisers, genetically modifying the crops—or it must abandon unproductive lands (Moore 2015, 270–286). Once the investment of keeping the impoverished soil no longer yields sufficient profits, capital expels these territories as bare land.

John Steinbeck and Ecological Class Politics

Post-humanist environmentalism provides illuminating insights on the ecological limits of capitalism, but a frequent complaint is that the elimination of clear distinctions between humans and non-humans is politically ineffective.[6] The addressees of any *publication* calling for an ecological class politics are strictly human, yet they are expected to enact ecological class consciousness through stories of the uprooting of rare mushrooms or faraway rainforests. Post-humanist environmentalism seems to require human individuals to transcend their anthropocentric identity in favour of an abstract extended self encompassing the entire biosphere. It is thereby confronted with an affective challenge: how does one generate a deeply felt and resonant connection between the human addressees of one's writings and a world too ancient, large and complex for the human brain to fathom? According to Chakrabarty, "we cannot place [the planet] in a communicative relationship with humans. It does not as such address itself to humans […] To encounter the planet in thought is to encounter something that is the condition of human existence and yet remains profoundly indifferent to that existence" (2021, 70). The environment at stake in ecological class politics exceeds the bounds of human intelligibility, constituting a hyperobject that resists easy representation (Horn 2020, 166). Tsing attempts to focus the challenge on a more manageable scale by zooming in on one entity, the matsutake mushroom, but even this simple being turns out to constitute a node in a bewilderingly complex network of relations.

More advisable is to assume anthropocentric strategic essentialism in conducting ecological class politics. Rather than trying to invoke compassion for faraway beings of a radically different nature from ours, Chakrabarty advises starting from a more familiar, human appeal. "Our creaturely life, collectively considered, is our competitive animal life as a species, a life that, *pace* Kant, humans cannot ever altogether escape" (2021, 90). Hence,

> any theory of politics adequate to the planetary crisis humans face today *would have to begin from the same old premise of securing human life* but now ground itself in a new philosophical anthropology, that is, in a new understanding of the changing place of humans in the web of life. (Chakrabarty 2021, 91, emphasis added)

Any effective response to the planetary crisis of today must start from an appeal to human beings' need to reproduce their way of life. Once this strategically anthropocentric appeal clarifies the stakes of the crisis on a cognitive level understandable for human beings, it can clarify why the political struggle for human reproduction necessitates an ontological shift of perspective in favour of a post-humanist ontology of the web of life. The affront of alienation-as-deracination and the subsequent ejection of bare land also affect human life. Alienation is hence not only a problem for Japanese mushrooms, but also for the human addressees of this book chapter. Focusing on this human fall-out first gives a more solid affective foundation to subsequently extend the analysis to other living beings. Once we viscerally accept the diagnosis of alienation-as-deracination for humans, it is easier to argue for its extension to the entire biosphere. John Steinbeck's novel *The Grapes of Wrath* shows potential in this endeavour. It was written in order to provoke outrage in Depression-era America for the uprooting of farmers and their lands under *laissez-faire* capitalism and it can still have this effect today (Seelye 2002, 30).

However, the politics of Steinbeck's book do not explicitly align with the programme of ecological class politics. Steinbeck was primarily a New Deal reformist (Dickstein 2004, 124). He believed that a stronger welfare state should integrate impoverished farmer-migrants into a broad and dignified working class (Yazell 2017, 507). This programme had no explicit environmental angle and held a strained relationship to Marxist class politics. Marxist critics generally like Steinbeck's social diagnosis, but they object to its reformist solutions (Beck and Erickson 1988, 44–57; Wang 2012, 1–31; Nez 2022, 97–84). Steinbeck's presentation of how the Joads are forced out of Oklahoma aligns well with Marx's theory of primitive accumulation and the expulsion of surplus populations (see Marx 1996, 503–545). According to Marx, British capitalism commenced when large landholders forcefully privatised common farming lands and drove off the local farmers. The latter migrated to the cities and became the urban working class. The Joads are the American equivalent of these proto-proletarian farmers. Droughts and debts make tenancy subsistence farming financially unsustainable. "A man can hold land if he can just eat and pay taxes; he can do that. Yes, he can do that until his crops fail one day and he has to borrow money from the bank" (Steinbeck 1993, 39). When the pressure of debt rises, a few large-scale landowners buy up all the land and forcefully expel their tenants. The latter move to California in pursuit of a better life, where they become a proletarianised industrial reserve army pushing wages down for other workers (McParland 2016, 84). The solution, however, is for Steinbeck not revolution but state reform. He does not wish to upend capitalism itself, but only to embed it within better government regulation. Marxist critics consequently accuse Steinbeck of containing rather than reinforcing working-class fervour.

Another element deviating from Tsing's ecological class politics is Steinbeck's Christian humanism (Dougherty 1962, 224–226). Steinbeck introduces one of the central characters, ex-preacher Jim Casy, as a man who, even amidst a deep crisis of faith, upholds Christianity via an appeal to love for the human neighbour: "Why do we got to hang it on God or Jesus? [...] Maybe it's all men and all women we love; maybe that's the Holy sperit—the human sperit—the whole shebang" (Steinbeck 1993, 29). Steinbeck's explicit love for humankind, created in the image of the Lord, animates the entire novel. His characters believe not in a post-human web of life but in an Emersonian humanistic Oversoul, a common immortal soul shared by all humanity, of which individual egos are only limited participants (Beck and Erickson 2016, 199). The novel is steeped in Christian metaphors and Biblical references. The title, for instance, refers not only to the abolitionist protest song *Battle Hymn of the Republic* ("Mine eyes have seen the glory of the coming of the Lord / He is trampling out the vintage where the grapes of wrath are stored"), but also to Revelations 14:19 ("And the angel thrust in his sickle into the earth, and gathered the vine of the earth, and cast it into the great winepress of the wrath of God.") (Gudmarsdottir 2010, 210). At the end of the novel, during Tom Joad's farewell speech to his mother, the elements of political protest and Christian humanism merge into a single faith in the humanist struggle for dignity. Tom argues that, by devoting his life to the downtrodden, his individual self will merge with the human Oversoul.

> A fella ain't got a soul of his own, but on'y a piece of a big one [...] then I'll be around in the dark. I'll be ever'where—wherever you look. Wherever they's a fight so hungry people can eat, I'll be there. Wherever they's a cop beatin' up a guy, I'll be there. If Casy knowed, why, I'll be in the way kids laugh when they're hungry an' they know supper's ready. An' when our folks eat the stuff they raise an' live in the houses they build—why, I'll be there. (Steinbeck 1993, 534)

Tom's devotion to the struggle against human suffering expresses a Christian faith in the dignity of humankind. By emptying his egoistic self and committing to the cause of humankind, he becomes part of the Oversoul that animates the love human beings show each other.

Given this explicit humanism and New Deal reformism, there is no point in arguing Steinbeck consciously was a post-humanist *avant la lettre* or a proto-ideologue of ecological class politics. Nonetheless, his anthropocentrism can be strategically useful if it remains compatible with post-humanist ecological class politics. Steinbeck's naturalism offsets some of the lofty humanism of Christianity and the New Deal, bringing him closer to post-humanist environmentalism. Steinbeckian characters tend to act very animalistically. Despite their Christian morals, they are not upstanding exemplars of the Protestant ethic but sensuous creatures craving fulfilment of their bodily needs. As early critic Alfred Kazin wrote disparagingly, "Steinbeck's people are always on the verge of becoming human, but never do" (quoted in Dickstein 2004, 118). Steinbeck held a profound interest in animal life and regarded human beings as just another species of animal (Kelley 2002, 255–265). Jim Casy, for instance, rejects the priesthood because he denies the sinfulness of bodily desire and fails to repress his sexual impulses. Casy preaches the faith of a carnal Oversoul revelling in bodily pleasure and sexual lust:

Here's my preachin' grace. An' here's them people getting' grace so hard they're jumpin' an' shoutin'. Now they say layin' up with a girl comes from the devil. But the more grace a girl got in her, the quicker she wants to go out in the grass. An' I got thinkin' how in hell, s'cuse me, how can the devil get in when a girl is so full of the Holy Sperit that it's spoutin' out of her nose an' ears. (Steinbeck 1993, 26)

The implicit undermining of Christian humanism continues throughout the novel. While the text abounds in Biblical references and presents itself as an American Exodus, the story of the Joads deviates sharply from that of the Mosaic Israelites by decentring human salvation (Seelye 2002, 20). Steinbeck emphasises the analogies to Exodus in the first chapters to present the migrants' lot as a transition from enslavement to the promised land. The evicted farmers think: "maybe we can start again, in the new rich land—in California, where the fruit grows. We'll start over" (Steinbeck 1993, 111). California, however, is not the land of milk and honey that the Joads deserve (ibid., 321). They just move from one enslavement to industry to another without liberation. In the final chapters, Rose of Sharon gives birth to the baby she has been carrying since the start of the novel. But again, salvific expectations are subverted, as the baby is stillborn and her uncle John sends it floating down the river during a flood like a macabre baby Moses, saying, "Go down in the street an' rot an' tell 'em that way" (ibid., 569). In Steinbeck's universe, there is no providential God looking out for the vulnerable and the weak. "An Almighty God never raised no wages" (ibid., 320). Only a combination of sturdy perseverance and dumb luck allows the Joads to survive the hardships of the road and the discriminatory violence of California (Seelye 2002, 22). In contrast to the promise of Revelations, where the heavy vineyards announce the wrath of God, there is no transcendent God to avenge the Oklahoma migrants. No one will save the downtrodden but the people themselves (Gudmarsdottir 2010, 214). If God is an Oversoul present in humankind, then only humankind can save itself from enslavement.

This anti-salvific message is where Steinbeck connects to the ecological class politics of Tsing and Latour. For the latter, the ecological class is the collective of living beings robbed of the means of reproduction. Capitalism ruins itself by undercutting the means of reproduction of life on Earth. The response to the dissolution of the web of life is a return to ecological relations. Even amidst the ruins of capitalism, living beings like the matsutake possess the potential to form new, mutually strengthening ecological relations with other organisms. For Steinbeck as well, the only adequate response left to the Joads is stubborn endurance, despite their livelihoods falling apart, and a continued commitment to mutual aid. By the end of the novel, the region is struck by a flood, the government refuses to send medical help, and the Joads have lost their car, on which their employment

and income depend. They are stripped from all means of reproduction. Yet the
book does not end in apocalyptic hopelessness. The final scene—so scandalous
the 1940 film adaptation chose to skip it—portrays Rose of Sharon feeding breast
milk meant for her stillborn baby to an old, starving stranger. Steinbeck's editors
urged him to delete the chapter or at least give the stranger a backstory, but Steinbeck refused, claiming that "the giving of the breast has no more sentiment than
the giving of a piece of bread [...] If there is a symbol, it is a survival symbol, not
a love symbol, it must be an accident, it must be a stranger, and it must be quick"
(qtd. in Seelye 2002, 18). As a symbol of survival, this uncomfortable nativity
scene emphasises that, in a Godless world, the relations of care living beings
nurture among each other is the only means of reproduction left.

The most explicit description of ecological relations as an answer to hardship
under Depression-era capitalism comes from Steinbeck's portrayal of the Joad
family. When living in their truck, for instance, Steinbeck writes about the Joads,

> As the cars moved westward, each member of the family grew into his proper
> place, grew into his duties; so that each member, old and young, had his place in
> the car [...] And this was done without command. The families, which had been
> units of which the boundaries were a house at night, a farm by day, changed their
> boundaries. In the long hot light, they were silent in the cars moving slowly west-
> ward; but at night they integrated with any group they found. (Steinbeck 1993,
> 250)

The family is a porous assemblage of living beings who develop cooperative relations through a back-and-forth rhythm that slowly generates a close-knit community of mutual aid. The boundaries of this family unit are not fixed in advance,
but change according to shifting circumstances. Along Route 66, for instance,
on their way to California, the Joads successfully cooperate with strangers to
form temporary camping sites. People spontaneously cooperate and thereby
form inclusive communities that support their members' well-being better than
anyone could have done on their own. Steinbeck revels at migrant cooperative
"techniques of building worlds" with their own rules and government (Steinbeck
1993, 248):

> Every night a world created, complete with furniture—friends made and enemies
> established; a world complete with braggarts and with cowards, with quiet men,
> with humble men, with kindly men. Every night relationships that make a world,
> established; and every morning the world torn down like a circus. At first the fam-
> ilies were timid in the building and tumbling worlds, but gradually the technique
> of building worlds became their technique. Then leaders emerged, then laws were

made, then codes came into being. And as the worlds moved westward they were more complete and better furnished, for their builders were more experienced in building them. (ibid.)

The slow calibration of immanent cooperative relations that Tsing observes in the matsutake's web of life finds here its equivalent in the spontaneous collaboration of migrants along Route 66. They establish new lifeworlds that sustain a viable enclave in hostile territory. Through the slow process of mutual affectation, these lifeworlds become richer and more supportive so that they allow their members to survive amidst the ruins of Depression-era capitalism. Though Steinbeck often prefers to use the language of Christian neighbourly love, which pushes him towards humanistic language, it takes no dogmatic post-humanist to call this 'making-kin.'

Steinbeck, a Post-Humanist Interpreter of the Land?

Showing that Steinbeck animalises his human characters or champions ecological relations among humans, however, does not make him a post-humanist. That requires an extension of ecological relations to non-human beings, which Steinbeck never explicitly does. However, there are more implicit clues for a post-humanist reading of *The Grapes of Wrath*. Some of Steinbeck's readers have, for instance, focused on the humanisation of cars in *The Grapes of Wrath* (Griffin and Freedman 1962, 569–580; DeLucia 2014, 138–154). The Joad family is not only composed of human members and pets, but also the family Hudson Super-Sex Sedan gets its own characterisation and biography. More pertinent is, however, Steinbeck's description of the entanglement between farmers and their land. As McParland observes, "we are introduced to the changing colours of the sky, the shadows of dust upon the land, and the life of animals and human beings who face the tumultuous transitions of the natural world. [...] Humanity is close to the earth, interdependent with an ecosystem that has been damaged" (McParland 2016, 75). Steinbeck describes subsistence farming as a close-knit cooperation of human and non-human life under adverse circumstances. For Steinbeck, 'ownership of the land' is not a legal title but a state of deep intertwinement with the soil through sustained labour and hardship (Steinbeck 1993, 41). By working (with) the land, one slowly develops a back-and-forth dynamic of bonding with the soil and its offspring. Though the words were obviously unavailable to a 1939 novel, today's post-humanists would call this 'making-kin' or 'ecological relationality.' Once these deep mutual roots of subsistence farmers and land are established, Steinbeck even argues that it is impossible to extract the farmers from this assemblage without fundamentally rupturing their individual identities. It is impossible for subsistence farmers to start over elsewhere, on new land, because they always carry with them personal histories that are embedded in a particular place left behind (ibid., 111). Steinbeck thus ultimately defends a place-bound ethics of human and non-human symbiosis. It is also in this area that Steinbeck presents a critique of capitalism as a process of alienation-as-deracination.

Alienation-as-Deracination in *The Grapes of Wrath*

Like Tsing, Steinbeck criticises capitalism as an uprooting force, but the focus shifts from the displacement of commodified mushrooms to that of farmers as commodified labour power. Steinbeck wanted to spark outrage among his middle-class readers through a blunt presentation of the hardships suffered by poor farmers and their land. Here, it is not the colonial plantation but its American successor, large-scale industrialised cotton farming, that is presented as the space of alienation for both workers and their land. Subsistence farmers are 'tractored off the land' and thereby transformed into a reserve army of abstract labour power readily deployed whenever their labour profits Californian industrial farmers. People are uprooted from the soil that raised them and turned into mobile carriers of labour power, leaving them without personal purpose or identity. They are robbed of the ecological relations that constituted their shared identity with their community and land. In the words of Jim Casy, "us, we got a job to do, an' they's a thousan' ways, an' we don' know which one to take. An' if I was to pray, it'd be for the folks that don' know which way to turn" (Steinbeck 1993, 184). Being reduced to for-hire commodities that move to wherever the labour market needs them dissolves people's bonds with the web of life.

The same applies to the bare land deserted by the emigrating farmers. This also suffers a loss of identity and resilience from being violently torn away from their cultivators. Not just human beings, but also the soil loses its means of reproduction, turning into a worn-out territory awaiting rejuvenating encounters with other organisms that never come. Steinbeck documents how a handful of companies monopolise the land and turn it into a passive profit-making vehicle. The choice of cotton production is, for instance, particularly damaging to the soil (ibid., 40). It exhausts the land more quickly than the latter can regenerate itself, reducing Oklahoma to a dust bowl. However, agricultural companies are not bothered with this looming environmental catastrophe. They plan for short-term profits, after which they either sell or abandon the soil as bare land. They are not interested in fostering a mutually beneficent lifeworld with the soil. Their business highlights accelerated profit-making rather than the slow mutual

affectation of ecological relations. According to Steinbeck, industrialised monoculture distinguishes itself from subsistence farming through its affective detach-
ment from the web of life that determines the soil's long-term fecundity.

> And it came about that owners no longer worked on their farms. They farmed on
> paper; and they forgot the land, the smell, the feel of it, and remembered only that
> they owned it, remembered only what they gained and lost by it. And some of
> the farms grew so large that one man could not even conceive of them any more,
> so large that it took batteries of bookkeepers to keep track of interest and gain
> and loss [...] Then such a farmer really became a storekeeper, and kept a store.
> (Steinbeck 1993, 298)

In chapter 5 of *The Grapes of Wrath*, Steinbeck gives a detailed analysis of how
alienation-as-deracination works in Depression-era America from the perspective of an outside observer (ibid., 138–148). The chapter documents how industrial monoculture replaces subsistence farmers with bare land. Surprisingly, no
one *wants* to upend the Oklahoma region, yet an entire self-propelling system
makes people so dependent on big banks and landowners that they have to do
capital's bidding. Steinbeck mentions the case of one of the people driving the
Joads off their land (ibid., 45). He admits that he does not want to operate as an
agent of the bank's violent interests, yet he must if he is to avoid his own children
starving. Even large landowners themselves do not want to evict their tenants,
and yet they have to. They are beholden to the big banks, their investors and
creditors. If landowners allow unprofitable farming on their territory, they will
ultimately pay a heavy price. At the bank as well, the employees hold no desire
to cause suffering to the countryside, and yet the dispossession of rural families
continues unabated. "The bank—the monster has to have profits all the time. It
can't wait. It'll die. No, taxes go on. When the monster stops growing, it dies. It
can't stay one size" (ibid., 40). The reproductive capacities of the region are stead-
ily undercut without anyone wilfully responsible for the outcome.

The alienation process Steinbeck describes dissolves the direct bonds people
have with each other and the land in favour of a centrally coordinated system
geared toward profit-maximisation. Individual beings are thereby transformed
into living accessories for a self-propelling system. It seems like none of them
are really in control of their own actions. "The monster isn't men, but it can
make men do what it wants" (ibid., 42). Capital is acting *through* them to pursue its own interests. These employees or farmers cannot take ownership over
their own decisions, because they are subsumed in a system that runs by its own
unaccountable laws. They are stand-alone cogs in a chain of commands that is
driven by an anonymous power. One either submits to these imperatives or one

is discarded. Bare land is purportedly collateral damage to be accepted to keep feeding the capitalist monster.

Ultimately, capital drives people to undercut the reproduction of the area and dissolve the bonds constituting the web of life until nothing but bare land is left.

> And all of them were caught in something larger than themselves. Some of them hated the mathematics that drove them, and some were afraid, and some worshiped the mathematics because it provided a refuge from thought and from feeling. If a bank or a finance company owned the land, the owner man said, The Bank—or the Company—needs—wants—insists—must have—as though the Bank or the Company were a monster, with thought and feeling, which had ensnared them. These last would take no responsibility for the banks or the companies because they were men and slaves, while the banks were machines and masters all at the same time. (Steinbeck 1993, 38–39)

In Steinbeck's novel, capital appears as a monster that instrumentalises the living beings that it subsumes. Living beings are reduced to "robots in the seat" (ibid., 43) *through* which capital enacts its own interests. "The monster that sent the tractor out, had somehow gotten into the driver's hands, into his brain and muscle, had goggled and muzzled him" (ibid., 44). Farmers no longer directly relate to their land or vice versa; capital rather acts *through* the farmers' hands, brains and muscles to take from the land what it can turn into profitable commodities. They are passive media for the self-actualisation of capital accumulation. This process dispossesses living beings of their own actions and puts them in a relation of dependency to an alien power. Capitalist accumulation operates as a self-propelling machine that dispossesses its agents of their autonomous agency to relate to their own lifeworld. These agents are turned into passive cogs powerless to change the monster's course—even when it is heading for disaster.

The Wrath at the End of the World

One should not too quickly identify Steinbeck as a post-humanist prophet, but he shares a number of affinities with post-humanist environmentalism that are helpful for the project of ecological class politics. Through a parallel reading of Tsing's *Mushroom at the End of the World* and Steinbeck's *The Grapes of Wrath*, I have sought to uncover these affinities. Firstly, both start from a relational ontology of ecological relations, though Steinbeck's version remains more wedded to humankind than Tsing's. The primary means of reproduction for living beings is their capacity to form cooperative ecological relations with other organisms

that strengthen their common resilience and chances of survival. Steinbeck's pre-
dilection for animalistic human characters struggling in a Godless world and
his naturalistic description of the Oklahoma soil as a character in its own right,
move the novelist closer to an ecological class politics. Steinbeckian characters
engage in ecological relations beyond the human sphere. Secondly, Tsing and
Steinbeck both lament alienation-as-deracination. Capital uproots living beings
from the web of life to mobilise them as stand-alone commodities in the capitalist valorisation cycle. This not only renders beings dependent on capital and its
pursuit of profit, but also condemns them to a fate of bare land once their value
for capital is exhausted. The strategic advantage of Steinbeck's anthropocentrism
is, on the other hand, that it facilitates affective understanding of the plight of
bare land. A politically effective response to the planetary crisis requires some
strategic anthropocentrism to first lay out the challenge of reproducing human
life on Earth before it clarifies how this struggle necessitates a shift of our human
solidarities towards other, non-human beings. Once readers agree with the diagnosis of alienation-as-deracination in the case of uprooted farmers, it is easier to
argue the same critique for the deracination of the web of life in general.

Nevertheless, Tsing and Steinbeck do not preach despair. Tsing is well aware
of the ruins at the end of the world, but she praises the matsutake because it
manifests a remnant capacity for ecological world-building that partly escapes
capitalist control. Life persists and renews its ecological bonds even under cata-
strophic circumstances. Steinbeck also affirms the inexhaustible capacity of living beings to form new relations of mutual aid. Despite all the hardships the
Joads encounter, they are "aimed right at goin' on" (Steinbeck 1993, 539). The
Joads start out as individualistic farmers who praise autarky and independence
above all else, but in the face of capitalist dispossession, this quest for autarky
mutates into an appeal to collective solidarity:

> Here is the node, you who hate change and fear revolution. Keep these two squat-
> ting men apart; make them hate, fear, suspect each other. Here is the anlage of the
> thing you fear. This is the zygote. For here "I lost my land" is changed; a cell is split
> and from its splitting grows the thing you hate—"We lost our land." The danger is
> here, for two men are not as lonely and perplexed as one. And from this first 'we'
> there grows a still more dangerous thing. (ibid., 193)

Marginalised labour migrants only stand a chance against alienation if they cultivate a 'we' of collaborative relations. They can form a counter-will to the instru-
mentalising force of capital and thereby resist their deracination and subsumption under capital's monstrous power. Though individually they can only oppose
their subjection at great personal cost, their collective organisation can tip the

balance in their favour. The capitalist monster would have to retreat when met by the superior strength of the web of life regenerated.

> And [resistant migrants] stand still and watch the potatoes float by, listen to the screaming pigs being killed in a ditch and covered with quicklime, watch the mountains of oranges slop down to a putrefying ooze; and in the eyes of the people there is the failure; and in the eyes of the hungry there is a growing wrath. In the souls of the people the grapes of wrath are filling and growing heavy, growing heavy for the vintage. (ibid., 445)

Notes

1. Marx himself became increasingly aware of the impossibility of separating the economy from ecology (see Saito 2017).
2. The concept 'web of life' comes from Moore (2015).
3. For the notion of 'affect' implying a simultaneous capacity to move and be moved by other beings, see Deleuze's interpretation of 'affect' in Spinoza (Deleuze 1981, 66–69).
4. See Marx (1996), especially chapter 15 on 'Machinery and Modern Industry.'
5. On the moments of friction and resistance to alienation, see Tsing (2011, 4).
6. See, for instance, Malm (2020).

References

Agamben, Giorgio. 1998. *Homo Sacer: Sovereign Power and Bare Life*. Translated by Daniel Heller-Roazen. Stanford: Stanford University Press.

Agamben, Giorgio. 2011. *The Kingdom and the Glory*. Translated by Lorenzo Chiesa. Stanford: Stanford University Press.

Beck, William, and Edward Erickson. 1988. "The Emergence of Class Consciousness in *Germinal* and *The Grapes of Wrath.*" *The Comparatist* 12, no. 2: 44–57.

Braidotti, Rosi. 2013. *The Posthuman*. Cambridge: Polity Press.

Brevda, William. 2016. "Specters of Joad." *Steinbeck Review* 13, no. 2: 196–209.

Chakrabarty, Dipesh. 2021. *The Climate of History in a Planetary Age*. Chicago: University of Chicago Press.

Deleuze, Gilles. 1981. *Spinoza: Philosophie pratique*. Paris: Editions de Minuit.

DeLucia, Laura. 2014. "Positioning Steinbeck's Automobiles." *Steinbeck Review* 11, no. 2: 138–154.

Dickstein, Morris. 2004. "Steinbeck and the Great Depression." *South Atlantic Quarterly* 103, no. 1: 111–131.

Dougherty, Charles. 1962. "The Christ-Figure in the *Grapes of Wrath*." *College English* 24, no. 3: 224–226.

Fraser, Nancy. 2022. *Cannibal Capitalism*. London: Verso.

Griffin, Robert, and William Freedman. 1962. "Machines and Animals: Pervasive Motifs in The Grapes of Wrath." *The Journal of English and Germanic Philology* 62, no. 3: 569–80.

Gudmarsdottir, Sigridur. 2010. "Rapes of Earth and Grapes of Wrath: Steinbeck, Ecofeminism and the Metaphor of Rape." *Feminist Theology* 18, no. 2: 206–222.

Haraway, Donna. 1998. *Simians, Cyborgs, and Women: The Reinvention of Nature*. London: Free Association Books.

Haraway, Donna. 2016. *Staying with the Trouble: Making Kin in the Chthulucene*. Durham: Duke University Press.

Horn, Eva. 2020. "Challenges for an Aesthetics of the Anthropocene." In *The Anthropocentric Turn*, edited by Gabriele Dürbeck and Philip Hübkes, 159–172. London: Routledge.

Kelley, James. 2002. "The Global Appeal of Steinbeck's Science." In *Beyond Boundaries: Rereading John Steinbeck*, edited by Susan Shillinglaw and Kevin Hearle, 255–265. Tuscoloosa: University of Alabama Press.

Laboria Cuboniks, ed. 2018. *The Xenofeminist Manifesto: A Politics for Alienation*. London: Verso.

Latour, Bruno. 2018. *Down to Earth: Politics in the New Climatic Regime*. Cambridge: Polity Press.

Latour, Bruno, and Nikolaj Schultz. 2022. *Mémo sur La Nouvelle Classe Écologique de Bruno Latour et Nikolaj Schultz*. Paris: La Découverte.

Lessenich, Stephan. 2019. *Living Well at Others' Expense*. Cambridge: Polity Press.

Malm, Andreas. 2020. *The Progress of This Storm: Nature and Society in a Warming World*. London: Verso.

Marx, Karl. 1996. *Capital: Vol. 1*. London: Lawrence & Wishart.

Marx, Karl. 2005a. *Early Writings*. Translated by Rodney Livingstone and Gregor Benton. London: Penguin Books.

Marx, Karl. 2005b. *Grundrisse: Foundations of the Critique of Political Economy*. Translated by Martin Nicolaus. London: Penguin Books.

McParland, Robert. 2016. *Citizen Steinbeck: Giving Voice to the People*. Lanham: Rowman & Littlefield.

Moore, Jason W. 2015. *Capitalism in the Web of Life: Ecology and the Accumulation of Capital*. London: Verso.

Morizot, Baptiste. 2020. *Manières d'être Vivant*. Paris: Actes Sud.

Mouffe, Chantal. 2018. *For a Left Populism*. London: Verso.

Nez, Thomas J. 2022. "Laborers Lost in The Grapes of Wrath." *Steinbeck Review* 19, no. 1: 67–84.

Nixon, Rob. 2013. *Slow Violence and the Environmentalism of the Poor*. Cambridge: Harvard University Press.

Saito, Kohei. 2017. *Karl Marx's Ecosocialism*. New York: Monthly Review Press.

Sassen, Saskia. 2014. *Expulsions: Brutality and Complexity in the Global Economy*. Cambridge MA: Belknap Press.

Seelye, John. 2002. "Come Back to the Boxcar, Leslia Honey: Or, Don't Cry for Me, Madonna, Just Pass the Milk." In *Beyond Boundaries: Rereading John Steinbeck*, edited by Susan Shillinglaw and Kevin Hearle, 11–33. Tuscoloosa: University of Alabama Press.

Steinbeck, John. 1975. *Steinbeck: A Life in Letters*. Edited by Elaine Steinbeck and Robert Wallsten. New York: Viking Press.

Steinbeck, John. 1993. *The Grapes of Wrath*. London: Everyman's Library.

Tsing, Anna Lowenhaupt. 2011. *Friction: An Ethnography of Global Connection*. Princeton: Princeton University Press.

Tsing, Anna Lowenhaupt. 2021. *The Mushroom at the End of the World: On the Possibility of Life in Capitalist Ruins*. Princeton: Princeton University Press.

Wang, Huei-Ju. 2012. "Becoming 'Migrant John': John Steinbeck and His Migrants and His (Un)Conscious Turn to Marx." *Cultural Logic* 19: 1–31.

Yazell, Bryan. 2017. "Steinbeck's Migrants: Families on the Move and the Politics of Resource Management." *Modern Fiction Studies* 63, no. 3: 502–523.

5.2
Interspecies Storytelling for Prudent Predation

JOERI VERBESSELT AND SYAMAN RAPONGAN

> Fish of the same species were comparable to flocks of birds living in trees—they did not slaughter one another. As to the food-chain issue, whether some fishes are eaten by others, or vice versa, is decided by the size of their mouths and has nothing to do with dominant or dominated classes, smart beings or stupid beings.
> —Syaman Rapongan (Rapongan 2015, 92)

> Someone who uses money to buy fish from someone else is the most useless kind of man.
> —Syaman Rapongan's father (Rapongan 2005, 44)

A Multispecies Precarity?

What can a predatory fish teach us about precarity, about the increasingly precarious interdependence of animal and human labour? For the academic conference that preceded this edited volume, I wanted to explore this question with the interspecies dimensions in the ocean writings by Tao novelist Syaman Rapongan. I felt stimulated by philosopher and queer theorist Jasbir Puar's question during an online "precarity talk" meeting in 2012: "can we think of precarity 'beyond' the human?" (2012, 171). And the response by philosopher and gender theorist Judith Butler, "we have to rethink the human in light of precarity, showing that there is no human without those networks of life within which human life is but one sort of life. Otherwise, we end up breaking off the human from all of its sustaining conditions (and in that way become complicit with the process of precarisation itself)" (173). While anthropologist Anna Tsing, in her study on the globalised commodity and human labour chains of matsutake mushrooms, introduces the term precarity rather loosely in a more-than-human context (Tsing 2015), literary scholar Nicole Shukin investigates more theoretically the conceptualisation of a politicised "becoming-species of precarity" (2018, 123). Shukin reads in Fukushima's rapidly reproducing radioactive wild boars, which impede the human impulse to repair malfunctioning infrastructures such as contaminated farmland, a "multispecies common in-the-making" (ibid., 117). According to her, the wild boars' perturbation of the "sovereign systems of the human and capital" (ibid.) resonates with cultural theorist Lauren Berlant's conception of "nonsovereign relationality as the foundational quality of being in common" (2016, 394). Shukin believes a theory of precarity is well suited to account for a multispecies common constituted by non-sovereign relationality because it can address the domination of animals by humans and capitalism by exposing the material and biological labour of animals (Hribal 2007), as well as their affective and immaterial labour (Shukin 2018, 120).

However, Shukin's theorising does not provide fertile ground for our chapter because it adheres to a paradigm of knowledge that is incompatible with Syaman Rapongan's animal writings. Shukin's article can be situated in the post-humanist multispecies paradigm currently dominant in the Western humanities. While post-humanism has undoubtedly helped debunk heteropatriarchal anthropocentrism and binary dualisms, we may wonder how this doctrine relates to non-Western knowledge. The premise of multispecies discourse is a Cartesian divide between sentient humans and mechanistic animals that has never existed in Indigenous lifeworlds (Bolter 2016, 2–3). Indigenous and decolonial scholars accuse post-humanist and new-materialist multispecies philosophers of theft and erasure: they pluck Indigenous knowledge from different Nations, cut loose its original roots and relations, repackage it in Western abstract models of knowledge, and then present it as a 'new' progressive theory in which the location of the philosopher and Indigenous epistemes are silenced (Sundberg 2013; Watts 2013; Todd 2016). The resulting reduction of Indigenous knowledge to a transferable analytic leads to its recolonisation within Western epistemology (Chandler and Reid 2020) and, as such, legitimises and universalises this epistemology as the only knowledge that matters (Sundberg 2013, 36). A side effect of this operation is the multispecies appropriation of animal lifeworlds as a theoretical resource to mythologically 'grieve' and transcend a human present in 'ruins' through speculation (Watson 2016; Chandler and Reid 2020).

In light of the critique on multispecies post-humanism, I return to Nicole Shukin's notion of a non-sovereign multispecies common. While countering sovereignty is understandable from the perspective of the "academic-industrial complex" that is dominated by Western epistemology, white heteropatriarchy and global capitalism (Smith 2010, 63), and while there is debate within Indigenous studies about the discourse of sovereignty as a Western conceptualisation (Martineau 2015, 22–30), Indigenous scholars regard sovereignty as a key concept for asserting their Nations' territory, resurgence and freedom (Simpson

2017). Quandamooka scholar Aileen Moreton-Robinson argues that Indigenous sovereignty cannot be ceded as "[b]loodline to country is about sharing the life force with the ancestors that created our land," and "[y]ou can put on our country anything you like, but we and the land remain sovereign" (Moreton-Robinson 2016).

Cree scholar Sharon Venne points out that while sovereignty denotes absolute power in Western epistemology, Cree sovereignty is "related to our connections to the earth and is inherent" (Venne 1998, 23). Anishnaabe and Haudenosaunee scholar Vanessa Watts elaborates that such relational sovereignty stems from Indigenous histories that locate humans as the last species arriving on Earth, implying that humans arrived in an already functioning non-human society with certain values and ethics. This meant that humans were dependent on non-human Nations with whom they had to make interspecies agreements to ensure their own survival (Watts 2013, 25). As such, sovereignty extends beyond the human, as Venne explains: "We call the buffalo, or the wolves, the fish, the trees, and all are nations. Each is sovereign, an equal part of the creation, interdependent, interwoven, and all related" (Venne 1998, 23). While Shukin pleas for a non-sovereign multispecies common to extend our self-determination beyond the human, without clarifying what such common might look like, Watts argues that within Indigenous histories the interwoven sovereignty of human and non-human Nations has always been essential in the "formation of governance" and an "obligation to original instructions from the earth" (Watts 2013, 27–28).

Indigenous sovereignty places limitations on what precarity theory can do. A conference debating the applicability of precarity theory in post-colonial studies highlighted the universalising dilemma of precarity (Hinkson 2020). Cultural theorist Simon During, who first argued for a reconsideration of the subaltern in light of "the precariat as a global group which includes people from many classes, religions and cultures as they are swept into capitalism's most recent phase [of global neoliberalism]" (During 2015, 37), acknowledged the limited applicability of this scope to particular and singular contexts (During 2020). Decolonial theorists Elizabeth Strakosch and Alissa Macoun argue against precarity theory by building on the seminal article "Decolonization is not a metaphor" by Unangax̂ scholar Eve Tuck and non-indigenous theorist K. Wayne Yang, in which the latter argue for "an ethic of incommensurability, which recognizes what is distinct, what is sovereign" (Tuck and Yang 2012, 28). Strakosch and Macoun state that "theoretical moves which abstract, analogise or universalise colonialism to a global theoretical register, disconnected from land and from local political relationships, [...] show how a certain type of political thinking can tend to erase the authority of Indigenous peoples and reproduce colonial epistemologies" (Strakosch and Macoun 2020, 507).

In their dedication and concern for perspectives beyond the human Western post-humanism and Indigenous studies may find common grounds, but the topic of my contribution requires me to privilege the arguments of decolonial and Indigenous scholars. In doing so, I seek to respect Dene scholar Glen Coulthard's notion of "grounded normativity" (2014, 13), which implies that the discussion of Rapongan's story "The Eyes of the Sky" in the following sections includes only Syaman Rapongan's own writings and the work of others who also identify as Indigenous Tao. I am also mindful of Nishnaabeg scholar Leanne Betasamosake Simpson's exhortation that the ethical practice of grounded normativity implies that one cannot simply take theories at face value but must engage with the people who embody those theories (Simpson 2017, 66). Following this guideline, I want to show who the gatekeepers of knowledge were and how I gained access to certain places, people and knowledge. I attempt to do so by approaching Syaman Rapongan's literature through what geographers Carrie Mott and Daniel Cockayne call a "conscientious engagement" with the politics of citation (Mott and Cockayne 2017, 956). Opposing quantitative positivism and problematic hierarchies of knowledge, Mott and Cockayne argue for citation as a performative technology that reveals how different voices relate to one another (Mott and Cockayne 2017). In the final section, I will expand my discussion of Rapongan's literature to recent insights from biological studies and how it prefigures not a multispecies class but an international interspecies alliance.

Interspecies Storytelling

I encountered the ocean writings by novelist Syaman Rapongan in the context of my doctoral artistic field research on the Pacific Island of Pongso no Tao (also known as Lanyu or Orchid Island). With my research, I wanted to counter 'precariousness' as the condition of our time threatened by ecological collapse. In particular, I wanted to analyse and create images to address the current imagination impasse between apocalyptic doomsday scenarios on the one hand and unabashed technological optimism with destructive consequences on the other. Pongso no Tao first caught my attention when I heard about the infamous case when the Taiwanese settler government installed a nuclear waste repository on the island in 1982. This facility is still active and has sparked several waves of protest, especially after Japan's Fukushima nuclear disaster in 2011. Syaman Rapongan is known for his opposition to such colonial ventures, and his novels express the Tao people's intimate bond with the ocean and their cultural heterogeneity. As a fisherman and novelist, Rapongan identifies as an Indigenous Tao in solidarity with other Pacific Island Nations (Huang and Rapongan 2021). I was Syaman Rapongan's neighbour during my two-month stay on Pongso no Tao in 2020. I returned to the island and his home several times, and we have an ongoing dialogue about how to position myself respectfully and consensually toward his work and Tao knowledge. This chapter is the result of that dialogue, a deep examination of Rapongan's translated writings, my immersion on Pongso no Tao, and countless dives into its ocean waters.

Syaman Rapongan's excerpted, abridged and translated "The Eyes of the Sky" from his novel *Eyes of the Sky* (2012) tells a story of colonial conflict and interdependent interspecies labour through the narrating point of view of a Cilat, a big silverish predatory fish also known as giant trevally or jackfish (Rapongan 2021). In summary, the Cilat fish sets off the narration by recalling Tao people's history. It recounts a time when the ancestral islanders transgressed "Heavenly Law" by cooking flying fish with other seafood, which led to sickness for humans and fish alike, threatening the first with extinction (ibid., 129). At the request of the gods, Mavaheng so Panid, the black-winged leader of the flying fish, explained to the humans the cause of the sickness and taught them how to classify the fish—what fish can be caught under which circumstances and eaten by whom. Since then, a healthy and sustainable bond has existed between the Tao people and the fish, which the Tao honour through sacred ceremonies and taboos (ibid., 129–30). The Cilat fish proudly states that until today, he is the Tao people's most prestigious catch as they "tell endless tales of fighting with" a "fierce and strong and handsome" fish like him. At the same time, the Cilat complains that his "old" meat is despised elsewhere, where it is traded as "cheap" fish, and sold cut up and mixed with other species as a mere breakfast supplement. A turning point in this lamentable evolution occurred when from 2000 to 2006, during the flying fish seasons, "fleets of death" came from the neighbouring island of Taiwan to Pongso no Tao to catch many tons of flying fish, threatening both predatory fish, such as the Cilat, and the Tao people with famine and extinction. These colonial operations continued until young Tao men with speedboats blocked the invading ships and prevented the impending extinction of the flying fish. The Cilat fish recounts that he was then free again to hunt flying fish, and stresses that he feels "deeply respected" by the Tao people who still follow the principles that Mavaheng so Panid once explained to them. The Cilat concludes that the ongoing agreement between the Tao people and the fish allows him to reach a "natural end" (ibid., 131–132).

Despite being among the sixteen Indigenous peoples that are officially recognised by the settler government of Taiwan (Silan and Munkejord 2022, 1), which is dominated by Han-Taiwanese people, the Tao people did not identify as Indigenous until recently, instead regarding themselves as ocean islanders. Indeed, the strong and dangerous Kuroshio Current historically separated Pongso no Tao from Taiwan and made other, more distant Pacific Islands easier to reach for the

Tao islanders navigating in non-motorised boats. As literature scholar Hsinya Huang elaborates on Rapongan's writings, "Tao ancestors used to move freely in the Pacific Ocean, following the migratory route of the flying fish that was subject to the flow of the Kuroshio/Black Current" (2016, 187–188). During the 2020 harvest festival of Pongso no Tao's Imorod tribe, I witnessed a public apology for the nuclear storage site made by the Taiwanese vice-president. This expression of remorse repeated the official apology by President Tsai in 2016 "[f]or the four centuries of pain and mistreatment" inflicted upon Indigenous peoples (Office of the President Republic of China (Taiwan) 2016). Cou scholar tibusungu'e vayayana points out that, compared to previously apologising settler states such as Australia and Canada, the Taiwanese apology was "more comprehensive due to the fact that Tsai apologized for specific mistreatments," such as the nuclear waste repository on Pongso no Tao, and "included the wrongdoings by each regime over the past 400 years." However, vayayana continues that the suffering from "the loss of language and culture" due to an "assimilationist education" policy seems to be "the sole aspect uncovered in Tsai's Apology" (2021, 36). It is to this violent process of "Sinicization" (Rapongan 2004, 16; 2000, 102; 1998) facilitated by Christianity and armed forces (Rapongan 2022, 58) that Rapongan's novels testify.

As becomes clear from the story in "The Eyes of the Sky," the Tao people cause a troubling obstacle for the Taiwanese fishing industry, which aims to deploy its extractive operations on Tao territory. As demonstrated by Tao people's resistance, only the erasure of the Tao people would establish the settler coloniser's ambition of fishing in the ocean waters surrounding Pongso no Tao. The Tao people have historically depended on Pongso no Tao's immediate sea environment for food, and more recently for tourism. In this ocean environment, the migratory flying fish shoals embody a key function as several human and non-human predators adapt their behaviours to their migratory movements. The Cilat fish, for example, as described by Rapongan, "[f]or the season of the flying fish […] comes back to the island" (2021, 130–131). According to the Tao ethnobiologist Syaman Misiva, the flying fish ('alibangbang' in Tao language) is the Tao's most important source of protein, and it is also the only fish "without gender [categorical] limitation," meaning that it is edible for "male, female, elderly, younger, pregnant women, and breast feeding mothers" (Misiva 2012, 6). The flying fish is a sacred fish given by the gods whose migratory movements structure the Tao's yearly cycle and ceremonies (ibid., 7). Rapongan's story shows that its black-winged leader taught the islanders that fish are sovereign beings that willingly give their lives to humans under certain conditions that must be respected as sacred laws. This interspecies relation has been established over many generations and reflects their historical interdependence inside the ocean's complex food webs.

Rapongan's choice of a Cilat, a predatory fish, as narrator calls for more discussion. To a reader unfamiliar with his novels, a non-human narrator seems a priori fraught. The general view is that humans cannot know what non-human species feel, let alone how they think or speak, because they have different body structures, organs and senses through which they experience their environment in a unique way. According to this line of thinking, any told feeling, thought or story of a non-human species must be anthropomorphic, a projection of human traits or behaviour onto non-human entities (Parkinson 2020, 1). According to critics, such anthropomorphism risks relational violence by denying difference and autonomy (Aloi 2012, 97; Weil 2012, 19). Rapongan is aware that his readers might share such anthropomorphic disapproval and might view a fish narrator with suspicion and possibly reject the story before it has even begun. Anticipating such a reaction, Rapongan has the Cilat fish introduce himself with a self-conscious remark at the beginning of the story:

> Now, a so-called "civilized" person like you needn't question how it is that I, a 'fish,' am telling this story. It is enough for me to say that you need not be cynical, need not sit in front of a computer or a television all day all year long and thereby presume to know everything there is to know about the world. (2021, 129)

Rapongan insinuates that the reader may not believe that one can know what a fish is thinking or saying, not because it is impossible or unethical to know, but because one cannot know by sitting in front of a virtual screen or, as he writes elsewhere in reference to his father, from "the uselessness of book learning" (2005, 44).

To understand how a fish thinks, against and beyond anthropomorphism, it seems necessary to embrace the idea that the ocean is a school from which one can learn by participating in the life-generating mechanism of predation. Aside from being a writer, Syaman Rapongan is an experienced fisherman and spearfishing hunter. In his autobiographical novel *Cold Sea, Deep Feeling: An Ocean Pilgrim* (1997), Rapongan writes extensively about how ocean hunting slowly shapes local ecological knowledge. Fish hunting requires critical skills and extensive expertise, such as sensing the relationship between the moon and the tides, the movements of currents, weather patterns, directions of winds, danger signs, or the different species of fish and their behaviours (Huang and Rapongan 2021, 70–71). Faced with the agony of being a novice hunter, Rapongan recounts the comforting words spoken to him by his spearfishing partner and cousin:

> Men who dive to spear fish have to be cheated by the fish many times, and those times are what count as your experience. The ocean floor is the world of the fish.

We are only strange creatures that occasionally come and take away their lives. If you chase a fish, it is naturally going to swim for its life, so you're not going to spear the big, smart fish. Aside from relying on our experience and strength, we must use some of our wisdom to understand the habits of each type of fish. That's the only way to make progress. (2005, 51)

These exhortations show how oceanic knowledge is shaped by the accumulated experience of predation, where understanding the behaviour of each fish effectively makes the fish into ocean teachers that can only be captured by inwardly simulating and emulating their skills.

Rapongan's cousin argues that this embodied knowledge must be supplemented by Tao wisdom, which denotes their ancestral knowledge mutually shared between humans and fish and shared collectively through stories told by fellow hunters and Elders. In his novel *Black Wings* (1999), Syaman Rapongan writes:

My great-great-grand father and all my forebears lived in this small island. The moment they were born, they fell in love with the sea, entertaining themselves by watching, worshiping, and adoring the sea. The sea-loving genes are already contained in my body, passed down from generation to generation. I love the sea fervently, almost to the degree of mania. (Rapongan 1999, 80, qtd. in Huang 2016, 188)

Such age-old oceanic understanding leads to the subversive representation of fish, as Hsinya Huang elaborates on Rapongan's literary work, from mere food for humans to being "pressed into the foreground alongside humans as creative agents and active participants" (192). As creative, active and, I would add, sovereign agents, it is no surprise that fish emerge as teachers and even narrators in Rapongan's stories that continually humble human agency or authoritarian knowledge.

Illustrative of the oceanic intuition of the Tao people is their origin history in "The Eyes of the Sky," in which the leader of the black-winged flying fish teaches the Tao people how to categorise fish, and through which a lasting agreement is established between humans and fish. Being Tao people's primal fish, and since catching them in large enough quantities requires a thorough understanding of their habits, it becomes clear why the flying fish serves as the cultural teacher of the Tao people par excellence. Mirroring the teacher of the black-winged flying fish, the Cilat narrator in turn becomes the appropriate teacher of the contemporary international fishing conflict for Rapongan's readership. It is striking how, in a story that recounts the rivalry between the Taiwanese fishing industry and the Tao fishermen over the catch of flying fish, a fourth character, the Cilat fish, is added to the story as an external but interdependent narrator. As mentioned, Rapongan acknowledges that his readers may have different assumptions and perceptions from his own. In addition to rejecting a Cilat narrator as anthropomorphic, readers might downplay the history of the Tao and its teachings about an ongoing interspecies agreement as mere myth, fantasy or superstition. Consequently, simply conveying that the Tao people resisted the invasion of the Taiwanese ships because of the teachings of the flying fish leader might not suffice to convince his readers of the importance of interspecies dependence or cultural heterogeneity. I argue that Rapongan not only emphasises his Indigenous Tao perspective, but that his choice of a Cilat narrator also allows him to make an ecological argument about the ocean's food webs.

Prudent Predation

In oceanic ecosystems, both humans and the Cilat are predators, and in its food web hierarchies, the Cilat occupies a position between fishermen (both Taiwanese and Tao) and flying fish. As such, the Cilat is particularly cognisant of the specific dynamics in the fishing relationship between the Tao and Taiwanese fishers and the flying fish, from the perspective of both predator (of the flying fish) and prey (of the fishers). The Cilat attests to its interchangeable position as prey/predator and points to the primordial predatory mechanism that sustains all life forms. Predation, as a reality and as a metaphor, has been wrongly demonised as a human evil, but, as Rapongan reminds us in another story, "whether some fishes are eaten by others, or vice versa, is decided by the size of their mouths and has nothing to do with dominant or dominated classes, smart beings or stupid beings" (2015, 92). Each animal participates in the exchange of the Earth's common substances to replenish its energy through the consumption of tissues from organisms other than itself, and although many species feed only on plants, herbivory could be understood as a form of plant predation (Petrakis and Legakis 2006, 87). Furthermore, ecological studies stress aquatic predators' essential ecological functions, such as controlling food webs, nutrient cycling, engineering ecosystems, disease transmission, mediating species invasions and even mediating climate change (Hammerschlag et al. 2019). In the complex food web of the story's ocean environment, both the Tao people and the Cilat fish act as top predators, perhaps matched only by the hammerhead shark.

Yet not all forms of predation are desirable, as the Cilat storyteller demonstrates when he recounts how both the unsustainable fishing practices of Tao's original ancestors and Taiwanese 'fleets of death' led to near-extinction. And while species extinction is sometimes inevitable in the evolutionary process, there is a strong scientific consensus on the vital role of biodiversity for species survival, ecosystem health and human well-being (Lajaunie and Morand 2017). Rapongan's claim that "if there is no ocean, there will be no fish and thus no wisdom" (2012, 29, qtd. in Huang 2016, 193) resonates with biologist Edward O. Wilson's argument that "[b]iodiversity as a whole forms a shield protecting each of the species that together compose it, ourselves included" (2016, 14). For years, scientists have sounded the alarm bells, speaking of a biodiversity crisis induced by human activity, which is leading to increased extinction rates (with background extinction rates one hundred to a thousand times the norm) (Lawton and May 1995) that may lead to a sixth mass extinction event (Kolbert 2014; Cowie, Bouchet and Fontaine 2022). If predation, especially apex predation, is known to be beneficial to biodiversity, how can we distinguish in ecological terms between the fishing practices of Tao fishermen and those of the Taiwanese fishing industry?

In their recent study on different predatory modes, biologists Orestes U. Gutiérrez Al-Khudhairy and Axel G. Rossberg contrast the models of inefficient, prudent and imprudent predation. While scientific consensus exists about in-efficient predation leading to predator extirpation, the above-mentioned biologists suggest a similar fate for imprudently aggressive predators who are "more likely to get competitively excluded by other consumers" (2022, 1065). Building on ecologist Lawrence B. Slobodkin's conception of prudent predation (1960), Gutiérrez Al-Khudairy and Rossberg label consumers (both predators and herbivores) 'prudent' if they eat sufficiently to sustain their populations, but not so much that overexploitation of resources becomes detrimental to the survival of their populations. They introduce the concept of "evolved prudence" that "arises through the consumer's adaptation to its native resource community by mutation and selection" (2022, 1055). Gutiérrez Al-Khudairy and Rossberg state that several studies demonstrate how, contrary to inefficient and imprudent predators, prudent predation evolved alongside "the emergence of a steady state in which, resulting from the evolutionary adaptation of the consumer's attack rate (or similar), consumers and resources coexist" (ibid., 1056). And their models, applied to empirical data, suggest that ecological communities emanate feedback mechanisms that lead to the extirpation of unfavourable (non-prudent) modes of predation.

These recent biological insights into different forms of predation are manifest in Syaman Rapongan's story excerpt. In its recounted origin history, the indiscriminate mixing of food sources by the Tao ancestors can be considered a form of imprudent predation. After the intervention of the black-winged flying fish teacher, the Tao people are guided back on the track of prudent predation through the agreement between sovereign human and fish Nations. The Tao people respect this bond in their treatment and categorisation of the fish and the ceremonial annual cycle. In the contemporary part of Rapongan's story, and similar to the transgressive behaviour of the Tao ancestors, the Taiwanese fish industry mixes the Cilat fish "with mangled shark, mahi-mahi, marlin, other" to sell as a breakfast accompaniment (Rapongan 2021, 131). The Taiwanese fishing boats, carrying with them the dimensions of colonialism and the commodity market of global capitalism, lead to serious disturbances in the ocean ecosystem of Pongso no Tao, and famine for the Tao people and predatory fish. In the contemporary conflict, however, the Tao fishermen took the role of intervention of the black-winged flying fish leader, affirming their interspecies bond of prudence, actively assuming their own cultural sovereignty, and resisting and blocking the invading ships. As a writer who tells this story cross-culturally to primarily Tao and Taiwanese (publishing mostly in Taiwan's official Traditional Chinese, and sometimes bilingually alongside the Tao language) and secondarily international (through translations) readers, Rapongan can be seen as adopting and advocating this role of sovereign and prudent intervention across human cultures.

While communicating cross-culturally in his novels, Syaman Rapongan stays close to the interspecies heritage of the ocean on which the entire Tao culture was founded and continues to evolve. By choosing a Cilat fish narrator, Rapongan stays true to the predatory mechanisms that sustain life and inextricably connect Tao people to the other species in their ocean environment. Today, this relationship between species is repeatedly threatened by human intraspecies and intercultural conflicts. Through Rapongan's literary works, we become aware of the importance of cultural heterogeneity and interspecies sovereignty that must be negotiated through prudent predation, allowing animals to be genuine, active, and sovereign beings, teachers and narrators who transmit essential ecological knowledge. Politically, this corresponds to the importance of countering the loss of Tao language and culture, and resisting colonial extractivism, such as industrial-scale fishing.

Toward an International Interspecies Alliance?

Inspired by the writings of Syaman Rapongan, I wonder if all humans can become prudent predators. Unlike Western multispecies discourse, I try to think and look for how I can live interspecies. The multispecies perspective provides us with the illusion of a morally safe position at a distance that seeks to make us contemplate the relationship between humans and animals in an abstract, analytical, metaphorical, transcendent, universalised, idealised or romantic way. It aims to represent all animals but lacks the relational, embodied and intimate grounding of life-generating acts, such as predation, that also make us animals. Rapongan's novels challenge this perspective by showing how capitalism needs colonialism to gain access to resources and how this extraction can only occur by destroying human–animal relations. As such, increasing precariousness can be fought together with animal Nations through an interspecies alliance united by the reversible mechanism of prudent predation. This implies that we respect the sovereignty of animals in a relational and reciprocal way, because if one wants to live with animals, one must also take into account the interests that make their Nations survive and flourish.

Guided by Indigenous and decolonial thinkers, we know that capitalism cannot be challenged without decoloniality. The Indigenous knowledges I encountered reflect an interspecies alliance that prudently and reciprocally respects all living beings, on the sovereign terms of the species that humans consume. I prefer the term alliance to an ecological or interspecies class because I am reluctant to absorb a variety of different actors and contexts under the same umbrella. The term alliance also complicates the solidarity of non-indigenous outsiders like myself, because you have to become a member of an alliance and this membership can only be established on the terms of those whose cause you aim to join. As Potawatomi scholar and activist Kyle Powys Whyte reminds us, such allyship requires abandoning privileges such as legal and moral domination, not in the least the white saviour syndrome, which conjures "the illusion that performing supportive but ineffectual actions is enough to merit and justify one's feeling innocent" (Whyte 2018, 237). As I learned from my own interactions with Syaman Rapongan, allyship must be negotiated during a slow process of relation building that takes several years. Likewise, Rapongan and his Tao ancestors needed more than a lifetime to negotiate and maintain the interspecies agreement with the fish around Pongso no Tao.

Storytelling has been an important medium for transmitting relational interspecies knowledge from generation to generation. Indigenous writers continue to use stories to demonstrate their cultural heterogeneity and ascertain their autonomy and self-determination. During my artistic field research, I encountered the lifeworlds of the grounded interspecies storytelling by Syaman Rapongan, Syaman Misiva, Husluman Vava (Bunun Nation), Topas Tamapima (Bunun Nation), Walis Nokan (Tayal Nation) and Ahronglong Sakinu (Paiwan Nation), among others. Their brilliant writings resonate internationally with the literature of other First Nations, highlighting cultural and contextual heterogeneity as well as political common ground for a potential interspecies alliance, resistance and resurgence indicated by the capitalised term 'Indigenous' (Garneau 2018, 26; Younging 2018).

References

Aloi, Giovanni. 2012. *Art and Animals*. New York: I. B. Tauris.

Berlant, Lauren. 2016. "The Commons: Infrastructures for Troubling Times." *Environment and Planning D: Society and Space* 34, no. 3: 393–419.

Bolter, Jay David. 2016. "Posthumanism." In *The International Encyclopedia of Communication Theory and Philosophy*, edited by Klaus Bruhn Jensen, Eric W. Rothenbuhler, Jefferson D. Pooley, and Robert T. Craig, 1–8. Chichester: John Wiley & Sons, Inc.

Chandler, David, and Julian Reid. 2020. "Becoming Indigenous: The 'Speculative Turn' in Anthropology and the (Re)Colonisation of Indigeneity." *Postcolonial Studies* 23, no. 4: 485–504.

Coulthard, Glen Sean. 2014. *Red Skin, White Masks: Rejecting the Colonial Politics of Recognition*. Minneapolis, London: University of Minnesota Press.

Cowie, Robert H., Philippe Bouchet, and Benoît Fontaine. 2022. "The Sixth Mass Extinction: Fact, Fiction or Speculation?" *Biological Reviews* 97; no. 2: 640–663.

During, Simon. 2015. "Choosing Precarity." *South Asia: Journal of South Asian Studies* 38, no. 1: 19–38.

During, Simon. 2020. "The Global South and Internationalism: The Geographies of Post-Subjectivity." *Postcolonial Studies* 23, no. 4: 457–467.

Garneau, David. 2018. "Can I Get a Witness? Indigenous Art Criticism." In *Sovereign Words: Indigenous Art, Curation and Criticism*, edited by Katya García-Antón, 15–32. Amsterdam: Valiz.

Gutiérrez Al-Khudhairy, Orestes U., and Axel G. Rossberg. 2022. "Evolution of Prudent Predation in Complex Food Webs." *Ecology Letters* 25, no. 5: 1055–1074.

Hammerschlag, Neil, Oswald J. Schmitz, Alexander S. Flecker, Kevin D. Lafferty, Andrew Sih, Trisha B. Atwood, Austin J. Gallagher, Duncan J. Irschick, Rachel Skubel, and Steven J. Cooke. 2019. "Ecosystem Function and Services of Aquatic Predators in the Anthropocene." *Trends in Ecology & Evolution* 34, no. 4: 369–383.

Hinkson, Melinda. 2020. "Refiguring the Postcolonial for Precarious Times: Introduction." *Postcolonial Studies* 23, no. 4: 431–437.

Hribal, Jason. 2007. "Animals, Agency, and Class: Writing the History of Animals from Below." *Human Ecology Review* 14 (June): 101–112.

Huang, Hsinya. 2016. "Re-Visioning Pacific Seascapes: Performing Insular Identities in Robert Sullivan's Star Waka and Syaman Rapongan's Eyes of the Sky." In *Landscape, Seascape, and the Eco-Spatial Imagination*, edited by Simon Estok, Jonathan White, and I-Chun Wang, 179–196. New York: Routledge.

Huang, Hsinya, and Syaman Rapongan. 2021. "Radiation Ecologies, Resistance, and Survivance on Pacific Islands: Albert Wendt's Black Rainbow and Syaman Rapongan's Drifting Dreams on the Ocean." In *Mushroom Clouds: Ecocritical Approaches to Mili-*

tarization and the Environment in East Asia, edited by Simon C. Estok, Iping Liang, and Shinji Iwamasa, 61–76. New York: Routledge.

Kolbert, Elizabeth. 2014. *The Sixth Extinction: An Unnatural History*. London: Bloomsbury.

Lajaunie, Claire, and Serge Morand. 2017. *Biodiversity and Health: Linking Life, Ecosystems and Societies*. London: ISTE.

Lawton, John H., and Robert M. May, eds. 1995. *Extinction Rates*. Oxford: Oxford University Press.

Martineau, Jarrett. 2015. "Creative Combat: Indigenous Art, Resurgence, and Decolonization." PhD diss., School of Indigenous Governance, University of Victoria.

Misiva, Siaman. 2012. *Animals in Tao's Eco-Cultural Meanings*. Hsinchu: National Chiao Tung University Press.

Moreton-Robinson, Aileen. 2016. "Speech at Clancestry Conversation 3 #SOVERIEGN-TYX." Accessed 14 November 2023. https://www.youtube.com/watch?v=RdjBMQ-0FPQ.

Mott, Carrie, and Daniel Cockayne. 2017. "Citation Matters: Mobilizing the Politics of Citation toward a Practice of 'Conscientious Engagement.'" *Gender, Place & Culture* 24, no. 7: 954–973.

Office of the President Republic of China (Taiwan). 2016. "President Tsai Apologizes to Indigenous Peoples on Behalf of Government." 2016. Accessed 14 November 2023. https://english.president.gov.tw/NEWS/4950.

Parkinson, Claire. 2020. *Animals, Anthropomorphism and Mediated Encounters*. London and New York: Routledge.

Petrakis, Panos V., and Anastasios Legakis. 2006. "The Role of Predation in Shaping Biological Communities, with Particular Emphasis to Insects." In *Predation in Organisms: A Distinct Phenomenon*, edited by Ashraf M. T. Elewa, 123–149. Berlin, Heidelberg: Springer.

Puar, Jasbir. 2012. "Precarity Talk: A Virtual Roundtable with Lauren Berlant, Judith Butler, Bojana Cvejić, Isabell Lorey, Jasbir Puar, and Ana Vujanović." *TDR: The Drama Review* 56, no. 4: 163–177.

Rapongan, Syaman. 1998. "The Call of the Flying Fish." Translated by Cathy Chiu. *Taiwan Literature: English Translation Series*, no. 3: 51–61. Originally published 1997.

Rapongan, Syaman. 1999. *Heise de Chibang* 黑色翅膀 [*Black Wings*]. Taichung: Chenxing.

Rapongan, Syaman. 2000. "The Wanderer Shen-Fish." Translated by Fan Pen Chen. *Taiwan Literature: English Translation Series*, no. 8: 101–106. Originally published 1995.

Rapongan, Syaman. 2004. "The Season of the Flying Fish." Translated by Mat Li-ming Tang. *The Chinese Pen* (Winter): 15–21. Originally published 1998.

Rapongan, Syaman. 2005. "The Ocean Pilgrim." Translated by Terence C. Russell. *Taiwan Literature: English Translation Series*, no. 17: 43–68. Originally published 1997.

Rapongan, Syaman. 2015. "The Birth of a Fisherman." Translated by C. J. Anderson-Wu. In *The Anthology of Taiwan Indigenous Literature: Short Stories (Part I)*, edited by Fang-Ming Chen, 86–115. New Taipei City: Lin Jiang-Yi, Council of Indigenous People.

Rapongan, Syaman. 2021. "The Eyes of the Sky." Translated by Tim Smith. *Ora Nui— Māori Literary Journal* 4: 129–132. Originally published 2012.

Rapongan, Syaman. 2022. *Les Yeux de l'océan / Mata Nu Wawa*. Translated by Damien Ligot. Paris: L'Asiathèque. Originally published 2018.

Shukin, Nicole. 2018. "Precarious Encounters: Philosophical, Cultural, and Historical Perspectives." In *Exploring Animal Encounters: Philosophical, Cultural, and Historical Perspectives*, edited by Dominik Ohrem and Matthew Calarco, 113–136. London: Palgrave Macmillan.

Silan, Wasiq, and Mai Camilla Munkejord. 2022. "Hmali', Rgrgyax and Gaga: A Study of Tayal Elders Reclaiming Their Indigenous Identities in Taiwan." *AlterNative: An International Journal of Indigenous Peoples* 18, no. 3: 354–363.

Simpson, Leanne Betasamosake. 2017. *As We Have Always Done: Indigenous Freedom through Radical Resistance*. Minneapolis, London: University of Minnesota Press.

Slobodkin, L. B. 1960. "Ecological Energy Relationships at the Population Level." *The American Naturalist* 94, no. 876: 213–236.

Smith, Andrea. 2010. "Queer Theory and Native Studies: The Heteronormativity of Settler Colonialism." *GLQ* 16, no. 1–2: 41–68.

Strakosch, Elizabeth, and Alissa Macoun. 2020. "The Violence of Analogy: Abstraction, Neoliberalism and Settler Colonial Possession." *Postcolonial Studies* 23, no. 4: 505–526.

Sundberg, Juanita. 2013. "Decolonizing Posthumanist Geographies." *Cultural Geographies* 21, no. 1: 33–47.

Todd, Zoe. 2016. "An Indigenous Feminist's Take On The Ontological Turn: 'Ontology' Is Just Another Word For Colonialism." *Journal of Historical Sociology* 29, no. 1: 4–22.

Tsing, Anna Lowenhaupt. 2015. *The Mushroom at the End of the World: On the Possibility of Life in Capitalist Ruins*. Princeton: Princeton University Press.

Tuck, Eve, and K. Wayne Yang. 2012. "Decolonization Is Not a Metaphor." *Decolonization: Indigeneity, Education & Society* 1, no. 1: 1–40.

vayayana, tibusungu'e (Ming-huey Wang). 2021. "Kuba-Hosa-Hupa: A Preliminary Exploration of Taiwan Indigenous Cou Cosmology and Pedagogy." In *Indigenous Knowledge in Taiwan and Beyond*, edited by Shu-mei Shih and Lin-chin Tsai, 35–54. Singapore: Springer.

Venne, Sharon Helen. 1998. *Our Elders Understand Our Rights: Evolving International Law Regarding Indigenous Peoples*. Penticton BC: Theytus Books.

Watson, Matthew C. 2016. "On Multispecies Mythology: A Critique of Animal Anthropology." *Theory, Culture and Society* 33, no. 5: 159–172.

Watts, Vanessa. 2013. "Indigenous Place-Thought & Agency amongst Humans and Non-Humans (First Woman and Sky Woman Go on a European World Tour!)." *Decolonization: Indigeneity, Education & Society* 2, no. 1: 20–34.

Weil, Kari. 2012. *Why Animal Studies Now?* New York: Columbia University Press.

Whyte, Kyle P. 2018. "Indigenous science (fiction) for the Anthropocene: Ancestral dystopias and fantasies of climate change crises." *Environment and Planning E: Nature and Space* 1, no. 1–2: 224–242.

Wilson, Edward O. 2016. *Half-Earth: Our Planet's Fight for Life*. New York: Liveright.

Younging, Gregory. 2018. *Elements of Indigenous Style: A Guide for Writing by and about Indigenous Peoples*. Edmonton: Brush Education Inc.

List of Contributors

Katrin Becker (M.Ed.) researches and teaches Anglophone literatures and cultures at the University of Siegen, with a particular focus on negotiations of class and classlessness in contemporary British fiction.

Olaf Berwald is Department Chair of World Languages, Literatures, and Cultures, and a Professor of German at Middle Tennessee State University.

Daniel Brookes is a lecturer in film and television at the University of Bristol whose research encompasses questions of form and aesthetics in documentary and feature narratives.

Tim Christiaens is an assistant professor of philosophy at Tilburg University in the Netherlands. He mainly works on critical theory and economic issues like the digitalisation of work, socio-economic exclusion and neoliberalism.

Christian Claesson is an associate professor of Spanish at the Centre for Languages and Literatures at Lund University, Sweden.

Deborah Dean is an associate professor at Warwick Business School (UK) and co-Director of the Industrial Relations Unit (IRRU) at Warwick University.

Markieta Domecka is a senior lecturer at the University of Roehampton and a former post-doctoral researcher within the ResPecTMe ERC AdG.

Marissia Fragkou is an assistant professor of theatre at the Aristotle University of Thessaloniki, Greece. She is the author of *Ecologies of Precarity in Twenty-First Century Theatre: Politics, Affect, Responsibility* (Bloomsbury 2018).

Liesbeth François is a teaching associate in Modern Latin American Literary and Cultural Studies in the Faculty of Modern and Medieval Languages and Linguistics at the University of Cambridge, and Fellow in Spanish at Downing College.

Irene Husser is a postdoctoral researcher at the German Department, University of Tübingen. Her fields of interests involve nineteenth-century to contemporary literature, media and cultural studies, political theory, sociology of literature, and popular culture.

Magnus Nilsson is a professor in comparative literature at Malmö University, Sweden, and the leader of the Research Environment "Precariat, Precarity and Precariousness in (Post-) Welfare-State Scandinavian Literatures," which is funded by the Swedish Research Council.

Sarah Pogoda is a senior lecturer in German Studies at Bangor University (Wales, UK), and founding member of the artist formation NWK-AO (Neue Walisische Kunst-Aufbauorganisation).

Valeria Pulignano is a professor of sociology, with expertise on work, labour (industrial and employment) relations and labour markets at the Centre for Sociological Research (CESO), KU Leuven. She is coordinator of the European Sociological Association (ESA) RN17 on Work, Employment and Industrial Relations and PI of ERC AdG ResPecTMe.

Syaman Rapongan is an award-winning author from the Pacific island of Pongso no Tao. As a writer-fisherman, he has published extensively on the distinct tradition of his oceanic Tao heritage in resistance to colonial operations.

Michiel Rys is a postdoctoral researcher of the Flemish Research Foundation (FWO Flanders) in the Research Unit of Literary Studies and Cultural Studies at KU Leuven, Belgium.

Christoph Schaub is a postdoctoral research associate in German literature and cultural studies at the University of Vechta.

Sula Textor was a teaching and research assistant at Potsdam University with a focus on cultural studies and comparative literatures before focusing on her work as a literary translator in 2023.

Joeri Verbesselt is an artist-researcher, and member of the Lieven Gevaert Centre (KU Leuven) and 'deep histories fragile memories' (LUCA School of Arts, Brussels).

Lander Vermeerbergen is an assistant professor of organisation design and development at Radboud University (Netherlands), Institute for Management Research and a former postdoctoral researcher within ResPecTMe ERC AdG.

www.ingramcontent.com/pod-product-compliance
Lightning Source LLC
Chambersburg PA
CBHW050631280326
41932CB00015B/2600